AN ENCYCLOPEDIA OF FURNITURE

AN ENCYCLOPEDIA OF
FURNITURE

Quantum
Books

A QUANTUM BOOK

This book is produced by
Quantum Publishing Ltd.
6 Blundell Street
London
N7 9BH

This edition printed 2004

ISBN 1-86160-954-X

QUMEOF

Printed in Singapore by Star Standard Industries Pte. Ltd.

Contents

• INTRODUCTION •

One of the interests in collecting antique furniture surely lies in the history that has developed alongside the evolving styles and decorative motifs. Each piece of every type of furniture detailed in this encyclopedia – chairs, sofas, tables and desks – has an individual design background, reflecting trends fashionable at the time of its construction. Necessarily functional, furniture over the centuries has been subject to design styles that closely reflect both social phenomena (political and financial) and artistic tastes of different cultures. The widening of communications around the world and the rapid development of man-made materials during the course of the last two centuries have radically quickened the pace of change, adding inspiration to the interpretations of individual craftsmen and innovators who have played an essential role in refining and reassessing furniture design. Indeed, the combinations of function and traditional use and the craftsmanship, techniques and materials used are all relevant to the way furniture shapes and designs have changed and developed over the years and continue to develop today.

Owing to the multitudinous strands of design which influence any one piece of furniture, strict classification can sometimes be difficult. European furniture design periods have generally been named after monarchies (Louis XIV, Queen Anne), architecture (Gothic, Classical), governments (Empire) or craftsmen (Chippendale, Sheraton, Hepplewhite); each of these can be further qualified by a country of origin, and will not necessarily refer to the same time span. American Queen Anne, for example, was produced in the United States some 50 years after the end of the reign of the English Queen in 1714 – its restrained elegance was very popular with the settlers. Many of these styles were revived at a later date, and either imitated with a contemporary feel (such as with Victorian Rococo) or reproduced using materials and construction techniques preferred by later craftsmen. Nonetheless, some form of descriptive classification is required, and if treated with caution, can be very helpful in identifying the underlying influences on a piece.

While the evolution of furniture styles can be classified according to external social developments, they also developed according to functional use and necessity. Unfortunately, due to the decaying of materials, we cannot be certain about the earliest origins of some types of furniture. Those included in this book each have their own history, interweaving both social and stylistic progressions with their developing role as functional items.

Sources

Having considered a few of the different types of furniture developed over the centuries, it is worth considering the sources of information on the style and conventions of the past.

People generally take little conscious note of the furniture fashions that are evolving around them, yet everyone carries with them a sense of what is 'modern' and what is outmoded. This presents no particular problem when talking about the 20th century, but the student of furniture history has to try to recreate a picture of evolving style from contemporary writing. Unfortunately, commentators often omit those commonplace details which would be of most interest, so that it is necessary to fall back on inventories of the contents of great houses.

Paintings and engravings are another good source of information, but the most influential sources have the furniture pattern books issued for the guidance of householders and furniture makers. These can usually be taken to reflect what was fashionable. By far the most famous is the *Gentleman and Cabinet Maker's Director*, published in 1754 by Thomas Chippendale. Chippendale's Director differed from earlier pattern books in that he intended it as a trade advertisement, showing potential customers what his firm could provide. His advertisement must be one of the most successful of all time, for his name dominates our view of a whole period of furniture history in Britain and America.

Pattern books and other specialized trade publications also highlight the problem of changes in the use of words. The word 'bureau', for example, is one of the most difficult in this respect. In France it is used to cover all types of writing furniture; in Britain today it is taken to refer to the traditional slope-front desk on a chest; Sheraton used it in that sense at the beginning of the 19th century; but half a century earlier, Johnson had defined a bureau as a 'chest of drawers', a sense which it retains in the United States. In many cases these difficulties can be circumvented by simple and accurate description, but some terms are used in specific contexts in reference books and sale catalogues, and most of these are listed in the glossary.

The illustrations in this book have been grouped in the order of chairs, sofas, tables and desks within each century, but the ends of the chapters do not necessarily indicate abrupt changes in form or fashion. Furniture evolves continually, as do the societies they were made to serve, and ideas take time to travel from one country to another; also, provincial areas always tend to lag behind the centres of fashion. It is only possible to get some idea of the range of furniture styles in a given period, and these are the examples explored in this book.

Chairs

From the earliest times, European chairs were divided into the purely functional turned or folding stool, and the more imposing throne for those in power – namely royalty, church and the law. Much of the furniture made before 1500 was of wood, and has therefore not survived, but evidence in paintings and sculpture shows that for the majority of the population in Europe at least, stools and benches were the norm.

However, refinement of design was clearly in force where there was money to be spent, and patronage of the arts and of craftsmen produced beautiful and functional chairs. As wealth became more widely distributed amongst the growing populations of Europe, a process greatly speeded by trade with the Orient and Europe's new colonies, and later by the far-reaching effects of the Industrial Revolution, chairs were in increasing demand. Delicate elegance, such as that seen at the courts of French kings Louis XV and XVI, was in many cases sacrificed to comfort, practicality and economy in the Victorian years.

Carving was the main form of decoration on wood, and continued to be so in the Gothic architectural movement and the Italian Renaissance. The Baroque movement, which also started in Italy, continued this penchant for carving, and the gilded and ornate work were the precursors of the Rococo movement. André-Charles Boulle established (possibly invented) an influential technique of brass and tortoiseshell marquetry, much used during the reigns of Louis XIV and Louis XV. Although France was to take the lead in setting design tastes for much of the 17th and 18th centuries, individual craftsmanship was at its peak in England. Holland, too, had developed its own distinctive national style from as early as the 16th century. The Dutch were among the earliest to explore different types of wood from their colonies, and marquetry and veneer were highly sophisticated by 1700.

Developing trade between East and West had a considerable impact, widening Europe's artistic boundaries. Japanning, for example, was widely adopted in the 17th century; the term describes European lacquer techniques attempting to copy work imported to England. Similarly, Chinese chairs of the 17th century were clearly of an elegance as yet unseen in Europe.

Just as trade increased contact between different cultures outside Europe, so political turbulence was responsible for the exchange of ideas within it. Religious exiles from France in the 17th century moved first to other European countries. taking with them their crafts, and then across the water to the newly-found America. The art of printing too, meant that as early as 1580, Hans Vredeman de Vries of Holland could publish pattern books of his furniture. The 18th century saw a spate of pattern books from the great English cabinet-makers Thomas Chippendale (1718–1779), George Hepplewhite (d. 1786) and Thomas Sheraton (1751–1806). This cross-fertilization of ideas increased in the 19th century as a vogue for international trade fairs (such as the Great Exhibition of 1851 at Crystal Palace) sprang up, and continued into the 20th century, with the important centres now expanded to include Milan, Philadelphia, Chicago and Vienna, as well as London and Paris. Wartime refugees to the United States sowed the seeds for the American post-war design boom.

The effects of the Industrial Revolution in the 18th century on chair design were immense. Larger and wealthier urban populations made new demands for space-saving pieces that provided comfort at a reasonable price. Machinery was developed that could take chair manufacture into new areas. Experimentation with metal tubing, chrome, plastics and fibre-glass have changed the face of chair design in the 20th century. The last two, for example, have led directly to the mass production of one-piece chairs, stemming from innovative designs by the Americans Charles Eames and Eero Saarinen in the 1940s. This revolutionary development produced a move away from decoration on chairs and towards fluidity of line.

This concern for line appears to be abating somewhat in the last quarter of the 20th century. Attention is focused instead on the widening division between unique and individual work from the designer-craftsmen on the one hand and the commercial demands of an ever-growing international market on the other.

Sofas

The generally more comfortable and appreciably larger sofa, as a somewhat more fluid piece of furniture for design interpretation, has assumed many guises over the years – and continues to do so. What can be more elegant than the simple lines of a Regency design, especially made to display the grace of a woman wearing a fashionable gauze dress? Or more comfortable and intimate than the feather-filled cushions of an Edwardian embossed-velvet settee with its atmosphere of opulence and comfort?

Due to its size, the sofa inevitably has been one of the focal points of a room's decorative scheme, and so has reflected in its development the influence of current fashions.

Since the 18th century, furniture historians have used various, and at times contradictory, terms to describe this item. The words 'settle', 'settee', 'sofa', 'couch', 'divan' and even 'day-bed' have often described almost identical objects. Occasionally there is some attempt to differentiate; one expert, for instance, suggesting that a sofa is to recline on, whereas a settee is intended for sitting upright. Other sources indicate that a sofa is used by only one person, but a settee by several. To some, a settle is a long wooden seat, to others it can have webbing or even springs. Some types have traditional terms that are in general use such as Knole, a Chesterfield or a chaise longue, but even these tend to be used loosely; one man's *conversation* being another's *indiscreet*. For the purpose of this book, the general term 'sofa' is used to encompass a broad spectrum of diverse seat furniture, from an Egyptian-style day-bed, to chair-backed hall seat to a formal structure in the Biedermeier manner.

All sofas, because of their size, were relatively expensive items, their construction relying upon good-quality hardwood that was necessary for strength. The costliest versions, in all periods, were those with detailed carving or inlay (indeed, it was only in the 20th century that the cult of expensive simplicity and functionalism developed). Drawing room sofas are, traditionally, display pieces, evidencing the taste and wealth of the householder. Consequently, the upholstery fabric was of prime importance and sometimes even more expensive than the frame. If fine materials, such as silk, were used for covers, they had to be laid over a heavy lining fabric that would take some of the strain, and this again added to the cost. When braids, fringes and tassels were popular, many of the most extravagant trimmings were produced in France, but these were so costly that they were only used by the most exclusive furniture makers.

Throughout its history, the sofa has mirrored the social attitudes and etiquette of its country of origin. Those made in Germany tend to have rather high seats, because the sofa was positioned behind a table in middle-class homes. Symmetrical, rather plain designs were preferred, as the mistress of the house sat at one end and the most important visitor at the other – a formality that was observed on all occasions. In contrast, French interiors were much less restrained, and sofas were grouped informally around the salon.

Many British and American mid-Victorian sofas, although large enough to seat several people, were only comfortable when used by one. In such pieces it was only the centre of the back that was fully padded, with the sides so heavily carved that they formed the most painful of back supports. Such sofas, with all the decoration rising to a crescendo in the middle, were superb fashion accessories for the crinoline-clad ladies of the 1850s and 1860s, and provided an excellent setting for receiving visitors. As behaviour became less formal and women abandoned the tightly laced corsets that forced them to sit upright, this relaxed attitude was reflected in the design of sofas, so much so that by 1900 there were feather-filled cushions and low seats.

From the 1840s, when sprung seats came into general use, writers on deportment tended to grumble about the lounging attitudes of men, who were often seen sprawling on sofas – even in the presence of ladies. Such complaints were even more vociferous in the early 20th century, when the low designs encouraged people to relax completely. By the 1920s, the arms on many sofas were broad enough to be used as side tables, and some designs included wooden or glass inserts suitable for an ashtray or a cup of coffee. Such luxurious designs are seen at their most extreme in the Hollywood interiors of the 1930s.

Today, there is a considerable divergence between the adventurous work of the artist-designer, seen in exhibitions and in a few exclusive shops, and the everyday, commercial products, whose basic shapes have changed very little since the 1930s. There are even firms specializing in the manufacture of reproduction pieces, some of which are so complex that they can cost more than the 18th- or 19th-century originals.

In general, there are not many fakes in the antique-sofa market, because the cost of reproducing some of the more extreme designs has been – and is – far too prohibitive. Sofas that do not have any show-wood, such as Chesterfields, are more of a problem, as a re-upholstered antique version does not look much different from a reproduction.

Tables

While the sofa's size is the element which most enhances its capacity for stylistic variation, the sheer diversity of the table in function, size and materials used in the making guarantees an even greater scope for interpretation. With their flat surfaces and straight lines, tables are open to an endless variety of ornament, and consistently reflect the changing tastes of their times. Craftsmen and designers have drawn from sources as diverse as religion, archaeology and nature in their search for inspiration, and the different design styles over the last few hundred years – Gothic, Baroque, Rococo, Classical – clearly indicate the breadth of influence. In some cases, the decorative function of a table is without a doubt more important than its practical use: the gilded 17th-century console table was originally designed to fill an unseemly gap on the walls of the Mirror Gallery in Louis XIV's Château de Versailles; the virtuoso marble-topped tables of the Italian 18th century were primarily made for display. Decorated Regency breakfast tables combine display and function, tilting down during the day when not in use, thus making the top fully visible.

During the 16th and 17th centuries, the use of tables became increasingly specific, reflecting the needs and status of the owner. The travelling life of much of the medieval nobility, and the poverty of much of the population, meant that little more was needed than the multi-purpose medieval bench, used variously for seating and storage, as well as a table. By the end of the 16th century, however, the European division between fashionable ornate tables found at court and the unchanging rough-hewn practical table of most or the populace was created and widened rapidly. It is the furniture of the fashionable that has lasted, coming from a more sheltered environment, and which is of most interest to us now. It was the aristocracy who commissioned the finest cabinetmakers and designers to create tables for their homes, and it was the wealthy that were keenest to keep up with the latest designs – a trend which continues today.

Soon after the beginnings of refinement in decoration at the time of the Italian Renaissance, separate table styles for separate functions began to emerge. Tables designed for writing were first found in Italy in the luxurious 16th-century palaces of Florence and Rome; dining tables developed away from the simple trestle and board; and the ornate courts of Louis XIV and XV saw the flowering of a myriad of small tables and desks – the writing table, the *table de nuit*, the dressing table, the occasional table, and after the introduction of tea from the Orient, the tea table.

The fact that tables were required for each of these separate functions gives the 20th-century observer a good idea of contemporary social developments. The influence of the Oriental trade routes – through the import of tea, but more importantly through the import of wood, materials and exquisite artworks – had a lasting impact on Europe, both artistically and socially. Delicate, round, candle-holding guéridons, first seen in the 16th century, were named after young black pages used mainly to hold lighting at the European courts, and are a reminder of the enormous wealth and status that growing trade through the Colonies brought to so many aristocrats and merchants – some of which was presumably spent on commissioning tables to decorate their splendid homes. The Georgian obsession with draughtsmanship, architecture and landscaping is reflected in their intricate gadgetted tables.

But although function and decoration are an obvious way to classify tables, the materials used are just as important. Generally made of wood, the very earliest tables from Ancient Egypt, Greece and Rome have rarely survived. Although the Egyptians prized ebony for its hardness and colour, the Romans probably used mainly light woods, such as pine and beech, which are easily destroyed by insects, damp and wear. In Europe, the native woods of oak and walnut were dense and durable, but even so, few European tables from before the 1500s have lasted today. The European tradition of carving, however, was developed during the Renaissance, as woods such as walnut were easily sculpted, and this art was readily adapted to the new, harder woods imported to Europe after the explorations of the 15th and 16th centuries. Ebony and the exotic zebra and rosewoods were ideal for the decorative art of veneer, a technique which uses thin strips of wood to create stunning patterns and designs, and which was to change the face and structure of furniture from the 16th century onwards. The designs of Chippendale in the 18th century made the best possible use of mahogany, showing its fine grain and deep colour to best effect.

In the 19th century, industrialization and newly discovered techniques of metalworking saw a proliferation of table styles, both structural and decorative. The Great Exhibition of 1851, held at London's Crystal Palace, was a showcase for imaginative – although sometimes excessive – furniture design, with tables made of cast iron, bent wood and papier mâché, amongst many others. Over the last century, synthetic materials have opened the door to another range of design possibilities, with aluminium and plywood preceding glass and plastic.

Desks

Although it may seem logical that the development of the desk or writing bureau would stem from the more commonplace table as a feature of functional, interior furniture design, writing furniture as such is a relatively recent invention. Desks were only commonplace in churches, monasteries and palaces before the 17th century, because in medieval times, when life for the majority was close to subsistence level, reading and writing played a very small part in people's lives. Those of noble birth lived in a way that was far from settled until the 17th century. The French word for furniture, *meuble*, is close enough to moveable/mobile to remind us of this mode of life. Thus furniture tended to be robust and functional, except for pieces with symbolic value like thrones.

Although furniture is recognized as a symbol of status in nearly all societies, writing furniture played no real part in the mainstream of this social code until the 18th century, when a great variety was to be found in the homes of well-to-do people. In his *Dictionary of the English Language*, published in 1755, Samuel Johnson defined several forms of writing furniture, but the most basic is the desk, which he described as 'an inclining table for the use of writers or readers, made commonly with a box or repository underneath it'. This seems to have been virtually the only piece of writing furniture found in homes before the middle of the 17th century.

Boxes of this kind remained a standard requirement of the traveller throughout the 18th and 19th centuries. They were made in all qualities, ranging from basic boxes to folding compendiums of presentation quality, featuring fold-out writing slopes, adjustable reading stands, inkwells, pounce pots, even candleholders. Although this simple medieval desk retained its own identity for centuries, it was also one of the building blocks for the more complicated permanent writing furniture. Other major ingredients were rudimentary writing tables and small cabinets of drawers with flaps that let down. The only real precedent for large and fixed pieces of furniture for reading and writing was to be found in churches or monasteries.

By the time Johnson published his dictionary, itself a pointer to growing literacy in the community, the proliferation of desks shows that these skills of reading and writing were already much more important in the homes of the upper classes. The general development of writing furniture for the home in the 17th century was part of a widespread improvement in trade, communications and technical skills, and specifically cabinetmaking.

The new impetus was first evident in continental Europe. Tables solely intended for writing were to be found in Italian palaces in the 16th century; in the Low Countries, compact writing cabinets seem to have appeared early in the 17th century. The new forms did not have much impact in Britain until the restoration of Charles II in 1600. By the end of the century, a variety of different desks forms were in circulation in Europe, and some had found their way to America. It is worth nothing how the prototype developed over the next two centuries.

Gateleg tables with fold-out flaps provided one starting point; the flaps on some early examples formed a space in which to store writing materials when closed. Another early solution was to mount the simple slope-front desk on a stand and to put the hinges at the bottom of the flap so that it became a large flat writing surface when folded down and supported – an arrangement which is instantly recognisable as a prototype of the slope-front bureau. This form became standard well before 1700, as did the fall-front secretaire, where the flap remained vertical when not in use, hiding storage compartments, then creating a generous writing surface when opened.

These different forms of fold-away desk were developed in parallel with an essentially different form of desk, based on the table, where the writing surface was always on view. Writing tables of this kind enjoyed their greatest popularity in France, where the *bureau plat*, which had appeared in the late 17th century French style took on fashionable features of the 18th and 19th centuries while remaining unchanged in practical terms.

The bureau Mazarin, a distinctive kneehole desk on legs characteristic of late 17th-century French style, lost favour during the 18th century, but equivalent combinations of base drawers and large writing surface became standard library furniture in Britain, as the pedestal desk. Like the *bureau plat*, this type was ideally suited to more public rooms and was designed to stand in the middle of the floor space. In the 20th century, the flat-topped library table is the general model for the office desk.

In more intimate rooms fold-away desks (most fitted with locks) have nearly always been the favoured form, reflecting a concern for compactness and secrecy. The grand houses of the 17th and 18th centuries tended to be fairly public places and written documents became more vulnerable as literacy grew.

In England, the firm preference was for the slope-front bureau with drawers underneath and often with a cabinet of drawers, or later a glazed bookcase, on top. There were many variations in size and design. The most striking are the large lacquer-decorated bureau-bookcases of the early 18th century, architectural in form and designed to stand against the wall. Such pieces are very different from the delicate little *bureaux en pente* favoured as ladies' desks in France at the same period. These were generally free-standing and raised on slender legs.

In 18th century America the combination of slope-front desk and bookcase was also the favourite form; an elegant echo of its generally more solid English counterpart. It became one of the most representative pieces of East Coast cabinet furniture, developing subtle but distinctive regional characteristics. This popular combination was adopted in Europe, though not in France. A distinctive Dutch form, with profuse marquetry decoration and a heavy *bombé* base with canted projecting corners remained popular throughout the 1700s, while German and Italian craftsmen developed fantastic Rococo forms. The exaggeratedly pot-bellied creations of the Venetians are hardly recognisable as kin to a more staid English equivalent.

The upright form of fall-front desk came back to favour in the second half of the 18th century, particularly in France, where it was known as a *secrétaire à abattant*. It lent itself to the more classical rectangular shapes which characterized the Louis XVI style and the French Empire style of the early 19th century. The same trends were evident in other countries, and the vertical fall-front was the normal form on fold-away desks of the Biedermeier period in Austria and Germany from the 1820s onwards. Here too the emphasis was on bold shapes and large undecorated areas of plain veneer. The basic *secrétaire a abbatant* forms a compact unit which can be adapted to fit many basic shells and which is unobtrusive when not in use, making it a favourite with 20th century designers struggling to escape traditional forms.

The large flat areas of these secretaires also present a broad canvas for decoration which has tempted designers of all periods.

A more modest 18th century development was the secretaire drawer, a feature made to look like any other drawer when closed, but which pulls out to become a fall-front writing compartment with pigeonholes at the back. Writing drawers of this kind were incorporated in all kinds of furniture. They became increasingly popular in Britain and America as the century waned and throughout the 19th century, as did the cylinder front which more or less replaced the slope-front in France after the 1760s and became widespread in England and America.

During the 18th century, France also took the lead in providing women with a great variety of well-thought-out smaller writing tables for everyday use. Very early the bureau Mazarin and its English and American counterpart, the small kneehole desk, seem to have served in the bedroom as dressing tables as well as desks. Small slope-front bureaux for ladies appeared on both sides of the Channel early in the 18th century, but the Paris *ébénistes* showed the greatest ingenuity and virtuosity in creating little *tables à écrire*. These were often work tables or delicate dressing tables, which also contained spaces for pen, ink, paper and a writing surface. No other writing furniture illustrates more clearly the importance of written communication in the pre-telephone era. Apart from these ingenious multi-purpose pieces, the French also created the most distinctive and practical of all desks for women, the *bonheur du jour*. This enjoyed a great vogue among French ladies in the 1760s, was taken up all over Europe and revived many times.

The early 1800s saw several influential desk types emerge. In England the Carlton House desk, a stylish adaptation of the French *bureau à gradin*, was a Regency favourite, and in the newly independent Federal America, tambour-fronted desks with fold-out writing flaps were fashionable and noticeably different from their counterparts across the Atlantic. The Davenport also appeared around the turn of the 18th century, a compact desk on chest immediately distinguishable from the slope-front bureau by being smaller, by the shallow angle of the writing surface and by the fact that the drawers are down the side. The first desks of this kind were seen in Britain in the 1790s, but they went on to become the typical item of writing furniture for the Victorian drawing-room. In later models, great ingenuity was used to pack in more features. The Victorian era saw many changes in the methods of furniture production. Rather surprisingly, it was fashion rather than improved design that obsessed the new masters of the furniture trade, who revived one style after another.

One landmark in the 19th century was the patent desk manufactured in large quantities at the factory of William S Wooton of Indianapolis. He created a closeable desk with over 100 drawers and pigeonholes. It was conceived on solid architectural lines and would be decorated according to the customer's pocket. Wooton's desk was practical and popular, but it also represents one of the dead-ends of High Victorian furniture design. The road to the office of the mid-20th century doubled back to reassess the styles and values of much earlier craftsmen.

It was the Arts and Crafts movement that actually led to the manufacture of simple, practical furniture that was an honest reflection of labour-saving production methods. The medieval inspiration of the Arts and Crafts pioneers produced some clumsy writing furniture, for of course there were no real precedents for domestic desks from that age, but in general terms their thinking influenced younger designers.

In America, the architect Frank Lloyd Wright was one of the most important of the new generation. He commissioned deceptively simple oak furniture to complement many of the private houses he designed. When he designed metal office furniture for the Larkin Building in Buffalo, New York in 1906, Wright was also setting the style for the mid-20th century workplace. Designers, free of classically inspired styles for the first time since the Renaissance, have explored the possibilities of plywood, plastic and tubular steel.

In the office, other technological advances, like the typewriter and the telephone, have tended to dictate simple flat surfaces with drawers beneath, especially as this form was suited to the trend towards clean, efficient design.

PRE 1600

Chairs

Before 1500, few Europeans (as we know them now) had ever seen a chair, let alone sat on one. Earlier chair design had existed, however, and one of the earliest recorded pieces of surviving furniture is a folding chair of ash with a seat of otter skin, in much the same design as a 19th- or 20th-century campaign stool. Found near Muldbjerg in Denmark, it is believed to date from before 1,000 BC. But this piece is particularly unusual, not just because of its early date, but also because climate has destroyed almost all wooden seat furniture made before 1500. Consequently, tracing the development of European furniture has to be through surviving paintings and art from over the centuries.

Surviving artefacts from the ancient Egyptian, Greek and Roman civilizations, for example, give clear evidence of contemporary seating. Chairs were standard practical equipment for the royal Egyptians – the Pharaohs were buried with several for use in the afterlife – and Greek and Roman drawings on vases and wall paintings show that they were in common use then too, although virtually none have survived. Indeed, Greek provided the English language with words for both chair (*cathedra*) and throne (*thronos*), and during the neo-Classical revival of the late 18th century attempts were made to reconstruct chairs from this time using the scant evidence available. The 'Klismos' chair in the Victoria & Albert Museum, London, is one of these.

In Europe, the use of formal seating was generally restricted to kings and bishops, the holders of power. Church influence on chair development is clear; what was possibly St Augustine's chair from the 6th century can still be seen at Canterbury Cathedral in England, and illuminated medieval manuscripts show Romanesque monks using chairs in the 12th century. England's Richard II is depicted on his throne towards 1500, and Leonardo da Vinci (1452–1519) painted Jesus' disciples on stools in the famous painting of the Last Supper. By 1550, boisterous peasants using stools in the fields appear in works by Brueghel, and just before 1600, Caravaggio places St Matthew in an identifiably X-framed chair in the tavern from which he is called to be converted.

Following the 13th-century Gothic style, design sophistication before 1600 reached its heights with the Italian Renaissances, initiated in Florence. The joined panelling technique developed in Flanders c1400. The 'Savonarola cross' chair, a folding chair with a high back fixed with leather or pane, was relatively plain, but other chairs, stools and benches made of planks were carved into more delicate shapes. Walnut was mostly used, but documents from the period show that the Italians were employing as many as 30 different types of wood in their furniture making at this time. Further north, the heavier Gothic style combined with the lighter Italian style to produce a rectangular mix of the two, typified in Hans Vredeman de Vries' pattern books published in Holland c1580.

The quality of 16th-century English furniture was not as high as elsewhere in Europe. Benches and tripod stools were used at meals, but chairs were reserved for the head of the household alone. Settles (benches with arms and backs) were large and more permanent pieces of furniture. Joint work developed, and in the mid-16th century, Henry VIII had started a trend of employing foreign craftsmen, many of whom produced magnificent walnut chairs in the 1540s. His daughter, Elizabeth I (whose reign lasted from 1559–1603) had chairs decorated with inlaid woods echoing the Renaissance styles dominant on the European continent, and seats were used in much greater numbers. Upholstery, too, developed, changing from the mere addition of a cushion to a wooden seat to a complete covering of the back and seat with tapestry and velvet.

Sofas

Despite the relative simplicity of their tools, craftsmen of the ancient Egyptian and Greek civilizations created day-beds and sofas whose designs have provided furniture makers through the ages with the most elegant of basic forms. Very little actual furniture from Pharaonic Egypt and ancient Greece has survived, however; the best-known collection was discovered near Luxor in 1922, in the tomb of Tutankhamen, who died c1350 BC. His golden throne, with lion-paw feet, exhibits a skilled use of inlay using precious stones, as well as the application of gold foil.

Bull's feet were used on furniture in the First Dynasty (c3000 BC), but by the New Kingdom (c1567–1070 BC) the lion-foot form had become more popular as shown by the funerary couches found in Tutankhamen's tomb. In an inlaid scene on the back of his gilded throne, the king is shown seated on an upholstered chair, suggesting that the craft of padded upholstery had its beginnings in Egypt. Most of these couches seem to have been low and sloped down to the foot, but those used by Tutankhamen were very high, perhaps an indication of his rank. Both cushions and linen covers appeared on couches, although the double benches that seated a man and his wife in tomb reliefs were left plain. Veneers, marquetry and inlay were also used by the Egyptians.

In ancient Greece, couches used for eating as well as for reclining on during the day were status symbols. At first Egyptian-style animal legs continued to be popular, but these were gradually replaced by rectangular legs that were sometimes extended to hold a mattress or pillow in position. Some of the scroll couches with scroll-decorated pillow rests were wide enough for two people to recline on for a banquet and were made comfortable with lone, matress-like cushions. From the 8th century BC, the Greek furniture makers were using very slim legs for couches, some of which were turned, a form of support that is found on Egyptian and Persian furniture of the period. Roman day-beds were even more closely related to Greek antecedents. Since couches were the most expensive items of furniture in the homes of well-to-do citizens, they were richly ornamented with bronze, ivory and bone. The sophistication of Roman furniture is seen in a sarcophagus of the 2nd century AD, which depicts a woman, lying on a couch that has turned legs, a long padded seat and a high back – a good design that was in fact imitated in the 1830s. Couches with both long and short legs were used by the Romans, although at meals it was usually only the head of the household who reclined; the rest of the family sat on stools and chairs.

By the end of the 1st century AD, the characteristic Roman style, with a high back and sides – the forerunner of the popular modern sofa – had emerged. The Roman love of colour and comfort was seen in the sofa's generously padded cusions and the brighly patterned mattress covers. The constuction of the more elegant Greek and Roman couches, which stood on delicate legs, was dependent on trained and disciplined craftsmen who carried their techniques across Europe.

Some of these skills were never completly lost in the so-called Dark Ages, and excavations continually reveal instances of work of a higher quality than was once considered possible. Because of the unsettled lifestyle of the nobility in the early medieval period, and the constant moves from one castle to another, portable furniture became highly important. The basic construction of couches was very simple, but the piece was given importance by the use of costly drapery and cushions. By fixing a wall-hanging above a bench, this basic structure was transformed into a seat of honour. Because people lived and slept in the same room, beds often doubled as couches.

Court life in the late medieval period was lavish and colourful, with furniture and walls hung with tapestry and embrioidery. By the mid-15th century, couches were found in rooms that also had a bed and they were obviously intended for daytime use. One low-backed French example had collapsible sides and was made more comfortable by the addition of tasselled cushions. Others had pierced-work of the great Gothic stone carvers. The typical Italian form of seat, the *cassapanca*, is also asociated with the 15th century, and was a development of the traditional chest, known as a *cassone*. The *cassapanca* was provided with a low back and a seat that could be lifted. It was either painted or elaborately carved, depending on the wealth and tastes of its owners.

Tables

In the pre-Christian world, it is probable that stools or benches served the same purpose as tables; judging by wall paintings and vases dating from the time of the Greeks and Romans, small tables resembling stools are clearly shown being used for eating and gambling. On the whole, these give the appearance of being very plain (although there are rare illustrations on the top surfaces), but more elaborate examples in marble have survived.

There is plenty of evidence that tables were in use in many other parts of the world, including Syria (tables are often mentioned in the Bible) and Western Asia. In China, tables were used well before the 1st century AD, and chairs and tables were employed ceremonially and domestically by the 10th century. In Europe, a brass stand from c100 BC was found at Pompeii, Italy, cast and chased elaborately in bronze, its three animal legs topped with sphinxes and joined by curving stretchers. Although it is not certain that it was a table, it resembles closely the form developed by the time of Christ and the Roman Empire a century later. A Romano-German sarcophagus from c300 AD is decorated with a carved three-legged table with a half-round top and, again, animal legs and feet, and by 400 AD free-standing, wall and cross-framed tables were all in existence.

Little is known of European furniture between 500 AD and 1,000 AD except through evidence from paintings and other artworks. Illustrated manuscripts from c1100 show monks and saints seated and writing on chair rests, but rarely using tables of any sort. The likelihood is that most were of rough construction, with thickly sawn planks for the top, and for legs. Tables were not used for storage as now, and were therefore less necessary than other pieces of furniture – possessions would have been stored elsewhere, in chests, coffers or in-built cupboards. In the Middle Ages, the bench served many functions – as a bed, a seat, and almost certainly as a table – and it was possible with the accumulation of wealth and more settled lifestyle that permanent pieces of furniture began to take root.

More examples have survived from after 1400 or so, however, although tables from well into the 16th century remain difficult to find. The plainness of the medieval table, often covered with cloths or table-carpets, was gradually embellished with the Renaissance vogue for ornament, first seen in Italy in the 15th century. These Renaissance examples were different in that the basic forms were decorated with abundant Classical motifs, among them swags, urns and grotesque masks, drawn from ancient Greek and Roman art and architecture, which continue to appear on Western furniture decoration. Renaissance Italy was a great trading nation, which exposed its designers to a variety of foreign influences: Venice's links with the Far East encouraged a taste for chinoiserie and the inlay of both exotic woods and ivory, and the city's proximity to the Arabic world resulted in the adoption of arabesque patterns. Such abstract motifs are widely used and have been perfected by Muslims, because their faith forbids the use of human and animal imagery.

As the Renaissance took hold throughout Europe, these same motifs are found on tables in France, Germany, the Netherlands and England. Elizabethan, 16th-century refectory tables no longer stood on simple trestles, but might well have sported bulbous, carved legs. Stretchers, added originally for strength, became an integral part of a table, providing additional surfaces for the favoured carved-wood decoration. Northern European nations were still influenced by the heavier Gothic style, but the influential Han Vredeman de Vries' pattern books showed tables employing a typically rectangular style evolved from a combination of Gothic and Rococo.

The 1500s witnessed a flowing of furniture in the Renaissance spirit, commissioned by the royalty and aristocracy of Europe. Fontainebleau Palace (built and furnished by France's Francis I, 1515-1547) contained some beautiful decorated tables, as did Henry VIII's Hampton Court Palace in England. However, the gap rapidly widened between court furniture for the wealthy who demanded the latest styles, and the

St Mark depicted in the Gospels of St Henry the Lion, a German gospel of 1175, sharpening his quill pen. He is seated on a medieval ecclesiastical throne, which has a 'dosser' or low back; they were frequently made of fabric stretched between the two uprights. The legs are very probably x-framed, hidden here by an embroidered cloth.

St Matthew (from the same illuminated manuscripts) shown writing his gospel on a high-backed throne, probably of panelled construction. The banker or cushion rests on boards forming the lid of a box beneath, which could then be used for storage. These thrones were often placed underneath a fabric or wooden canopy.

rough, practical all-purpose table for the poorer population, which remained unchanged as the centuries passed.

Desks

European writing furniture dating from before the 17th century is relatively rare. To find the most common and substantial survivals, it is necessary to look in places where reading and writing were accepted as part of everyday life and, from the fall of the Roman Empire onwards, these were churches and monasteries.

Not only were medieval churchmen more commonly able to read and write than the rest of the population, they also enjoyed a status that to some extent separated them from the hurly-burly of everyday life, allowing them to maintain libraries which would have been out of the question even for the lay gentry, who were frequently caught up in wars and internal power struggles. The continuity of life in religious orders has meant that a good deal of ecclesiastical furniture has survived. The simple lectern, a book slope on a tall stand intended for reading aloud from the scriptures, remains a symbolic and practical item in churches today, but it was essential as a support for massive and heavy early books.

This practical use of the slope with a supporting ledge along the bottom edge influenced desk design right into the 20th century. It is to be found in more massive form in monastic settings, often as fixtures in libraries, and examples with panelled bases show great affinity with the later slope-front desks, except that they did not allow room for the knees of anyone who wished to sit at them and write.

Renaissance and earlier depictions of scholarly gentry or saints in their studies often show them at a bookstand on a pillar with a pen in one hand and an ink pot in the other, while weights were sometimes added to prevent the leaves of the book from turning over. Alongside this precarious and inconvenient arrangement one also sees illustrations of the more practical, low table desk in use, which allows papers and books to be spread around.

While books remained rare and expensive, private libraries were few, and large writing desks seem to have been absent from the homes of even the most rich and powerful. Palaces were furnished to impress, but state beds with luxurious hangings and the tiered buffets for the display of valuable possessions were more important to the career of a public figure than a show of scholarship. In the largely public atmosphere of a court which was frequently moved around, small writing boxes seem to have been the rule, intricately fitted with all the necessities like ink and pens. Some, like the magnificently decorated sloping box of drawers and compartments made for Henry VII of England in about 1525, which survives in the Victoria and Albert Museum, were luxury objects; others were more utilitarian.

It was with the development of smaller private chambers in great houses that the appearance of the domestic folding desk was most intimately connected. As Renaissance ideas spread North through Europe from Italy, private scholarship became fashionable and the nobility aspired to closets or studies. The Renaissance man collected natural curiosities, as well as coins, medals and books which created a need for somewhere to store and study them.

Some of the earliest chests of small drawers with a single flap that fell forward and could be used for writing (as opposed to doors) came from Spain. These rectangular travelling cabinets, known as *vargueno* from the 19th century onwards, came into use in the 16th century. They were often plain on the outside, apart from elaborate clasps, but tended to be luxury objects with extravagantly decorated interiors showing a strong Moorish influence.

The banks of small drawers and cupboards were often arranged like architecture in miniature, but emphasis on concealed intricacy of this kind is characteristic of much of the writing furniture of later periods.

A Greek two-handled bowl of the 6th century BC decorated with a cock-fighting scene. The two spectators sit on folding x-stools known as diphros okladias, *a light portable seat that could be carried by a slave and set up when needed.*

A Greek amphora of similar date showing Zeus sitting on a throne with animal claw feet. Such chairs, derived from Egyptian or Asian originals, were used by the Greeks as seats of honour in theatres or other public places.

The Winter Parlour (c1582) from the Swiss Castle of Wiggen shows the range of 16th-century styles available in Europe. The trestle table is Gothic, the chair backs are carved with Renaissance scrolls and shells, and the door is framed by revived Classical columns. The overall effect is slightly busy and confused, lacking the clarity of 18th-century Classical revival which is clear and cool. It is an excellent use of pine giving a homely but interesting result.

PRE-1600

A . The State Throne of Tutankhamun, *c*3000 BC

This is a reconstruction of one of the earliest free-standing chairs. The original was excavated from the tomb of the Egyptian Pharaoh in 1922. Beneath the embossed metal and enamel it has a simple wood frame, basically identical to those found in most Western homes today. There are many good examples of Ancient Egyptian chairs and stools in the Cairo Museum, perfectly preserved because of conditions within the tomb.

Little is known about Greek and Roman chairs other than from the designs on contemporary vases and paintings; the next reliably dated examples of chairs are European, from the late Middle Ages onwards.

B . A 16th-Century English Four-Legged Stool or Table, *c*1580

The clover-leaf top of this piece is something of an enigma, and probably unique. It is certainly strong enough to be a stool and the carved columnar legs are identical to joint stools of the Elizabethan period. However, the top is relatively thin, therefore probably too weak to be a seat. Whether a chair or a table, it is very rare, very early and a very pleasing relic from the times of Drake and the Armada.

C . An Oak Joint Stool, *c*1580

This beautifully decorated stool is not only early but extremely rare. The arcaded rails are characteristic of the Elizabethan era, but in this case the arches were filled with a carved scallop shell; still seen on the end of the stool, although the others have broken, this was probably a unique feature. The fluted legs are also unusual in the way that the beaded ring forms the capitol; it is interesting to note how a typical Renaissance decoration is interpreted by the English craftsman. There may also have been an applied border of decoration in between the arches on the square-sectioned legs, forming a continuous arcade.

B

C

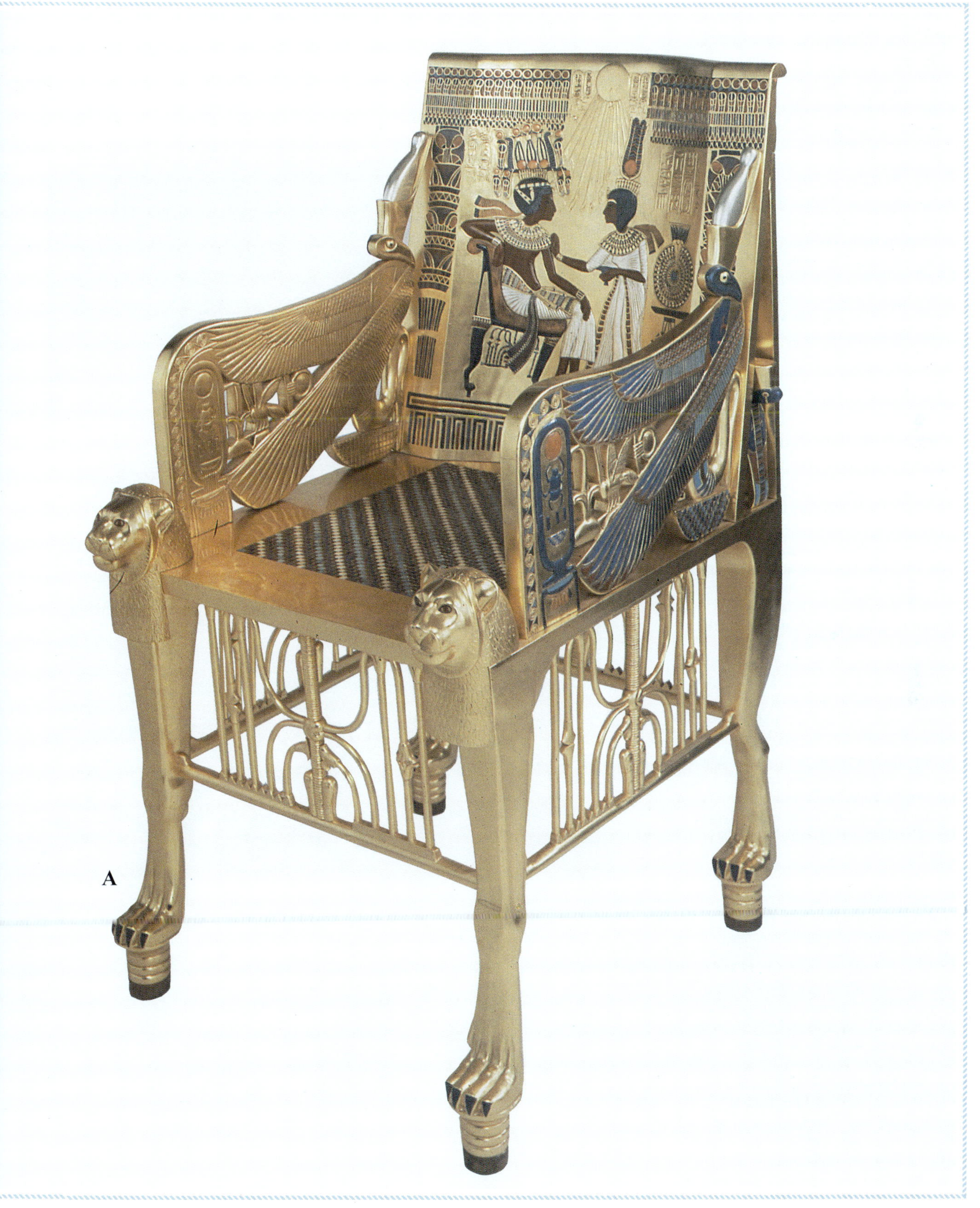

A

A . An Ancient Egyptian Painting, featuring a Sofa with Animal Feet, c1000 BC

Ladies Listening to a Harpist are the subject of this Egyptian tempera painting of c1000 BC. It comes from the Valley of the Nobles, Thebes, and dates to the XXth Dynasty. From the Tomb of Inkerkha, it shows the deceased listening to a harpist and seated on a small, straight-backed sofa. The strutted framework beneath the seat was a popular construction method and acted as a brace as well as a decorative device. The animal-leg feet in this instance are quite simple, but in some seat furniture massive and well-carved lion-paw feet were used. Cheap woods were often gilded or painted to create a more lavish effect.

B . Modern Painting of Cleopatra by John Collier, featuring Early Egyptian Sofa with Animal Feet, c50 BC

In his interpretation of *The Death of Cleopatra*, John Collier (1850–1934) shows the Queen of the Nile reclining on the type of couch that could have been used in the period. Early Egyptian sofas were very simple, but by the 1st Dynasty legs with bull's feet were used. Lion-paw feet, in combination with lion masks at the head, appeared in the Middle Kingdom on the beds or settles of people of high rank. In the main, native woods such as tamarisk or acacia were used, although cedar and juniper were also imported. Sheet gold and gold leaf on gesso were employed (in this instance, gold enhances the headrest section). By the time of Cleopatra, couches were used for both daytime reclining as well as nocturnal sleeping. These ancient forms appear to have persisted and influenced much Roman furniture.

C . An Ancient Roman Wall Painting, featuring a 'Love Seat' c50 BC

In *Noblewoman Playing a Cithara*, a fresco dating to c50 BC, a woman sits on a small sofa, similar in size to love seats of the 18th century. The seat is supported on turned legs, strengthened with a brace, and its slatted back is curved for greater comfort. This piece reveals the complexity of form that was possible at the time. These early furniture-making methods were carried across Europe by the Romans but were lost during the Dark Ages, after which the development of modern European construction methods began.

B

C

A

PRE-1600

A . A Gothic Oak Coffer, *c*1500

Although some of the richer residences of this date might have had separate tables, in the majority of houses the coffer was used as a general piece of furniture serving as storage space, bench, table and even bed. The distinction between coffers and chests was minimal, although generally a chest travelled and a coffer did not. A coffer could be as large as 12ft (3.65m) long and 4ft (1.2m) wide. In 1438, the Company of Coffee Makers asked Richard III to prohibit the import of Flemish furniture in order to protect their home market.

This English example is set off the ground (to keep it away from damp and insects), and has a simple hinged top. The planks are joined with tongue-and-groove timber, and the front shows typical deep-carved 'tracery' decoration (so-named after the patterned windows of churches and cathedrals).

B . A French Henri II Walnut Centre Table, *c*1580

As in the rest of Europe, France produced little furniture of note before 1400. The few chairs, stools and tables that did exist were largely plain and Gothic in style, made of thick planks and joined with pegs. This changed with the Renaissance, which spread from Italy throughout Europe during the 15th century, revolutionizing all branches of art. During the reign of François I (1515–47), the prevailing decorative style in France changed from Gothic to Italian-influenced Renaissance designs; the showpiece of the new style was the Chateau de Fontainebleau outside Paris. This was the centre for the school of Fontainebleau, greatly influenced by the Italian, Francesco Primaticcio (1505–70), and responsible for introducing Italian designs in furniture production. These included carved motifs and table friezes, which were decorated with designs such as slender naked nymphs, chubby angels with garlands of flowers, satyr masks, strapwork and scrolls.

By the time Henri II (1547–59) succeeded François I, the applied arts in France were in turmoil. Apart from the highly decorated pieces displayed at Fontainebleau, another style, geometric and simple, was emerging in reaction to Renaissance excess.

This table belongs to the simpler French style, which stressed the architectural elements of the Renaissance movement. Based on an overall geometric plan, the legs, shaped like columns, are distinctly non-Gothic. Although there is a small amount of turned ornament, there is very little carving.

C . An Oak Court Cupboard, *c*1600

This early type of sideboard takes its name from the French word, *court*, meaning short. English-made, cupboards such as this are first mentioned in documents from the reign of Elizabeth I (1559–1603), and in Shakespeare's *Romeo and Juliet* servants are told to 'remove the court cupboard and look to the plate' – meaning to clear the furniture and utensils after eating so as to leave space for dancing. The drawer in the frieze probably would have been used to store linen or valuables, and the top would have displayed food and plate.

The traditional English court cupboard usually had three tiers – here, for example, there may well have been another tier on top of the two remaining, but furniture was constantly altered and adapted. The drawer is decorated with 'stop fluting', and the front legs are bulbous compared to the flatter back legs. The cupboard is solidly built, with mortice-and-tenon joints throughout pegged with wood – the pegs can clearly be seen on the bottom rail.

D . A Spanish Walnut Table, *c*1600

This table is typical of many produced in Spain during the 17th century, and may well date from very early in the 1600s. Plain, with elegant bobbin-turned legs, it has the S-shaped iron stretchers that were found on a great deal of Mediterranean furniture of this period. Iron stretchers are elegant and stronger than wood, as well as pliable, so it is perhaps surprising that they were not adopted elsewhere in Europe before the 19th century. The tops of these tables were often attached to their trestle legs by a loose mortice-and-tenon joint. This allowed the whole table to fold when the stretchers were removed.

There is a noticeable lack of carved or other decoration here, although it was not due to a lack of skill. Spain and Portugal were at the peak of their power in the mid 16th century, and many finely carved and inlaid cabinets date from both the 1500s and 1600s. A more likely reason is that the table would have been covered with an embroidered tablecloth or table-carpet showing mythological, biblical or folklore scenes, and would therefore require less embellishment. This was a continuation of a custom common all over Europe, as can be seen from the very fine 'table-carpets' in the Victoria & Albert Museum, London, which date from the late medieval period onward.

C

D

PRE-1600

A . An Early Medieval Table Desk
It is made of faded hardwood, with a carved top about 10in (25cm) square, set at a gentle slope on turned baluster legs, which are joined by stretchers with further small turned columns along each side. This well-made and rare survival from the Dark Ages is known as *Le Pupitre de Sainte Radegonde,* following traditional belief that it belonged to Radegonde, wife of Clotaire, King of the Franks in the mid-6th century. Radegonde forsook the corrupt life of the royal family and founded the Sainte Croix monastery at Poitiers, where the desk is still preserved. Whether or not it belonged to a saint, this is a good example of an early desk of the type seen in prints and paintings of the Middle Ages and the Renaissance. Like most early desks it has an ecclesiastical origin, emphasised here by the carved decoration: the Lamb of God at the centre, with the symbols of the four evangelists in the corners, Latin crosses to each side, a Maltese cross at the bottom and Christ's monogram at the top. The underparts, which are of mortice and tenon construction, are decorated with chevron bands and rows of dots and circles.

B . A Small Table Desk
It is 1ft 4in (41cm) wide and is thought to have been made for Henry VIII of England in the 1520s. Here the sloping lid has been thrown back and the front dropped down to reveal the painted and gilded decoration of the interior. The inside of the lid is embellished with looped strapwork containing the badges of Henry and his first wife, Catherine of Aragon. The inside of the front flap bears portrait medallions of 'Paris de Troy' and 'Helen de Greci' and opens to reveal three drawers, the centre one divided by partitions and the other two fitted with sliding lids. There is a further small partitioned drawer in the bottom of the righthand side. The desk is now covered on the outside with shagreen and mounted with gilt metal, work which dates from the early 18th century.

Small table desks seem to have been the favoured form of writing surface until the 17th century, and this is a fine example of sumptuous work befitting a royal palace.

C . A detail of the Henry VIII table desk, with the second lid thrown back to reveal two lockable compartments with lids. The one at the back bears a medallion of the head of Christ and the one on the right depicts St George with the slain dragon at his feet. The inside of the lid bears the coat-of-arms of Henry VIII supported by two putti with trumpets, flanked by the figures of Mars on the left and Venus with Cupid on the right. This highly sophisticated piece of furniture shows a strong Renaissance influence and may have been the work of a foreign craftsman working in England.

D . A Late 16th-Century Inlaid Oak Table Desk
This is an English piece, fitted on the inside with a nest of eight drawers and with an old iron lock and the original strap hinges. The bog oak and light wood decoration is inlaid in the true sense of the term (that is, let into grooves cut into the solid carcase rather than laid on as a patterned veneer) and continues right round the box in a series of stylised palace façades and abstract geometric motifs. The form of this slope-front desk is typical, with a moulded ledge along the front edge to prevent books from slipping off. It is 2ft 3in (69cm) wide.

E . A Spanish 16th-Century Painted and Partially Gilt Vargueño
This 3ft 6in (1.48m) wide example has a chest base with a pair of drawers over a pair of cupboards, rather than the more commonly-seen trestle base. Behind the fall front there are 12 small drawers grouped around a cupboard with three more drawers inside. Notice the shell-fronted lopers pulled out to support the writing surface.

A

D

B
C
E

1600 *to* 1700

The period between 1600 and 1700, a time of wide-sweeping social, economic and historical change, saw the beginnings of many highly embellished and ornate furniture styles, as well as a continuing growth in the craftsmanship, skills and techniques used to produce these pieces. Such design changes and refinements were often swift and clearly documented in each of the major furniture types, and thankfully, many fine pieces from this period survive to chronicle their development.

Chairs

The refinements in chair design which had begun in England and France in the mid-16th century continued in the 17th century, and by 1640 chairs appeared showing the influence of clothing fashion on their design. The Farthingale chair, for example, was armless, to allow women dressed in the voluminous costumes of the time (sometimes as much as 4ft/1m 22cm wide) to sit down. Politics, too, had a considerable influence, seen both in the plain, no-nonsense lines of Puritan Roundheads in England and in the refined design of the glittering court of Louis XIV of France at Versailles.

French style at the turn of the century showed good proportion, clear design, restraint in ornament and a high degree of refinement; workmanship was of the very highest order. Flemish and Italian craftsmen, imported into France at the turn of the century by Henry IV, had taught their crafts to apprentices, and within 50 years or so, the French had outstripped their masters. By 1640, chairs were low-backed, as in Holland and England, those with high backs developing at court. In general, chairs were of simple design, and with finer turning in France than in neighbouring countries; their chief decoration was their upholstery.

In contrast, Louis XIV furniture was opulent, classical, and highly symmetrical. The development of marquetry using brass and tortoiseshell (known as boulle since André-Charles Boulle established the technique in France) was just one of many decorative techniques developed during Louis XIV's reign. French court chairs of the time were generally carved in oak and polished or gilded softwood and were notable for their hierarchy: armchairs (*fauteuils*) or chairs without arms (*chaises*) were reserved for the king alone, a stool (*tabouret*) was a privilege for the courtiers, and folding stools were reserved for the duchesses. In well-to-do private homes, upholstered armchairs and wing chairs were generally high-backed, with finely carved arm supports and legs.

Oak was the dominant wood in English 17th-century furniture up to around 1660. Charles I had made efforts to align England with the arts movements on the continent, but the Civil War and 11 years of Puritan rule (1649-1660) had a profound influence on styles. Despite this, upholstery became more widely used during this time, and Elizabethan carving excesses were toned down. The development of regional chair styles suggests a wider use of seating than previously, as does the widespread production of the turned (or thrown) chair and the stick-back chair (now known as the Windsor chair). But it was Charles II's restoration to the throne in 1660 which made a dramatic difference to English design. The monarch's links with overseas tastes and craftsmanship during his years in exile were maintained when he returned to England, and flourishing trades – with apprentices – were soon well established. Trade and overseas colonization created enough wealth to follow latest styles such as veneering (detailed work which required finer craftsmanship than anything before, and led to the emergence of the prestigious cabinetmaker) and lacquer work, based on the exotic oriental work being imported from the Far East.

An important cross-fertilization of ideas between England and the rest of Europe took place through the religious persecution of the French Protestant Huguenots by the Catholic authorities. William and Mary (who came to England from Holland in 1689 to reign) invited the persecuted Huguenots, many of whom were master craftsmen, to take refuge in England. The new king and queen also brought with them several of their own outstanding craftsmen, one of whom was the renowned Daniel Marot.

Consequently, by 1700, English woodworkers were working with the very latest in cabinetmaking techniques.

Furniture produced in America during the 17th century mainly reflected tastes and styles of the mother countries of the settlers. Indeed, furniture was scarce at the start of the century and few pieces remain, although at the time chairs with straight back-posts and rush seats were widely used: refinement was seen in the turning rather than the overall shape. Towards the end of the 17th century, designs were filtering over from Europe, and especially England, but American colonial styles remained very much their own, simpler and more functional than their fashion-conscious European counterparts.

So, by 1700, there were gilt chairs in France, marquetry in Flanders, sculptural carving in Italy, regular trade between Europe and the Far East, and constant contact between Europe and the Americas. By the end of the century, the chair was no longer a symbol of power - it had become the seat of the populace.

Sofas

In contrast, by the beginning of the 17th century, the couch had become the seat of honour in important houses. Sometimes canopied, it would stand against a tapestry - or needlework-hung wall, and so did not need a back. The arms on the finest examples were adjustable and could be lowered by either a ratchet system or a series of rods. The 'Great Couches' of this type were either pained or covered with padded leather or fabric. The most famous example, popularly known as the 'Knole' sofa, dates to the second quarter of the century and is a later development, as its original high back shows that the piece was intended as a freestanding item. Settees of the chair-back type were a development of the earlier court fashion of standing a row of chairs against one another on either side of a seat of honour or a state bed. Both carved and upholstered versions are characteristic of the second half of the 17th century, the most superb examples still retaining their original needlework or Genoa-velvet upholstery. The finest work of the period was created by French craftsmen, who fashioned prestige pieces for the court with gilded carving, sumptuous cushions, tassels and fringes. The upholsterer's craft is seen at its best in the finest sofas of the late 17th century. Intended only for the very wealthy, they boasted opulent cut velvets, brocaded silks, fringes and tassels exported from France and Italy, thus allowing one piece of furniture to exhibit the products of several countries. After the revocation of the Edict of Nantes in 1685, French weavers and cabinetmakers, fleeing religious persecution, took their skills to other countries. By the end of the 17th century, French furniture makers had begun to produce almost every type of basic sofa. The most characteristically French design was the *lit-de-repos*, with ornate gilded carving. Some versions had only one arm which acted as a back rest and was obviously intended for reclining, while others had two sides so they could seat several people.

Tables

At the onset of the 17th century, there emerged three main types of everyday table in the homes of the wealthy. A large communal dining table was used in the great hall of a stately home (this could seat up to 50 diners); a smaller, private table, made of thick timbers and often of oak, for writing or dining; and the folding table, its flap supported by the relatively sophisticated gate leg and requiring hinges. As the century progressed, and homes generally became smaller, tables which could be extended for occasional use became popular. Although formal public life for royalty took place in massive chambers – as epitomized by Louis XIV's Château de Versailles – smaller private apartments and informal chambers required a different style of furnishings.

The Château de Versailles, built during the reign of Louis XIV (1643–1715), became the standard for European taste. The showpiece of the Sun King was filled with furniture which included tables as extravagant in their size and colour as the palace they occupied (the creation of such court furniture often fell within the domain of the architect). The 'weight' of these pieces strongly impressed itself on a room, and furniture form became an integral part of interior design. A heightened overall effect was achieved by the use of the innovative console table in particular, which stood against a wall, often surmounted by a mirror forming a pattern with the now larger vertical windows. Large palaces needed private apartments, and for these too smaller tables were made, some compact enough for the bedside, and including drawers to hold cosmetics and writing materials. Likewise, the ritual of dining became more complex, and so side and serving tables were devised, as were wine tables and games tables.

France itself had benefited from the skills of Flemish and Italian craftsmen, particu*larly* in the setting up of the *Manufacture Royale des Meubles de la Couronne* at Goubelins on the outskirts of Paris in the 1660s. Here Louis XIV sponsored workshops that not only provided the interior decoration for his ambitious palace-building programme, but also produced future generations of native craftsmen of the highest calibre.

In England, the move towards extravagant European fashions was halted by the execution of the king, Charles I (ruled 1626-1649), and the establishment of a Puritan state under Oliver Cromwell. Tables reverted back to being plain, uncarved and functional. But with the restoration of the monarchy in the 1660s came an influx of continental practices.

Tea was introduced from the Orient during the 17th century, and the ritual for taking tea became part of the aristocratic social life. Ham House, outside London, the residence of the Countess Lauderdale, was fully refurbished in prevailing European styles in the 1670s. An inventory dating from 1679 suggests that tea parties were already well established, listing an 'Indian furnace for tee garnished wt silver' [sic]. And as well as tea tables, there were card tables, tables for lighting and occasional tables that were unfolded when necessary.

English tables began to sport carving and gilding, these handsome embellishments often executed by Hugenot craftsmen such as Daniel Marot and the French carving family, the Pelletiers. A further continental influence in the move towards flamboyant decoration, and structure based on beauty, not support or function, came once more from Italian sources, and the naturalistic forms of the Baroque fashion. Italy dominated European taste with its Baroque furniture design, perpetuating the Renaissance love of decoration. At its best, it created colourful and dramatic tables on sweeping, scrolling gilt supports; at worst, it produced heavy clumsy tables with little functional value. Italian tables tended to be of soft wood, sometimes poorly carved, although there are some finely carved examples by the sculptor Antonio Corradini in Venice.

France had already established it own style influenced by the Baroque affection for colour and the exotic. The decorative art of veneering, originally known to the ancient civilizations of Egypt, Greece and Rome, allowed highly skilled craftsmen to make full use of the finely figured hardwoods which arrived with the opening of world trade routes. The French term *ébeniste* (cabinetmaker) refers to the preference of early veneerers for ebony. Ebony seems to have been the first hardwood sawn into thin sheets and applied to the surface of a carcase with glue; although it later ceased to be widely used in the art of veneering. Veneers were adapted for marquetry and parquetry (naturalistic or geometric designs respectively), and cabinetmakers were keen to exploit the decorative possibilities of wood grains and other materials.

By 1700, tables of bright-red patterned marble on carved wood bases of shells, figures and foliage were no more surprising than examples featuring Boulle inlay, or constructions of solid silver. Among the factors leading to such ostentation were the increase in new wealth and sheer love of show. There is no doubt that, compared to their medieval counterparts, tables had come of age, in terms of both design and decoration.

Desks

Visitors to large stately homes often remark upon the scant privacy that the finely decorated interconnecting rooms afforded their wealthy creators. The arrangement of successively grander rooms in long suites with a bedchamber at the end makes the modern observer uneasy, not to say uncomfortable, for it is hard to imagine everyday life carrying on in such showy surroundings.

This luxurious discomfort may seem incongruous, but it results from social rather than practical considerations. In the 17th century the standard arrangement of rooms in these large houses imitated the layout of Royal palaces. They were often the showplaces of ambitious couples, where richly decorated collecting cabinets were on view, but nothing so practical as a writing desk appeared in the state rooms. To find the real living quarters in such houses it is necessary to look behind the scenes, where one finds a growing concern for privacy and convenience. As at Versailles, beyond the farthest, grandest chamber in each suite at Ham House there is a closet, a small place of retirement where the formalities of public life could be relaxed.

Such chambers had been provided for important guests at a much earlier date, but at Ham House the Duchess created more than a bolt-hole. She had two adjoining private rooms, double-glazed against the cold and connected by back stairs to a bathroom. The inventories of the time indicate that these were rooms for informal gatherings such as tea parties. Also listed at the same time are two writing desks, one in each room, and another in the Duke's closet. There is no writing furniture at all mentioned in the 1645 inventory.

The desks themselves, described as 'scriptors', were small and simple cabinets on stands, filled with little pigeonholes and drawers. They were beautifully made, probably in Holland, with veneers of oystered kingwood, set off by small silver handles and mounts, but they are among the least overtly showy pieces in the house. They represent the innermost sanctuary within an already private room. The french word *secrétaire* draws attention to this idea of the desk as a place where papers and possessions can be locked away and kept secret.

The large double-domed bureau-cabinets which began to appear in Britain and Holland at the end of the 17th century and became standard items of furniture in the early years of the following century seem a long way removed from the diminutive scriptors, especially when they dominate the room with mirrored doors and brightly coloured lacquer decoration. The techniques of veneering were also applied to many of these bureau-cabinets for writing, giving a much grander appearance then their predecessors. They do, however, fulfil the same role, and when opened out their size makes them almost closets in themselves. They represented a personal domain to which a gentleman could retire to sort out his affairs, even in a large room frequented by family and servants.

It was not only a desire for increased comfort in the home that brought about the great increase in the amount of writing furniture available by the end of the century, but the influence of increased trade also played its part, as there was an increased scope for experimentation in design from the ideas and embellishments of foreign craftsmen. Many of the desk forms found at the end of the 17th century can be seen as part of the experimental process that produced the more assured and practical writing desks of the 18th century.

1600-1700

A. An English Oak Chair, *c*1600

This unusual design is probably from the late 16th or early 17th centuries, and one of just a very few made. The notion of forming the back from an architectural arch is extremely original, and the details are strikingly carved. The Renaissance gave rise to a number of architectural details such as the 'arch' back supported on columns. This is a very English version, though, with little of the Italian elegance. The wear on the uprights and plain columns forming the front legs indicate an early date.

B. An English Oak Armchair, *c*1640

This chair certainly dates from the first half of the 17th century, since its proportions and construction are so typical of that period. It is most notable for its beautifully carved back, the design of which depicts a double-headed eagle with outstretched wings. The eagle motif forms part of the arms of Prussia, although these may be the indistinct arms of the northern English Speke family; early armorials and crests are often difficult to identify from mere decoration. The chair also bears the initials T.W., probably added during an owner's inventory. Still showing the influence of earlier throne-like chairs, this tall armchair is 3ft 8ins/112cms high.

C. English Inlaid-Oak Joined Chairs, *c*1650

Chairs such as these were made throughout England from the end of the 16th century, and are perhaps the first generation of chairs as we know them today. They take their name from the joiners who made them, applying the same simple construction to chairs as they did to buildings. The mortice and tenon joints are held together by pegs from the outside, quite clearly seen on these chairs at the bottom of the front legs. In the earliest examples, the members were heavy, with some decoration, and the stretchers almost touched the ground.

The chair on the left is fairly sophisticated, and although sometimes produced in walnut, this example is oak. Its back is decorated with carved scrolls on the arch and also has inlaid central panels with stylized marquetry flowers, probably using bog-oak, holly and other fruit woods. This chair also has turned legs, which lighten the legs at the front, and undulating arms.

Although similar, the other chair is probably from a slightly earlier date. It bears the initials 'I.T.', which probably refers to the owner of the chair, since coats of arms were rare at this time. The panelled back is in the form of an architectural Roman arch

C

D

A

B

surrounding a stylized vase of flowers of geometric fruitwood inlay. These chairs are likely to have been restored since they are of very great age, and some of the new pieces may themselves be over 200 years old. The seat rail and parts of the legs may be later, betrayed only by their slightly uncharacteristic look and lightness of wood.

Although oak is now less fashionable, it was once thought to be the most desirable of woods. Chairs and joint stools such as this from the 17th century were often forged and adapted with timbers. Forgers were extremely enterprising both in the 19th and 20th centuries, often burying timbers in bogs for years to give the right texture, dryness and colour. A good 19th-century fake may now be nearly 200 years old, so beware!

D . A Pair of Ming Dynasty Chairs, *c*1600

The Ming Dynasty lasted from 1368 to 1644AD, and these chairs probably date from the late 16th or early 17th centuries. The contemporary European equivalent would have been a throne or possibly an early caqueteuse. Although the caqueteuse also has a U-shaped back, these Chinese chairs are particularly harmonious, with gentle curves balanced by the out (the curving end of the arm). It is interesting to note that below the front of the seat the rail is carved with a scrolling pattern similar in some respects to the aprons on Georgian chairs. The construction of the back also resembles European chairs of this design, with a central splat (back panel) which is decorated. Chinese chairs are known in other forms from at least the 13th century AD, which suggests that the development of the chair in the East may have been parallel to that of the West, or, more likely, influenced European designs. This same design continued to be made in China well into the 19th century, also appearing with a square back. That the same basic design has been used for so long is a marvellous example of Chinese reverence for tradition.

1600-1700

A . A 17th-Century English Turned or Thrown Chair, *c*1675

Thrown chairs appeared very early and were widespread, extending beyond Europe. They are thought to be based on a Byzantine model, although many examples are found in Scandinavia. The earlier designs have triangular seats and are three-legged, similar to early joint stools. As can be seen, each individual component is turned on a lathe to form the desired shape and then fitted like a peg into the frame.

This wonderful sculptural object, with its lovely geometric rhythm, could easily have been made by a craftsman of 20th-century Vienna Secession. It is probably late 17th-century English, and is made from the traditional woods of oak and ash.

In England, the Guild of Turners can be traced back to the 14th century. One of the main functions of a trade guild was to ensure that specific work was carried out by its own members, although in provincial England, such rigidity was infrequently enforced: during the reign of James I, for example, the Shuttleworths of Gawthorpe employed a dish-thrower to make them a turned chair; as the name suggests, a dish-thrower made plates and bowls by turning them from wood, a practice which continued even into the 19th century. Clearly in Jacobean Gawthorpe, dish-throwers could turn their hands to anything, but in 16th-century Germany, where the Reformation banned the carving of religious images, the Guild of Carvers, who were consequently unemployed, were forbidden to carry out other carpentry work such as building.

B . A North Country Marriage Chair, 1675

The arched back rail as seen on this chair is a feature which is normally associated with the counties of either Yorkshire or Derbyshire, England. This chair has the added interest of three carved initials and the date. According to convention, the upper initial, M, represents the surname and the two lower initials are for the Christian names of the couple to be married during that year, 1675. This highly original chair would almost certainly have been a marriage gift.

C . Two 17th-Century Yorkshire Chairs, *c*1680

These two rather spectacular chairs are of a fairly typical 17th-century design. Solidly built, heavy timbers form the rails with mortice and tenon joints, and the front legs and cross stretchers are bobbin-turned to give a lighter look, although also retaining solid mortice and tenon joints. Their more remarkable aspect are their backs, which are typical of chairs from the Yorkshire area. Regional chairs, like oak furniture, are areas of study of their own. The scrolling finials on the uprights, combined with the characteristic double-crescent decoration, are very typical; so too is the vigorous carving in low relief with a variety of scrolling lines, and interlocking symmetrical monsters, seen here on the right hand chair. The designs remained fairly local well into the 18th century, and even into the 19th century in isolated areas. Presumably passed on from craftsmen to apprentices, they provided sturdy chairs for an undemanding market.

D . A 17th-Century English Oak Armchair, *c*1680

The armchair in its simplest form had fully emerged before the beginning of the 17th century, and had progressed from the box-chair, little more than a coffer fitted with a back, to this rather more sophisticated, joined piece. The structure remained essentially unchanged, however, and this chair is still massive in construction; consider, for example, the size and weight of the stretchers. There is little in the way of refinement here apart from a small frieze of carving along the top of the seat, echoed along the seat rail. New features can be seen, though; the arm supports and front legs are now baluster-turned, and the arms have some shape.

This chair could have been made as late as 1700, since rural areas often continued to use earlier, unrefined designs. That the chairs were functional and enduring is clear from the fact that they are relatively common today. Their production may well have continued alongside much fancier, lighter, pierced, carved and caned chairs of the period, which used less wood but needed more skill in their making. It should be stressed that at this time chairs were still fairly rare, and that most homes would only have had stools for seating

D

A

C

B

1600-1700

A . A Pair of Late 17th-Century English Giltwood Chairs, *c*1680

The under-frames of these chairs are clear evidence of the French and Dutch influence on English design towards the end of the 17th century. The Huguenot craftsmen who fled the court of Louis XIV increased the taste for gilt furniture and for scrolling sculptural design. Similarly, Dutch craftsmen were imported with the Dutch Prince William of Orange when he arrived in England to become William III. Dutch influence on these chairs can be seen in the square-sectioned baluster front legs; note, too, the sculptural feel to the cross-stretchers which curve upwards into a pronounced scroll. The high backs, arched above and below, and the seats, are still covered with the original upholstery, a rich damask velvet with a frothy braid surround. It is possible to date these chairs to the last two decades of the 17th century, as they precede the cabriole legs and simplicity of design that began towards the end of the 17th century.

B . Two Louis XIV Walnut Armchairs, *c*1680

These two French *fauteuils* date from a time when chairs were becoming increasingly popular in Europe, and were being produced both in much greater numbers and of better quality. Note the beautiful turning on these barley-twist stretchers and arm supports, and the curving arms. They are in particular much lighter than previous designs, although still sturdy in appearance. In England, the chairs of Charles II's reign (1660–1685) imitated French design as the English monarch was keen to copy the court of the Sun King. These two, however, are fairly plain examples for their date, and are not especially courtly; they may even be from Flanders.

C . A Chinese Lacquered Armchair, *c*1680

Dating from the reign of the Chinese Emperor Kangxi, the unfamiliar design of this curious-looking low chair had a lasting effect on European furniture. Its construction is relatively sophisticated, lacking the rectangular frame of almost all European chairs of the same date, and using very few straight lines. This would have been built for an aristocrat in China, and has a heavy emphasis on decoration, less on supporting the structure, as seen in the pierced carving, a stylized representation of scrolling foliage.

The type of lacquer decoration seen here is traditional Chinese porcelain designs of the Song and Ming dynasties. It uses deep, strong colours and still conveys great natural beauty; note the design on the seat. Europeans were already copying this type of lacquered work, although the concern with patterns made with interlacing curves and piercing was not approached in Europe until the height of Chippendale, a century later.

D . A Charles II Walnut Chair, *c*1680

With the restoration of the monarchy after England's Puritan Commonwealth in 1660 came an emphasis on decorated style. Charles II reigned from 1660–1685, and design during this time was particularly influenced by the craftsmen of the European continent generally, and by those of the court of the Sun King specifically.

This beautiful example shows traces of a plainer English tradition, seen in the turning of the rails which support the back, but is ornamented in the new style. Typical of the period is the caned back, and so too are the explosive crestings on the top of the back, the cross-stretchers, and the slightly absurd scrolls at the front of the chair. Until the contemporary design explosion of the 1960s, the 'old fashioned' carved scrolling which this chair epitomizes was considered the height of antique quality. It is still a splendid chair.

D

B

C
A

A . A William and Mary or Queen Anne Walnut Chair, *c*1690

The most striking feature of this chair is its characteristic bulb-turned legs and the cross-stretcher. The turning of the legs tapers to form a central baluster while the contrasting curves of the stretchers produce an elegant pattern. This form of leg is a curious combination of prevailing continental influences with an enduring love of turning; a similar combination can be seen on the thrown chair and joined stools of the period.

The overall appearance of the chair may seem quite plain, but it might well originally have had brightly-coloured needlework upholstery acting as a foil to the walnut below, as on a similar chair in the Victoria & Albert Museum, London. The style of leg used here appeared for only a relatively short period of time, either in its plain form, or sometimes as a much more angular carved and gilded baluster; it was soon replaced by the more popular cabriole.

B . A William and Mary Painted Armchair, *c*1690

This rare example of a gilt and blue-painted William and Mary chair, with its original upholstery in very good condition, came from Godmersham House in Kent. Most striking with this armchair is its sculptural element: the arm supports and legs are elaborately carved with their edges heightened in gilt, and the front legs take on the form of herm shown with cherubs, a common subject for the many marble statues that might have been found in baroque gardens of the period. Note also the decoration on the arms, known as egg and dart moulding, another direct application of an architectural detail to furniture. Although more restrained than the work of Andrea Brustolon who created sculptural chairs on the continent, the influence of European craftsmen is overwhelming, and it clearly shows the richness it brought to English furniture design.

C . A William and Mary Lacquered Armchair, *c*1690

This chair, one of a pair, is particularly significant as it is one of the first design revivals to be seen in England. This model was originally produced in 1600, and is similar to one of that date from Knole, Kent. Knole, a stately home near London, retains most of its original 17th-century furniture, and has England's best collection of early chairs. From the Duke of Leeds' collection at Hornby Castle, York, there were originally six chairs

A

D

and at least one stool. It is an indication of the progression in chair design during the 17th century that by 1700 chair-makers were ready to re-think earlier forms, having achieved the complexities of twisting columns, caned seats, carved stretchers and even winged chairs.

This example in the scarlet and gold lacquer of the period is distinctly three-dimensional; the top of the chair back echoes the shape of the legs, and contrasts with the upturned bow of the seat. Despite looking back to the designs of the past, the stretchers which join the legs are beautifully baluster-turned and square-sectioned, a feature which very much belongs to the end of the 17th century. This product of adventurous designers confident in their sense of line, and in the technique of their craftsmen, heralded the great period of English chairmaking – the 18th century.

D . A William and Mary Walnut Miniature Chair, *c*1690

It is extremely rare to find a miniature chair of this period, but this example seems to have all the authentic characteristics of a full-size one of the same date: the outstretched arms, the scrolling front legs, the square-sectioned back legs and the arcaded front stretcher. The original needlework of anglicised oriental design was clearly executed by someone who had never visited the Far East. Measuring less than 18ins/46cms high, it was probably too small for a child to sit on and might have been for a doll.

1600-1700

A. An English Gilt-Wood Day-Bed, c1695

This day-bed, from Temple Newsam House in Leeds, was made c1695 for the Duke of Leeds. A sofa at its most princely, it is part of a suite, also incuding a high-backed sofa with arms (see Ill. 8), which was made for the Duke's manor, Kiveton Park, in Yorkshire. Both this day-bed and the sofa have stretchers in the same form and are upholstered in Genoa silk velvet in reds and greens on a typical cream background. It was an interest in comfort that fostered the construction of such day-beds; this gilt-wood example, with its tasselled fringe, is especially fine, in that attention was given to the carving of its frame as well as to its upholstery.

B. An English Gilt-Wood Settee, c1695

This fabulous settee from Temple Newsam House is one of the great classics in the history of British furniture. Made c1695, it is over 7 ft (2.1 m) long and made in the princely manner. Matching the day-bed (Ill. 7) and, like that piece, very much in the French taste, the straight back is crested by three escutcheons bearing the cipher and coronet of the 1st Duke of Leeds (Thomas Osborne, created duke in 1694). It is upholstered in Genoa velvet, one of the most fashionable coverings of the period, and is elaborately fringed and tasselled. Although the upholstery is original, it was rearranged in the 20th century, perhaps to conceal areas of heavy wear. The extravagant use of fringe and braids is typical of the period, although the cost was so high that furniture in this manner would only have been owned by the very wealthy. The day-bed and settee were originally made for Kiveton Park in Yorkshire, home of the 1st Duke of Leeds, but both are now at Temple Newsam House in Leeds.

C. An English William & Mary Upholstered Sofa, c1690

Dating to c1690, this sofa of the William & Mary period is of that style's typical form, wherein each seat area is reflected both by legs and supporting stretchers. The simple square shape is embellished with bobbin-turning to the legs and stretchers, while the upholstery of the back, seat and arms is finished with a deep fringe, the standard decorative practice at the time. Such pieces could only have been afforded by the relatively wealthy, and consequently few have survived; those that do appear on the market now command high prices.

C

C

B

A . An English James I Oak Dining Table, *c*1620

In the medieval period, dining halls consisted of a 'high', or 'top', table raised on a platform. At this table, which held the salt, sat the most important diners; the rest of the eaters sat at other tables, 'below the salt'. During the transition from this tradition to a single large table, as seen here, trestle tables which could be folded away were used – Penshurst Place in Kent, England, contains three famous oak trestle tables from the late 15th century.

By 1580, however, joined tables had arrived. They generally had a fixed top, six legs and stretchers between the feet, used as both foot rests and to stack away the benches or stools which were sat on. In the late 16th century, these tables were often heavily carved with elaborate frieze decorations, but by 1600 they were plainer and more stylized.

This example is fairly typical, with a little turning on the legs, some carving on the frieze where the rails meet the legs, and mortice-and-tenon pegged joints throughout. By the end of the century, the realization that these tables were too large led to the development of extending flaps. Tables such as these were also used to play 'shovel board' in Tudor times, a game closely related to 'shove halfpenny', wherein coins are pushed along a flat surface with the palm of the hand.

B . An Oak Folding Table, *c*1620

This table uses the simplest of mechanisms to open out. The top is opened like the lid of a box, with wrought-iron hinges fixed with nails, and the back leg swings out as a support, ie 'gate leg'. It has standard features for its time, including hexagonal shape, plain but slightly tapered legs and a drawer in the flat, stylized frieze.

Tables such as this appeared in almost all inventories of the big houses of the period. For example, the 1641 inventory of Tart Hall noted 'an ovall Table of wanscote with falling sides'. 'Wanscote', or 'wainscot', is derived from the word 'wain', or wagon. During the 15th century, wainscot came to mean 'wagon wood' (ie a wagon load of wood or timber); hence its use to refer to any wood for furniture or panelling.

C

D

C . A 17th-Century Folding Table, *c*1630

This folding table makes use of two gate legs, one on each side. The double gate leg was generally employed where the table was larger, as here, and so needed more support. By 1670, tables seating as many as 10 were made, with two gate legs on each side to accommodate extending flaps. Another popular variation allowed the table to fold away altogether. This utilized gate legs which pivoted, and a top that tilted in the manner of 18th-century breakfast tables.

This fairly basic example shows many standard features of James I and Charles I styles. The legs are solid and only very slightly turned, but the decoration is more pronounced; there is strapwork on the lower stretcher, and a running frieze of scrolling just below the top. Mortice-and-tenon joints secured by pegs can be seen on the inside of the legs.

D . A Spanish Table of Refectory Type, *c*1650

This refectory-style table was the alternative to the Spanish trestle table. It is of heavier build, with a large, overhanging top, and a deep frieze with two drawers. The table's stout baluster-turned columns are joined by a substantial H-shaped stretcher; pieces of similar design were also made in France during the early 17th century.

Much of the decoration shows Moorish influence. The southern third of Spain, which included Granada and Seville, was occupied by the Moors and their Islamic culture until the fall of Granada in 1492. The decorated panels on the frieze are quite geometric, as if influenced by Italian Renaissance design, but the carving has an Arabic asymmetry to it, as do the drawer decoration and iron escutcheon around the keyhole.

B
A

A . A Charles II Oak Low Dresser, c1670

From its earliest origins in the medieval period, the dresser had a ceremonial function as an early sideboard. A dictionary of 1611 defined it as 'a court cupboard only to set a plate upon', and early accounts of court life describe how a gong was sounded to summon courtiers to the dresser before the strict ceremony of carrying dishes to the master of the house.

Elsewhere in Europe, the dresser was often painted and highly decorated, although many of the earliest examples through the 16th century would have been covered with tapestries or cloths. Originally carved, by the late 17th century the decoration was generally simple, as seen here. The dresser would have sat against a wall in the hall, with dishes and jugs of pewter, etc, sitting on it. It may have had a set of shelves attached to the wall above it – a basic form of Welsh dresser, in fact. Low dressers were generally made of oak, and sometimes yew.

From the 18th century onward, many dressers had an attached structure for shelves, closer to the dresser of today. It also became a more informal piece of furniture, found in the kitchen rather than the hallway.

B . A Louis XIV Lacquer and Boulle *Bureau Mazarin*, c1670

The elaborate decoration, bright colours and gilt work associated with Louis XIV's reign had in fact been popular for some time before his succession as ruler in 1661 at the age of 23. After the Renaissance influence decreased in France at the end of the 16th century, it fell to Henry IV (1589–1610) to re-establish the furniture industry by importing foreign craftsmen and setting up workshops in Paris. Under Louis XIII, Mme de Medici brought an Italian influence to the French court, combined with an interest in Flemish art. The flamboyant Italian style was reinforced by Cardinal Mazarin, himself an Italian, who ruled as Regent for the child Louis XIV from 1643–61.

Cardinal Mazarin gave his name to the eight-legged *bureau,* a form which later developed curved sides. The *bureau Mazarin* was invented in the second half of the 17th century, and was at first used as both a writing desk and a console table. This example is relatively light compared to many pieces, but is typically ostentatious with its lacquer and boulle decoration. The use of lacquer was promoted by Louis XIV's Minister of Arts, Colbert, after he formed the *Compagnie des Indes* in 1664. Through the company he imported lacquer and other art works from the Orient.

A . An Italian Baroque Marble-topped Side Table, *c*1670

One of a pair of high Baroque side tables from the Palazzo Massimo in Rome, this example boasts an impressive combination of colour, vigorous curves and lines pointing in all directions. The top is made of Siena marble, which creates its own pattern by variety of shade and colour, and its supporting frame consists entirely of curving lines. The legs bow, the stretchers curve in six different directions before meeting at the centre, and the apron is decorated with foliage and plumes. The contrast between the gilding and red paint is also dramatic; the table is the epitome of the Italian Baroque spirit, truly *con brio* (literally, 'with noise').

High Baroque was at its peak between 1630 and 1680 and was centred on Rome; the sculptural vogue was strong – this was the heyday of the renowned papal sculptor, Gianlorenzo Bernini (1598–1680). Papal influence exerted itself in other ways, too; an increase in wealth among new merchant dynasties brought life to the furniture trade, and nepotism saw the rise of several powerful families, including the Barbèrini, Borghese, and Rezzonico families. The latter were based at the Palazzo Rezzonico in Venice, where the established sculptor, Antonio Corradini (1668–1752), carved much of their furniture.

B . A Charles II Oak Gate-leg Table, *c*1670

Charles II reigned for 25 years (1660–85) following the Puritan Protectorate, led by Oliver Cromwell. This table clearly shows the Puritan influence on design, with plain lines and a total lack of carved decoration. The shapes are geometric – the top is round, the stretchers rectangular – and even the turned legs are simple. The only decorative elements are minimal – the aprons hanging from the frieze.

This table has two single gate legs, one on each side, and a drawer in the frieze. The advantage of two flaps is that the table folds away to a small size. Tables such as these were made for a variety of purposes, from card playing to dining, and in a variety of sizes. The Windsor Castle accounts of the 1680s refer to 'an ovall wanscott table 6′ 6″ long and 4′ 6″ broad with a turned frame (the table made to fould)' supplied by one William Cleere.

After 1660, most tables were made in oak, although some were walnut, some yew, and in the countryside some of fruitwoods. The fashion for formal gate-leg tables died away in the early 18th century, but saw a revival after 1770 or so; they continued to be produced up to the mid 19th century, especially for country and common use.

C . A Charles II Oyster-veneered Table, *c*1670

This unusual decoration of small circles of veneer (hence the term 'oyster') is produced by cutting the branches of a tree across the grain. Like trunks, branches show annual growth rings, and an economical way of making the most of a special tree was to slice the branches and enclose the rings in a frame of lighter wood. This was generally found on English furniture, with woods as varied as laburnum, lignum vitae, olive-wood and various fruitwoods. The shape of this table is standard for the period, with barley-twist legs, inward curving cross-framed stretchers and bun feet.

From the 1680s onward, English furniture was marked by a return to decoration after Puritan plainness. There were strong influences from the court of Louis XIV, and William of Orange was accompanied by Dutch craftsmen, including Daniel Marot (1663–1752), when he came to the English throne in 1688. As a result, English cabinetmaking became truly European, blossoming with a new interest in decorative styles.

Inlay and marquetry were highly popular, using techniques such as 'seaweed' marquetry (made from very fine panels of marquetry resembling strands of seaweed), floral panels, and ivory and tortoiseshell inlay. In France at this time, André-Charles Boulle was developing the brass and tortoiseshell inlay that was named after him.

A . An English William and Mary Gilt Side Table, *c*1690

Originally from the Dutch royal family, William of Orange came to the throne of England through his marriage to Mary, the daughter of James II. He reigned from 1688 to 1694, bringing with him a greater European influence in the area of design than had ever been seen before in England. This influence was from two main sources: the French court style of Louis XIV (1643-1715), which became increasingly gilded and ornate as the century progressed; and Daniel Marot, the famous Huguenot craftsman who was William's main adviser on interior decorating (Marot had fled French persecution of the Protestants in the 1680s and taken up residence in Holland).

The rich combination of Dutch, Flemish and French influence can be seen on this table in terms of its ornateness. The table top is elaborately carved in relief with a cartouche, a departure from the English tradition of plain, functional tables which probably would have been covered with a cloth. The deep frieze has rows of lobes (rope-twists motifs) that were commonly found on Italian *cassoni* (marriage chests) and other Renaissance furniture. The legs are four 'S' scrolls, a change from the usual English turned, round-sectioned or barley-twists legs.

B . A Baroque Gilt Side Table, *c*1695

The full repertoire of Baroque decoration can be found on this side table. It is designed to take a heavy marble top (although this is possibly too slight to be the original), and wild foliate scrolls bearing unusual figures hang from the apron. There is also a figure in the centre of the cross-framed stretcher; holding a sheaf of corn, she may represent Ceres, the Roman corn goddess, or simply be an allegory of summer.

In the 17th century, sculptural allegories – and their application to furniture – were a popular Baroque feature. Consider the two main figures on the front legs of this table. On the left, another Ceres-types figure is dressed in classical drapes, representing summer, and on the right, a shivering, bearded man symbolizes winter. The likelihood is that this is one of a pair of console tables: the other would have shown spring, probably as a young girl with flowers, and autumn most likely would have been personified as Bacchus, the god of wine.

The origin of this table is not clear, particularly as some restoration work may have occurred on the front figures. The carving of the man, with his narrow Alpine face and the naturalistic branch beneath his arm, suggests Northern Europe: naturalism was characteristic of those countries. But generally big, scrolling Baroque tables are thought of as Italian. Established trade routes between Germany and Italy had been functioning since the Middle Ages, and so had the exchange of design ideas. This table probably comes from Austria, southern Germany or northern Italy, all of which, thanks to shifting national boundaries, shared similar styles.

C . A Boulle Table Top, *c*1695

The art of boulle (or 'buhl') work was named after its inventor, André-Charles Boulle (1642–1732). He was the most celebrated cabinetmaker during the reign of Louis XIV, and from 1662 onward he worked continuously for the royal family refurbishing the various palaces, especially Versailles. He originally trained as a cabinetmaker, architect, engraver and bronze worker, and published a series of engravings which helped to promote his work throughout Europe. Boulle never signed his pieces, and despite the fact that they sold for several thousands of pounds, a vast sum then, he was often in debt, thanks to his passion for collecting works of art: his enthusiasm for Renaissance art plunged him from surplus into crippling debt on several occasions, from which the King repeatedly protected him, much to his annoyance.

His technique used a combination of metals and tortoiseshell worked in one of two basic ways. *Première-partie* utilized background sheets of red or dark tortoiseshell decorated, through cut-outs, with underlays of various metals (including brass, pewter and copper). *Contre-partie,* as seen here, reversed the process, with a background of metal and tortoiseshell underlay. Boulle work remained popular in France from this time on, peaking in the 18th century and experiencing a revival in the 19th.

One of its disadvantages is that it damages easily; as the different metals expand at different rates, the work can lift off the table surface and is very difficult to replace. The wrinkle across the central oval has been caused in this way, but this is still a very fine example of 17th-century boulle work, showing a wealth of decoration: the central armorial, mythological figures, strapwork, floral and scroll inlay, and engraving all enhance the medley of bright colours.

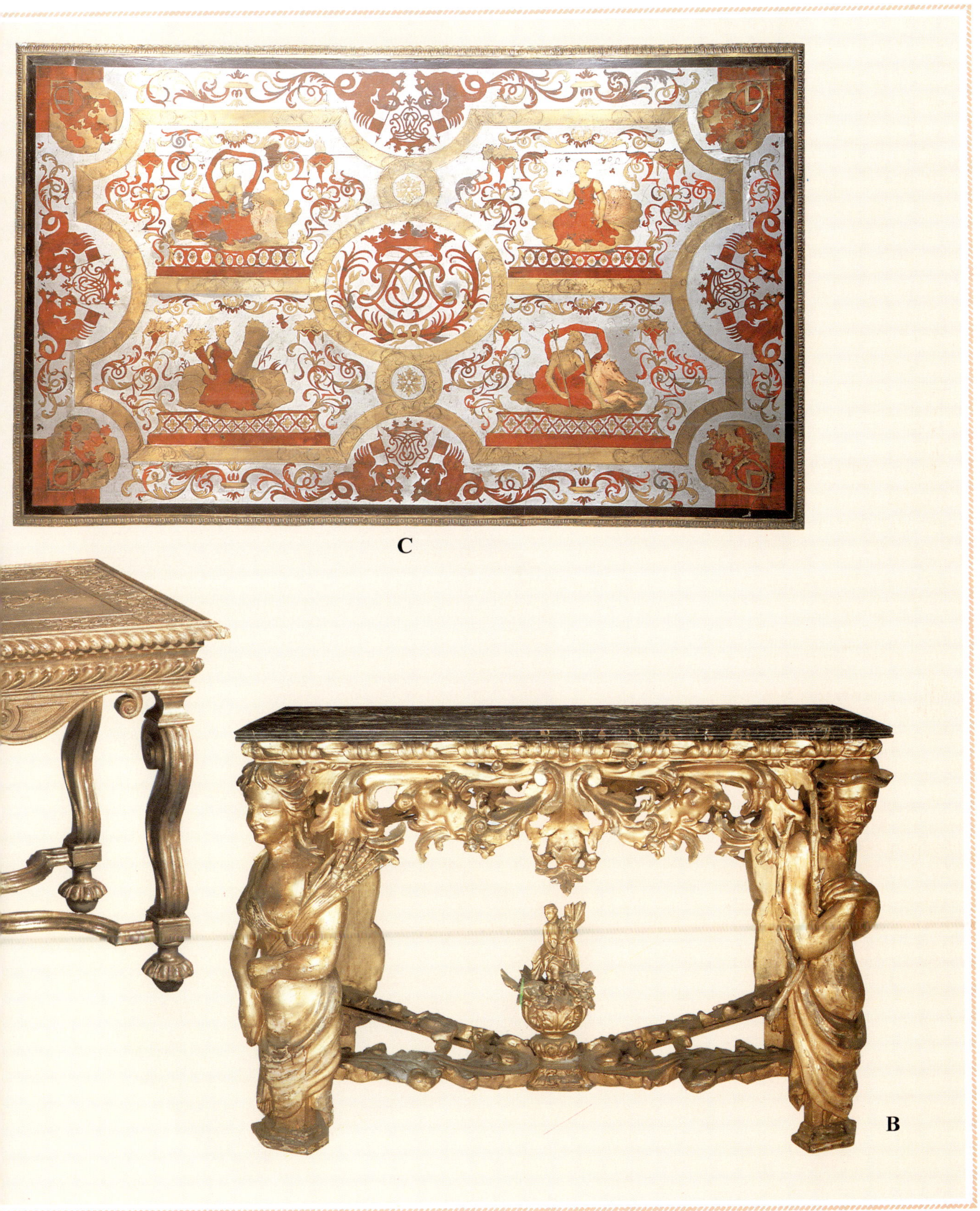

C

B

1600-1700

A . An Early 17th-century Spanish Walnut Vargueño

This example has a trestle stand and a fitted interior of drawers and cupboards. The fall front is supported on lopers in the stand when lowered. It is 3ft 9in (91cm) wide. Though the complex pierced hinges, locks and fittings are typical of these distinctive Spanish pieces, the overall plainness of the exterior reflects the origins of the vargueño as a travelling chest. The interiors, however, are generally much more decorative and reflect the Moorish influence of the time. Intricate geometric designs are often built up from small pieces of ivory, ebony, tortoiseshell and other inlays. Trestle stands, known as *puentes,* are most common, but chest bases are also found, and the vargueño would seem to be the earliest form of the fall-front secretaire that was to become popular all over Europe in later centuries.

B . An Early English 17th Century English Carved Oak Table Desk

Fitted with an external bookrest and a shelf and two drawers beneath the lid, this desk is carved at the sides with triangular panels of vine leaves and bunches of grapes above a frieze of carved roses and lozenges. Carving was the principal method of decorating English oak furniture up until the end of the 17th century, when the crafts of veneering and lacquering were introduced from the Continent. It was also during this period that table desks of this type began to be incorporated as the tops of larger and more permanent bureaux with chest of drawer bases. This example is 2ft 1in (63.5cm) wide.

C . An American Oak and Pine Bible Box of the Mid-17th Century

1ft 11in (58cm) wide, it is carved along the front with a series of rosettes and scratched with the initials AG and the date 1644. It stands on turned maple feet. Simple table boxes with hinged lids for the storage of books and valuables were the nearest things to desks to be found in American homes before the end of the 17th century.

A

D

C

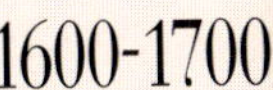

B

E

D . An American Carved Oak Desk Box, *c*1670

The box is only 14¼in (36cm) wide, with a sloping pine lid. The sides are carved with leafy branches and the initials *MF*. This rudimentary table desk has been attributed to Thomas Dennis or William Searle; both craftsmen worked in Ipswich, Massachusetts in the second half of the 17th century producing finely carved, joined furniture. Such pieces would have been used for storage, but the slant lid meant that they were also useful for reading and writing.

E . The Oak Writing Table Made for Samuel Pepys's Library in London

It is possible that 'Simpson the Joyner', who made bookcases for Pepys's Library, also made this writing table. The desk top, 5ft 5in (1.65m) wide and carved with moulding to match the bookcases, is supported on massive twin pedestals which are actually glazed bookcases intended to house Pepys's largest volumes. Pedestal desks did not become standard furniture in English libraries until the 1720s.

A . An English William and Mary Slope-Front Bureau in Oak

The way in which the top overlaps the gateleg base is typical of such desks, and a similar arrangement is found on many late 17th century examples with chest of drawer bases. The two centre front legs, which are neatly recessed into the body when closed, swing forward to support the writing surface. Inside the desk there are shelves, four drawers and a storage well, and three small drawers in the frieze provide additional storage space. After years of standing on damp floors, the feet of old pieces of furniture are often the first things to suffer, and on this desk some of the feet have been replaced.

B . An English William and Mary Black Japanned Kneehole Desk, c1695

This desk is decorated with a variety of Chinese-inspired scenes and stands on unusual bell-shaped feet. One of a pair, the desk has a single long drawer above a kneehole containing a cupboard and a small drawer, with three more small drawers on each side. Japanning, the imitation of Oriental lacquer work by European craftsmen, became popular in Britain in the late 17th century and remained an exotic, and expensive, form of decoration well into the 18th century. It is 2ft 11in (89cm) wide.

C . An English Late 17th- or Early 18th-Century Writing Chest

The whole desk is japanned in black and gold with chinoiserie landscapes and birds. The hinged top folds forward to form a lined writing surface supported on gatelegs which swing out from the body of the chest. The base has a concealed compartment with three drawers below, flanked by cupboards containing drawers and pigeonholes. This is an interesting hybrid combining the features of a bachelor's chest and an early gateleg desk. It is 3ft (92cm) wide.

F

C

B

D. An English William III Mulberry Wood Bureau, *c*1700
It is 3ft (92cm) wide, with two short and two long drawers below a writing compartment fitted with drawers, pigeonholes and a well. (This was a space used for storage found under the writing surface which doubled as a lid.) By the end of the 17th century the distinctive form of the English slope-front bureau was well established. This example, with its contrasting burr veneer and pewter stringing, is very much in the manner of Coxed & Woster, cabinetmakers who set up in business at The White Swan, St Paul's Churchyard, London, around the turn of the century. They are two of the best-known makers of their period, simply because they were among the few who labelled their work; several examples of different sorts of writing furniture bearing their name have survived. The pewter inlay with crossbanded veneer and the crossbanded framing around the sides of the pieces show the influence of Gerrit Jensen, the leading cabinetmaker of the period, who introduced such decorative elements to England from France in the late 17th century.

E. An English William and Mary Double-Domed Bureau Bookcase
This piece is 3ft 5in (1.04m) wide, with mirror-panel doors and is decorated with gilt chinoiserie scenes on a red ground, and topped by five silvered flower-vase finials. The base of two short and two long drawers also incorporates a hidden well beneath a slide in the writing compartment and there are candleslides in the upper section beneath a fully fitted interior of pigeonholes, drawers and cupboards.

F. An English William and Mary Marquetry-Decorated Writing Cabinet
This piece is 3ft 4in (1.02m) wide. The base is of two short and two long drawers beneath a fall-front writing compartment containing drawers and pigeonholes arranged around a central cupboard. There is a further concealed drawer with a cushion shaped marquetry front in the frieze just below the overhanging cornice. Fall-front desks of this kind are often referred to as escritoires today, but might have been known to their first owners as scrutoires. They were fashionable in the late 17th century, but seem to have been generally superseded by the bureau-bookcase in England early in the following century. Luxuriant floral marquetry of this kind is also typical of the period, inspired by the veneering skills of immigrant craftsmen from Holland and France.

A . A French Louis XIV Boulle Bureau Mazarin

This is a typical design, 5ft 2in (1.58m) wide, with a pair of pedestals containing three bow-fronted drawers each and a single frieze drawer in the centre. It is veneered on almost every surface with a brass-on-ebony design of fanciful scrolling foliage with swags, birds, figures, flowers, vases and other motifs. This distinctive style of late 17th-century decoration is often called *bérainesque,* a reference to the French architect and designer Jean Bérain, who worked with Charles-André Boulle and was one of the principal creators of the Louis XIV style. Bérain's fantastic populated scrolls are regarded as precursors of rococo decoration, but his designs always remain balanced and symmetrical. The usual brass, here combined with ebony and tortoiseshell, was by no means the only material used for decorative effect, although this became the favourite when the boulle technique was revived in the 18th and 19th centuries.

B . A Louis XIV Bureau Mazarin

This unusually large example, 5ft 11in (1.8m) wide, is veneered in kingwood and inlaid with pewter on ebony grounds. Most bureaux Mazarins are much smaller and serve as simple pedestal desks without fitted writing compartments, but this example is of a type that was popular in England and Holland as well as in France during the late 17th century. The rectangular top, with a large central medallion of pewter strapwork against ebony, is hinged down the middle and folds back to reveal a secretaire compartment. The top drawers are dummies which fold down to form the front of the writing surface. Both flaps are locked shut by means of two locks which are placed, rather unusually, between the simulated frieze drawers. Inside, the fittings are rudimentary compared with the many-drawered writing cabinets of the same period, having only three pigeonholes extending back under the rear part of the top. The decoration of the interior is particularly fine, however, with a marquetry coat-of-arms flanked by flowers and pewter and ebony monograms beneath coronets on the underside of the flap, and similar panels inlaid in *contre partie* on the writing surface.

C. A Boulle Marquetry Bureau

Not all magnificent furniture is easy to attribute or even to date. This mother-of-pearl, brass and stained shell boulle marquetry bureau had been stored in an attic at Knole Park in Kent, disregarded for many years before it came up for auction in 1987 and sold for £1.21 million.

The bureau is 2ft 11in (89cm) wide and 4ft 1in (1.25m) high including the upper section of three drawers, which are inlaid across the front with chinoiserie groups symbolising Astronomy, Painting and Geography, and at each side with a sculptor and a stone cutter.

The flap is inlaid with a landscape filled with courtly chinoiserie figures and a host of mother-of-pearl birds, and is lined on the inside with blue morocco leather. The interior holds a stepped arrangement of seven drawers in purpleheart above a walnut-lined well.

The base has a serpentine front in three parts, inlaid with five musicians in the centre and two rather puzzling garden scenes at each side. There are two small drawers at the bottom of the centre section and, on each side, a small drawer over a cupboard disguised as drawers and containing a kingwood *coffre fort* with a hinged top and a concealed drawer. The sides of the body are also decorated with garden scenes. The back is flat, indicating that it was intended to stand against a wall.

So unusual is the overall jewel-like effect that the origin of the bureau remains as mysterious as the distant dreamy scenes which cover it. As craftsmen travelled from court to court and no inventory entry for this or the only other similar known piece has turned up, present attributions range from a late-17th century Paris workshop to a South German one, *c*1720.

D. A French Louis XIV Bureau Mazarin

This bureau in the manner of André-Charles Boulle, with fruitwood and pewter marquetry, 3ft 9¼in (1.15m) wide, is supported on the capped tapering legs with curved X stretchers typical of this type of desk. This example also has the usual cupboard in the back of the kneehole recess, as well as the less common lockable writing compartment beneath the hinged top. The rosewood and fruitwood veneered interior is secured by means of a single lock at the centre of the frieze, which drops flat in use. This arrangement provides only limited space for paper storage and fell from favour with the bureau Mazarin by the early 18th century.

1600-1700

A . A French Louis XIV Ebony Bureau Plat

This bureau is of massive design, with heavy ormolu mask and rosette mounts along a shaped frieze without drawers. The rounded rectangular top, 5ft 6in (1.68m) long, is supported at the corners on four female masks, a feature found on the early bureaux of makers like André-Charles Boulle and Charles Cressent. The bureau plat began to appear in French interiors in the late 17th century, and early examples show the monumental style of the period.

B . A French Louis XIV Boulle Bureau Plat

It is 6ft (1.83m) wide, with a rectangular leather-lined top, three frieze drawers and heavy cabriole legs with scrolled leaf toes. The inlay is in *première partie* with brass on an ebonised ground, and mounted with large masks at each end and on the corners. It is not possible to assign this high-quality desk to a particular workshop, for like many late 17th or early 18th-century pieces it is unmarked. None of the products of the workshop of André-Charles Boulle himself was marked, although this desk shows many similarities to a drawing thought to be by him. Work of this quality would only have been commissioned for palaces and great houses, in which the bureau plat was already becoming a standard item of furniture by the late 17th century.

A

B

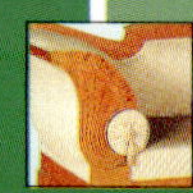

1700 to 1800

The year 1700 marks no great and sudden leap in the development of furniture, but if one takes the turn of the century to mark the middle of the period 1650–1750 and looks at what had been achieved between those two dates, the difference is immediately obvious. A gentleman of the 1650s would have been astonished by the quantity, quality, convenience and style of the furniture available by the 1750s.

Chairs

Although France was without doubt the dominant influence over taste at the beginning of the 18th century, different political climates did produce their own styles. Rococo was the style of the time, with veneers, marquetry, ormolu mounts and oriental lacquer. In France, two main styles of chair prevailed, the *siege meuble*, immovable and set against a wall, and the lighter *siege courant* which could be moved as and when required. Armchairs had their arms set back to accommodate the hooped dresses of the period, and lounging became popular, so the sofa and chaise longue developed accordingly.

Rococo was at its height around 1730, characterized by asymmetry and organic forms such as rocks, shells, scrolls and foliage. A notable feature of the time was the exchange of ideas between different nations, leading to Dutch influence on English work, japanning in Italy, and traces of Chippendale and Queen Anne in Spain. George III chairs were closely imitated in Denmark and Hepplewhite shield backs could be found in Naples.

In England, the period 1690–1715 produced a return to sobriety in decoration – the basis of the Queen Anne style with higher-backed chairs and with vertical lines and plain splats. Then came the Georgian period of furniture (1714–1779) which found its main medium in the mahogany imported from the West Indies, c1725, overtaking walnut in popularity by 1750. The use of mahogany encouraged a return to carved decoration, and this can be seen in the work of Thomas Chippendale (1718–1779), the most famous of English cabinetmakers. His pattern book, *Gentleman and Cabinet-maker's Director* of 1754, spread his fame throughout Europe and the world, and was a main cause for the movement of styles across Europe.

The second half of the century saw a move in Europe towards neo-Classicism. Robert Adam, a Scottish architect, followed in the steps of William Kent (1685–1748) as an architect concerned with the interior decorating of his buildings. George Hepplewhite also published a pattern book *The Cabinet-Maker and Upholsterer's Guide*, published in 1788, whose elegant, well-proportioned furniture is a fair representation of taste in the latter half of the century. By the end of the 18th century, English chair designs were imported, copied, adapted and widely admired in countries throughout the world, from America to Russia, and Norway to Spain.

With Louis XV's succession to the French throne in 1723 came the lighter, more elegant Rococo style. When in turn Louis XVI and Marie Antoinette came to the throne in 1774, the flat surfaces and linear shapes decorated with lacquer and ormolu drew heavily on classical influences. The 1780s saw a vogue for English design; mahogany was introduced on a larger scale; neo-Classicism and Rococo merged until the traumatic Revolution of 1789. From then till the turn of the century the plainer Directoire furniture was seen.

The growth of industry and trade in America by the start of the 18th century meant an increased exchange of ideas with Europe. The William and Mary easy-chair at the start of the century began to merge with more sophisticated Queen Anne chair designs around 1725, and American Queen Anne chair design showed the style at its best. The variety of skills required in chair making (upholstery, carving, turning and joining) reached their height in Philadelphia in the mid-18th century. The influence of Thomas Chippendale arrived in America around 1760, and his name is synonymous with Rococo in American design.

The American Revolution interrupted the flow of

ideas from Europe, but Robert Adam's designs provided the base for the classical revival seen in the United States after the Revolution from around 1780 onwards.

New England Chippendale is much more linear than English Chippendale, and different areas show distinct stylistic characteristics. Regional differences in Chippendale chair design are complex and well documented. In Newport, for example, the mid-century furniture trade was dominated primarily by two families, named Goddard and Townsend, who incorporated many Queen Anne features into the New French style. The pilgrim's shell motif became a recurrent theme carried from Queen Anne through to Chippendale furniture, particularly the striking block-front cabinet furniture. Newport Chippendale is often a more heavily decorated variant of Queen Anne; elsewhere in New England are strong stylistic variants, such as the work of the Dunlap family in New Hampshire who specialized in a rather anarchic use of the shell combined with a mixture of styles. In terms of manufacture, the towns of Salem and Boston tended to produce rather slender, vertical styles, though of a construction which necessitated the now out–moded stretcher.

Sofas

In the early 18th century, the most progressive seat furniture was made for great houses and palaces but, by the 1760s, up-to date designs for the homes of gentlefolk of moderate means became available. This gradual shift in emphasis, from the taste of the nobility to the needs of a growing middle class, resulted in a great increase in the number of manufacturers, many of whom are known through the labels and marks they applied to sofa frames. French furniture enthusiasts are especially fortunate, since, after 1751, every item was required to be stamped with the maker's name, a system that was not enforced in Britain or America.

Some of the most splendid 18th-century sofas were designed as components of large suites of furniture. Intent on creating interiors of perfection, architects such as William Kent developed furniture styles that were in accord with the structure of a room; thus, tables, stools and massive pairs of sofas were all conceived as part of a grand composition. Kent dominated fashionable taste in the early years of the century; his sculptural sofas, ornamented with shells, animal heads, sphinxes, cherubs and leaves, resembled stone monuments rather than functional furnishings, and when gilded or painted, were usually made of relatively cheap pine.

As mahogany became more widely used, the styles of seat furniture became much lighter. No longer was upholstery fabric seen as the most important element of a sofa as in the 17th century. Instead the show-wood came to dominate a piece; and makers competed to produce the most delicate creations. By the 1750s sofas were an accepted part of the furnishing of any gentleman's house, and there were various styles for the hall, drawing-room, boudoir or library. The simplest were given drop-in seats and wooden backs, a type that remained popular for use in entrance halls until the 20th century, when many reproductions of early styles were re-introduced. The chairback type of sofa, first seen in the 17th century, was very popular. Some of the more interesting pieces were upholstered in needlework depicting biblical or classical scenes. Most of this needlework was produced commercially, but occasionally sets of gros- or petit-point covers were worked by the ladies of the house.

Thomas Chippendale designed some of the most elegant sofas of the chair-back type, perhaps the most characteristic being in the ribbon-back form, a delicate style especially suited to mahogany. More in sympathy with general European taste were Chippendale's upholstered sofas which revealed the increasing importance of comfort. In general, Chippendale furniture was made on a scale more suitable for houses than castles, and his sofas varied from 6 to 10 ft (1.8m to 3m) long. For additional comfort, he suggested a matching bolster at each end, as well as square back cushions. Despite this interest in the general market, Chippendale sofas in the grand manner – whose gilded, carved cherubs and classical figures created an atmostphere of opulence – were still deemed necessary for splendid rooms. Chippendale's 'couches', in fact comfortable armchairs with the seats extended and supported on six or eight legs, are among the most elegant of sofa designs.

In 18th-century Europe, French furniture styles were all important. Elegant sofas made in the Rue de Cléry area of Paris were exported to Germany and Russia for the homes of the most discerning. These sofas were made of oak, beech or walnut, and were polished, painted or gilded. Among the large variety of sofa styles made was the curved *confident*, or *tête-à-tête*, on which two or three people sat facing in opposite directions, thus enabling them to whisper discreetly. Such pieces often formed a part of the large suites of salon furniture, which could also include several sofas and *lits-de-repos*, all upholstered in Gobelins tapestry or ravishingly coloured Lyons silk brocade.

The period of revolution in Europe heralded a new classicism, which favoured simpler antique forms once used by the Egyptians and the Greeks. Embroidered and brocaded covers were discarded, and sofas were finished in restrained fabrics more suited to the new democratic lifestyle. This classicism was seen at its most refined in northern Europe, but British and American designers favoured the cleaner, more academic lines that revealed the quality of workmanship rather than obscuring it with ornament.

Tables

Whereas the 17th century had been marked by its vast variety of table shapes and adornments, the 18th century was distinguished for its craftsmanship. Indeed, the 1700s saw a quality of manufacture never since equalled, with the added introduction of American craftsmen and designers as a force to be reckoned with. By 1730 in France a variety of tables was an essential and valued part of the furniture of the aristocratic household. During the Régence period, there had been an increasing interest in the quality of manufacture as the range of decorative options declined. Stretchers were disappearing, and veneering with plain wood grain and lacquering was on the rise. In no time a new curved style, of which Régence is considered the first phase, fully emerged – Rococo.

The gifted French *menuisiers* and *ébénistes* such as Charles Cressent (1685–1768) and Bernard van Risenburgh (fl.1730–1770), together with their fellow craftsmen – the mount-makers, guilders, etc. brought about a golden age of furniture making. The new look for tables favoured eccentric curving, light-hearted constructions in light-coloured woods (often with parts cut out) and, especially in France, finely chiselled gilt-bronze, or ormolu, mounts. More table types were developed in France, notably small specialist ones such as the *table en chiffoniére* (a work table with a high gallery) and the *table à ouvrage*, for needleworkers.

The Rococo in Italy and Germany essentially followed the lead of France, but in England a trend for plain, dark woods, which began in the 1600s with the Britons' love for their native walnut, and continued later with furniture made of dark, red-brown mahogany, available from the colonies without any export duty after 1720. The new wood carved easily and also yielded beautiful grain patterns, known as 'figuring'. The Chippendale style developed, with Rococo patterns applied to a plethora of English tables – among the favoured motifs were leaf carving, pierced latticework and Chinese motifs. As an extension of this fantasy element, the Gothic style was revived; a medieval cathedral could be evoked on a table, whose legs might be carved as clusters of architectonic columns beneath arches in the structure's frieze.

Although there had been pattern-books of designs for furniture in the past, Thomas Chippendale's *Gentlemen and Cabinetmaker's Director* which contained over 200 designs, started a new vogue for 'Anglomania' in Europe and also set the precedent for American cabinetmakers to copy later (post-1780) Hepplewhite and Sheraton table designs into the 19th century.

In France and England in the 1760s and 1770s, tables were now being designed in the neo-classical style popularized by the architect Robert Adam (1728–1792), who had toured Roman monuments and borrowed classical architectural details for his interiors. In Adam designs, tables often played a crucial part, frequently being fixed near windows, thus giving symmetry to the formal room layouts. Rococo curves disappeared, and new straight lines characterized the tables of 1780s Britain – perhaps with the added enhancement of fluted legs emulating the columns which supported the roofs of Roman temples. The tops and aprons of tables tended to be flatter, often of plain mahogany or with restrained, geometric inlay; cabriole legs and hoof feet also disappeared toward the end of the century. Around 1700, American settlers used either tables brought from their homelands in Europe or, as was more often the case, made them of native woods in the style of the Old World. Since early Americans were preoccupied with living rather than luxury, furniture design in the colonies, they favoured simple but elegant plainness in keeping with Puritan values. By the 1780s and 1790s, after gaining independence from Europe – and thanks to Chippendale's pattern books and to increased emigration – colonial table production began to catch up with the Old World, developing its own distinctive character. By 1800, North America boasted thriving centres of high-quality production of European-style tables with local variations, such as different styles of inlay and ball-and-claw feet. These were concentrated in Philadelphia, New England and New York; in the latter, Duncan Phyfe (1678-1854) was one of the best-known producers of Federal tables, some of which still bear his original label.

Desks

In 1650 most writing in Europe and America would have been done on a table, or at a simple table-top desk; by 1750 it was possible to choose from a range of established types of desk. In Britain, the large bureau-cabinet with drawers beneath and paper storage above was a standard piece by the mid-century. It was ideally suited to the day-to-day business of a household, and it was adaptable. Later in the century the upper part tended to be glazed, but the form of the typical English bureau meant that it could also be dispensed with altogether without spoiling the appearance of usefulness of the desk.

Smaller versions with single doors in the upper part were popular for use in ladies' bedrooms or dressing rooms, although here a little kneehole dressing-table-cum-desk was also common. In the library, itself a specialized room of growing importance in the 18th century, large pedestal desks that could be placed in the centre of a book-lined room were found most convenient.

Much of the 18th-century furniture was very feminine. Upholstered chairs and sofas appeared alongside a clutter of little tables for sewing, reading and writing, reflecting the middle-class woman's occupations in the home. Where a large desk was required (more generally for the use of the male householder), the simple *bureau plat* was always popular in France and could be used in conjunction with a separate filing cabinet or cartonnier. The French equivalent of the slope-front bureau, the *bureau en pente*, was still popular in 1750, but it was soon to be displaced by the *secrétaire à abattant* and the *secrétaire à cylindre*. In the very best writing furniture produced by the Paris *ébénistes* there is an attention to detail seldom found elsewhere. Creations such as the Bureau de Roi created for Louis XV by Oeben and finished by his successor Riesener combined elegance, convenience and ingenuity to a standard that was unmatched, even by the tour de force exhibition piece seen in Europe a century later.

The cylinder front of the Bureau du Roi was in itself a technical innovation, and the many mechanical surprises it embodies are a reminder that 18th-century France was fascinated by science and technology, but such mechanical intricacy was expensive. The limited means of the middle classes in France, as in other countries, were stretched to more modest interpretations of the court style.

In America, elegant writing furniture in the form of slope-front desks and book cases were part of the move towards a more comfortable life.

1700-1800

A . An American William and Mary Bannister Back Chair, New England c1710

This fine example of American baroque is beautifully carved, with its pierced crest on the back, vase-turned legs and bulbous stretcher all forming contrasting tight curves, as do the out-turned 'Spanish' feet. Clearly an American version of a William and Mary chair, it is probably by John Gaines of Ipswich, Massachusetts. Other chairs of this set are in the Metropolitan Museum of Art. The Bannister Back chair gets its name from its balusters. Made of a mixture of woods, including maple and ash, a similar armchair in the Henry Ford Museum, Michigan, is ebonised; English chairs of the same design can be seen at Knole, in Kent.

American William and Mary style became popular during the first quarter of the 18th century, approximately a generation later than in Europe. Seventeenth-century Puritanism lingered, and few American chairs of the style are as elaborate or outrageous as European examples. They do have common features, however, notably turned stretchers and bannister backs, particularly those from Rhode Island. The Delaware River Valley also produced good turned chairs, often of plain woods with ebonized and painted decoration and complex turning. Another distinct style to become popular all over the United States was the Boston Chair. This usually had a leather splat which curved in towards the back in a similar fashion to English Queen Anne 'Chinese' examples. All of these different chairs generally used the mortice and tenon joint, sometimes with good bulb-turned stretchers.

It can be hard to distinguish between American and European chairs of this date. American designs use slightly different proportions, variations in decoration and raw materials, and have a greater simplicity.

B . A pair of Queen Anne Japanned Chairs, c1710

The form of these chairs, compared with the decorated style immediately before and after this date, is delightfully simple and draws elegance from the oriental designs which it emulates. It is very rare to find such chairs in good condition, since the frame of soft wood, probably beech, was often ravaged by time, and English lacquer was water-soluble and quite brittle.

The chairs' curves are very gentle, with the elegant cabriole legs giving outwards as much below the knee as above, thus creating a restful balance which ends on a simple square foot. Note how the back sways to fit the sitter, and how its broad central splat is decorated with oriental motif; surely an inaccurate attempt at a Chinese painted scroll. The anglicized Chinoiserie is evident on the seat rail also, which is scattered with various objects from the Orient – fans, baskets and so on – and the leaves on the legs are painted rather than carved, as might be expected on later Georgian chairs.

C . A Queen Anne Oval Walnut Stool, c1710

Although similar to rectangular stools of the same date, the oval seat in this example adds immeasurably to the harmony of line. Traditional English stool design of the highest quality, the curves of the seat are convex in contrast to the concave curves of the stretcher, and the out-turned feet are plain and dignified. An enchanting feature of this stool is that at the joints, where traditionally English blocks give way to a stretcher of undulating shape apparently inspired by oriental designs of the period. The stretcher is carved with a tobacco leaf of such simplicity that it is almost stylized, resembling the foliage on oriental porcelain imported during this period. The combination of such natural form and controlled curves on this disciplined design shows the touch of a master. The period needlework, with its graphic pattern, highlights the pattern of the undercarriage.

D . A Queen Anne Walnut Stool, c1710

The primary virtue of this early 18th century stool is its simplicity. Although at this date it might have been made as a stool on its own, it would probably have accompanied a suite of chairs. Its construction was sufficiently robust to be able to dispense with the stretchers, and this made the design far less cluttered. The legs taper elegantly to a slightly pointed pad foot, which has the simplest of line decorations. The simple linear motif on the knee of the cabriole is reminiscent of the decoration of contemporary silver, known as 'cut-card work' and from that line, flanked by a pair of scrolls, it hangs in a single husk. This particular needlework seat is later than the date of the original stool, but it would have had a similar design, which complemented the rich colour of the wood.

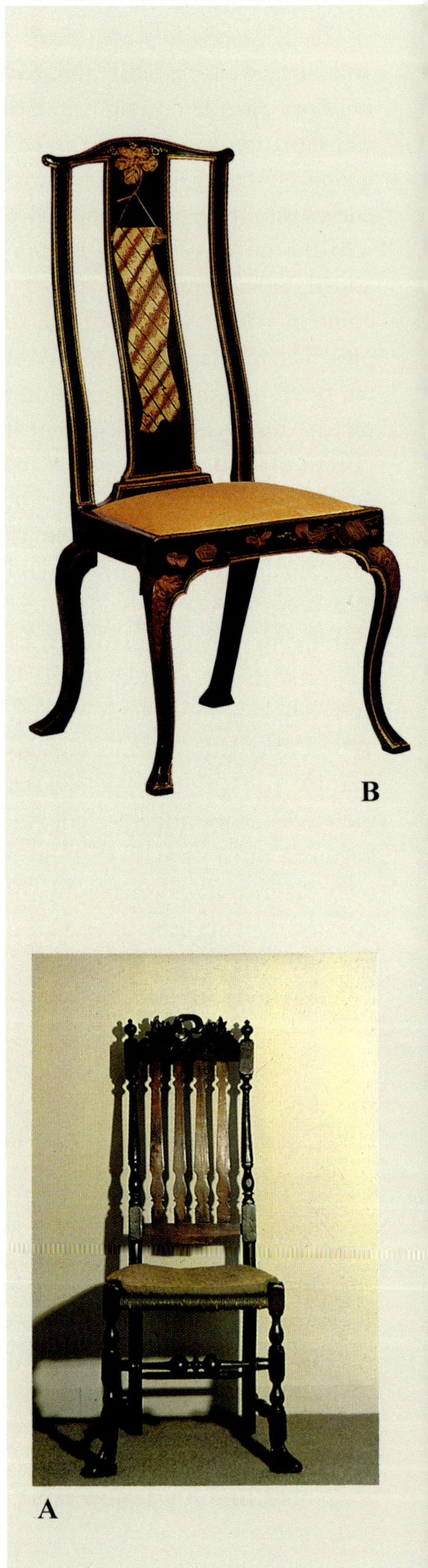

B

A

C

D

1700-1800

A . A Queen Anne Walnut Shepherd's Crook Armchair, *c*1710

This chair is as beautiful as it is unusual. Shepherd's Crook armchairs, a well-defined model of distinctive pattern, were produced primarily in the first quarter of the 18th century with some minor variations. This good early example still has stretchers, and in fact an unusual crinoline stretcher, supposedly designed to accommodate the dresses of the time. The simple tapering legs with pad feet and delicate blocks are typical late Queen Anne or early George I. As can be seen, this is little more than a stool with a superstructure added on. It is particularly pleasing in this case to see the period embroidery seat. The looped arms that give the chair its name; made in two pieces, they are joined by a figured simple walnut back.

B . A Queen Anne Child's High Chair, c1710

This functional child's high chair stands at just over 3ft/91.5 cms high, and would have seated a relatively wealthy child at table. Made primarily of walnut, the elms side rails are turned and square-sectioned, allowing a strong mortice and tenon joint; chamfered back legs are an extra sign of quality. It is authentically constructed like a full-size chair of the period, although it is made more robust by its extra cross-pieces. The undulating apron and simplified arms are nice touches and the slight wear on the foot rail conjures up scenes of the generations of infants who may have fed here.

C . A Régence Walnut Armchair, *c*1715

Régence describes the period 1715–1723 in France when the Duc d'Orléans was acting as Prince Regent for Louis XIV. Interestingly, it corresponds to the first few years of George I's reign in England and shows how French furniture developed during the reign of Queen Anne. As we have seen in England, Queen Anne's reign was a period of harmony, restraint and simplicity in chair making. There was a reversal of the trend towards decoration which characterized William and Mary's reign; in France, however, late 17th-century styles matured smoothly during the first quarter of the 18th.

This fauteuil, one of a pair, has many 17th-century continental characteristics; for example, the curving x-framed stretchers, the cabriole legs, the hoofed feet and the gently curving arms.

The open arms and contrasting curves give the chair a light, airy feel, and this effect is

A

B

C

D

heightened by the high decoration; the scallops on the arms are echoed by the scallops and trellis work on the seat rails. There is also an extra finesse in the scrolled feet which rest on their own feet below. The mellow combination of the warm-coloured walnut against this tapestry upholstery represents an elegant high point in neo-baroque European furniture.

D . A Queen Anne Walnut Embroidered Wing Chair, c1710

Here, as with other examples of Queen Anne chairs covered in elaborate embroidery, the eyes are attracted to the pattern of the upholstery rather than to the woodwork or overall shape. The embroidery themes can vary from biblical scenes to simple scrolling floral patterns which lead off the edge of the chair, or local traditional pastimes; in this case the hunt. The simple cabriole legs immediately indicate the chair's age, as they are almost identical to those on the rectangular Queen Anne stools of the same date. The square-sectioned cabriole leg at the back adds an overall balance to the chair, and although disguised by the needlework, the outward scrolling arms and billowing wings which come from the high back are typical of this period.

A . An Early 18th-Century Georgian Wing Chair, *c*1720

It is difficult to be precise about the date of this chair but by comparison with the Queen Anne wing chair from the same period, these front legs are more highly decorated, with shell moulding, slight scrolls and have squarer feet. These back legs are much simpler than the front ones, perhaps indicating poorer quality craftsmanship, or perhaps a later replacement; this could only be determined by examining the frame beneath the upholstery. It is similar to the Queen Anne version in having the same high back, curving wings and outward scrolling arms.

B & C . A George II Red-Lacquered Chair, *c*1720 and a Pair of Round-Backed Chairs by Giles Grendey

Lacquering, or japanning as it is also known, reached its height of popularity and excellence in England during the first 30 years of the 18th century. Of the many workshops manufacturing and decorating in these styles at the time, Giles Grendey (1693–1780) is the craftsman best known today. He has given his name to this style of English lacquering which includes characteristically Anglicized oriental figures. Grendey established for himself a dominant share of the profitable export market in English lacquer, notably to Spain and Portugal. He was working at a time when British craftsmanship was at its height, and his empire grew to generate new trading partners. Grendey also made furniture in walnut and mahogany as well as small, neat pieces elaborately decorated with idiosyncratic motifs and shaped panels. English lacquer was generally of higher quality than that of the Dutch, a main rival at this time.

During the 1730s, Grendey supplied a suite of lacquer furniture similar to this chair (**B**) for the Spanish Duque del Infantado to furnish his castle at Lazcano, near San Sebastian in northern Spain. There are also similarities to a set of four dining chairs at Godmersham Park, Kent, which have similarly-designed cross-stretchers, back legs and shell motif. (Godmersham Park is thought of as one of the last great chair collections to be broken up.)

In spite of many illustrious associations, Grendey was a furniture maker for the well-off English middle-classes rather than the aristocracy. His life was a combination of ambition and idiosyncracy. He was apprenticed in 1709, and by the 1720s had already taken on his own apprentices (whom he seems to have treated with great cruelty). In 1747 he became upper warden of the Joiners Company, describing himself as a

B

C

cabinetmaker in St John's Clerkenwell, London. By 1766 he had become Maitre of the Company, but was admonished the very next year for poor attendance.

He is perhaps best remembered for the enthusiasm with which he promoted scarlet lacquer furniture, which became a symbol of opulence and quality. As examples of his different styles, and to explain the attribution of these chairs to his workshop, it is interesting to compare the figures on the splat of the high-backed chair to those on the vase splats of the more homely,round-backed examples (**C**) which are similar to a set at Temple Newsham, near Leeds. Both scattered with English-looking orientals, which came to be his trademark, in fact the overall effect bears little resemblance to an oriental scene; perhaps therein lies the charm.

D . A George I Mahogany Dining Chair, c1720

This original and striking design has been attributed to the hand of Thomas Chippendale's father in the past, but there is little evidence to substantiate this: it perhaps resembles the work of Giles Grendey (1683–1780). The legs and seat are of a standard type though the carving is excellent – the detail on the leafy knees adding great texture – and the back is quite extraordinary. Its two flat side rails resemble something between a lyre and a sabre, and flank the highly imaginative splat. This affecting combination of lightness and baroque vigour is difficult to surpass.

1700-1800

A . A George I Walnut Sidechair, c1725

This one of a pair of early chairs has two interesting features: its back and its carving. Although each side of the back is made up of two opposing scrolls, there is a high degree of horizontality about the design as a whole, and even the corners of the scrolls are sharp and angular, as is the splat. This emphasizes the horizontal lines in what is essentially a vertical arrangement, and gives the impression of extra breadth which was very characteristic of early Georgian design. These were broad, solid, chairs with an unrockable stability about them.

The chair's carving, on the other hand, is distinctly baroque. Consider the maskheads on the knees of the legs: these are not naturalistic, but nature is used simply as the model or inspiration behind the decorative lines. Later in the century the move towards rococo and truly organic forms led to lighter and more realistic carving, which often carried less impact.

B . An English George I Walnut Gilt Chair, *c*1725

This chair is from an important set which is now divided between the Metropolitan Museum of Art, New York, and the Colonial Williamsburg Museum, Virginia. It is a spectacular example of a really good walnut chair; beautifully carved, the back with small and expressive scrolls, a large expansive seat, and decorated with gilding, which is extremely rare. The chair has an undefinable exuberance which is rarely equalled.

C . An Early Georgian Stool or Bench, *c*1730

Although this stool may appear at first to be unusually low, it is in fact of normal height but is designed to seat more than one person which makes it rare. The wonderful legs are the height of contemporary style, powerful lion-paw cabriole with a splendid rococo cartouche on the knee, surrounded by a variety of foliage on splendid, hairy ball-and-claw feet.

A

C

B

1700–1800

A . An Early Georgian Walnut Dining Chair, *c*1730

The tall, slender back of this beautifully carved dining chair indicates that it probably dates from George I's reign. Its exceptional feature is the elegantly carved lions' heads on the knee of each cabriole foot. These are distinctly naturalistic, and this kind of realism was a typical English characteristic which gave carving tremendous life.

B & C . English Cock-Fighting or Reading Chairs

Probably from the late George I or early George II period, this delightfully eccentric chair (**B**) stands out amongst all others because it is used back to front, is also a table and, as in one of the examples, has a drawer, or sometimes hinged flaps or trays. The flap can be adjusted to place the book or paper in the right position, and the flush, lockable drawer in the front rail and flaps which swing out from the sides would have held writing materials such as quills, quill cutters and pounce pots.

The lack of stretchers and decorated cabriole legs suggests that the chair with the drawer is from the 1730s. The tightly-curved edges of the rounded seat tapering to the back, and the padded yoke, are very typical of the early 18th century. The studded leather upholstery is also period, and the stout pad feet kicking out at the back give the chair a robust feel.

It is interesting to compare this chair with a later example (**C**). Here, the yoke and back are no longer padded, the back is reeded in late 18th-century manner, the lines are severe, and even the kicking-back legs are restrained. The later design has none of the assertive confidence of its ancestor; its lines are carefully measured and restrained, but there is a loss of elegance in the loss of simplicity.

Very sculptural and very English, there seems little evidence to link these chairs with cock fighting, although the back-to-front pose is often seen in contemporary paintings of the sport.

D . A Shepherd's Crook Armchair, c1730

A later example of a Shepherd's Crook armchair with a more interesting shape of back. Note too the absence of stretchers. This style of chair was also revived in the 19th century.

B

C

A

D

A . An Early Georgian Shepherd's Crook Armchair, *c*1730

The Shepherd's Crook arm of this chair is a fine example of the style, and is fitted to what is probably the carver from a set of dining chairs. The flatness of the rails and scrolls is typical of the George I period. While it is a three-dimensional chair in that it is high, deep and shapely, each individual element is carved in one plane only; for example, the splat scrolls outwards but not backwards or forwards, and likewise, the top of the cabriole leg is flat and stylized, not at all naturalistic. It is as if it is made of a variety of pieces of card which are cut out into silhouettes; it has an excessive, over-decorated look and may be of Irish origin.

B . Two George II Walnut and Burr Walnut Dining Chairs

These excellent examples of chairs of this period are part of a set of eight, which had by then become standard. They display many clear features of George II chairs; note especially the beautifully figured burr splat of double-baluster form, with dimunitive scrolls which match those on the ends of the arms. The veneers, chosen from cross cuts of the tree, have been carefully matched. The front legs carry the Astley family crest and are scrolled above hairy paw feet, and the back legs kick out to a simple pad. It is interesting to note the dimensions. While the armchair is of normal height – 3ft 4ins/101 cms – its width of 2ft 8ins/81 cms is unusual, making it almost cubic in proportion. The generous seat was designed to take the full coats of the period.

C . A George II Mahogany Irish Elbow Chair, *c*1730

This chair has many qualities associated with Irish craftsmanship in the 18th century. Although basically English in design, there is an overall heaviness in the combination of shepherd's crook arms and elongated back, in the slight disproportion of height to depth, and in a surfeit of carving, which often accompanies Irish work. Even though the back legs are somewhat clumsy, the chair shows the charm of Irish Georgian furniture, especially with its original petit and gros point needlework seat which sets off the deeply-coloured wood.

Generally Ireland, like other English colonies of the time (particularly America), followed prevailing English styles and adapted them to local taste. Ireland did not enjoy the prosperity brought about in England by the Industrial Revolution. Design advanced much more slowly, and therefore George II styles, such as this chair, lasted well into the reign of George III; in turn, severe late Georgian chairs continued to be made further into the 19th century than in England.

D . A George II Walnut Shepherd's Crook Armchair, c1740

This armchair exhibits every type of George II decoration. Originally one of a set of six, one is now in the Victoria & Albert Museum, London, and four are at Clandon Park in Surrey. The back is a fairly typical shape, formed from scrolls but crested with a delightful spray, like a peacock's tail, which sits above a solid, vase-shaped splat, inlaid within a strung border. The arms are in the shape of a shepherd's crook and the legs are cabriole.

What really makes this chair exceptional, however, is its carving. The legs are carved with open leaves which look a little like scallop shells, hung with closed leaves, and the foot really resembles a scroll of paper. There is a fan-shaped anthemion on the seat rail, and to lighten the overall effect the seat, still covered in contemporary needlework, is upholstered in bright and white tones.

D

A

C
B

A & B . A George II Love-seat and Two Single Chairs from a Suite of Mahogany Seat Furniture

This excellent suite, originally from Aspley House, Bedfordshire, comprises a pair of love seats and six chairs. They are from the great period of English chairmaking, and the fundamental structure of the pieces contained with their scrolls characterizes early English rococo. The love-seat pictured here is an example of a form which reached its height in the first half of the 18th century. It was certainly a social form of furniture, falling between the large carvers of this period and the double chairback settee; the ideal frame for an intimate conversation in a formal salon.

The large C-scroll, which forms the back and ends just above the seat, is carved all over with rocaille and acanthus. The splats are similarly decorated in low relief around the central interlacing strapwork: this baroque motif continues throughout the century. The arms of the love-seat can be seen to be carved both outwards and then in, and also upwards and then down. The front legs are cabriole with a cabochon on each knee, terminating in hairy hooves. The beautiful red brown tone of this early Cuban mahogany is quite irrepressible: colour is one of the most crucial determinants of age.

C . An American Queen Anne Walnut Chair, c1740

Interesting to compare with the other Queen Anne chairs illustrated, the shell carving, general shape and cabriole legs of this Philadelphian chair are very similar. The scrolls on this chair, however, have an extraordinarily sinuous effect and the splat is finely figured to create a delightful combination of simplicity and decoration. American Queen Anne chairs clearly mark the development of an indigenous style. In New York (originally, of course, New Amsterdam), elaborate baroque Dutch style tended to produce rather bulbous splats and an abundance of foliage carving, particularly on the crests, whereas in New England, and particularly Massachusetts, British conservatism favoured a vertical look with higher backs and often with a stout rear stretcher between the legs. (There is a good example of a Newport chair in the Winterthur Museum in Delaware.) Oriental lacquer became increasingly popular and there are some notable Queen Anne chairs with slightly elaborated European-Oriental decoration. Thomas Johnson, who described himself as being 'Japaner at the Golden Lyon in Anne Street, Boston', was notable for this kind of work.

D . Two George II Mahogany Dining Chairs, c1740

These beautiful chairs are from a set of two armchairs and six singles which originally also had stools and triple-seat settees. Good examples of George II dining chairs, the first notable feature is the excellent colour and figuring of the wood, striking even in a photograph. The second is the tremendous virtuoso carving, particularly of the seat and top rails. It is deep, crisp and luscious, embellishing its undulating seat rail; this shape of seat rail is sometimes known as the Vitruvian Scroll. The armchair's unusual combination of curved timber forms a pattern of interlacing lines, giving these large chairs a light and elegant appearance. Even if the baroque decorating is exaggerated, these examples of early rococo are a credit to the ingenuity and craftsmanship of the time.

E . An English Provincial Chair, c1745

While of beautiful quality, when this chair is compared to the London chairs of the same period, it seems a little gauche. The carving, for example, fails to reproduce convincingly the form of the swags of cloth it is trying to represent.

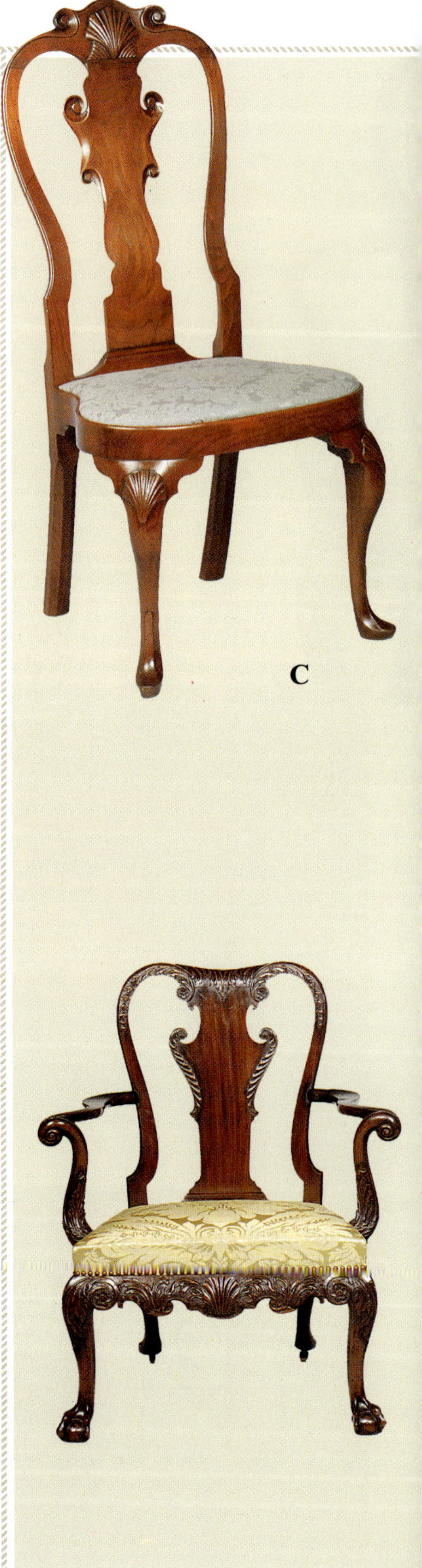
C

E
A
B

A . A George III Giltwood Armchair, *c*1750 by the Cabinetmaker William Gordon

This chair is from part of a considerable suite of 30 armchairs, four sofas, 16 single chairs, two stools and a waisted library table made for Spenser House in the 1750s. The suite represents the epitome of mid 18th-century taste and style, derived by a traditional partnership of the patron (in this case the first Earl of Spenser), and a designer (John Vardy) who directed the overall look. Vardy duly commissioned the great cabinetmaker William Gordon to make the chairs.

Although William Gordon primarily worked with another craftsman, John Tait, in a firm of cabinetmakers which operated in the 1760s and 1770s, he had already made a mahogany suite at Althorp similar in design a decade before. He subscribed to Chippendale's *Director* (1754), a hugely influential source of inspiration to the furniture trade. The firm of Gordon and Tait appear in several London Directories at various addresses, two of which were in Little Argyle Street and in Swallow Street. Between 1770 and 1779, there are several detailed bills for work at Althorp and also at Wimbledon. The partners later divided; Tait continued working in Piccadilly for the Royal Household during the 1790s.

The suite is representative of mid-century English rococo, a style which remained more constrained than the European styles. Here, the rails are curved, the legs cabriole on scrolling feet, and almost every surface is extensively carved.

B . A Windsor Chair, *c*1750

The term 'colonial furniture' broadly refers to pieces made before the American Revolution of 1776. Prior to that date, design influences came from two main sources, England, and Europe generally. Each nationality of immigrant – the Dutch perhaps most influentially – imported not only furniture but also a traditional affection for that style; the styles combined to give rise to recognizably American-made designs, particularly after the Revolution. American-manufactured chairs, even more obviously than English ones, fall into two categories: rustic, which by definition were the chairs that most Americans used, and formal, more rigorously based on popular styles and particularly imported ones.

The Carver Chair is a good example of Jacobean American, based on a chair which was supposedly brought over by John Carver, the first Governor of the then British colony. The chair has a typically English 17th-century, slightly baroque, look. The Brewster chair is an elaborated version of the same design, and both were used as models, widely copied in a variety of woods – oak, cherry, hickory and walnut. This Windsor chair is clearly related to its English cousins. The Ladderback Country Chair, which appeared in England and on the European continent, often with a rush seat, also became Americanized for everyday use, and is still made by the Shakers today. It should be remembered that many of the first immigrants to sail to America were fleeing religious persecution (such as the Pilgrim Fathers) and were generally Puritans wishing to avoid Catholic oppression. Their Puritanism is reflected in generally plain designs and an inherent conservatism.

C . An American Queen Anne Chair, *c*1750

This elaborate example of a Rhode Island chair shows clearly the change in style from heavy, earlier forms to this light backed seat; it has a slender splat, but still retains its heavy stretchers. The change can be seen too in the style of carving on the knees, the pendulous ball-and-claw feet with the claw at the back, and the crested top rail with a fan shell, this last in the style of Englishman Giles Grendey.

D . An American Queen Anne Walnut Chair, *c*1750

This exquisite example of simple Pennsylvanian design with typical shell decoration is probably by Philadelphian James Bartram, who was the original owner and from whom it had passed to his descendants until sold in New York in 1985. Bartram was listed in 1726 in the Delaware County Deedbook as a joiner in the Marple Township; it is extremely rare to find a chair with such a history on the open market. Particularly remarkable are the delicate cabriole legs ending in what are known in the United States as slipper feet and which show a marked French influence when compared with the stern, strong, English back.

D

C

B

A

1700-1800

A. A George II Giltwood Armchair, *c*1750

This is one of a superb suite of eight armchairs and a sofa (56) originally at Rudding Park, near York. It displays all of the best aspects of English rococo, with a design openly indebted to the style promoted by the court of France's Louis XV. It is quite small and light (3ft 4ins/101cms high), and the arms are upward swept on leafy scrolls, echoed on the four cabriole legs which terminate at a scroll at the toe. The rails are serpentine-shaped and carved with leafy decoration in relief, with central cabochon and all the varieties of rocaille decoration. The rich effect created by this gilt underframe is countered by the severe shape of the upholstery, giving an overall balance to the chair.

B. A George II Giltwood Sofa, *c*1750

This sofa comes from the same suite as the armchair from Rudding Park, near York. It is interesting to see how the rococo is translated into a larger piece of furniture. It is expansive (8ft 8ins/264cms wide), and although it has the structure of chairs joined together, with eight legs altogether, full use has been made of the sculptural possibilities. The back, arms and feet scroll effusively in every direction exhibiting a freedom which the chair, being full, heavy and more baroque, does not enjoy.

C. A George II Mahogany Settee, *c*1745

This good example of an English rococo sofa is light and elegant; even the padded seat is slender, perhaps not as robust as others. The expanse of the back, and its squareness, is moderated by the gently waving sides; the woodwork is of a high quality too, beautifully carved with typical scrolls, and delicate cabriole legs. Typical of English rococo, the sofa is not excessively decorated and forms a suitable companion for a suite of chairs because it would not dominate the set excessively.

A

B

C

A. A Pair of George II Mahogany Chairs

From the transitional period between the early Georgian solid, carved and decorated look, and the later George III light, linear and elegant pieces, the style of these chairs sows the seeds for chair design of the second half of the 18th century.

Here, the backs are still fairly flat, with broad rails and a broad central splat; the splat is pierced with a symmetrical design, a rococo element, and the uprights are straight, giving a slimmer look which is lightened by carving. The legs are still cabriole, and carved on claw-and-ball feet, but are much longer and lighter than their predecessors. The seats remain balloon-shaped, but the rail is shallow with only an ear remaining of what was previously a bold, undulated wave. The period embroidery provides a sharp contrast to the dark and more sober frame.

With very minor adjustments these remaining curves could be straightened to make the whole effect rectangular and severe: it is possible to see Robert Adam and George Hepplewhite beckoning from the future.

B. A Philadelphia Chippendale Chair, *c*1775

These chairs are part of a set, part of which is in the Winterthur Museum, Delaware, US, a house originally used by George Washington. Made in the American Chippendale style (although not based on drawings from Chippendale's *Director*) they were produced in America during the same period of 1750–1780. They are primarily mahogany but also include some poplar and pine. Most striking is that they are excellent examples of Philadelphia carving, which can have a dazzling, almost expressionistic, quality. Although the motifs are based on nature, they appear as tight, parallel curves or outward-moving lines which are very striking.

Philadelphia was the second largest English-speaking city in the world in the mid-18th century. Its output of furniture polarized American furniture production between Pennsylvanian and New English design. The popularity of decorated European styles was greatly accelerated by the arrival of Thomas Affleck from London in 1763. He worked with Philadelphians such as William Savery, James Gillingham, John Shoemaker and the celebrated Benjamin Randolph. American Chippendale indulged in more curves and sculptural form (such as the universal ball and claw feet) than the English Chippendale style, and indeed sometimes seemed more continental than English in flavour. Like their English predecessors, the pieces tended to be on a large scale, and especially those from the Delaware River Valley which are sometimes rather plain, in the Queen Anne spirit. Shoemaker and Savery both produced chairs with wonderfully undulating rails and sometimes retained the crisply-carved shell motif, again an anachronistic Queen Anne motif. Around 1770 Randolph produced a set of sample chairs which are full-blown rococo, or as it was frequently described, in 'the new French style'; these have Gothic tracery to the backs, bow-shaped top rails, pronounced cabriole legs on scrolling toes, a rare feature, and all manner of carving. The chairs are now in Colonial Williamsburg Museum in Virginia, US, which like the Winterthur Museum in Delaware, has an excellent selection of chairs of this period. The link with central Europe is particularly in evidence in Pennsylvanian rustic furniture with its bias towards decoration, whether on the painted German marriage chests, the naïvely carved hall chairs, often clearly decorated on the homestead by amateurs, or the dozens of other country designs drawing on influences as diverse as the Tyrol and the Italian Renaissance.

C. A Mid-18th Century Chair-Back Settee in the manner of Thomas Chippendale, c1750

This design is a classic of its kind, and it is interesting to compare it to the George II love-seat illustrated earlier (47). Little more than two chairs joined together, it is notable for its elegance, rather than its comfort. The 'chairs' are typical Chippendale, with elaborate, interlaced, ribbon backs, leafy back rails, and all on gothic, triple-column front legs. Much of the woodwork is ornamental rather than structural. Consider, for example, the small corner struts between the legs and the front rails; in the form of a Gothic, crocketted arch, they give style but little strength.

The importance of this design is that it is a stepping stone between the love-seat and the fully upholstered sofa that we have today. This settee design could be adapted to be two, three or four chair-backs long and in spite of its slightly comic, three-legged appearance, it is an important step in the development of seat furniture.

A

B

C

A . A Chippendale Wing Chair, c1750

This interesting variant in the progression of the wing chair combines traditional characteristics and original ideas in a particularly Chippendale way. Although still sculptural, it is different to a Queen Anne chair in that it is much squarer; the wings resemble those of 17th century chairs, which were often hinged, and with arms scrolled upwards instead of outwards.

Here, however, legs and stretchers indicate the age quite clearly. Harshly rectangular, the only curves to be seen are the decorative struts between seat rail and leg. These features are distinctly English, bearing no resemblance to the open armchairs of the 1730s and 1740s which were much influenced by France. The reintroduction of the stretcher is a curious characteristic since stretchers had ebbed in popularity since the early 18th century, but it was perhaps necessitated by the lighter frame, or perhaps solely for decoration.

B & C . A Pair of George II Gainsborough Armchairs, *c*1756

These fine examples of mid-century comfortable armchairs by John Gordon (**B**) were of a style supplied to a number of great houses at the time. There is a set of eight of these chairs at Blair Castle, Scotland, also known to have been made by John Gordon of Swallow Street, London, in 1756; he was of the Gordon family of the firm Gordon and Tait who were also associated with the gilt Spenser chairs. The original documentation at Blair describes, 'eight mahogany chairs carv'd frames in fish scales with a french foot with a carv'd leaf upon the toe.' They cost just under £4 each.

Although they are of the same comfortable proportions as armchairs today, they are of unusual design. The arm supports down to the seat seem to emulate a dolphin motif found on contemporary French and Italian chairs, here delightfully understated. The seat rail, in the form of a Cupid's bow, alludes to classical motifs of an earlier period and sweeps down into the simple cabriole with the nicely detailed leaf. The fishscale decoration is also from the organic baroque vocabulary of the earlier century, and the reeded edges and restrained lines of the upholstery show wider European ideas adapted to English taste. There is an obvious similarity between these chairs and the hall chair pictured (**C**) also by John Gordon.

D . Two Georgian Mahogany Armchairs, c1756

This spectacular pair of armchairs is from a suite of seat furniture based on a design by Thomas Chippendale. Similar chairs are illustrated in his *The Gentleman and Cabinet Makers Director*, Third Edition, published in 1762. The chair backs appear on Plate 10, and the chair rails and legs on Plate 13. These highly original chairs are possibly the most sculptural examples of 18th-century English chairs, and show the possibilities that the Chippendale pattern books presented.

A good example of a Rococo suite, these chairs fall between Grotto furniture (which has backs and seats based on shell forms) and early George II, heavily-ornamented neo-Baroque chairs. Note the carved coat of arms in the back – those of Bassett of Tehidy Park, Cornwall. These chairs were made for Sir Francis Bassett who married Elizabeth, daughter of Sir John St Aubyn, in 1756, 20 years after Tehidy Park was built.

E . Two Chinese Chippendale Chairs, c1760

These are good examples of a type of chair known as Chinese Chippendale from a set of twelve from Elvden Hall, Norfolk. Here, the term 'Chippendale' is used in the broadest sense, for these are not after a design by Thomas Chippendale. As can be seen, the chairs bear very little resemblance to actual Chinese pieces, which to this day remain more or less the same as the oriental chairs illustrated earlier. Here, there are strong elements of Gothic decoration on the arches on the splat. This style reached its height between 1750–1770, and produced some very elegant chairs.

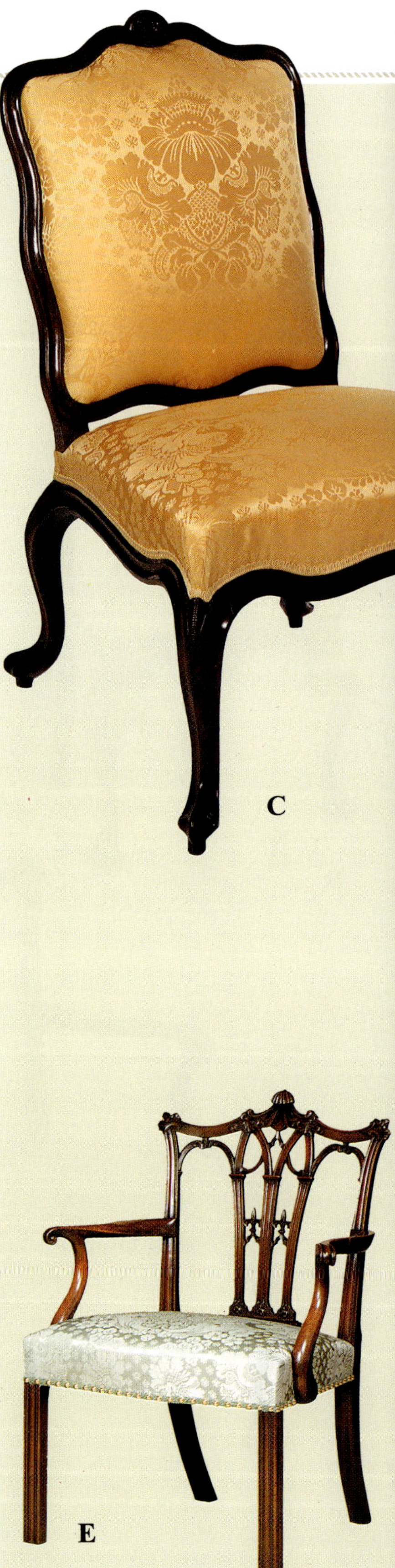

C

E

A
B
D

1700-1800

A. An American Queen Anne Armchair, *c*1760

The term 'Queen Anne' as used here refers not to the reign of Queen Anne, nor the English style of that time, but to the style popular in America during her reign at the beginning of the 18th century. It corresponds more to the European William and Mary style; note the bow-shaped top rail, and the many curves in the chair's outline. The chair was probably made by John Elliott of Philadelphia, and shows three beautiful examples of the American scallop shell motif. A curiosity of this chair is that the inscription on the back of the crest spells OIL, probably for Oliver Ingraham Lay, a New York, 19th-century artist who obviously had a reverence for the antique, but was not too shy to adapt a piece for his own satisfaction.

B

B. A Pair of Gothic George III Windsor Armchairs, *c*1760

These are classic Windsor chairs made of elm and yew in country style, upright and sturdy. Windsors often adopted prevalent styles of the period in which they were made, and these are Georgian Gothic Revival. Just as Horace Walpole transformed his country house at Strawberry Hill outside London by changing the façade with the addition of Gothic battlements, towers, and other Mediaeval paraphernalia, so Gothic architectural details are used here to make these chairs seem Mediaeval. The backs are in the shape of a Gothic arch, and the splats echo the Gothic tracery pattern to be found in cathedral windows. These are nothing like real Gothic furniture which consisted of little more than primitive stools and rough tables.

C. A Louis XV Single Chair, *c*1760

This is one of a set of 12 single chairs by Nogaret of Lyon. With its curved sides and elegant cabriole legs, it is the epitome of French elegance of the time, envied and copied all over Europe, and especially in England, which dominated the chair market throughout the 18th century. Although graceful and shapely, the chair decoration is more discreet than much Louis XV, marking a move towards more sober tastes.

E

D. An American Queen Anne Walnut Armchair, *c*1760

This Philadelphian armchair is the product of some of the best craftsmanship seen before American Independence. The curvaceous design with a dramatic top rail is loosely based on chairs from the reign of William and Mary in England; the splat and cabriole legs are early Georgian; and the reeded lines carved on the edge of each rail are a unique adaptation of a Queen Anne idea. The construction is substantial without being heavy and the effect is sculptural, although not as excessive as some English George II chairs are. The beautifully figured splat and carved shells are delightfully American.

E. A Giltwood Bergère, *c*1764

This impressive bergère, the French term for an armchair with upholstered sides, was probably made by Jean-Baptiste Tilliard the Elder who worked between 1740 and 1760. While it still shows some rococo curves, the basic chair shape is being straightened to become more expansive and cubic; a little more neoclassical. It is on this type of bergère that Robert Adam and other English designers based so many of their own versions.

It is interesting to notice the variation in style of arms found on bergères. They are sometimes the same height as the back, forming a kind of tub, or can be much smaller as here.

A. A Louis XV Giltwood Chair, c1765

This chair, now one of a pair, would have been part of a salon suite, which may well have included sofas. It was made by Jean-Baptiste Tilliard who came from a well known family of Parisian *menuisiers* (joiners). He became a maître in 1738 and was attached to the Garde-Meuble for several years before founding his own workshop in 1741. He supplied the French court with chairs and various other pieces of cabinet furniture. The elder Tilliard retired in 1764 but his son, Jean-Baptiste II, took over the workshop and continued to make furniture into the reign of Louis XVI.

This chair is absolutely typical of a style established in the first half of Louis XV's reign (1723–1774) and which has been popular ever since. The fundamental structure of the frame is a series of serpentine curves which form the seat rails, the sides of the backs, the legs and the arms. The back, which is rectangular, gives the impression of solidity and stability. The combination of white paint and gilt had tended by this time to replace the pure gilt of the luxurious first part of the reign. This is a basic example of the model which the English adopted and which set new standards for elegant solidity.

The French crown throughout the 18th century had a voracious appetite for furniture to decorate the great palaces; Tilliard, Jacob and others were the suppliers and, in part, promoters of the French style.

B. An American Chippendale Chair, c1765

This chair, made in New York, clearly shows the influence of English Chippendale and has many characteristics from Chippendale's pattern books. There is the New York balance between decoration and plainness, its roots in the designs of the original Dutch inhabitants, but it is also moving towards an increasing Anglicization.

This chair was made for one Elias Boudinout of New Jersey.

C. Two George II Mahogany Dining Chairs, c1765

Taken from a set of 14 by Robert Manwaring, one could be forgiven for looking at these chairs and shouting 'Chippendale'. Chippendale has come to mean mid 18th-century mahogany furniture of this type, although not pieces necessarily by Thomas Chippendale, or from his workshop. Robert Manwaring designed and probably actually made the chairs. In 1765 Manwaring published *The Cabinet & Chairmaker's Real Friend & Companion* and the following year *The Chairmaker's Guide*. From these we know more about his work than about him, though we know he was active in the 1760s and specialized in chairs.

Manwaring's design is generally rather more solid and 'masculine' than that of Chippendale. Certainly, this furniture has a frontal appearance. The rails are broad and flat, and the effect is not lightened by the fretwork carving and attempts to orientalize the design. While rather earthbound compared with Chippendale, these are really excellent chairs.

D. A pair of George III Mahogany Stools, c1765

This well-known model of stool is probably based on a design by Thomas Chippendale. Generally of good quality and with examples distributed right across the country, this style originated from the 1760s. There are 26 of them in the Christchurch Upper Library at Cambridge University, which are believed to have been supplied by Thomas Chippendale in July, 1764. The fact that they are in the library clearly indicates that they are seat furniture and certainly not foot stools, fulfilling the same function as sets of joint stools in the 17th century, and upholstered stools at the beginning of the 18th century.

The elegant bowed seats, in the form of an extended scroll, are standing on unusual, curved legs joined by a Gothic arched stretcher with a central patera. Stark in comparison with earlier upholstered stools, they are an interesting combination of Gothic and rococo scroll, and like other furniture of this period, tend towards severity. It is interesting that a similar design is found in a set of painted rococo hall furniture at Petworth House in Sussex, which shows their flexibility of function and appearance. An aquatint of a library from Ackermann's history of Oxford and Cambridge universities shows stools of a very similar design.

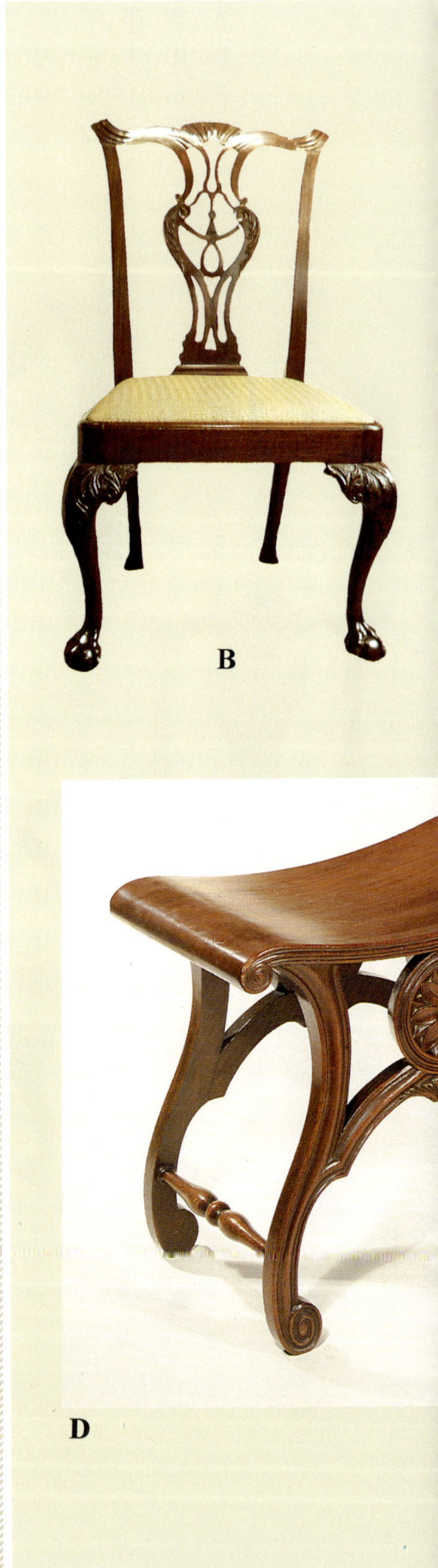

B

D

C

A

A . A pair of George III Mahogany Sidechairs, *c*1770

It is interesting to see this unusual integration of the armorial escutcheon painted in the centre of the interlacing reeded straps which form the back; in addition the family crest is carved into the toprail. Although the painting of family arms on chair backs, or carving them on the knees, is not uncommon, it is usually on the solid backs of hall chairs which were traditionally made in pairs or sets. Although these appear to be from a dining set they have very shallow seats and so may have been intended as very elaborate hall chairs. The slightly top-heavy proportions which derive from their transitional style. The rectilinear backs are in contrast to the Hepplewhite shield form. They have as many broad horizontal lines as vertical, giving a massive appearance. The weightiness was necessary to support the central plaque. The legs and rails are crisply carved which reduces their mass, and serpentine to reduce the impact of the horizontal; the tapering to a waisted foot makes the uprights seem longer. The heavy back on a lighter base typifies the transition between heavy and light Georgian.

B . A Philadelphia Chippendale Sidechair, *c*1770

This splendid chair is crisply carved on a plain strong design, all lightened by the cabriole legs and the interlacing pierced back, which is taken direct from Chippendale's *Director*, Plate XVI (lower right), published in 1762, which shows how rapidly English influence penetrated abroad.

The chair was one of a set made for Charles Thompson, Secretary of the Continental Congress during the American revolution, and there are four very similar sets, one of which is in the Winterthur Museum, Delaware, US. This chair, with its fully documented history, represents the peak of American mid-eighties furniture taste, and fetched a world-record price in 1987 of over US$250,000.

C . A pair of George III Giltwood Chairs, c1770

This pair of chairs belongs to a large suite of 12 chairs and a sofa from the collection of the Hon. Mrs Aileen Plunkett, from Luttrellstown Castle, Dublin. Made in the 1770s, these chairs are relatively restrained compared with the large, French-influenced, Louis XV pieces so popular at the time. Even so, the gilt legs are ornate, with anthemion sprays and an unusual looped swag decoration above the fairly straight cabriole legs. The appeal of these chairs is that the legs contrast with and thereby heighten the effect of the simple lines of the upholstery.

These chairs can be compared to a suite of giltwood armchairs supplied by Chippendale for the Couch Room at Harewood House, Yorkshire. The Harewood chairs are even more neo-Classical in taste, and both are good examples of the parallel inclinations towards simplicity and decoration which mark the period.

D . A pair of Hepplewhite Mahogany Armchairs, *c*1775

These are one of the most elegant variants of a style known generally as Hepplewhite, although they do not necessarily appear in George Hepplewhite's own pattern book. The shield-shaped backs are particularly lightened by the carved details at the top, and by the vase-shaped frames containing a notional fleur de lys motif. The legs are fairly standard, tapering to give a slimming effect, and the feet are smart sabots. Most spectacular are the arms: beautiful wide loops which are probably too high for practical use but add a kind of bravura elegance. The neat appearance of the chairs comes from the pattern of lines formed by the frame; by curving back in to themselves rather than jutting outwards, they give the chairs a calm, lyrical balance, even if in practice they are neither comfortable nor robust.

E . A Pair of Philadelphian Chairs, c1775

These are not only an excellent pair of Philadelphian chairs by the well-known maker Thomas Tufft, but they are perfectly documented. They were part of a suite which were entered into an account book by Richard Edwards of Lumberton, New Jersey, US, who recorded purchases both for his General Store at Lumberton and for his own household. The Chippendale suite comprised a high chest of drawers, a dressing table and this pair of chairs. The Edwards-Harrison family sold them in 1987 for US$ 1.76 million.

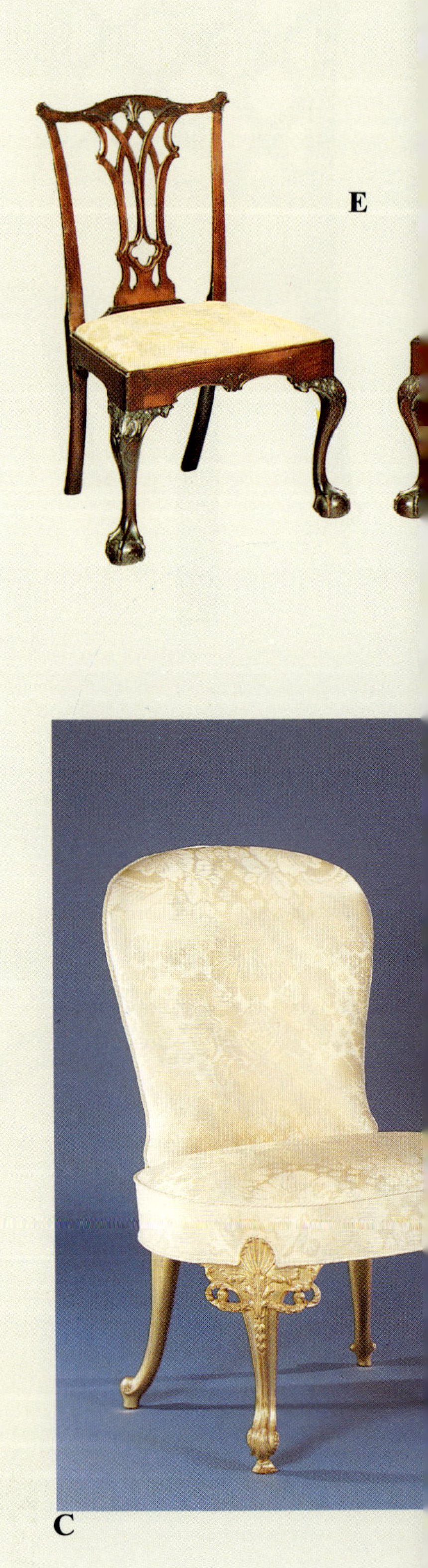

E

C

D

B

A

1700-1800

A . An English Giltwood Armchair, *c*1770

This chair, now one of a pair, was formerly part of a suite from the home of the Dukes of Argyll at Inveraray Castle, Scotland. It bears all the hallmarks of French taste which so influenced English chairmaking during the third quarter of the 18th century; compare it, for example, with Tilliard's Louis XV giltwood chair (70). Both are substantial, with large expanses of flat, rectilinear surfaces, and both are lightened by the elegantly curving rails and legs. Here, the decoration on the rail is particularly refined, emphasizing the serpentine shape with reeding (the small moulded line at the edge of the rails); this increases the rails' apparent length. The line is continued past the indented knee to the scroll toes, balanced on their own peg-top feet.

B . A Provincial George III Dining Chair, c1770

Provincial chairs of this date differed from their London-made cousins both in the material, which is not mahogany, and in the pattern. Although the shape is similar, this chair, for example, lacks refinement of carving and the light, strong framework. It is slightly heavier in appearance and retains the outdated square legs and stretchers. It is possibly by a provincial chair-maker following a London pattern: consider, for example, the motif resembling a scroll on the top corners of the seat back. The cabinet-maker seems to have followed the pattern without understanding that this should resemble a piece of scrolled paper, having never seen an original. This chair would originally have been part of a suite.

C . A Chippendale Dining Chair, c1765

This interesting chair from a set of 12 originally came from Kippax Park, Yorkshire, and is probably by the Yorkshire firm of cabinet-makers Wright & Elwick of Wakefield. Both partners in the firm were known to subscribe to Chippendale's *Director* and this is similar to many of his designs. The two partners worked together between 1745–1771; Wright probably came from London to join Elwick, a man of plain tastes. Together they founded a firm which dominated cabinet-making in northern England throughout the second half of the 18th century.

D . A pair of English Gilt Armchairs, c1765

While rococo began to wane in Europe, in England it was at its height, as is seen in the third edition of Thomas Chippendale's *Director*. This pair of armchairs are two of the best of their kind, with exaggerated curves, heavily carved with rocaille, and with a pronounced cabriole at the back. Although fundamentally rectangular, they have used as many of the exaggerated rococo curves as the English dared. To some, this is an acquired taste, but it is still worth admiring these chairs for their excellent craftsmanship.

E . An American Chippendale Wing Chair, *c*1770

This chair could easily be English, although documentation proves that it comes from Newport, Rhode Island, US. It is in spirit very close to English Queen Anne Wing chairs; the upholstered parts are the same shape as those of its English cousins and the cabriole legs have claw and ball feet joined by turned stretchers which end in substantial blocks. This frame is in mahogany, whereas the English Queen Anne chair would probably be walnut-framed. The stretchers of this chair are delicately turned, like the spindles on some American Windsor chairs, and the ball and claw carving is typical of Rhode Island. Its date of 1770 shows the conservative American affection for earlier styles, as it is some 50 years behind English designs. The title 'Chippendale' here refers to the Chippendale taste popular at this time in America.

F . An English 'French Hepplewhite' Bergère, c1770

This English-made chair is typical of the new style imported from France, which emphasized comfort as much as the look of the piece. Designed to support an ample frame, the arms have become a part of the back, and it is easy to imagine a Georgian *bon-viveur* collapsing in one of these in the library after dinner. These are the forerunners of the English tub chair, and are clearly different from the open armchairs and wing chairs which had preceded them.

F
E
D
C

A . A Pair of Chairs by Georges Jacob, *c*1770

Similar to the pair of Jacob chairs illustrated, these bear the *ébéniste's* (cabinetmaker's) stamp on the woodwork beneath. They would originally have been gilded and were perhaps stripped during a change of taste away from their elaborate cousins from Jacob. Naming chairs with a maker's label or stamp became increasingly popular throughout the 18th century, particularly in France after 1750, and toward the end of the century elsewhere: it has continued until the present day.

B . George II Gilt Armchairs in the style of Robert Adam, c1780

These handsome chairs were taken from Powerscourt, County Wicklow. They are archetypal Adam, with their oval backs and nicely-carved back legs. The unupholstered example here shows both the construction of the chair and the type and age of wood used. The frame is the only part not covered in gilt or, in the case of mahogany, polish; it should be just like this – dry and hand-sawn with a light, mellow look to it. The seat rail is joined to the legs by invisible mortice and tenon joints which are screwed or pegged at the corners for added strength (although used here, pegs were considered old-fashioned by this date and were often discarded after 1750). The oval back was probably made in four pieces, again pegged for strength. The nail holes on the frame shows where the stuff-over seat had been fixed. This oval back panel had been nailed to the frame, though on European chairs, it was often fixed with a catch and removable, a practical detail which shows a kind of refinement rarely seen on English chairs.

C . A George II Mahogany Dining Chair, c1785

This chair came from a set of 12, which could also have originally had two armchairs with it. Good examples of quality Hepplewhite suites, the design may well have come from his famous pattern book *The Cabinet Maker & Upholsterer's Guide* of 1788, published two years after his death. Hepplewhite was an apprentice of Gillow of Lancaster and his somewhat conservative pattern book epitomized the furniture of the 1780s and 1790s, utilizing classical motifs in a restrained, English way. Although, according to Ambrose Heal who wrote on English furniture makers, 'his contemporary reputation as a maker was in no way exceptional,' he gave his name to a style of furniture of lasting appeal, regularly reproduced even today.

A

D

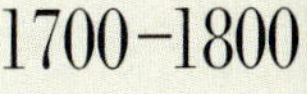
1700–1800

B

C

Hepplewhite laid claim to the three Prince of Wales' feathers motif as being of his own invention, even though it was in general use at the time. The shield-shaped back, however, is very much Hepplewhite's style, as are the serpentine-front seat rail and tapering, reeded legs.

D. An American Chippendale Wing Chair, *c*1780

The Queen Anne style continued to be popular well into the American Chippendale period which dominated fashion during the second half of the 18th century. This is very much a transitional chair; the upholstered parts resemble traditional Queen Anne chairs, with high backs and outward-scrolling arms, whereas the visible frame (the legs and stretchers) are very much Chippendale, with straight lines and of square or rectangular section. The front legs are fluted, an architectural motif revived in furniture design by Robert Adam. After the War of Independence, America very swiftly re-established contact with, and reproduced, European fashions. It is known that Chippendale's pattern books were available, and designs such as this were popular alongside earlier Queen Anne styles.

A. A Pair of Louis XVI Giltwood Armchairs, c1780

These classic late 18th-century French chairs came from a suite of six *fauteuils* (covered armchairs) by Georges Jacob; broadly speaking, the style corresponds with that of Robert Adam in England. The two craftsmen shared an architectural spirit and taste for classical ornamentation as applied to these salon chairs. Just as Adam was one of the great chair designers, Jacob was one of the great furniture makers, specializing in chairs. He was not only an *ébéniste* (cabinetmaker) but also a *menuisier* (chairmaker or joiner).

Born in Burgundy in 1739, by 1765 he had become a *maître ébéniste* and his reputation soon spread. From 1773 onwards he received numerous commissions from the crown, and in 1781 he was appointed *ébéniste ordinaire* to Monsieur le Comte de Provence (who afterwards became Louis XVIII). He was one of the great French cabinet makers and his work is well represented in the Louvre, the Palais de Versailles, and at Fontainbleau in France, and in the Victoria & Albert Museum and the Wallace Collection in London. (The latter is one of the finest collections of French furniture and works of art.)

The general horizontal feel of the chairs comes from their breadth, and from the backs roughly forming square panels. All the rails are profusely decorated and carved: neoclassic architectural friezes, a ribbon twist around the main rail, the beading on the arm supports, and fluting on the tapering legs.

B. A Louis XVI Giltwood Sofa, c1780

Made by Georges Jacob, the constant tension between elaborate decoration and control, as seen here, was common to all Western European designs during the 18th century. This sofa has an enclosed, sheltering quality which is emphasized by its curves. The controlled carving of interlaced ribbons forms a constraining border for the plush interior, and the sofa is supported by an unobtrusive set of stubby legs. It is interesting that, although a later replacement, this fabric is identical to that used by Louis XV, and is actually from the same source.

Jacob, who was extremely versatile, was himself influenced by English standards, presumably of constraint, and at Windsor Castle there is a suite bearing his stamp in distinctly English taste. He was also known to use ungilded mahogany with an effect reminiscent of English brown furniture.

C. A George III Mahogany Armchair, c1785

This unusually elaborate armchair has an intriguing combination of motifs. The pierced back is carved with a most unusual splat of a central urn above an anthemion with interlaced ribbons. The front legs are distinctly Adam, and the arms have an elegant pronounced scroll in the French taste, clearly showing the fashionable influence of the time. However, the classical urns and architectural references are details imposed on what is basically a carved English chair.

D. A George III Mahogany Dining Chair, c1790

This would originally have been the armchair from a suite of anything from six to 32 chairs; generally, most of them would have been single with one pair of armchairs such as this. Relatively plain and undistinguished, they are still elegant, with the rectilinear back decorated only with stretchers of opposing curves, making the chair light and serviceable. It is the arm supports and turned-baluster legs which indicate a date towards the end of the reign. These were clearly extremely popular; and there are many mid-range chairs of a similar pattern readily available today. Because of their popularity, designs such as this were produced well into the 19th and 20th centuries.

E. A Sheraton Painted Armchair, c1790

This is a classic example of late 18th-century beechwood furniture. Typical of the type illustrated in Thomas Sheraton's pattern book, published in the early 1790s, its frame is a basic shield-shape with various motifs forming the splat. In this case, two arrows either side of a tall chair and a laurel wreath are all tied by a ribboned bow. The rest of the frame is painted with swags, husks and other piecemeal decorations from Thomas Sheraton's repertoire. It is very characteristic of the elegant, classically-inspired patterns of this time, with an added sophistication in the black painting and extra colour. Although nowadays these chairs are found singly or in pairs, they were originally supplied in reasonably large sets. Their design marks one of the peaks of late 18-century decoration. From this point on, they began to be over-decorated and thus excessive in a heavily coloured and textured room.

D
C
A

A . A Pair of Anglo-Indian George III Ivory Chairs, *c*1790

Since the 17th century, the Orient acted as a valuable source of exotic materials. While lacquer is associated with China and Japan, the abundance of Indian elephants provided a plentiful source of ivory of the whitest colour and the purest texture. During the late 17th century, Anglo-Indian furniture consisted mostly of cabinets and caskets of local woods, such as ebony and coromandel, inlaid with figurative and geometric designs. At the start of the 18th century the move toward austerity during the reign of Queen Anne halted this trend, and furniture of the mid-century was primarily carved from mahogany from the Western Empire, especially Cuba and Honduras. Towards the end of the 18th century, more elegant designs and the taste for dramatically-coloured furniture brought forth a variety of small ivory-veneered objects such as tea caddies and games boxes, often with the stained decoration characteristic of the industry based in the province of Vizagapatam.

India under British rule produced some veneered furniture based on contemporary British designs. Often with slight variations, these were veneered in ivory rather than being solid mahogany, rather in the style of walnut veneers of the early 18th century. However, these particular chairs are solid ivory. Of considerable weight, the Hepplewhite-style frame is painted with orientalized gilt foliage. They could almost be mistaken for cream lacquer, and are clearly associated with the white-painted furniture and lacquered chairs of the end of the 18th century, which in turn heralded the exuberant Regency taste of Thomas Hope and George Smith.

B . Two American Federal Armchairs, *c*1795

These armchairs are unusual in being American Louis XVI, which was fashionable before the French Revolution – no doubt as a product of the strong French-American links during the latter part of the 18th century. The French versions would probably be gilded or painted. From a famous set – probably of 12 armchairs originally – they were once owned by the family of Alexander Hamilton. They are almost certainly by the Philadelphian cabinet-maker, Adam Hains, and were made between 1793 and 1797. Other chairs from the set were probably made for use in The Vale, the country home designed by Samuel McIntire for Theodore Lyman of Boston: they are now on view in that house. Other chairs bear Hains' own maker's label, and some of

the set may well have been used by George Washington in the Presidential Mansion in Philadelphia and are now in the White House.

C. A Pair of Ebonized and Gilded Sheraton Armchairs, c1798, and Preliminary Drawings

Although these chairs are not identical to the design which Thomas Sheraton has signed on the engraving (bottom left), the similarity is probably as great as with any chair. The back panels are caned rather than covered with fabric, and the pastoral panel (which genteelly reflects the aristocratic preoccupation with rustic, idealized life) differs from the drawings. However, the turned legs, rope-twist arms and carefully-drawn proportions are the same. Close examination of the engraving shows that the top of each of the legs is different, which reveals Sheraton's intention to provide a guide rather than designs to be copied; in his *Cabinet Dictionary* of 1803, he notes, 'It is very remarkable the difference of some chairs of precisely the same pattern, when executed by different chair-makers, arising chiefly from the want of taste concerning the beauty of an outline, of which we judge by the eye, more than the rigid rules of perspective.' The book plate shows his skill as a draughtsman, although he clearly did not underestimate the maker's art; which is perhaps why his name is synonymous with late Georgian taste today.

D. Two American Hepplewhite Chairs, *c*1790

The chair on the left is from Rhode Island, and the other from Salem, Massachusetts. The latter was probably made by Samuel McIntire, but their similarity shows how standardized furniture design had become by this date; it is likely that they were both inspired by Hepplewhite books or other similar publications. However, there are differences; the Salem chair is lighter and more elegant, with no stretchers and, arguably, a finer back with more pleasing design. Both are good chairs of carved mahogany, typical of the Federal period, which corresponded to English Regency.

A . A French Régence Gilt-Wood Canapé, 1700–35

From a suite of Régence furniture, this fine canapé was made in France in the 18th century. The cresting of the back rail is especially decorative, and there is an equally ornate apron to the seat front. The term 'Régence' is often used rather loosely to cover the period from 1700 to 1735, The suite also included four *fauteuils* (upholstered chairs with open arms). Upholstered in leather and standing on six cabriole legs, this Rococo piece's construction is derived from chair-back forms. Rarely does furniture of this quality appear on the international market.

B . An English Queen Anne Walnut Love Seat, *c*1710

A small early 18th-century walnut sofa, this piece is reupholstered in saffron silk. This version, with a rectangular back, has well-shaped low scrolled arms and stands on cabriole legs with hoof feet, enriched with restrained carving on the knee. Known as a 'love seat' because of its small size, such sofas were sometimes constructed in the chair-back style, with pierced central splats which must have made them very uncomfortable. Others have needlework upholstery, sometimes in combination with gilt-wood, giving them a regal effect. Less romantically, it seems probable that these sofa/chairs were made to accommodate the voluminous skirts of ladies of fashion more comfortably.

C . An English George I Mahogany Love Seat with Needlework Upholstery, *c*1720

Small-sized sofas such as this one were popularly known as 'love seats' and were ideal pieces for the display of needlework. This particularly attractive George I example, with gros- and petit-point needlework, was made *c*1720. The mahogany sofa has a shaped back and high scrolled arms with curvilinear supports. It stands on cabriole legs with carved volutes. Such sofas were mainly used in reception rooms and could be placed near a tea or card table.

B

D

D . A French Régence Beechwood Sofa with Needlework Upholstery, c1720

Early 18th-century French furniture was lighter and more sophisticated than its British counterpart. This sofa, carved in beechwood, was made in the Régence period (1715–23) of Louis XV's reign. The delicacy of its scrolled legs, joined by waved cross-stretchers carved with flowers, is typical of the best work made within the guild system, which encouraged the development of the various crafts involved in the construction of seat furniture. The sofa's value, however, depends not so much on the carcase as on the quality of the superb needlework upholstery, which depicts Venus attended by nymphs and putti, together with animals, shells, leaves and flowers. The rich design is executed in gros- and petit-point needlework in wool and silk on a dark brown background. The panel on the serpentine seat shows a lion chasing a stag.

A . A Dutch Painted Hall Bench, *c*1720

Furniture that is especially made for hall seating is, almost invariably, highly decorative but extremely uncomfortable. This green-painted hall bench dates from the early 18th century and was part of the furnishings of a Dutch home. The houses of the Dutch merchant classes in the 1700s were much more lavishly equipped than those of their German or English counterparts, and in the main reception furniture was intended to impress. This hall bench has an ornately carved large central shell centred among attractive pierced work. The shallow carving of the decorative apron is a typical Dutch feature of the period.

B . An English George I Walnut Settle, *c*1725

The height of the back of this double chair-back walnut settle is relatively low, a good feature that suggests a date of around 1725. The flat uprights are given more interest by the carved decoration at the top, and the line of the back uprights mirrors the shape of the back splats, thus giving the piece a pleasing unity. The cabriole legs have the typical shell-carved knees and the ball-and-claw feet that were so popular with British makers, and the gentle shaping of the back made the chair quite comfortable as well. A weak feature, however, is the shallow seat rail, which lacks ornamentation.

C . A French Louis XV Gilt-Wood Canapé, *c*1725–30

This fine early Louis XV gilt-wood canapé dates to the second quarter of the 18th century. The term 'canapé' refers to high-backed French sofas in Louis XV style, although it is also used more loosely to describe any French-style sofa with closed sides. The serpentine top rail is carved with flowerheads and scrolling acanthus leaves, flanked by shells and wave motifs. The down-swept armrests are carved with foliage and shells and incised with latticework. The carving to the serpentine front of the seat complements the back rest, which is also decorated on the reverse with shells and foliage. The cabriole legs end in foliate carved scrolled toes. The canapé was once in the collection of the Art Institute of Chicago.

C

A . A French Louis XV Walnut Canapé

The close nailing of the upholstery makes a positive contribution to the design of this small French canapé. Made of walnut, the canapé stands on six moulded cabriole legs with scroll feet. The shaping of the seat front is reminiscent of the chair form, although the back is made in one piece. The moulded outset arms feature scrolls and padded elbow rests. The sofa is upholstered in rose damask, with a needlework fruiting-vine border with ornamental corners continuing on the squab cushion. The originality of the upholstery makes this canapé especially appealing.

B . A French Louis XV Walnut Canapé with Tapestry Upholstery

A delicate and small canapé, this piece was made in France in the 18th century. The undulating double curve of the back rail is repeated, unusually, on the lower edge of the back rest. Made of walnut, the canapé stands on delicate cabriole legs. The double serpentine fronts of the seat rail are centred with carved motifs. The tapestry upholstery is in good condition and depicts figures in a colourful landscape.

C . An English George II Gold- and White-Painted Beechwood Sofa, *c*1735

Painted in white and gold, this dramatic beechwood sofa was made c1735. A sofa such as this would have been an integral part of a complete decorative scheme, commissioned by a very wealthy patron. All the woodwork was covered and rich fabrics used for the upholstery, so that the magnificent effect of an Italian palace could be re-created. The use of carved swags, shells, mythological beasts, fruit and leaves set against abundant scrolls was all typical of the designs of William Kent (c1686–1748) and his followers. Kent's influence extended into all spheres of educated taste, even though it was retrospective in idiom and demanded a degree of craftsmanship that was extremely expensive. Complete suites of furniture in the heavy Baroque taste that marks this sofa filled the homes of many wealthy British noblemen.

B

C

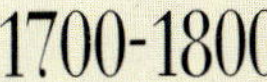

D

E

A

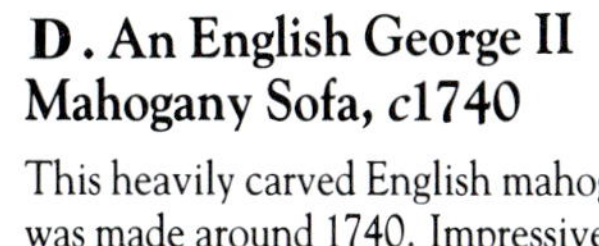

D. An English George II Mahogany Sofa, *c*1740

This heavily carved English mahogany sofa was made around 1740. Impressive pieces of this kind were often constructed as one of a pair and would originally have been upholstered in silk or velvet. Shaped high backs of this type are usually completely upholstered, the carved arm supports thereby adding interest. Originally one long squab cushion would have been fitted rather than the three replacements. The carved cabriole legs are finished with heavily ornamented volutes. Though somewhat florid in construction, the piece would sell well as it is so typical of the period.

E. An English George II Mahogany Sofa, *c*1740

From around 1740, the arms of sofas and chairs became much higher and, as in this example, are often a virtual continuation of the back. This English George II mahogany sofa has nicely shaped cabriole legs, terminating in ball-and-claw feet. The shallow seat rail is decorated with central carved motifs. It has six legs to give added support because of length; hence it clearly shows how the sofa form developed from the chair-back types. The seat-rail pendants give added interest, although obviously the piece would be much more valuable if it had the original, or a later tapestry or needlework, covering. In the mid-18th century, both damask and leather were used, as well as velvet.

1700-1800

A . An English George II Double Chair-Back Walnut Sofa, *c*1740

Made in England *c*1740, this George II walnut double chair-back sofa has a somewhat clumsy form. Originally the seat would have been upholstered in needlework or velvet: the unattractive striped upholstery is especially unfortunate. The out-scrolled arms are raised on acanthus-carved supports, whereas the well-shaped cabriole legs are carved at the knees with a mantled cabochon flanked by acanthus leaves; they terminate in paw feet. The chair backs have pierced-work splats decorated with flowerheads and acanthus leaves. As flat splats are much more common, an example with this amount of ornamentation always commands interest, especially, as in this case, when the sofa is one of a pair.

B . An Italian Walnut Sofa from the Palazzo Rezzonico, Venice, *c*1745–50

Sofas of this type were made for use in Italian ballrooms or the very long rooms that extended the depth of a Venetian palace. This most elegant example dates to the mid-18th century and was made for the Palazzo Rezzonico in Venice. The undulating, carved back rail is centred with a shell and supported on a pierced splat. The carved apron of the seat rail contributes to the overall delicate effect. This sofa is part of a matching set of furniture, which also includes a larger version with three back splats and standing on ten cabriole legs. Large sofas of this type were ideal for use in a ballroom as they could be moved easily to allow for dancing.

C. An Italian Triple Chair-Back Gilt-Wood Sofa, *c*1745–50

A triple chair-back gilded sofa made in Venice in the mid-18th century for the Palazzo Rezzonico. The chair backs are centred with carved foliate crests, devices that are repeated on the seat rail. By the mid-18th century, French influence on Italian furniture was very strong and the Italian nobility began to use smaller items of furniture for the more intimate types of rooms which were becoming more fashionable. For many years the heavy, palatial styles associated with the 17th century remained popular in Italy, but gradually lighter furniture began to be made by native craftsmen who had often been trained in France. In thier imitative work they often exaggerated the decorative forms to create pieces that were sufficiently impressive for the Venetian palaces.

C

B

A

1700-1800

A . An English George II Sofa with Needlework Upholstery, *c*1750

A nicely proportioned English-made sofa of *c*1750, its shaped back and high, scrolled arms characterize the period. It stands on simple square legs united by plain stretchers. Sofas of this type were ideal for the display of needlework, which was often worked by the women of the household – although a large number were also commercially produced. After 1775, needlework covered sofas were replaced with silk or tapestry upholstery. In the 19th century it again became fashionable to work sets of covers for antique furniture, a practice that has continued to the present day.

B . An English George II Ebonized-Wood Sofa, *c*1750

From a suite of George II furniture, this sofa with a plain rectangular back has an ebonized finish. The cabriole legs are carved with acanthus leaves. Close nailing is used to accentuate the square form of the seat padding.

C . An English George II Gilt-Wood Sofa, *c*1750

This mid-18th-century gilt-wood sofa was later reupholstered in velvet. Massive, heavily carved sofas were usually part of a large saloon suite, all parts of which would be covered in matching fabric. The architectural style of the piece is reminiscent of William Kent's work. A very ornate back crest was a feature of many sofas of the George II period, as this impressive detail gave the piece added importance. This was still furniture in the grand manner, intended for mansions and castles. As the carved wood was covered with gesso and gilding, cheaper materials – especially pine – were used for the construction.

D . An English George II Gilt-Wood Sofa, *c*1750

The very pleasant curve of this sofa's serpentine back, in combination with its fairly deep seat rail, contributes to a highly pleasing piece of mid-18th-century English furniture. Made during the reign of George II, the gilt-wood sofa has out-scrolled arms centring a rectangular seat. The seat rail is carved with Vitruvian scrolls terminating in square motifs. The well shaped cabriole legs are carved with pendent bellflowers that are flanked by scrolls; the feet are also scrolled. The later upholstery does not detract from the value of such a fine example from an especially favoured period.

A

D

1700-1800

A . An English George II Double Chair-Back Mahogany Sofa in Chippendale Style, c1750–60

This superb carved-mahogany, double chair-back sofa of the mid-18th century is similar in form to examples designed by Thomas Chippendale (1718–79). The ribbon-back of this sofa, so called because the carving was made to resemble crimped ribbon, makes the piece highly desirable. Chippendale made several sets of what he termed 'Ribband-Back' chairs, all of which had given 'entire satisfaction'. In his *Gentleman and Cabinetmaker's Director*, he suggested that the seats could be covered with red Morocco leather for an especially fine effect. This sofa incorporates sections from several of the chair designs in the *Director*. The Victoria and Albert Museum, owner of this example, considers it to be the work of Chippendale himself, who was a master woodcarver. In the highly ornamental Rococo designs of this type, Chippendale was following the French styles first seen at the court of Louis XV. Such exquisite 18th-century work is unsurpassed.

A

B

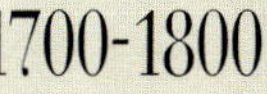

C

B. An English Georgian Oak Settle, *c*1750–60

Oak settles of this type were originally intended mainly for use in large halls, but are now popular for dining rooms. In this simple 18th-century design, the back has four plain panels. The shaped legs that are continued into the turned arm supports are of unusual form, as is the centre leg that seems almost an afterthought to provide additional support. The squab cushion rests on wooden slats, although in some versions cord was strung across the seat. There are many variations on this basic form, as country makers in each area made these very practical pieces in some number. Throughout the 19th and early 20th centuries similar pieces were made, especially for use in hotels and pubs.

C. An English George II Sofa, designed by Thomas Chippendale, *c*1759

This is one of Chippendale's most elegant designs for a sofa, published in 1759. He recommended that the structures be made from 6 ft to 9 or 10 ft long (1.8m to 2.7–3m long). The depth of the seat from front to back, he suggested, should be 2 ft 3 in to 3 ft (.7m to 1m), and the height of the seat (including the castors) 1 ft 2 in (.4m). He felt that the seats should be deep enough for the sofa to be used as an occasional bed. In his design book, Chippendale claimed that all the drawings could be executed by a skilful workman, although at the time many complained that some of the more extreme creations, especially those in the Chinese manner, were almost impossible to copy. This type of sofa was of a plainer form, however, and has been constructed, with adaptations, by generations of cabinetmakers.

1700-1800

A. An English George II Sofa, designed by Thomas Chippendale, *c*1759

The larger versions of this 1759 Chippendale sofa design were provided with a bolster and pillow at each end and cushions at the back 'that may be laid down occasionally to form a mattress'. The 'circular' back corners of this design were obviously considered very progressive by the designer and exhibit the influence of French taste. An inset drawing suggested that this seat could be made in the Gothic style by using rectangular-type legs decorated with quasi-ecclesiastical carving. The line drawings naturally make the sofas seem very light and delicate: when constructed, they have a much heavier effect, as the wood probably could not be worked so delicately by other cabinetmakers. Chippendale claimed that in his workshops every design could be improved 'both as to beauty and enrichment'.

B. A French Louis XV Gilt-Wood Day-Bed by Jean-Baptiste Tilliard, second half of 18th century

An ornate and typically French 18th-century day-bed of carved and gilded wood, this example bears the stamp of Jean-Baptiste Tilliard (1685–1766). Its apron's decoration echoes that of its back, and a drop-in squab cushion provided the comfort that furniture buyers were demanding at the time. Cushions of this type were usually filled with curled horsehair. In 1743, French master craftsmen were obliged to stamp their work, an aspect of the strict guild system that has made it possible to trace the development of style, even within individual families. Tilliard *père* and *fils* were among the leading *menuisiers* who passed the craft from father to son.

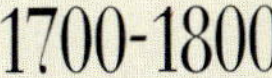

C

B

C. A French Louis XVI Beechwood Canapé en Corbeille, c1750–75

Made in the manner of Nicolas-Quinibert Foliot (1706–76), this fine beechwood canapé en Corbeille dates to the third quarter of the 18th century. Its complex serpentine back is centred with a flower-filled urn flanked by acanthus leaves. The arms have voluted supports carved with trailing, budding veins. The padded, upholstered seat has a conforming seat rail carved with ribbon-tied floral bouquets and the apron is carved with laurel and scrolling foliage. The cabriole legs end in foliate scroll toes. Similar sofas are known with the stamp of 'N. Q. Foliot'. The Foliot family were members of the guild of the *menuisiers* who passed their skills from father to son and worked according to strict rules delineating the functions of the various furniture craftsmen.

D. An English George III Triple Chair-Back Walnut Settle

Chair-back settles evolved from the practice of placing a row of chairs close together, against walls or on either side of a state bed or a seat of honour. Despite the fact that they were often not very comfortable – as in this model, intended for three people to sit together – the form continued to be popular until the 1900s. This triple chair-back settle, in attractively figured walnut, is not as well proportioned as the best early 18th-century examples and the shaping of the top of the central leg is weak. Also, the carving of the top of the shell on the uprights is too fussy, as is that of the joining shells between the chair backs.

A. A Continental Parcel-Gilt Triple Chair-Back Settee in Rococo Style, *c*1760

Each section of this triple chair-back settle, made *c*1760, is centred with a carved crest, and the knees are robustly carved. Although highly decorative, the parcel-gilt structure lacks the elegance of some of the best English work; rather, it reflects the more ostentatious Continental Rococo taste which was practiced in Italy and imitated in Germany.

B. An English Georgian Hump-back Settee in Chippendale Style, *c*1760

Typically Chippendale in style is this mahogany 'hump-back' settee with scrolling spandrels. Made in England *c*1760, the settee's seat rail is decorated with the blind fret that characterizes so many Chippendale designs. The sofa designs illustrated in the master's *Director* reveal his most complex and expensive work, but simpler constructions such as this were also made in some number for sale through his shop in St Martin's Lane, London, and to the many customers for whom he furnished entire houses. Chippendale trained a large number of craftsmen who imitated his designs when they set up their own businesses, some in America, where furniture in the classical Chippendale style was also produced. The Chippendale furniture style, whose effect depends on fine materials and good craftsmanship, has never gone out of style.

C. An English George III Sofa in Chippendale Style, *c*1760

Dating to the reign of George III, this mahogany sofa is constructed in Chippendale style. In his *Director*, Chippendale illustrated a chair with similarly shaped arms and an upholstered back with small side projections; such chairs were described as 'French chairs'. This double chair-back sofa stands on square legs linked by plain stretchers. The brackets joining the legs and seat are a feature of pieces in Chippendale style.

A
B

A . An English George III Mahogany Sofa, 1760s

This Georgian sofa presents a striking appearance because of its exaggerated scroll-arms. Made of mahogany, it dates to the 1760s. The square chamfered and stop-fluted legs are joined by plain stretchers. Mahogany only came into general use in the British furniture trade after 1750, when Cuban as well as Jamaican imports became available. Honduras mahogany was also used extensively in the late 18th century. Mahogany was an ideal wood for sofas, as it remained strong even when heavily carved or when thinly cut to form slender legs or delicate stretchers. As the qualities of the wood became more appreciated, stretchers were no longer a necessity and were included more for their decorative qualities than to give added strength to a piece.

B . An English George III Mahogany Corner Sofa, 1760s

This George III mahogany sofa was especially made for use in a corner position. Dating to the late 1760s, the piece is unusual because of its shape. The settee is also of good general quality and has a shaped padded back, terminating on either side with scroll elbow supports, and a moulded mahogany frame, standing on square front supports. The castors are later, as is the coiled springing of the seat. When reupholstered in the 18th-century style, this sofa would present a much finer appearance, especially when the unsightly rectangular, fringed cushion is eliminated.

C . An English George III Sofa Design by Robert Adam, 1762

Robert Adam (1738–92) designed this delicate sofa in 1762 for Lord Scarsdale. The classical details on the arms and back rail are typical of Adam's interpretation of the styles of Greece and Rome. Simple neo-Classical furniture of this type brought a refreshing lightness into English drawing rooms and Adam's designs were soon widely imitated. Adam's sofa designs were intended for pieces about 12 ft (3.6 m) long that were to be gilded. This specific example was also executed for a 'Mrs Montagu in Hill Street'. London furniture maker John Linnell (c1737–96) was responsible for the construction of many sofas to Adam's drawings, but his interpretation was often quite exuberant and used as a vehicle to display his carving skills.

D . An English George III Mahogany Sofa, c1765

An English-made mahogany sofa, this dates to around 1765, to the reign of George III. The serpentine cresting rail of the back continues, in a well-defined curve, to the sharply downward-sloping arms, which are padded. The attractive gadrooned border is repeated on the front of the serpentine seat. The cabriole legs are headed by mantled cabochons and end in delicate scrolled feet. As this Georgian piece is only 5 ft (1.5 m) long, its size makes it especially desirable. Its somewhat restrained interpretation of the exuberant French Rococo style is more in accordance with British and American taste.

E . An English George III Mahogany Sofa, 1770s

From a suite of furniture, this George III mahogany sofa stands on long cabriole legs with carving and scrolled feet, lending it slightly ungainly proportions. Such high sofas were used as seating around card tables or for eating supper, and sometimes appear unsatisfactory or awkward when seen in isolation. The curved padding of the front is more typical of the work of French upholsterers.

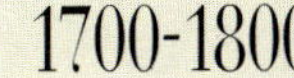

E

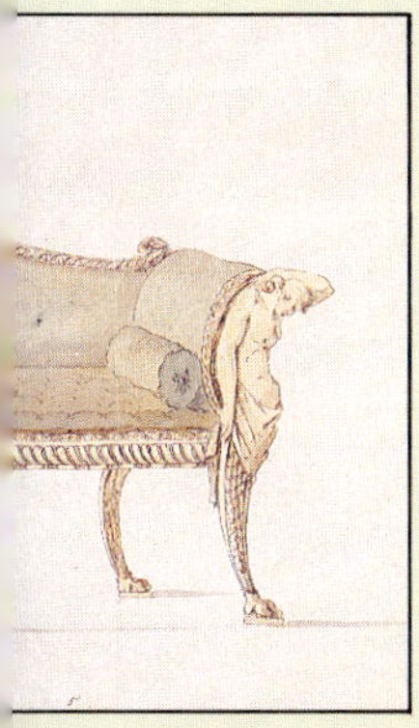

C

B

1700-1800

A . A French Louis XVI Gilt-Wood Canapé by Georges Jacob, *c*1775

This canapé is part of a suite of Louis XVI gilt-wood furniture also comprising four armchairs. Although made as one of a set, the sofa's rectangular back is in complete contrast to the rounded chair backs. The frame of the canapé is carved with leaf tips and continuous laurel banding, and its conforming seat rail is sculpted with leaf tips and berried laurel. It stands on circular, stop-fluted legs that taper and are headed by paterae and gadrooned capitals; they end in *toupie* (or 'top') feet. The suite is stamped 'G. Jacob', the mark of Georges Jacob (1739–1814), an innovative maker of carved seat furniture who introduced more formal, rectangular elements into his work in the last quarter of the 18th century.

B

Mahogany Settee with Needlework Upholstery, *c*1775

A very elegant George III settee with an attractive serpentine curved back rest, this piece dates to around 1775. It has beautifully scrolled arms of slim form that contribute to its elegant structure, and the square-shaped legs are carved with mantled cabochons. With mahogany show-wood, the sofa is especially desirable because of the needlepoint upholstery, worked in gros- and petit-point and depicting various exotic animals, including an elephant. The shaping of the centre of the front rail is an unusual feature. It is probable that the squab cushion was also originally covered with matching embroidery.

C . An Italian Neo-Classical Gilt-Wood Settee, *c*1775–1800

With its superb craftsmanship, Italian and French furniture design dominated Europe in the 18th century. This gilt-wood settee dates to the third quarter of the 18th century and was possibly made in Piedmont. Many Piedmontese craftsmen had originally worked in France, so they often adapted French designs in a more ornate, typically Italianate manner. This neo-Classical example has a curved back that continues in a firm curve to form the arms. A portrait medallion, framed with ribbon-tied twin cornucopias, centres the back. The arms end in rams' heads above acanthus-carved supports. The seat rail is carved with leaves above trailing scrolled foliage and husks that centre yet another portrait medallion. The spiral-fluted cabriole legs are sculpted with acanthus leaves and terminate in acanthus-carved scrolled toes.

A

C

B

1700-1800

A. A French Louis XVI Gilt-Wood Canapé, attributed to Georges Jacob, *c*1775–1800

A very formal French gilt-wood canapé, this example dates to the last quarter of the 18th century. Made in a gentle interpretation of the Renaissance manner, it features a rectangular back, which was more popular in Germany and other northern European countries than in France. The sofa is attributed to Georges Jacob (1739–1814) who was one of the leading *menuisiers* of the time. He originally worked in a typical Louis XV style, but gradually introduced neo-Classical features into his work. In the last 25 years of the century, when this canapé was made, Jacob was continually adding new elements to his seat furniture. The curves of the Louis XV style were steadily abandoned and, by 1800, straight, more formal lines were preferred. The frame of this sofa is carved with festoons of fruit and flowers and the slightly out-scrolled armrests have laurel-decorated columnar supports. It stands on circular fluted legs that gently taper.

B. An English Cream-Painted and Parcel-Gilt Sofa in Hepplewhite Style, *c*1780

This Hepplewhite-style sofa was made *c*1780. By the last quarter of the 18th century, squab cushions were no longer very fashionable, although they continued to be used occasionally. In this version, the seat padding is fixed to the seat rail. In his *Guide* of 1788, Hepplewhite suggested that the woodwork of sofas should be 'either mahogany or japanned in accordance with the chairs'. As he considered the sofa to be part of a suite of furniture, he also advocated the use of matching coverings. This cream-painted and parcel-gilt version is in the more severe taste associated with the period. The back is almost rectangular but softens at the corners before it sweeps down to the straight sides, which are fitted with elbow rests. The sofa stands on turned and fluted legs, and its seat rail is carved with a central decoration.

C. An English George III Settle, *c*1780

Settles of this type were especially made throughout the 18th century for use in halls and garden rooms. As they were only intended for occasional seating, they were not provided with cushions or upholstery. This George III example is of a much higher quality than usual and is given additional interest by its arched central panel. The arms are well shaped and the carving of the seat rail also indicates a quality piece, one that no doubt originally occupied the hall of an important house. In the 19th century, the central panels of hall settles were sometimes overcarved with a family crest or even a royal cipher.

D. An English George III Mahogany Sofa, *c*1780

The simple and uncluttered line of this late 18th-century English sofa has a timeless quality. Such furniture does not move in and out of fashion but is considered classic, always favoured by the more conservative section of the antique trade and attractive to the investment buyer. Made around 1780, during the reign of George III, the sofa is of mahogany and is fitted with a squab cushion. Its serpentine back is padded and is continued to form the arms, which are fitted with elbow rests. It stands on square, fluted legs which taper and end in spade feet.

A . A French Louis XVI Walnut Canapé with Tapestry Upholstery, c1780s

The effect of much French seat furniture depended largely on the tapestry or needlework upholstery covering it. The Gobelins factory produced sets of tapestries that included panels for chairs and firescreens, as well as wall-hangings. Good quality French tapestry was made throughout the 19th century and was often employed to re-cover much earlier furniture for use in the drawing room or salon. The oval back of this walnut canapé is an ideal vehicle for the display of a romantic landscape. The light structure of this late 18th-century sofa and its rounded form were the marks of a French style that was to be copied and adapted in Britain; Robert Adam, in particular, favoured this type of structure.

B . A French Louis XVI Gilt-Wood Sofa, 1780s

In this Louis XVI gilt-wood sofa, the transition from the organic serpentine designs of the mid-18th century to the rectangular forms that characterized the late period can be seen. This two-seater sofa comes from a salon suite and is bordered with foliate carving. Padded armrests make a concession to comfort. Such sofas were intended for formal use, although they could also be used at card tables. Seating of this type, but in a much simplified form, was made for many middle-class homes in the early years of the 19th century.

C . An English George III Painted-Wood and Soft-Upholstered Sofa, 1780s

By the late 18th century, English sofas were made with a greater awareness of comfort. The square-sided cushions and the straight front to the seat of this George III sofa are elements of a particularly English upholstery method of the period. To create the 'square stuffed' effect, layers of padding were stitched above one another to give a crisp edge, which could then be accentuated with piping. Soft settees of this type were often criticized, as they were said to encourage indolence and lounging. The tapered legs of the 1780s sofa are painted.

B

1700-1800

A. An English George III Mahogany Settle, *c*1780–90

This late 18th-century mahogany high-backed settle features three fielded panels on its back. The balluster supports to the arms are in 17th-century style. Extra stability was given by the thin seat rails with their cross supports. Country pieces of this type are difficult to date precisely as designs in remote areas changed little until the mid-19th century and, as well, construction methods were somewhat static.

B. An English George III Carved and Painted Sofa, *c*1780–90

The formal elegance of this late 18th-century sofa would appeal to any buyer furnishing a home in George III style. The shaping of the serpentine back is pleasing, as is the line of the scrolled arms. The sofa is supported on carved and painted cabriole legs, which feature unusual Gothic-style tracery in combination with acanthus-leaf decoration on the feet. It is now reupholstered in damask and is fitted with the usual squab cushion.

C. An English George III Mahogany Sofa, *c*1785–95

This simple late 18th-century sofa stands on tapered legs of square form united by stretchers. It has a serpentine back and high padded arms. Plain but well-made furniture in mahogany was preferred for the furnishing of gentlemen's homes in Britain and the United States and this basic style has been adapted and reproduced throughout the centuries. Because of the honesty of their construction, pieces in this restrained George III manner were favoured when more ornate sofas were discarded.

D. An English George III Gilt-Wood Sofa, *c*1785–95

This George III gilded sofa comes from a late 18th-century drawing-room suite. The graceful curve of the serpentine back is broken by the upholstered armrests. Sofas with arms that are a continuation of the back were derived from French canapés. In Britain, Robert Adam popularized an even lighter form with turned, fluted legs. Silk damask was one of the favourite upholstery materials of the period, although the colours were much stronger than in this re-covered example, 'crimson India silk' or brilliant yellows being among the preferred hues.

D

A

C

B

A. An English George III Painted-Wood Sofa, *c*1785–1800

A late 18th-century sofa, this features a padded rectangular back and a wooden border with padded armrests. Painted in pale grey, the sofa stands on slim, reeded legs with spiral balusters extending to the fronts of the arms; the reeded legs are very typical of the period. The severity of the rectangular form of the back rest points towards the more geometric designs of the turn of the century. In the 1780s and 1790s, comfort was still an adjunct of wealth and luxury, and the seat was supplied with a mattress-like cushion – an expensive item, as upholstery frequently cost more than the wooden frame.

B. An English George III Gilt-Wood Sofa, *c*1790

Standing on eight cabriole legs, this George III gilt-wood sofa has a serpentine back. The knees and the front apron are decorated with shell and foliate carving. This sofa is in the manner of John Linnell (1729–96), a carver, cabinetmaker and designer, who worked out of London for many wealthy clients and also made furniture to Robert Adam's designs. Many of his original drawings have survived. So fine is some of Linnell's work that it is difficult to ascertain whether he or Robert Adam was responsible for certain pieces, notably at Osterley Park in Middlesex. This sofa is obviously one made 'in the grand manner', and was intended for a very wealthy customer.

C. A Continental Gilt-Wood Sofa showing Adam influence, *c*1790

The large rooms of Italian palaces and German castles in the late 18th century demanded a dramatic style of furniture. This gilt sofa, c1790, would have been sufficiently ostentatious to satisfy any ruler of a small German state. Standing on ten tapered and fluted legs, the heavily carved and gilt structure is in the sculptural style originally associated with Italy. The carved back rail is crested with a device incorporating a shield and a quiver of arrows, and the arm supports terminate in stylized heads. The putti were also a very popular form of decoration, especially on the Continent. Pine was often used for heavily carved furniture of this type which was intended to be gilded or painted.

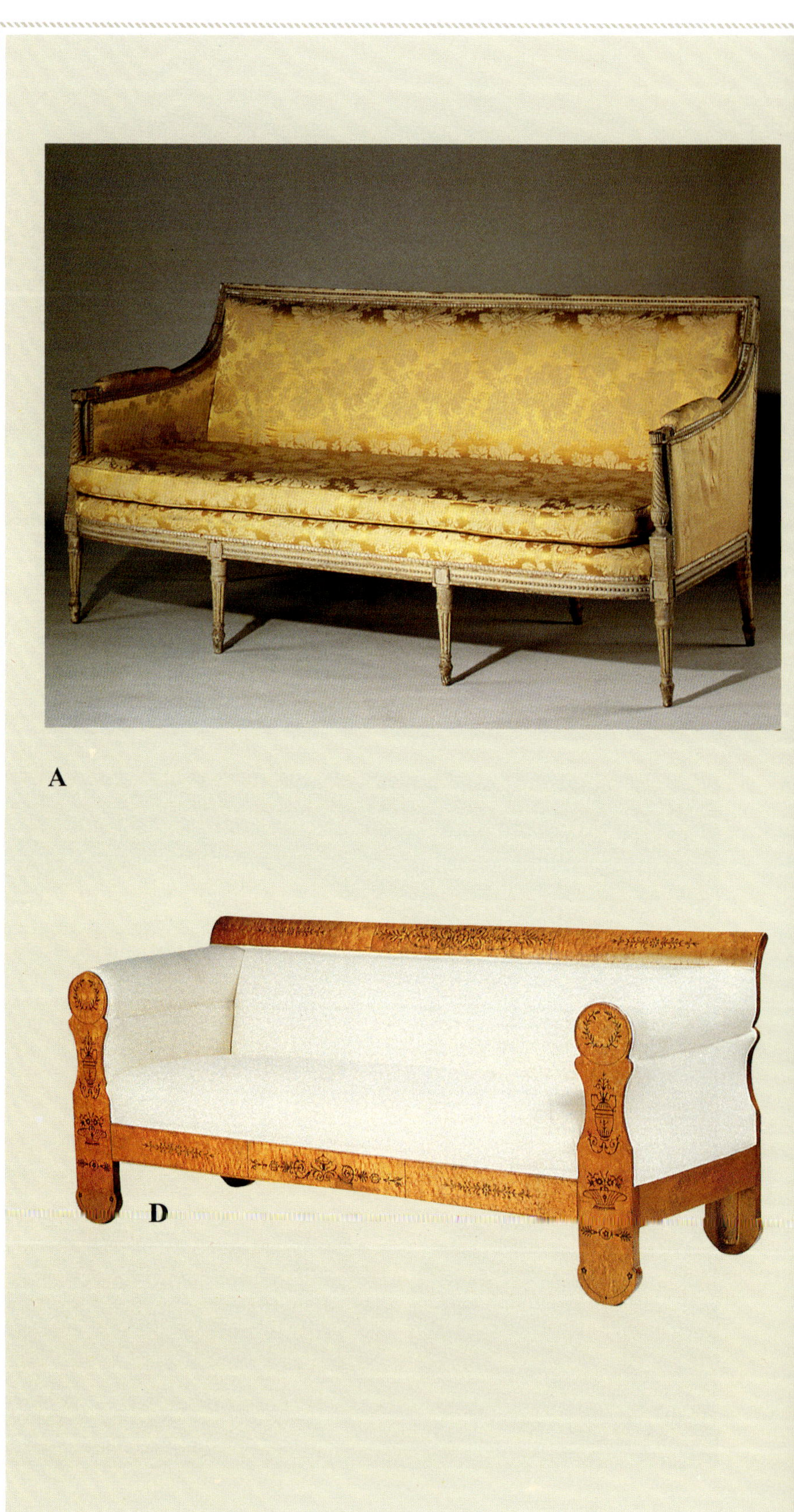
A

D

D. A French Empire Bird's-Eye Maple Sofa, 1790s

The severe form of this French Empire-period bird's-eye maple sofa originated in the Republican period. Napoleon and his court were influenced by the restraint of earlier design styles, and especially took a great interest in Classical architectural forms. The light-coloured woods, such as maple, which were favoured in Germany were also preferred in France, and the use of flat shapes and curves within a single plane was common to progressive furniture makers in both countries. This version is made with great simplicity and reveals a use of basic shapes and materials suggestive of the much later Bauhaus philosophy.

A. A Dutch Neo-Classical Mahogany Sofa, *c*1790–1800

By the closing years of the 18th century, the simplicity of neo-Classical forms, first popularized in France, influenced the design of furniture for middle-class use. In the Low Countries, French influence was especially strong, although the love of ornament for its own sake, rather than to augment the classical inspiration of a piece, was never abandoned completely. This marquetry-decorated mahogany sofa was made in Holland and stands on semicircular moulded bracket feet. In marquetry the ground is a veneer rather than solid wood, making it possible to apply the decoration in a sheet. The favourite woods for use in marquetry were sycamore, plane, holly and poplar, although other light woods were sometimes dyed to give a greater variety of colours. Sofas of this form, but without the inlay, were especially popular in the early years of the 19th century.

B. An English George III Mahogany Sofa with Tapestry Upholstery, *c*1790–1800

By the last years of the 18th century, sofas and chairs had become much squarer in form. The strength of mahogany was especially suitable for slim, tapered legs. Frequently, the complete back and sides were upholstered, but this version is made more interesting by the front legs, which are extended to form the fronts of the arms. The seat is padded and fringe-decorated. Tapestry was still a much-favoured upholstery material; it was woven in Britain as well as in France.

C. An English George III Sofa, c1795

The design for this late 18th-century English sofa anticipates the simplicity of European post-Revolutionary structures. The intersection of the arms with the long, rectangular back is quite geometric compared to the fluid lines of earlier pieces. The square, tapered legs are continued to form the turned arm supports, a device that became very popular in the early 19th century. It is upholstered in brocade. Damage to replacement upholstery does not affect the value of sofas of this period, as they are usually re-covered to suit a decorative scheme.

C

B

A

1700-1800

A . An Italian Gilt Side Table, *c*1700

The strong Italian sculptural tradition meant that most artists and craftsmen could turn their hand to carving decoration. This table is similar to pieces by Filippo Juvarra (1678–1736), who worked in the Palazzo Reale, Turin, in the 1730s. But it is often difficult to date furniture produced between the end of the 17th century and the beginning of the 18th – as a whole, it is grandiose, gilt and scrolling. Italy clearly led the way in design during this period, but despite this the quality of workmanship was not often high.

The carving on the table support uses natural forms, such as the central scallop shell, thus demonstrating the roots of the Rococo movement, which was to emerge fully between 1730 and 1750. The legs are scrolling, dolphin-like forms, and the support seems rather large for the small marble top. The likelihood is that the top is not original to the piece: as good seams of marble are increasingly rare and usually limited, it was often difficult to replace a smashed top with marble of the same quality.

B . An English Yew Table, *c*1710

The use of yew for this table, made during the reign of Queen Anne (1702–14), was an unusual alternative to walnut, the preferred wood until 1720. After that date, a relaxation of import duty from English colonies allowed mahogany to be bought more cheaply and competitively, and so it became used in greater amounts. With a tightly patterned grain and a bright yellow-gold colour, the yew provides a subtle accompaniment to the simple shape of the table.

The top is inlaid with the design of a house, an example of the interest in homely motifs – hunting, country life, etc – in the Queen Anne period. It is surrounded by a cushioned edge, another Queen Anne feature, above an undecorated frieze, and is supported by straight legs ending in pad feet. There is no stretcher, which gives a lighter feel to the table, and the only ornament is a slight scroll where the leg joins the apron. Even the scroll seems restrained compared to the earlier fussy Baroque scroll, and it is this air of understatement and subtlety which characterizes Queen Anne furniture.

B

C

C. A French Régence *Table à Gibier,* c1720
20. A French Régence Side Table, c1720

The term *Régence* specifically refers to the early years of Louis XV of France's reign. On the death of Louis XIV in 1715, a Regent was appointed to rule the country until Louis XV came of age. In furniture, however, Regence style covers the first few decades of the 18th century, and shows a reaction against the heavier, more ornate furniture of Louis XIV's reign from 1643 to 1715.

With the *table à gibier,* the stretcher remains heavy and square-sectioned, but the square edges of the top are slightly rounded, and the architectural, square-sectioned legs curve, which give a lighter feel. The table's frieze is ornate, as on earlier tables, and is decorated with scallop shells from which pierced foliate scrolls extend.

The Régence side table dates from a few years later, and shows clear signs of Rococo influence in its tapering legs and lighter, curved stretchers. The deeper frieze on the top gives the piece a vertical feel which makes it seem taller than it actually is, and the restrained decoration makes it feel lighter.

D. An Italian Gilt Wood Side Table, *c*1720

Figure sculpture has always been part of the Italian artistic tradition. In consequence, Italian tables are more often supported by human figures than those from any other country. One of a pair, this table shows considerable High Baroque influence. Overall, it seems fairly heavy, and is vaguely in the style of Antonio Corradini, who worked in the early 18th century. A sculptor, Corradini carved some of the furniture for the Palazzo Rezzonico in Venice, and specialized in beautiful human and mythological figures, sea monsters and angels in the Baroque style. He was already a well-known and highly rewarded sculptor of his time, and it is a reflection of the importance placed on figural work that he, not a furniture carver, was chosen for this important commission.

This table is clearly a side table intended to be set against a wall, as the two rear legs are decorated in front only.

1700-1800

A. A French Régence Oak Console Table, *c*1720

By the end Louis XIV's reign in 1715, almost all courtly furniture in France was gilded. During the reign of Louis XV, much design was still influenced by his predecessor, who was known as the Sun King because of his passion for gilt and other visual extravagances. However, France had long had a tradition of carved, natural wood, which had flourished at the beginning of the century under Louis XIII (1610–43) and the Government of Cardinal Mazarin. Throughout the reign of Louis XV, the two different styles developed, as can be seen clearly on this table.

Made of oak and one of a pair, this bare wood table has been carved with courtly mask decorations, an ornate frieze and heavy, square-sectioned stretchers. Originally it may have been gilt, but it has since been stripped, perhaps during the 19th century (it was unusual, however, for gilded furniture to be made of a dense wood such as oak, which is harder to carve than a softwood). It is unlikely that the marble top seen here is the original; that probably would have been a more finely patterned marble of more exotic colours.

B. A pair of French Régence Painted *Torchères* and a Blackamoor *Guéridon*, *c*1725

Torchères such as these were used to augment the main lighting of a room in a similar way to a spotlight today. The chief source of light would have been in the form of a chandelier (literally, candleholder) or sconces (wall-mounted candle brackets). This substantial pair are cream-painted, heightened with gilt and feature sculptural carving. They are probably made of a softwood, such as beech, and are in the Régence style – popular in France and England in the first few decades of the 18th century.

The blackamoor is a 19th-century copy of a late 17th- or early 18th-century Italian or French figure. Although purely decorative here, an original would have held a candlestand in place of the basket of fruit. Black pages were very fashionable in 17th-century courts around the Mediterranean and were generally recruited from the Moors, the Arabic-Berber races from North Africa. There was supposedly a servant called *Guéridon* who gave his name to such candlestands, and which was later applied to any small round table.

D

A

B

C

C. A Louis XV Ebony Table, c1725

This chic and elegant table from the time of Louis XV uses the classic combination of ebony veneer, ormolu mounts and brass stringing. It is the stark contrast of colours which gives the table its particular style (a look often associated with this date of French furniture), and the lack of stretchers contributes to its lightness. The black veneer manages to both slim down the already slender cabriole legs and give weight to the top.

The French Régence period in furniture refers to the first few decades of the 18th century. It saw a sharp reaction against the heavy, over-decorated pieces of the end of the 17th century, as seen in the bulbous, colourful work of André-Charles Boulle.

D. A French Régence Ebonized *Bureau Plat*, c1725

The *bureau plat* was the leading form of writing table in the Régence period, whose styles prevailed over the first quarter of the century. Earlier 17th-century writing tables were generally eight-legged, with a deep frieze and three vertical drawers. This cubic design was epitomized by the work of the French architect/designer, Jean Bérain (1638–1711).

Around the turn of the century, the simpler *bureau plat* was introduced, replacing earlier heavy, boulle (inlaid brass and tortoiseshell) pieces. This table is ebonized, using paint and polish to resemble ebony. The mounts are ormolu, but functional rather than decorative, and the top is tooled leather.

Régence was the French style of c1720, not to be confused with the English Regency period of c1810.

1700-1800

A . An English George II Console Table by William Kent, *c*1730

This is one of a pair of console tables in the Italian-influenced style which Kent (1684–1748) and his friend and patron, the 3rd Earl of Burlington (1685–1753), were largely responsible for in the first half of 18th-century England. Of heavy, often gilt and richly carved wood, Kent's furniture was based on Italian Baroque work and is known as Palladian, after the work of the Italian architect, Andrea Palladio (1508–80).

Kent himself began his career as an apprentice coach-painter, but was sent to train in Italy as an artist on several occasions. There, he met Lord Burlington and the two went on to become arbiters of English taste and fashion in the 1720s and 1730s. Kent worked as a painter, sculptor, architect, interior decorator and landscape gardener, although his chief influence was on architecture and the decorative arts. He was responsible for the design of London's Horse Guards Parade, and worked on the interior of Kensington Palace. Not everyone was impressed by his work, however. Referring to his painting, the artist William Hogarth dismissed him as a 'contemptible dauber', and Horace Walpole spoke of his work as 'immeasurably ponderous', although he also mentioned that its overall effect was 'audacious, splendid and audacious'.

B . A Louis XV Walnut Console Table, *c*1735

Asymmetry was a crucial element of Rococo design. Applied to furniture, this meant that neither the two sides nor the top or bottom of a piece bore identical shapes. If a 17th century table, for example, was divided down the middle, the two parts would be mirror images. Here, that is clearly not the case. The cartouche in the centre of the frieze is not symmetrical, nor is the ornamented stretcher. The table top is as far from being rectangular, and is obviously of greater weight than its base. Another type of symmetry, although less precise, compares the visual 'weight' or mass of an object. Typically, the heavy top of a 17th-century bureau is balanced 'symmetrically' by the 'weight' of heavy scrolling stretchers.

This style of furniture is sometimes called *con brio,* which translates as 'noisily' (in music it means 'with movement'). The table is walnut, a rich wood that is easily carved, and the decoration is rocaille – motifs taken from nature, as opposed to the classical, architectural motifs seen in the 17th century.

C . A Louis XV Gilt Iron Console Table, *c*1740

Mainland Europe – France in particular – has a lively tradition of fine ironwork, which started in the 16th century and continues up to today. Iron stretchers on tables were in use in Spain as early as the 17th century, although Great Britain and the United States only adopted the idea of metal furniture in the 19th and 20th centuries.

This console table and its iron leg supports use hammered-steel strips to form a single cabriole leg. The pierced frieze imitates wood-carving, but allowed craftsmen greater freedom to experiment because of the strength of metal. The decoration here is not hammered or wrought when hot, like the frame, but made from a separate, thinner sheet of metal which is more pliable. The scallop shell and pendent flowers have been cut out as silhouettes and bent into shape using a gentle applied heat.

D . A Louis XV Console Table, *c*1740

This is a good example of a Rococo gilt wood and gesso console table. The console table originated from the reign of Louis XIV – the *Galerie des Glaces* (Gallery of Mirrors) at the Palais de Versailles is lined with them, alternating between windows and mirrors along the walls – and was at that time fairly square in shape, with straight, square-sectioned members.

This piece, however, is pure Rococo. All curves and very asymmetrical, its legs taper inward and its stretcher bears a highly elaborate, floral design. Much of the decoration is rocaille (motifs taken from nature), a reaction against the solid, monumental design of the Baroque-influenced 17th century.

E . A Louis XV *Table à Ouvrage,* *c*1745

The name *table à ouvrage* ('work table') often refers to needlework tables such as this one. The top is leather-covered, as are the drawers, which held scissors, thread, etc, and the table is decorated with elaborate Rococo inlay designs of organic motifs in kingwood.

This would have been considered the height of Rococo taste, restrained but lively. Pieces such as this were produced by the cabinetmakers. Bernard Van Risenburgh, who worked between 1730–1770 and stamped his work 'B.V.R.B.' (and whose identity was only revealed in 1957), and Roger Vandercruse, known as Lacroix (1728–99), who used the stamp 'R.V.L.C.'.

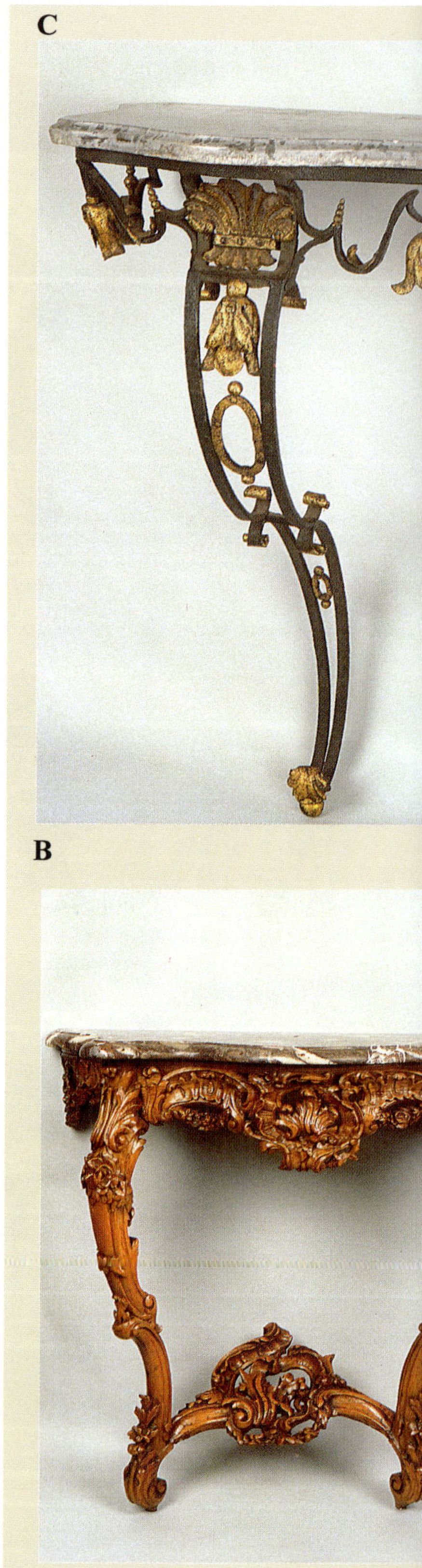

A

E

D

A . One of a Pair of Chinese K'ang, or Low, Tables, *c*1750

This low table stands only a few inches off the ground, and was made as an accompaniment for a K'ang (a Chinese low platform), from which it takes its name. The K'ang was in use as early as the Han dynasty (*c*200 BC), and consisted of a central rectangular section supported on a structure of frames. K'angs were used for both sleeping and sitting; when sitting, the K'ang table, as seen here, was placed on the K'ang (platform), which was at the right height for reading or writing.

K'angs and K'ang tables were generally made of rosewood, carved out of as few pieces of wood as possible. They were usually very simple, using no nails or dowels, but instead disguised mortice-and-tenon joints. Lacquer, made from the sap of trees, was popular as a defence against damp and insects, as it dried to a hard resinous finish. The lacquer was then often decorated with incised designs, and sometimes gilt or set with ivory inlay. Other tables used by the Chinese included square or round versions for eating, and high rectangular tables set against a wall as a stand for a *ch'in* (or lute).

The lacquer decoration on these tables became a highly refined art form in the East, and the source of inspiration for European chinoiserie decoration from the 16th century onward.

B . A Finnish Pine Dresser, *c*1750

This table with a cupboard below comes from the National Museum of Finland in Helsinki. It is the legacy of a medieval model which continued to be made well into the 18th and 19th centuries for everyday use, despite the fact that the Renaissance arrived in Scandinavia in the 16th and 17th centuries (brought by artists, such as Albrecht Dürer (1471–1528), who travelled widely around Europe spreading Italian styles. The continued popularity of traditional forms was due to a lack of tools and money, which meant that pieces needed to be strictly functional.

The uneven top and edges are proof that the timber was cut with a primitive saw and an adze probably was used in shaping the pieces, which were then pegged together. As this would have been one of very few pieces of furniture in a home, it would have performed a variety of functions – as a table, seating, storage for valuables and food, etc. It is clearly the basis for some of the forms of contemporary pine furniture produced today.

C. An Italian Rococo Console Table, *c*1750

This Italian version of a Louis XV console table would have served the same purpose as a French example: part of the integral decoration of a room, it would sit between or beneath windows, possibly with a mirror above it.

Painted rather than gilded, the motifs on this table are largely 'grotesque', taken from designs found in ancient Roman grottoes excavated from the 15th century onward. The unusual shapes were pounced on by enquiring 18th-century artists once the influence of Renaissance and Baroque designs wore thin. One such was the Renaissance artist, Raphael (1483–1520), who employed this grotesque style to decorate galleries in the Vatican in Rome.

So similar were grotesque motifs – shells, garlands of flowers, scrolling fungus-like forms and exaggerated curves – to those of the French Rococo rocaille repertoire, that it is unclear whether Rococo originated in France or Italy. French pieces tend to be more restrained, Italian more exuberant.

This table possibly originated in Genoa, in the north of Italy and near to the French border, and seems to combine the best characteristics of both versions – resulting in an elegant, original piece.

D. A Mid 18th century South German Card Table, *c*1750

This sculptural table shows the influence of the German Neuwied school of cabinetmaking, whose famous sons David and Abraham Roentgen were producing from their workshop from the mid 18th century onward. Sculptural wood-carving had long been a speciality of the region, reaching its zenith with religious Renaissance carving of *c*1500; subdued under the anti-Catholic Reformation movement in the 16th century, carving remains central to South German art to this day.

Made of walnut, the table has a marquetry top exhibiting several Rococo motifs – bell-flowers, garlands, even a parrot; the overall effect is somewhat darker and more architectural than that of English marquetry, although in both a variety of woods is used. The whole table has a slightly sculptural feel to it. The hoofed feet are typically South German, and the projecting rounded corners would have been hollowed out to support a candlestick when the table was open. The top unhinges from the centre to reveal the baize-covered playing surface.

A . A Mid 18th century German *Table à Ecrire*, *c*1750

This table is titled in French because of its obvious debt to French design. Germany at this date consisted of numerous small states and principalities rather than one unified country. This led to considerable regional variations in furniture design and quality of craftsmanship, one of several reasons why French fashions had so much influence. The Seven Years' War (1756–63), involving much of Europe, also led to a severe loss of Saxony's territory and income, which meant yet more reliance on France for furniture production.

This piece is discreetly Rococo, with gently curving legs and apron, and upturned toes. The German influence can be seen in the inlay and marquetry, less clear than French work and utilizing the unusual combination of kingwood, yew and amaranth. Although French craftsmen almost always marked their works, tight guild regulations in Germany left most pieces anonymous.

B . A Louis XV *Bureau Plat*, *c*1750

The *bureau plat,* introduced during the Régence period, proved very popular and became a standard form in French furniture. The finest examples of the 18th century are associated with the French cabinetmakers, Charles Cressent (1685–1768) and André-Charles Boulle (1642–1732); the latter was successful at adapting 17th-century designs to 18th-century tastes.

This example is relatively simple and severe in its line, but has definite Rococo asymmetrical tendencies. Its edges are curved, its legs cabriole, and the top is not rectangular. Veneered in a typically French herringbone pattern of tulipwood and kingwood, it is simply decorated with beautifully executed ormolu mounts. The mounts on a piece of furniture such as this would have been made by members of the guild of *ciseleurs;* the guild was devoted to working up bronze mounts before they were gilded.

C . A Louis XV Marquetry Small Table, *c*1750

During the second half of the century, the fashion for women to receive visitors while dressing led to the manufacture of numerous small, beautifully decorated occasional tables. These ranged from high tripod tables, which stood about 5ft (1.5m) high and held mirrors – used when standing to dress hair, especially in Italy – to small dressing tables such as this. Both practical and decorative, they were often finely finished with inlay and marquetry.

A good example of restrained Rococo, this table concentrates on shape rather than elaborate decoration. The legs are elegant and outswept, and the apron is in the form of a Cupid's bow. The frieze contains a brushing slide (which extends to hold brushes), and the lid lifts to reveal compartments for make-up, powders, combs, etc.

D . A Louis XV *Table de Nuit*, *c*1750

This simple and functional piece of furniture held a chamber pot and sat next to the bed. Night tables were used extensively throughout Europe during the second half of the century, and later models became increasingly sophisticated, using fake drawers and closing doors to disguise their real function.

Although this piece is from Louis XV's reigh, which was renowned for ostentation, it is relatively discreet, discarding the earlier addiction to ormolu.

E . An English George III Chippendale Sideboard Table, *c*1754

The name 'sideboard table' comes from Thomas Chippendale (1718–79) himself, as first seen in his *Gentleman and Cabinet-maker's Director,* 1st edition, published in 1754. A guide to which cabinetmakers subscribed, a pattern-book such as Chippendale's provided a detailed drawing of a piece of furniture, giving a series of options for decoration: this allowed furniture makers to either copy or adapt the original idea. Plate LX in the first of Chippendale's three editions illustrates all the characteristics of this table, although the original drawing is slightly asymmetrical due to the different suggestions it puts forward.

The piece is typical of English Rococo tables, although its top is later than its other components, possibly due to damage. The frieze is covered in interlaced blind-fret cusps, an ogee and criss-cross ornamentation using foliate scrolls; its centre acanthus-leaf cartouche has an apron pendant hanging below. The table legs are elaborately Gothic, with a central column supported by four smaller columns, all joined by crocketed arches and ending in architectural feet.

This well-known sideboard table, which is discussed in Percy Macquoid's *The Age of Mahogany, 1720–1770,* is relatively modest in size (6ft 6in/198m wide) and would have stood against a wall to be used for serving. It falls between the more heavily constructed early 18th-century side tables and the lighter, more elaborate sideboards of George III's reign.

E

C

D

A

B

A . A Louis XV Table, *c*1755

This dignified table is plain by French standards. It is part of the general style which covered the move from Rococo furniture through transitional designs to the neo-classical influence. It shows very little decoration; there is no ormolu, and the inlay and cross-banding are both unobtrusive.

Rococo influence can be seen in the colour, shape (curved legs and bow apron) and lustre of the table, but the overall lines are distinctly more sobre, following a lead by Charles-Nicolas Cochin (1715–90), which he took in the late 1740s after touring classical Rome.

B . A Louis XV Tulipwood Writing Table, *c*1755

This table is from the transitional period between the Rococo and neo-Classical styles. The lightness, colour and curving lines are all Rococo, as are the asymmetrical cartouche on the top and the herringbone pattern created by the alternate stripes of light and dark tulipwood. The table's cabriole legs still curve, and the apron bows. But the cleaner lines of the neo-Classical period are here, and the ormolu decoration is not excessive.

The piece is probably from the Dubois, a dynasty of cabinetmakers established by Jacques Dubois (*c*1693–1763), and continued by his brother, Louis (1732–*c*1790), and nephew, René (1737–99). René worked for Louis XVI and Marie-Antoinette before opening a furniture shop in Paris in 1779.

C . A Louis XV *Coiffeuse, c*1755

During Louis XV's reign the frivolity of the French aristocracy reached a peak which is difficult to imagine today. The paintings of Jean-Honoré Fragonard (1732–1806) depict the indulgencies and excesses in both lifestyle and personal appearance of the rich. *The Swing* (*c*1766), for example, was commissioned by a baron for his mistress; Fragonard was requested to paint her on a swing being pushed by a bishop, with the baron in a place where he 'could have a good look at the legs'.

Elaborate hairstyles were all the rage, and a *coiffeuse* such as this was sat at to create them – the name is taken from the French verb *coiffer,* meaning to dress the head. The central panel of the top raises to reveal a mirror, flanked by compartments for make-up, powders, etc. The three frieze drawers are also compartmentalized, and the slide over the central drawer pulls out to hold brushes.

D . An 18th-century Florentine Scagliola Table Top, 1756

Scagliola is a man-made composition which imitates marble and other ornamental stones, and takes its name from the Italian *scaglia,* the number of small pieces of hard and semi-precious stones used in *pietra dura* work. It is made of finely grained plaster of Paris mixed with glue, and coloured as required. Traces have been found in ancient Roman artefacts, but the art was revived by Guido del Conte (1584–1649) and became very popular in the 18th century (it was almost always produced in Italy).

This beautiful table top is one of a signed pair, and in consequence is very rare indeed. It is inscribed 'D P Belloni A Florentia F 1756', or 'Don Pietro Belloni at Florence made this (F=fecit) 1756', and is of excellent quality. Showing the Rococo style at its best, it uses light colours, particularly pale blues and greens, and the border features flowers, scallop shells, small animals and human figures intertwined. The central rustic scene is typically romanticized – in reality, the life of an 18th-century shepherd was not so idyllic.

In England in 1664 the diarist John Evelyn wrote 'I have frequently wondered that we never practised this in England for cabinets', but it was first seen in the Royal Household in the 1670s. In 1790, scagiolia was much in demand as a cheap way of imitating rare marble, and a factory producing it was opened in London. It was used by both Robert Adam and George Smith; the latter recommended it for the tops of small tables in his book, *Household Furniture,* of 1808.

A

B

D
C

A . An American Queen Anne Tray-top Table, *c*1760

This tray-top table is almost identical to a walnut tea table illustrated in the *Shorter Dictionary of English Furniture* by Ralph Edwards, dated 1715 (towards the end of Queen Anne's reign). The American table, however, has a skirt beneath the rectangular top with protruding apron, a late Queen Anne feature, and is made of cherry wood, which has a smooth grain and tends to be less finely figured. It was made in New England, probably Connecticut, where such skirting and pad feet were popular.

American cabinetmakers often used native fruit woods, which sometimes included walnut and mahogany, although it would be very rare for an English cabinetmaker to use cherry wood for a fine-quality piece such as this. Native English woods almost always indicate provincial manufacture. Queen Anne American furniture was made well into the 1760s, even though the monarch herself had died nearly 50 years earlier.

B . An Italian Louis XV *Lacca contrafatta* Side Table, *c*1760

Much Italian furniture in the 18th century was influenced by French artists, particularly in the northern areas of Piedmont and Liguria. On the whole, designs were slightly exaggerated – curves were greater, decoration more colourful – compared to the French pieces, and craftsmanship was often poorer.

In this case, the decoration on the table top is uniquely Italian. *Lacca contrafatta*, as it was known, consisted of printed paper cut-outs, often of rustic or Oriental figures. These were attached to furniture which had generally been painted with a cream or yellow base, and the whole surface was then varnished. The firm of Remondini, of Bassano del Grappa, was renowned for this style of work, which was cheaper and less difficult to produce than lacquer. A variety of Italian furniture ranging from bookcases to tea caddies was treated in this way. The technique is largely associated with Venice, but, as with other forms of lacquer, it was practised throughout northern Italy.

Also typically Italian is this table's sculptural quality: the Louis XV cabriole legs start with an angelic head at the top, and the feet are carved into leafy hooves. It has two tiers, and is a variant on the *chiffonière,* a table form which had space for books and often a drawer for needlework.

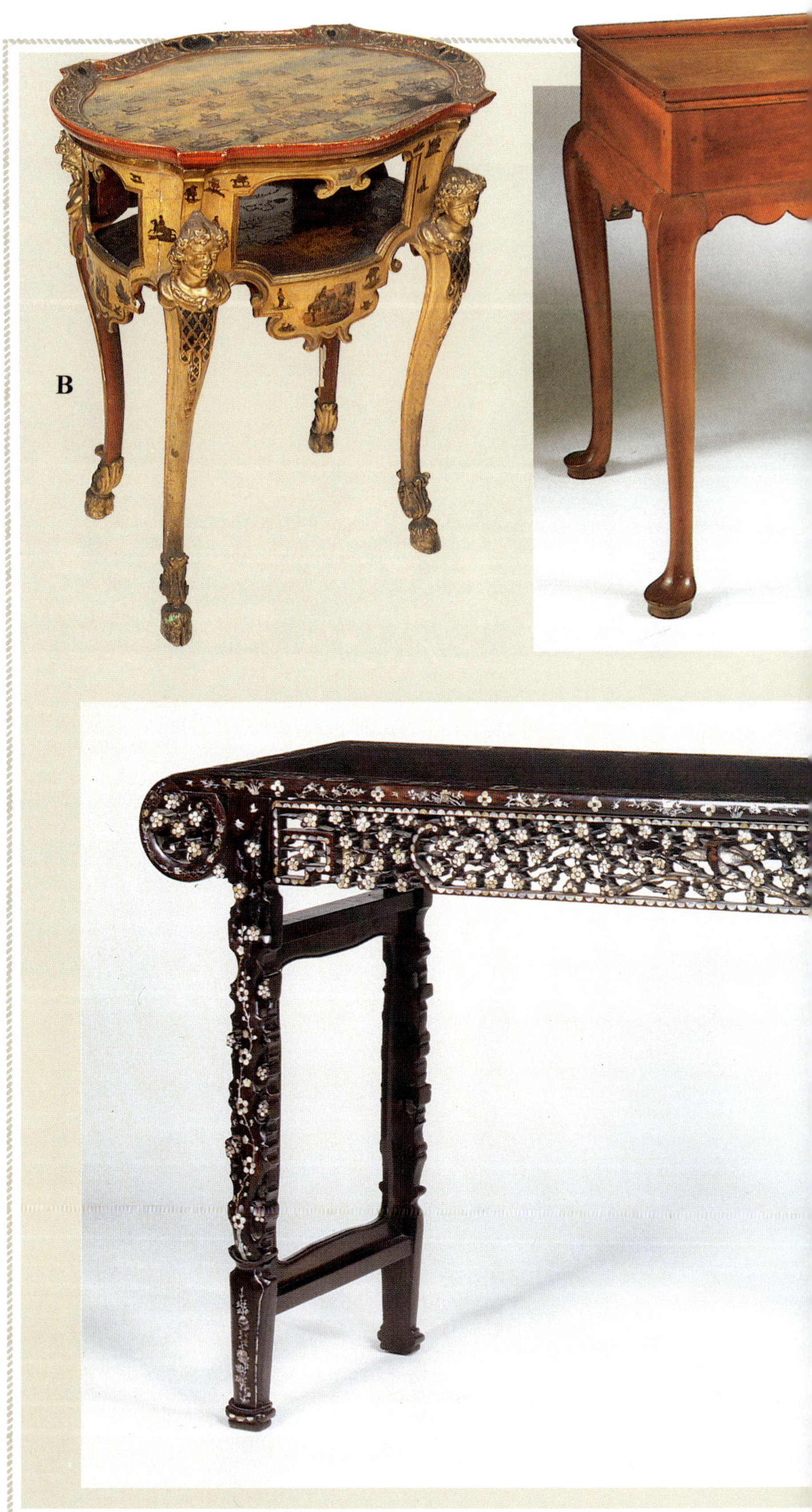
B

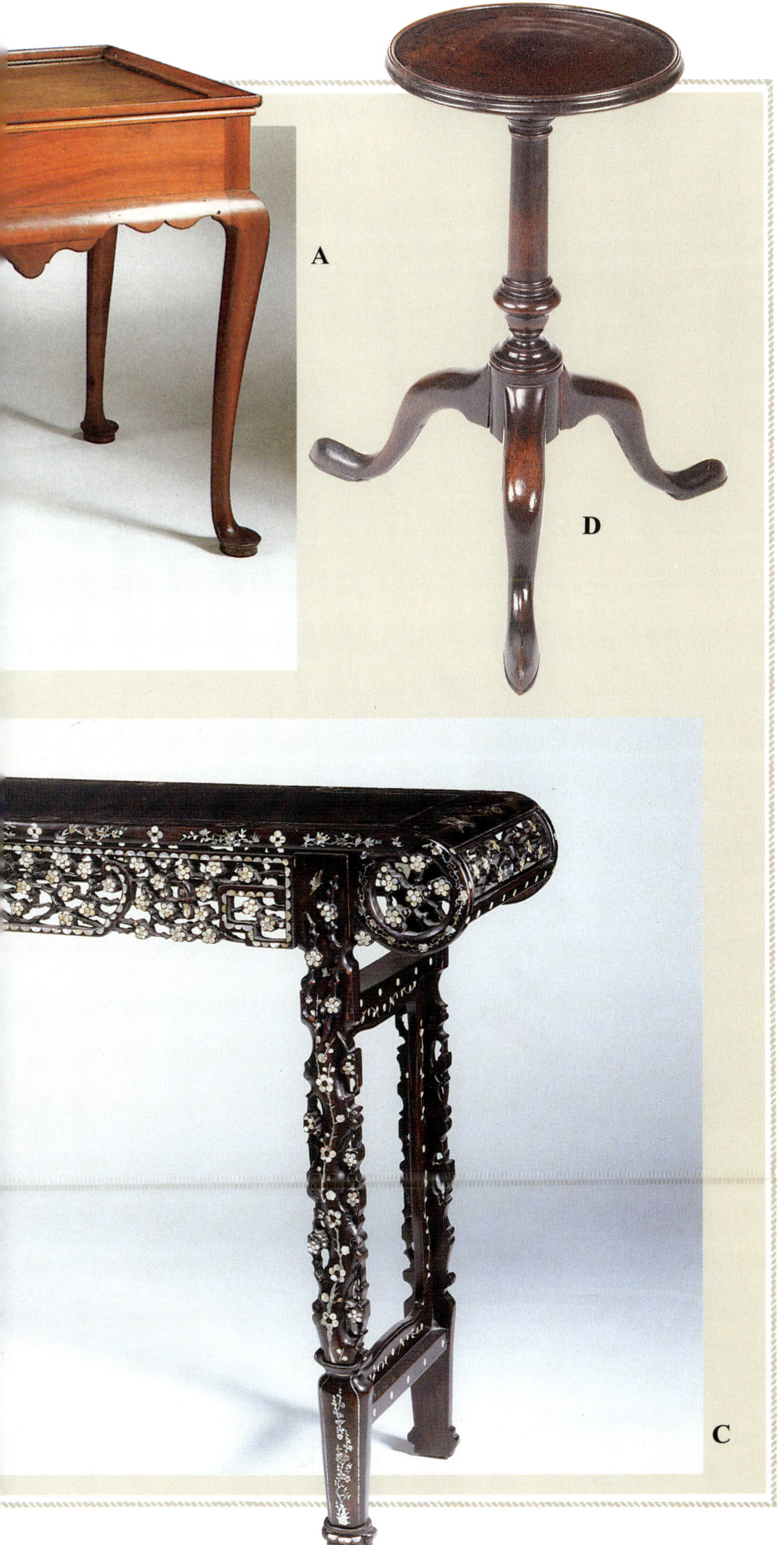
A

D

C

C. A Chinese Hardwood Altar Table, *c*1760

The use of tables had been fully established in China since the days of the T'ang Dynasty (AD618–906), although they served a different purpose to those in Europe. Often appearing in pairs, they would be set along a wall to hold incense burners or a *ch'in* (Chinese lute); in a formal room this would be on the east or west walls as the main entrance was always in the south wall, but in a less formal setting they may well have been placed asymmetrically. Generally, Chinese table models changed little over many centuries, although their decoration, as evidenced here, tended to increase as the years passed and Western influence grew.

The size of China meant that many woods were available, but among the most valued was *hua'li,* a hardwood similar to rosewood. In the south, bamboo was used, often varnished with lacquer to prevent damage from insects. On the whole, Chinese furniture followed simple, elegant lines made to fit together without dowel or nails. This high-quality piece shows an unusual amount of decoration, with extensive carving on the apron below the top. The top itself is pierced with a naturalistic design of the branches of the prunus tree, and the apron is dotted with prunus blossom inlay.

D. An English George III Occasional or Wine Table, *c*1760

In general, Georgian furniture fell into two main streams – the controlled, veneered pieces which were adapted from the popular pattern-books; and the more natural, flowing pieces which represented the originality and traditional craftsmanship of English 18th-century cabinetmaking at its best.

This small table belongs to the second category. Its charm comes from its own elegantly functional shape and simplicity, and does not rely on either a pattern book or a contrived setting to look its best. The wood is a good colour, and the top is simply decorated with a reeded dished edge, to prevent glasses from falling. It is also hinged, which allowed the snap top to fold down when not in 'occasional' use. The column is plain, with two small collars above the slender tripod, and the legs sweep gracefully down to the rounded pad feet with a small carved disc around each toe.

A . An American Chippendale Tea Table, *c*1760

The tilting top of this tea table is similar to that of its English cousin, and is released by a 'bird cage' mechanism – the latch is surrounded by tiny turned columns, like a cage. These are just visible at the top of the column support.

Made of finely figured walnut, it has a slight upturned edge to accommodate the crockery and is beautifully angular. The slender column has a knop known as a compressed ball and sharply curving cabriole feet. The ball-and-claw feet on this table have the pronounced shape typical of Philadelphia, and on the whole the piece is a refined, elegant example of that city's style.

B . Two French Bedside Tables, c1760

These two night tables are typically Rococo, with their swelling outlines, uneven curved galleries above the top, and asymmetrical ormolu mounts, castors and fine sabots.

The spaces were meant to hold chamber pots, and the handles on the left-hand example and spaces on the right-hand one are for carrying the tables. Nicolas Petit (1732–91) made the table on the right. A successful Parisian businessman, he both made and sold furniture in his workshops in Faubourg St-Antoine, marking both his and other works he sold with his stamp.

C . A Transitional *Guéridon, c*1760

Although the word *guéridon* referred to a tall candlestand in the 17th century, by the middle of the 1700s it was used to describe a small round table such as this. It is in the transitional style, derived from the more extreme Rococo, with legs that gently curve from a pointed 'knee' just under the frieze. It is made of tulipwood with herringbone cross-banding.

Note the return of the stretcher, here used as a second tier. It is not structurally necessary for a table of this design, and has been introduced for decoration. The source of transitional table design is clear: from Louis XV in the 1740s to Louis XVI in the 1780s.

A

E

D. A Louis XV *Table à la Bourgogne*, c1760

The mid 18th century saw a fascination for gadgetry in furniture, both in France and England. The future Louis XVI of France had a considerable influence on furniture design long before his succession to the throne in 1774. He was particularly interested in technical design and mechanical devices, an interest shared by the Georgians in England, as seen in their writing desks.

When closed, this table appears quite ordinary, with a deep frieze. When opened, however, a fitted interior with four small drawers and compartments for writing utensils pops up, and the leather-lined flap provides a writing surface. Also known as a *secrétaire à capucin,* this form was often associated with the Parisian cabinetmaker, Roger Vandercruse, known as Lacroix. A fine example of his work from around the same date can be seen in the Musée Nissim de Camondo in Paris.

E. An American Chippendale Tea Table, c1765

This table comes from New England, and is strikingly similar to English tea tables from the end of George II's reign, c1750. Its simple, dignified form, circular top, turned column and tripod base are all European features. It is made of mahogany, the favoured English wood of the time, and is probably from Boston, Massachusetts, which was – and still is – proud of its English heritage, and whose cabinetmakers were keen to emulate English styles.

In Boston, for example, chair backs are found as direct copies of the work of Chippendale and Robert Mainwaring. Two other distinct Boston characteristics are the decoration on the knees of the cabriole legs – a Rococo scrolling style made with a punch rather than carved with a chisel – and the rat-claw feet, broadened to look more like a rat's paw than a lion's (as with ball-and-claw feet).

A . An American Chippendale Mixing Table, *c*1765

The contrast between the harmonious curves of the stand and patterned marble top of this table is striking. Although marble-topped tables had been popular since the 16th century in Europe, a combination of a crude slab and walnut such as this is unlikely to be found in English furniture of the same date. It is unusual in European furniture to find marble combined with anything other than a lightly decorated and coloured base of gilt or painted wood which complements the natural formation of the stone. In America, however, marble was highly valued and thought of as exotic.

Known as a slab-top table, this piece was commissioned by Benjamin Franklin for his daughter (according to family tradition), and is still in the family. The marble is Pennsylvanian, and the base is typical of Philadelphia cabinetmaking – with its undulating apron, long cabriole legs with tightly clasping ball-and-claw feet, and a carved scallop shell on each knee. The retention of the shell from the Queen Anne period was characteristic of Philadelphia work, particularly carved in this naturalistic way.

B . A Louis XV *Guéridon, c*1765

This small round table shows the standard marks of the neo-classical style. It has a pierced brass gallery around both tiers, the straight edges of the drawer front are emphasized with ormolu, and the legs, rather than being cabriole, are virtually straight with a bend in them.

It was probably made by Roger Vandercruse (1728–1799), who was better known as Lacroix and who stamped his work 'R LACROIX' or 'R.V.L.C.'. He was from a family of cabinetmakers, headed by his Flemish father, François Vandercruse. Three of his five sisters married well-known cabinetmakers, (the eldest married first Jean-François Oeben and then Jean-Henri Reisener, another Simon Oeben, and the third, Simon Guillaume), his brother was a master clockmaker, and his son, Pierre, became a *maître ébéniste.*

This table is also very similar to the work of Charles Topino (1742-1803), who excelled at making small pieces of furniture. His use of marquetry was often highly original, with his trademark garlands and foliage often repeated in the ormolu mounts. He worked for nobility, dealers and fellow craftsmen.

C . A Louis XV Transitional Console Table, *c*1765

French design dominated world furniture fashions throughout the reigns of Louis XIV and XV, moving from the heavy Baroque styles at the beginning of the period to lighter, more elegant Rococo by the end. By 1760, French influence was waning, and England emerged as a new influence. Toward the end of the century, the dominant style, restrained and neo-classical, was the very opposite of Rococo.

This table comes from the transitional period between the two, and combines elements of both. The legs, for instance, still curve but are definitely straightening. The symbols on the frieze and stretcher are swags, festoons and urns – all classical motifs. But the table as a whole is moulded into the shape of a Rococo console table.

During the mid 18th century, many European designers travelled to Italy to study the emerging neo-classical styles. These included the Englishman, Robert Adam, who studied in Rome in the 1770s, the Marquis de Marigny, Madame de Pompadour's brother and Charles-Nicolas Cochin from France in 1749. Cochin (1715–90) was later to become Director General of Buildings in France and championed a return to 'the way of good taste of the preceding century'.

D . A Louis XV Reading Table, *c*1765

This stunning example of craftsmanship is unattributed, although it was possibly made by Léonard Boudin (known to have worked on similar pieces), perhaps with marquetry by Gerreit Jensen, renowned for his sophistication and use of ivory. There is a table of the same type in the Louvre in Paris, stamped by Christophe Wolff. A number of other craftsmen were working to this remarkably high standard around this date: Jean-François Oeben was known for his inlay pictures, and J-C Delafosse published a book of marquetry designs in the 1760s.

This table, which opens to reveal three sliding panels for reading, writing, etc, shows two strands of influence: its roots lie in the Rococo movement, with its curved outline and marquetry pictures of landscapes and mythological scenes in mother-of-pearl, ivory and wood. But it also shows neo-Classical dignity in its elegant legs, which although curved are almost straight; its curved top, which is fundamentally rectangular; and its inlay on the legs of husks and geometric florets. These contradictions are characteristic of the so-called transitional period between Rococo and neo-Classicism during which the table was made.

C

B

D

A

1700-1800

A . A Rosewood Writing Table by Thomas Chippendale, c1765

This beautiful table is rare, both because of its remarkable kidney shape and because all the documents surrounding its original sale from Thomas Chippendale to one Winifred Constable still survive. That invoice, 'to a large horseshoe table of black rosewood neatly inlaid with other woods and in a neat frame at £10 10s (10 guineas)', also specifies a damask leather cover at 18s; 89½ft (27.3m) of packing case at 3d a foot, total £1 2s 3d; and deal, screw and packing for 4s 6d. The total for the order was £12 14s 9d.

Chippendale is known to have spent much time working in the large house at Burton Constable for which this table was made. The house has spectacular bay windows, and the table may well have been designed to fit one of them, hence its unusual shape. It is discreet and uncluttered by Chippendale standards, its decoration relying on the contrast of grains and the inlaid fan-shaped patterns linked by a single line of husks. This motif is repeated on the tapering legs.

In many ways, the table is similar to furniture of mid-century France, concentrating on an elegant shape, minimal decoration other than wood grain and a bold, curving line.

B . An American Chippendale Dining Table, *c*1770

Probably from Philadelphia, this table was made during that city's time as the nation's capital and its prominence as the centre of Rococo-style furniture production in America. Thomas Affleck's arrival from London in 1763 boosted this first real flowering of American style, although many local craftsmen, such as William Savery, Jonathan Shoemaker and Benjamin Randolph, were also working in the same vein.

Philadelphia had a tradition of generously proportioned furniture, seen here in the beautiful long, curving drop leaves, emphasized by the arch in the apron at the end, and the bold, curving cabriole legs, which end in magnificent ball-and-claw feet. The table shows a new angularity after the preceding Queen Anne style, reflecting the confidence of Philadelphia's cabinetmakers.

B

D

C. An American Chippendale Card Table, Rhode Island, *c*1765

This mahogany card table is probably by John Goddard (1723–85) of Newport, Rhode Island. It is a good example of the transition between American Queen Anne and American Chippendale taste. Queen Anne is associated with plainer forms, flat, undecorated surfaces, and simplicity, as seen here on the top and apron. The shell decoration which characterized this Queen Anne-influenced local form can be seen on the front cabriole leg of this card table. American Chippendale looks more to English Rococo – cabriole legs, ball-and-claw feet, decoration and outlines with tight curves. All of these influences could have been found in Thomas Chippendale's *Director,* known to have been available in America during the 1760s.

Such pieces were usually of carved (but rarely inlaid) mahogany, and the carcasses were sometimes made of secondary woods – a clue to the main furniture-making centres. Philadelphia, then the nation's capital, was famous for its cabinetmakers, Thomas Affleck, William Savery, Jonathan Shoemaker and Benjamin Randolph, all of whose Rococo furniture rivalled the best of European work. Newport and Boston created Chippendale furniture with its own distinctive style, adhering to a linear tradition and a tending toward tall, thin proportions.

John Goddard was one of over 20 members of the Goddard and Townsend furniture-making dynasty, interrelated Quaker families which dominated the trade between 1760 and 1780.

D. A Pair of George III Satinwood Card Tables, *c*1775

Designed to sit against a wall, this pair of *demi-lune* (half-moon) card tables have a less obvious function – card tables when in use, they were also intended to fill wall space between the numerous windows in Georgian houses. This use is similar to that of pier tables (so-named after the architectural term 'pier', which refers to the supporting wall between two windows), although these were sometimes more elaborate and generally shallower than card tables, so they protruded less from the wall.

Satinwood, which was lighter and less sombre than mahogany, was a favourite with the Georgians. The bands of foliate inlay on a mahogany background which edge the table tops are heightened by the use of harewood, a sycamore veneer stained grey-green. Although the table aprons are plain, the decoration at the top of each leg uses the oval motif which was so fundamental to Georgian design.

A . A George III Sycamore and Gilt Gesso Side Table, c1775

Robert Adam (1728–1792) and his contemporaries in the mid 18th century were to have a profound effect on the history of furniture. Adam himself was a real innovator, often producing furniture with no precedent whatsoever; inevitably, some of his experiments were more successful than others. When considering furniture of this period, it must be remembered that much was designed for a specific setting, providing an essential background for the piece.

This style of table, for example, never became popular. The combination of an all-wood top on a gilt gesso base feels slightly wrong (the top would look better with tapering legs, the base with a marble top). The textured frieze decoration, too, clashes with the finely grained sycamore top, showing neo-Classical motifs of a central vase form and scrolling leaves on a background of satinwood. Perhaps if restored to its original brilliant gilt state and put in a sympathetic setting, the table could be seen in a different, more positive light.

B . An English George III Mahogany Serving or Side Table, c1775

A handsome and functional piece of furniture, this 5ft (1.52m) wide table would have stood at the side of a room and been used for serving. Its serpentine front in a bow shape tempers its rectangular form, and was a feature of English design of the 1770s and 1780s. The two frieze drawers with handles follow the same line.

As a concession to the elaborate carved furniture of the 1760s, there are small, carved oval decorations above the table's stout but tapering legs; these are echoed at the top of the legs themselves. This transitional period in design was beginning to anticipate the change during the 1780s and 1790s from three-dimensional (carved) ornamentation to flatter surfaces with applied decoration in the form of paint, lacquer or inlay.

The slightly heavy proportions and stout block feet of this table suggest that it might be Irish, but furniture was produced on such a grand scale, and generally from pattern books, that it is hard to be certain of its origin. Pattern-book drawings had a tremendous influence on design, the most renowned among them being Thomas Chippendale's *The Gentleman and Cabinet-maker's Director,* which was published in three editions between 1754 and 1762.

A

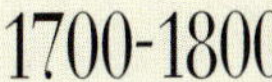

C

B

C. An English George III Mahogany Architect's or Drawing Table, *c*1780

This elegant and restrained work table is typically English, reflecting both the Georgian fascination with mechanical furniture (as seen in contemporary exercise chairs and bureaux with discreet drawers in their base) and the aspirations of the Georgian Renaissance man.

The simplest of a series of writing tables, it has two ratchets which allow the working surface to lie completely flat, like a desk, or to be set at any angle required. The understatement in the design is particularly clear in the tapering legs and the drawers – the latter have no handles, and are only distinguishable by the cock-beaded outlines.

Educated Georgians were often concerned with the planning of their own properties (Lord Burlington, for example, was largely responsible for the design of Chiswick House, London, in the mid 18th century) and architectural tables date from this time, a concrete reminder of Georgian interests.

1700-1800

A . A Louis XVI Marquetry Table by Charles Topino, *c*1780

This beautiful chest of drawers was made by Charles Topino (1742–1803), who specialized in very high-quality pieces of small furniture. It has three drawers which are disguised by the superb marquetry decoration; the top and front have landscape panels, the sides are decorated with garlands and foliage, including typical neo-classical motifs such as sheaves of wheat and flowers. The discreet lines of the furniture are slightly negated by the effusive decoration and colour.

Although originally successful, Topino, like many cabinetmakers, suffered at the hands of the French Revolution and was declared bankrupt in 1789.

B . A Louis XVI Gilt Wood Console Table, *c*1780

In design history, the Louis XVI period saw a considerable exchange of ideas and craftsmen between England and France. This piece is very similar to many console tables used by Robert Adam in his interiors for the English aristocracy during the 1770s and 1780s. The French *ébéniste* (cabinetmaker) Georges Jacob was known to be working for the English Royal Family over the last part of the century, and pieces of his from this date can still be seen at Windsor Castle, near London.

The table has a half-moon top and fluted legs, and its frieze is heightened by a *guilloche* and egg-and-tongue decoration, architectural forms and motifs favoured by the English. But there are signs of its French origin: the legs seem stouter for the frieze than would usually be seen in England, and the stretcher is heavy. Both features give the table a more solid appearance which is quite antithetical to the spirit of Adam's designs.

C . A French Iron *Guéridon*, *c*1780

This piece is difficult to date accurately, but the curved legs suggest a possible date of c1760. It is close to the *guéridon's* original function as a candlestand, with a narrow top designed to hold candelabra and an adjustable shaft which allowed the height of the light source to vary.

The contemporary English craftsman, Matthew Boulton (1728–1809), produced similar pieces in his workshops in London and Birmingham, although these tended to be in gilt bronze of very high quality, following the French lead in ormolu. This is virtually the only form of metal furniture found in England during this period, although some exotic silver furniture exists at Knole in Kent, made for Charles II.

D . A Louis XVI Steel *Guéridon*, *c*1780

This most unusual table follows the design of wood-tripod *guéridons*, which were generally more popular in England than in France. Its style, with gallery and marble top, is similar to that of Louis XVI, but it is difficult to be sure of its date without documents.

Even though the French had a continuous tradition of metalworking from the Middle Ages onward, the finely turned steel stem on spindling, curving tripod legs had little precedent, and seems contemporary enough to have come from the 20th century, perhaps the Art Deco period of Bauhaus school.

E . An English George III Sycamore Pembroke Table, *c*1780

This delicate table embodies the height of Hepplewhite or Sheraton ideals of decoration. Made of sycamore, which itself has a shimmering grain, the table is cross-banded in tulipwood. The detail illustrates nearly the entire Georgian vocabulary of decoration: a large shell-shaped inlay is framed by an anthemion and urn-draped foliate scrolls; this in turn is surrounded by portrait medallions, hung from ribbons and joined by swags of husks. The tapering legs on castors are also classically Georgian, and the table has a single drawer in the frieze.

According to Thomas Sheraton, Pembroke tables take their name from 'that lady who first gave orders for one of them, who probably gave the first idea of such a table to the workmen'. Introduced during the 1750s, they have two flaps supported by hinge brackets and were originally rectangular, although later pieces are more often oval or have serpentine edges. Pembroke tables are essentially practical items, as can be seen from Adam's designs; wherein console and side tables were clearly for decoration but Pembroke tables such as this one were in constant domestic use.

A

C

E

D

B

A. An English George III Mahogany Envelope Games Table, *c*1780

This rare envelope card table is far more unusual than other *demi-lune*, D-shaped or serpentine-fronted games tables of the period, and is particularly distinguished for bearing the name of its maker – C Toussaint. Although it is certainly an English-made piece, the maker's French name implies that he might have been one of a number of French craftsmen who went to England during the 18th century to learn the trade at a time when English fashions were very popular in France.

The table is typically George III, with its squareness, straight lines and tapering legs. The cross-banded pattern in satinwood and tulipwood on the top is very much of the period, as is the circular decoration in boxwood radiating from the centre. As expected in a card table, the leaves fold out to increase the size of the playing area, but it is very unusual for the closed leaves to form the pattern of an envelope.

The table is photographed here to show it both open and closed, and it can be seen that its playing area is bare wood. As most card tables are thought of as being baize-lined (although there are exceptions to the rule), it is possible that this might have been designed as an occasional or tea table.

B. An English George III Satinwood Hepplewhite Dressing Table, *c*1780

From the front, this table appears to be a small commode (chest of drawers), with a drawer which pulls out and a sliding flap to the side which extends to hold the paraphernalia of dressing and make-up. In fact, the front is a dummy drawer, and the hinged lid, decorated with the typical neo-classical decoration of an urn surrounded by scrolls, lifts upward to reveal a fitted interior.

The pronounced serpentine edge of the table top and the elegant cabriole legs veneered in cross grain both owe a debt to French design of the time. This was a period when many ideas were exchanged across the English Channel, and in fact this style is sometimes known as 'French Hepplewhite'. Both Sheraton and Hepplewhite included a range of similar tables in their pattern-books, many of which included Georgian gadgetry such as roll tops or full-length ratcheted mirrors.

The stylishness of the piece could well be due to a habit women had at this time of receiving guests while dressing – thus requiring a dressing table that was both decorative and functional.

A

B

C . An English Hepplewhite Pembroke Table, *c*1785

Although the history of this table is unknown, there is a documented card table which shares many of the same characteristics. If, as is likely, the two were supplied together, they would have come from a leading cabinetmaker of the Hepplewhite era.

Three unusual features which the tables share are the dappled mahogany grain of the veneer (mahogany contours are usually broad); the geometric loops of the drawer handles, which have chamfered corners where the washers meet the wood; and the contrast of flat, two-dimensional figuring and crisp carving, seen here on the legs.

The table also has striking folding leaves with instepped quadrant corners. Its shape, which falls between circular and rectangular, is unusual. A superb example of a Pembroke table, this piece shows the refinement that was possible on even the most standard of table designs.

D . An English George III Satinwood Painted Card Table, *c*1785

The second half of George III's reign is sometimes known as 'The Age of Satinwood' and is considered by many to be the finest period of English decorated furniture. This beautifully executed table, probably one of a pair or even from a set of four, would have been very expensive even in its own time.

The table is covered in all types of Georgian painted decoration, including the centre panel, filled with musical trophies (instruments displayed artistically); the frame of floral garlands and ribbons, and the cross-banded edges of tulipwood and burr yew wood. The legs and sides are painted with similar motifs.

D-shaped, this piece follows the classic format for a card table of this date: a rear leg, hinged in the middle of the table back, swings out like a gate to support the top, which when unfolded reveals a baize-lined interior. A decade earlier the *demi-lune* (or half-moon) table was preferred, but by 1785 the D-shaped table had increased in popularity.

1700-1800

A . A Pair of English George III Caskets on Stands, *c*1785

The late Georgian period was one of considerable experimentation in design, exploring gadgetry and placing a variety of furniture on stands. The closed casket here is a work box, with room for needles, material, cottons, etc, and the open box is a teapoy, or tea caddy. This has two compartments on each side for different flavours (of mainly china teas), and two canisters which often still bear the labels 'Green' and 'Bohea', the two main varieties of the day. Tea was a very expensive commodity and was therefore locked away. A box like this also contained a blue glass bowl for the ritual of blending tea.

Both caskets have hinged lids and are decorated with cut-steel clasps. Some of these frame medallions were made by Matthew Boulton (1728–1809), who was best known for his silver and ormolu workshops and who specialized in metalwork.

B . A Marquetry Table by David Roentgen, *c*1785

David Roentgen (1743–1807) was the son of Abraham Roentgen, the renowned Saxon cabinetmaker who retired from his workshops at Neuwied on the Rhine in 1772. He was succeeded by David, who became Germany's most famous cabinetmaker of the time and was hugely successful, with established markets for his work in Berlin, Vienna and Paris. He became a *maître ébéniste* in France in 1780 and subsequently adopted the stamp 'DAVID'. His fame rested mainly on his inlay marquetry techniques – he created shadows by using different shades of wood, so that his finished work resembled mosaic. Previously, cabinetmakers had either engraved or burnt shadows into their pictures.

This simple oval table with disguised drawers is typical of his work. He collaborated with Pierre Kintzing, a famous mechanical toy and clockmaker, and specialized in hidden drawers such as these. In this case, one long drawer reveals four hidden ones when a secret catch is opened at the end of the table. Although the shape is clear, the inlay and colour on the top and sides detract from the simplicity of line, a typical pitfall when German craftsmen attempted neo-classical pieces such as this, perhaps because of the still-strong influence of the Rococo in Germany.

C . A Louis XVI *Table en Chiffonière, c*1785

The *table en chiffonière* is generally thought of as a small case of drawers on legs, sometimes with a writing slide. It is related to the *chiffonier,* a tall chest of drawers made in large numbers in the middle of the 18th century.

Straight-edged, this example has a pierced brass gallery, a marble top, and sides and drawers veneered in tulipwood and kingwood. Its only decoration is the ormolu surrounding the escutcheons and capping the feet. The bottom halves of the legs are the only curving lines on the entire piece.

In England, Thomas Chippendale noted the supply of 'a neat shiffener writing table, japanned in green and gold with a drawer and cut bottles' in his accounts in the 1760s, the first such reference to this French source.

D . A Louis XVI Inlaid Writing Table, *c*1785

The second half of the 18th century witnessed a trend throughout Europe toward smaller, more intimate rooms, which required appropriate furniture. Many small tables were made to meet this need, often less than 3ft (91cm) long. This table has two clear indications of its approximate date: the frieze has a *guilloche,* a gilded bronze band which is directly associated with neo-classical architectural ornament; and it is relatively plain for Louis XVI, and could therefore have been made after the Revolution in the 1790s.

It does, however, show typical Louis XVI elements. The leather writing surface in the centre of the top is plain, but is surrounded by a sophisticated band of interlacing marquetry of tulipwood and kingwood. The frieze is decorated with ormolu, and the legs, cross-banded and bordered in a darker wood, finish in neat brass caps.

A

D

C

B

A. A Louis XVI *Table à Ouvrage,* c1785

This piece is in the full-blown Louis XVI style. The characteristic brass gallery around the top of and undertier gives the table horizontal emphasis, contributing to the effect of straight lines and solidity which was typical of this time. The stretcher or tier here is used decoratively, to balance the weight of the box on top, and it functions as a shelf as well.

It is a sewing table, and the side flap folds down to reveal a fitted storage space with room for sewing equipment and materials. The marquetry decoration on the side is realistic, and in contrast to earlier tables has a clearly bordered, neat, floral pattern. The restraining border helps to give the table a more subdued feel than that of earlier, similar Rococo work boxes, in effect holding the design 'still'.

B. A Pair of Small French Console Tables by Georges Jacob, *c*1785

These small cupboard tables are typical of the contemporary passion for small furniture and for things English. *Anglomanie,* or Anglomania, was at its height during the 1780s, and these tables are basically French Chippendale; it is the brass gallery and marble top of these console tables which indicate that they are not actually English.

The carving is probably by Georges Jacob (1739–1814), the foremost carver of the period who worked in plain, gilt and painted woods. He was the founder of a line of cabinetmakers which included two sons, the younger of whom changed his name to Jacob-Desmalter and carried on the family business into the early 19th century. Born the son of a peasant in Burgundy, Jacob was a favourite of Marie-Antoinette's and reached his peak at the time of the Revolution. His closeness to the royal family meant that he was denounced several times during the Revolution, this despite his attempts to gain credibility, which included making gun stocks for the Revolutionary army. He died in a hospital asylum.

C. A Louis XV *Guéridon,* c1785

Although correct in all its individual elements, this piece somehow manages to give the impression of being assembled. The general elegance of the period is missing, and the *guéridon* features too many decorative ideas – none of which sets the tone for the whole table.

Almost all the elements were standard in the 1780s – the brass gallery, the heavy ormolu mounts around the drawers, the curved apron under each tier and the cross-

banding and marquetry inlay. So too were the curious outward-bowing supports above the cabriole legs, although if straight supports had been used, the whole table would have a much cleaner outline.

D. An American Federal Candlestand, *c*1785

This table was made specifically to hold candelabra or candlesticks and has a small drawer below to accommodate lighting equipment such as a tinder box and wax tapers. The candlestand dates from around 1785, which was technically the 'Federal' period following American independence in 1783. New styles being developed in England by Robert Adam were slow to arrive in America due to the war, and so are not reflected here.

The Queen Anne style was still being produced in America up to this time, and neo-classical furniture was fully absorbed in American style a decade or so later. This period is confusing because so many styles were made at the same time; country makers tended to be conservative.

This elegant table was probably made in Connecticut, and is of beautiful red cherry wood with an even grain. The beginnings of neo-classical influence can be seen here in the fan-shaped inlay on the top, the urn-like column, and the graceful angular tripod with small feet which are known as pointed snake feet.

E. An American Chippendale Card Table, *c*1790

The general construction of this table is closely based on a model popular from the 1770s and 1780s in England. The top hinges backward and the rear gate leg swings out to support it; the top edge has a chequered, key-fret moulding; the frieze above the legs has a cross-hatched edge; and the fluted, tapering legs end in Marlboro feet.

While the table is made up of English elements in an English construction, the decorative motifs are combined in such a way as to make this table very American. The frieze decoration is not a true classical motif, and the legs are fluted in a solid manner slightly out of keeping with the table top.

Probably from Connecticut or Rhode Island, it is made of cherry wood, in keeping with the Americans' extensive use of fruitwoods, and is from the transitional time between the Chippendale and Federal periods – the former associated with carving and decoration, the latter with neo-classicism and architectural detail.

A . A Russian Oval Table, *c*1790

The inspiration behind this table is clearly the French neo-classical style of the 1780s. Much Russian furniture followed designs from Western Europe, although they were often imbued with a regional flavour. In this case, for instance, the top of finely figured mahogany, the extensive use of linear ormolu decoration and the unusual stretcher are all Russian additions, although the basic shape of the table, the pierced gallery and the details on the legs are standard neo-classical features.

Similar examples to this are to be found in the Pavlovsk Palace near Leningrad, and several inventories from before the Russian Revolution of 1917 include many French pieces of this date.

B . An English George III Mahogany Pembroke Table, *c*1790

This standard round-top Georgian Pembroke table is the more desirable of the two main models, ie, round – and rectangular-topped. A good early example, the table is circular when the flaps are extended, and has tapering legs. Later Regency and Victorian Pembroke tables often have turned legs, and use a lesser mahogany than the well-figured wood here.

Tulipwood – a striped wood from Brazil used almost exclusively for banding – was a favourite with the Georgians, and is used here in the cross-banding around the table edge. Satinwood too is used, a contrast with the dominant darker mahogany. Other classic Georgian decorative motifs can be seen in the oval inlaid panel at the top of the legs, which terminate in brass capping and castors.

C . An English George III Mahogany Architect's Table, *c*1790

This practical architect's table has a sophisticated double ratchet with an unusual mechanism. It also contains a frieze drawer that is divided into compartments for inks, paper, etc, and two drop-leaf wings on each side which can be extended to increase the working surface.

Nicely detailed, with castors for moving the table around the room and a ledge on the work surface to support the drawings, this piece is made from classic Georgian flame mahogany, so-called after the enormous contours of the wood which result in a flame pattern.

D. An English George III Mahogany Artist's Table, *c*1790

This elegant baize-lined table has a lighter frame than most other architect's tables. It also has a double-ratcheted mechanism which withdraws into a tailor-made mahogany cover, secured by a loop. When folded, the table covers an aperture to hold a palette, and the undertier is shaped to fit the knees of the artist.

Showing all the signs of a Georgian gadget, this adjustable artist's table is indicative of the contemporary vogue for sketching, watercolours and oil painting – 'during the 18th century such tables were seen as very healthy for those who stand to read, write or draw'; *The Dictionary of English Furniture* (1st Edition) captioned a similar table from the Noel Terry Collection in York, England. The same type of table was used by the Reverend Edward Hoyle, who stands reading at one in a 1760 painting by the renowned English portrait painter, Arthur Devis.

E. An American Federal Pembroke Table, *c*1790

This sombre, utilitarian Pembroke table is made of mahogany. It follows the English patterns popular at this date, and is probably by John Townsend (1732–1809) of Newport, Rhode Island. Much influenced by Chippendale, he came from one of the important Quaker cabinetmaking families of Newport, and is thought to have settled in Connecticut.

The construction and inlay decoration of this table are similar to other pieces by Townsend. Its severe rectangular look is relieved only by a little inlay at the ends, with 'book end' inlay (fluting) above the carrot – and line-inlaid legs with cross-banded cuffs (the small decoration at the end of the legs).

F. A Sheraton Mahogany Drum-topped Table, *c*1795

Understatement was an essential characteristic of Georgian design: the art lay in what was not stated. The success of this table, which is extremely simple, lies in its excellent proportions. The diameter of the top almost exactly matches the diameter of the splayed tripod legs (which are cleanly stopped with brass-capped castors), and no jagged edges, scrolls or carving break the severity of line. In fact, there is very little decoration at all, apart from the natural grain of the wood and the neat ivory escutcheons around the keyholes.

A. An English George III Triple Pedestal Mahogany Dining Table, c1795

The extendable English dining table went back to the middle of the 17th century, when there was a change in style from large, static oak tables placed in the great hall to mobile, lighter furniture. Woods such as walnut and oak, used in the 17th century, were increasingly replaced by mahogany for almost all dining tables after 1720, when import tax on colonial woods were lifted.

The pedestal dining table, such as this example, belonged to the second half of the 18th century, and had the advantage of being infinitely extendable. At Hardwick Hall in Derbyshire, for example, there is a dining table with five four-legged pedestals supporting it on turned reeded columns. It is rare nowadays to find tables with more than two pedestals; the leaves and pedestals of such tables are often replaced, broken into small arrangements and reassembled with different veneers. These tables can be almost entirely dismantled, as the pedestal fits into a block on the underside of the leaves, usually with removable brass bolts.

This example has all the essential late Georgian characteristics: strong, red-coloured top with matching veneer; turned columns on the pedestals; elegant sabre legs; and brass claw castors. The style continued into the 19th century, albeit in a more angular form.

Georgian design was much occupied with construction and proportion.

B. An English George III Library Drum Table, c1795

In the early 18th century, library tables intended as decorative furniture became more specialized. They were large, grand and stood in the centre of the room, often without drawers. This more practical example, however, has a tooled-leather surface for writing and eight drawers – an impressive piece of cabinetmaking, as four of these are rectangular, the other four triangular. Much smaller than early 18th-century examples, the table swivels on its central turned support and rests on three splayed legs. This circular form is known as a drum table because of its shape.

C. A French Porcelain and Ormolu *Guéridon*, c1795

Small round tables such as these were popular in France at the end of the 18th century and during the Empire period of the early 19th century. They were both functional and of very high quality, often using porcelain plaques decorated individually by known artists. The Impressionist painter, Pierre-Auguste Renoir, for example, painted porcelain plates during the mid 19th century to make a living.

In this case, the central plaque shows French 18th-century porcelain at its best, decorated with breathtaking realism. It is supported by a finely wrought ormolu base, with the legs pared down to simulate bamboo and a slender three-pronged stretcher which would be hard to reproduce in wood. The table is in the style of Adam Weisweiler (c1750–c1810), who probably trained with David Roentgen before moving in the 1770s to Paris, where he worked until around 1810.

D. An English George III Pembroke Table, c1795

This stunning and refined Pembroke table clearly demonstrates the meeting of two eras in furniture design, that of the Georgian 'Age of Satinwood' (1770–1800) and the Regency 'Age of Rosewood' which immediately followed. This serpentine-edged table has a centre of dark rosewood surrounded by an apron of bright satinwood, the two slightly separated by tulipwood cross-banding.

Difficult to date precisely, the table's small oval fan inlays are a classic Géorge III motif, which implies a time around the turn of the century, and the table shows a concern with style typical of Georgian furniture. Many specialists claim that the late Georgian/early Regency period represented the peak of English craftsmanship and design; pieces such as this are at the height of late Georgian taste.

E. An English Late George III Card Table, c1795

This attractive serpentine-fronted card table with inward-curving sides opens out into an elegant star shape. Confusingly, it has a combination of different decorative styles: the loop swags on the frieze in boxwood inlay are reminiscent of the 1780s; the star inlay and fluted legs are both typical Regency figures; and the elegant tapering legs are slightly sculptural, a feature normally associated with the very early 19th century. Nevertheless, the overall shape of the piece is appealing, and it is topped with well-figured mahogany.

B
D
E

1700-1800

A. An English Queen Anne Walnut Bureau

This bureau is 3ft (91cm) wide, with a base of two long and two short drawers supported on bun feet. Walnut was the veneer selected by British cabinet-makers for most good-quality work until the 1730s. Timber from native trees was supplemented by imported European walnut, but the severe frosts of the winter of 1709 are said to have destroyed most of the walnut trees in Central Europe and by 1720 it had become so scarce that its export from France was banned. The problem was solved by the importation of black walnut from Virginia and by the almost universal adoption of mahogany as a veneer in the latter half of the century.

This bureau shows several signs of its pedigree. The heavy bun feet are a reminder of the late 17th century Dutch influence, whereas simple bracket feet were normal on most English bureaux by the mid-18th century. The bold dividing moulding around the centre of the body shows that this piece was conceived very much as a desk on a chest. The space from the level of the flap to the moulding (a well) could be used for storage: the opening was in the bottom of the writing compartment and closed by a lid.

B. An English Queen Anne Oak Bureau of *c*1710

This example is very compact at only 2ft (61cm) wide and equipped with a stepped interior and a well beneath the fall-front.

Honest oak pieces such as this continued to be made by country craftsmen to the traditional pattern right through the 18th century and beyond. Original handles and original feet are features to look out for on such pieces. Feet tended to wear out quickly with rough use and standing on damp floors; the tall brackets on this example are later replacements.

C. An English George I Walnut Bureau, *c*1715

This is a fairly early example of a standard English bureau of good quality.

It is veneered throughout with carefully-selected burr-wood, feather-and cross-banded, with two short and three long drawers graduated in size from top to bottom and cock-beaded around the edges. There is a fitted interior behind the fall front, which is supported on lopers when opened. The whole framework is supported on bracket feet and is 3ft 2in (96cm) wide.

Desks to this basic design continued to be made throughout the century.

A

B

C

1700-1800

A . An English Queen Anne Walnut Bureau Cabinet, early 18th century

Shown open and closed.

The double-domed mirror-glazed upper section contains 20 drawers of varying size, twelve of them with concave fronts, grouped around a central niche. The Corinthian pilasters have gilt capitals and bases and are partly stop-fluted. The arrangement of drawers in the base is fairly standard for the period, as are the mirror panels. The mirrors helped to magnify the light of candles placed on the slides which can be seen above the fall-front. This is a large desk, 3ft 3in (99cm) wide, and would have made an imposing fixture in any room, but the carrying handles suggest that it was considered portable.

B . An English Queen Anne Lacquered Bureau-Cabinet

This desk is 3ft 5¼in (1.04m) wide, decorated with a variety of chinoiserie scenes including large birds, figures in landscapes and flowering plants. The commanding double-domed cabinet is typical of early 18th-century English desks of this type, as are the arched mirrored panels on the doors. Other features which are commonly found at the beginning of the century but which die out later on are the candle slides beneath the mirrors, the ledge along the bottom edge of the fall-flap which allowed the slope to be used as a lectern for supporting books, and the deep space between the slope and the top drawers. Access to this space is via a lidded well in the bottom of the writing compartment. In later examples this space is more often occupied by further drawers.

Exotic japanned furniture remained popular in the early part of the century, having been introduced from Holland after the Restoration and explained to English craftsmen in Stalker and Parker's *Treatise of Japanning and Varnishing* of 1688, which included 'Patterns for Japan-work in imitation of the Indians for Tables, Stands, Frames, Cabinets etc.' Japanning also seems to have been considered a suitable occupation for the amateur artist.

A

B

C

D

C. An English Red-Japanned Bureau-Cabinet, early 18th century

Supported on gilt hairy paw feet; the bureau has a base of two short and two long drawers, and a writing compartment over a storage well.

This is a fine example of the most extrovert of all 18th-century English furniture forms, markedly different from the staid mahogany bureau-bookcases which became the standard Georgian product later in the century. This bureau is unusual in that the mirrored outer doors, when opened as here, reveal three glazed panels, the central one hinged as a door. The cabinet behind the panels is unfitted but splendidly decorated; the brilliance of the gilt butterflies, and grape clusters on their bright red ground is a reminder of the original effect of the whole before light and dirt dimmed the exterior. The width of this piece is 3ft 1in (94cm).

D. An English Queen Anne Red Lacquer Escritoire

The fanciful chinoiserie scenes in gold are a spectacular form of ornament which is relatively common on bureau bookcases of the period but rare on escritoires. There are two short and two long drawers in the base, a long concealed drawer in the cushion cornice at the top, and a variety of small drawers and pigeonholes around a cupboard in the upper section. The fall-front is fitted with a rising velvet-lined writing slope. It is 3ft 7in (1.09m) wide.

A . An English George I Walnut-Veneered Chest

Chests of this kind, in which the top folds out to form a table or desk supported on lopers like those found on English bureaux, were made throughout the first half of the 18th century and are usually referred to as "bachelor's chests", which may be a contemporary term. The design provided storage and a place to sit for those with limited space.

This piece is 2ft 8in (81cm) wide, with a heavy hinged top.

B . An English George I Walnut Kneehole Desk, *c*1720

An unusual feature of this desk is the fitted writing compartment behind a fall-front. It also has a folding top. The lower section, with three drawers in each pedestal and a cupboard at the back of the kneehole, is the normal pattern for desks of this type, but it is rare to find an 18th-century English piece with a lockable writing compartment of this kind. The width of this desk if 3ft 1½in (95cm).

C . An English George I Walnut Kneehole Bureau

Beneath the flap, which is decoratively quarter-veneered and baize-lined, the writing compartment is fitted with a cupboard, four drawers and pigeonholes. This early 18th-century piece, perhaps intended for a lady's bedroom, clearly shows its ancestry, being a simple combination of the commoner kneehole desk and the slope-front table desk, divided all round by a moulding. This example is 2ft 5in (74.5cm) wide, and has six small drawers flanking another drawer over a cupboard in the kneehole. Such pieces often doubled as dressing tables; some are fitted for that purpose.

D . An English Portable Table Desk, *c*1730

Shown open and closed.

Under the flap are five drawers and three pigeonholes, and the single base drawer has a shaped block front cut from solid beech. The main carcase is of pine, red japanned and decorated with chinoiseries in gold and silver. It is 1ft 3½in (39cm) wide.

E . An English Walnut-Veneered Table Bureau, c1705

The diamond-and leaf-inlaid fall-front opens to give access to a fitted interior and forms a writing surface supported on a pair of tiny lopers with ring handles. Similar ring handles are fitted to the chevron-banded drawer below. This desk is a slightly more sophisticated reminder of the simple slope-topped boxes of the previous century.

D

B

A . An American William and Mary Slope-Front Desk, *c*1720–30

This desk was made in Pennsylvania, and is walnut-veneered with two short and two long drawers in the base. It is 2ft 9¾in (86cm) wide.

With its one-piece design and shaped, stepped interior of small drawers and pigeonholes around a central cupboard, this desk has all the basic characteristics of the typical piece of writing furniture of the 18th century. Tell-tale early features are the turned ball-and-cone feet and the brass pear-drop

B . An American William and Mary Slant-Front Desk, *c*1710–1725

The carcase, 2ft 10in (86cm) wide, is of pine and maple, with a simple open compartment beneath the slope and two drawers in the frieze. The whole desk rests on a joined stand, with turned legs and is mortice and tenoned together.

C . A French Régence Period Bureau Plat, *c*1720

Veneered in kingwood and mounted with gilt bronze espagnolettes, masks, foliate scrolls and leafy handles, this 6ft 7in (2m) wide desk is a good example of the so-called Régence style, which represented a gradual transition from the massive and formal baroque of Louis XIV's reign to the light and fanciful rococo of Louis XV's mid-reign. Three drawers are fitted into the frieze along one side, but those on the other side are dummy drawers.

D . A French Louis XV Bureau Plat, *c*1730

This desk was made by Charles Cressent, who was *ébéniste* to Philippe, Duc d'Orléans, regent for Louis XV until 1723. (He was also an accomplished sculptor and was taken to court and fined on several occasions for modelling, casting and gilding his own mounts, which, under guild regulations, was explicitly the province of the *fondeurs* and *doreurs*.) As the leading *ébéniste* of the Régence period, Cressent presided over the gradual lightening of the more formal Louis XIV style which was a feature of the early years of the 18th century. This bureau retains a certain stately quality, not least because of its width being 6ft 9in (2.05m), but this is countered by the characteristic rococo C-scrolls of the drawer handles, with their sprigs of wayward leaves, and by the sweep of the central escutcheon. It has a leather-lined top with three drawers in the shaped frieze and is mounted with finely-modelled caryatids at the angles and bearded masks flanking the central drawer.

C
D

A. An American Queen Anne Blockfront Mahogany Kneehole Desk, *c*1730–40

There are three drawers on each side of the kneehole cupboard and one long drawer across the top, giving an overall width of 2ft 8in (81cm). The delicate stringing and multi-coloured star inlay (four-pointed on the cupboard door, twelve-pointed on the top) is of a type found on many American Queen Anne pieces and was probably copied from London cabinetmakers. This example was made in Massachusetts.

During the American Chippendale period carving became the dominant form of decoration, but contrasted veneers were used a great deal during the Federal period.

B. An American Queen Anne Walnut Kneehole Desk, *c*1745

Made at Newport, Rhode Island, it has a width of 2ft 9½in (85cm). Supported on bracket feet, the desk has one long frieze drawer, small deep drawers down each pedestal and a panelled cupboard in the back of the kneehole.

C. An American Queen Anne Mahogany Desk-and-Bookcase, *c*1735–1750

From Boston, Massachusetts, this double-domed desk is 3ft 4½in (1.03m) wide, and is in two parts, with carrying handles on the sides of the top and bottom sections. It has a four-drawer base beneath a fitted interior with small drawers, pigeonholes and document drawers behind the two pilasters with flame finials. In the centre is a cupboard, often called a prospect drawer in America. The shelved upper section is unusual in that it has gold-painted shells decorating the alcoves behind the arched mirror-panelled doors. One of the candleslides is shown in use here to demonstrate how the mirrors helped to reflect light back into the room.

D. An American Queen Anne Maple Desk-and-Bookcase, *c*1740

There are compartmented shelves and pigeonholes behind the panelled doors in the upper section and a stepped fitted interior without a central cupboard. This is a good example of the plainer style of Rhode Island cabinet-work, without any of the shell carving or blockfronts usually associated with the more famous Newport craftsmen. It is 3ft (91cm) wide.

E. An American Walnut Desk-and Cabinet, *c*1745–50

This early example of block-and-shell carving from Newport, Rhode Island, is 3ft (91cm) wide.

The panels of the cabinet doors are raised and headed with convex carved shells, while concave shell carving is used to enrich the block-front interior of the desk. The base has a plain, straight front of graduated drawers resting on ogee feet.

F. An American Queen Anne Black Walnut Desk on Frame

This is a fairly sophisticated version of the rudimentary slope-front desk mounted on a lowboy, which was to be found in the American colonies from the beginning of the 18th century. This example is 3ft 2½in (98cm) wide and was made in Philadelphia c1750. Here the lowboy has the usual arrangement of two small and one long drawer, while the desk is stylishly fitted with little serpentine drawers and pigeonholes to either side of a cupboard containing four more drawers. The drawers are all fitted with spurs to prevent them being pulled out inadvertently. The simple scalloped apron on the base is a traditional form of decoration, but the cabiole legs with ball-and-claw feet and the quarter-columns in both desk and base reflect the growing sophistication of the late Queen Anne period in America.

E

F

A
C
B
D

A . A French Louis XV Rosewood Veneered Bureau Plat, *c*1750

This large and handsome desk is traditionally supposed to have belonged to the Compte de Vergennes, Louis XVI's Foreign Minister. Certainly the bureau was amongst the furniture in the *Ministère des Affaires Etrangères* in 1901 when it was moved to the Louvre for public display. It was made by Pierre II Migeon and Jacques Dubois and has gilt bronze leafy mounts, three frieze drawers and a shaped leather-lined writing surface which is 6ft 6in (1.99mm) wide.

B . A French Louis XV Bureau Plat

This tulipwood and kingwood desk was made by Bernard II van Risenburgh. It is 6ft (1.83m) wide. Below the shaped serpentine top, the three frieze drawers are balanced by three dummy drawers on the opposite side. The marquetry flowersprays which decorate the featherbanded kingwood drawer fronts and the sides of the desk are typical of van Risenburgh, who was one of the most accomplished *ébénistes* of the Louis XV period. He was known only by his abbreviated *estampille* of BVRB until the late 1950s, when his full name and identity were finally discovered.

C . A French late Louis XV Green *Vernis Martin* Bureau Plat

This desk has a matching *cartonnier* and inkstand, and all were made by René Dubois, *maître* in 1754. The bureau is 4ft 8½in (1.43m) wide, the *cartonnier* 6ft 10in (2.08m) high. Bureaux plats were often made with matching *cartonniers* or filing cabinets. Some are no more than small *gradins*, designed to stand at one end of a large desk, but this magnificent example is free-standing. Here it has been turned at an angle to show the gilt decoration of martial trophies on the bottom panels, but it was intended to stand at one end of the desk within easy reach of the writer and the cupboard doors are on each side rather than the front. There are also small drawers in the frieze at each side, while the top section is divided into three velvet-lined compartments. The details of the ornament are all gilt, crowned by the embracing figures of Cupid and Psyche on a spirally-fluted drum with Peace and War to either side. The trophies on the doors in the base represent Learning and Agriculture.

D. A French Louis XV Secrétaire à Abattant

The secrétaire à abattant first came into fashion as a large piece of case furniture in the 1750s, but examples in rococo style like this one are far less common than those of a few years later in the more formal neo-classical style. This tulipwood-veneered example, does, however, show all the features of the more typical Louis XVI secrétaires. The large shaped flat in the upper section folds down to give access to six small drawers and pigeonholes decorated with sprays of flowers tied with ribbons to echo the exterior end-cut marquetry, and there is a two-door cupboard in the base. Just beneath the serpentine marble top, nearly 5ft (1.50m) from the floor, there is a shaped drawer in the frieze. It was made by Christophe Wolff, who became *maître* in 1755.

E. A French Mid-18th Century Kingwood Secrétaire à Abattant

Pieces like this one, which show the rounded, rococo characteristics of the Louis XV period combined with the sterner lines of the Louis XVI period, are often referred to as being in Transitional style, a term which emphasises the gradual way in which French furniture styles tended to evolve in the 18th century. This example has a brown marble top veined with white above a fall-front with rounded corners which conceals an interior of shelves and four drawers, one of which is fitted with an inkwell and a pounce pot. The doors below hide more shelves and a *coffre fort* (strong box). It was made by Jean Demoulin, maître in 1749, and is 2ft 8in (81cm) wide.

F. A Small French Late Louis XV Secrétaire à Abattant

This piece is 3ft 2in (97cm) wide, veneered in a variety of woods, mounted with gilt-bronze lion heads and masks, garlands and swags and with plaques of flower-painted Sèvres porcelain. It is probably from the workshop of Martin Carlin, who specialized in porcelain-mounted pieces. Small secretaires like this one, in the form of *meubles d'entre deux* (a cupboard with curved shelves on each side), enjoyed a period of popularity in France in the third quarter of the 18th century and they were later copied by English makers. Sheraton illustrates one, described as a lady's cabinet in his *Cabinet-Maker and Upholsterer's Drawing-Book* (Plate XVI).

A . A French Louis XV Kingwood Parquetry Secrétaire-de-Voyage

In this picture it is shown open to reveal a few of its many secret drawers. The block of drawers on the right normally forms the interior of the double-doored cabinet in the base, but a secret catch allows it to be removed to reveal many more drawers with leather tab handles on the inside. The central drawer of the removable section is here taken out to show the further drawer which normally lies behind it. There are yet more little drawers in the well in the floor of the writing compartment, a long drawer in the side of the desk just above the carrying handle and a further slide below the fall. It is quite small (1ft 4in (41cm) wide), but every space has been put to use.

B . A French Secrétaire à la Bourgogne

This is a form of mechanical writing table that was in vogue in Paris in the 1760s. Though only 2ft 8in (81cm) wide, it is packed with displays of technical virtuosity and decorated with no fewer than 24 marquetry panels, covering almost every surface, including those normally hidden in the body of the table.

The top is inlaid with a picture of a classical ruin and one of the pieces of fallen masonry conceals a lock which releases the front half of the top. This folds forward to form a writing surface with a leather lining.

The whole of the back half of the top rises at the touch of a button to reveal a bank of small drawers and a central niche with a tambour front. All the drawers are themselves opened by spring catches, and a catch behind the tambour releases a collapsible bookrest which can be pulled out and used as required.

More surprises spring from the body of the front half of the desk, with a central nest of six small drawers flanked by hinged lidded compartments.

This desk is unmarked but similarly complex examples are known to have been made by Jean-François Oeben and other German cabinetmakers working in Paris who were known for their mechanical expertise.

C . A French Mid-18th-Century Secrétaire à Culbute

The cherrywood this piece is made of is inlaid with geometric lines and a central Maltese cross in amaranth. This fairly humble piece, 2ft 1in (64cm) wide, is a rare survival of an interesting form of folding desk which proved more ingenious than practical. The hinged top is adjustable, allowing the desk to be multi-functional: as shown here, with the lid closed, it is a small side table. For reading, the top can be lifted to the angle desired and held by single strut, while a small section in the middle of the front can be hinged upwards to form a convenient rest for the book. The top can also be hinged open completely to form a leather-lined writing surface (see detail). The sloping box underneath can then be lifted upwards from the well of the desk to reveal itself as a fitted compartment with drawers and shelves for storing writing accessories. In practice the hinged mechanism proved fragile and the drawer section was heavy and inconvenient to lift into position. This desk seems to have originally been fitted with a sliding fire screen at the back and candleholders in the brass sockets at the tops of the front legs.

D . A detail of the Secrétaire à Culbute, viewed from above, with the leather-lined flap folded forward and the hinged compartment ready to be lifted into position. Note the strut on the right for adjusting the slope of the top when in use as a bookrest.

E . A Louis XV Rosewood, Tulipwood and Satinwood Meuble à Écrire Debout

This was made by the Paris *ébéniste* Joseph Baumhauer for Count Karl of Cobentzl, a minister for Empress Maria Theresa in the Austrian Netherlands. Baumhauer received a royal warrant c1755.

It is a most unusual piece and was made to a very high standard, with particular attention paid to the matching of the ormolu framing and the cabinetwork. The main body has an interior of shelves, veneered throughout with rosewood. The concealed drawers at each side have fronts disguised as part of the ormolu framing of the marquetry panels. On the top is a fixed leather-lined slope with a small drawer in the side. It is 3ft 5in (1.05m) wide and 3ft 10in (1.18m) high, so that a person can stand at it and write. This desk is a typical example of the way in which much Paris furniture of the time was supplied to foreign patrons. It was sold on 9 August 1758 by the *marchand-mercier* Lazare Duvaux to M. de Meulan, who was the Count's agent. He then dispatched the cabinet to the Count in Brussels.

C
E
A

A . The Bureau du Roi Louis XV

This elaborate bureau à cylindre, perhaps the first ever made, took nine years to complete. It was begun by Jean François Oeben in 1760, and when Oeben died in 1763 the work was carried on by his successor in business, Jean Henri Riesener. The bureau is signed in marquetry at the back *Riesener H. 1769 à l'Arsenal de Paris.* It was designed for the study or *cabinet intérieur* of Louis XV, where it stood until the Revolution.

The exterior, dominated by magnificent gilt-bronze mounts, is decorated with fine marquetry panels. The roll-top itself is decorated with three cartouches representing Learning and the Arts flanked by Dramatic and Lyric Poetry. The frieze and the double drawers on each side of the kneehole are decorated with ribbon-tied flower sprays, as are the corresponding panels on the sides and the back. The upper side panels are decorated with military trophies, and at the back there is a central gilt-bronze plaque depicting putti holding up a portrait medallion of Minerva, flanked by marquetry panels emblematic of Mathematics and Astronomy. Documentary evidence suggests that the blue and white *biscuit de Sèvres* plaques of the Three Graces on the lower side panels replace royal ciphers which were defaced during the French Revolution. The clock in the centre of the gallery is double-sided.

Oeben, in common with many Paris-based German craftsmen, was renowned for his use of mechanical devices to release hidden drawers and convert furniture to other uses. In this desk the tambour slide opens at the touch of a button to reveal small drawers flanking a pigeonhole and a writing surface divided into three leather-lined panels. The centre panel is raised by a button to form a reading stand, and beneath it is a well containing three drawers. There is also a secret drawer on the lefthand side of the interior.

The desk, for many years on view at the Louvre in Paris and now back at Versailles, was much admired during the 19th century and several replicas were made to a very high standard.

B . Details of lion pelt mounts from the three desks

The hanging lions' pelts used as mounts above the knees of the legs on all three desk. The original from the Bureau du Roi (a) was meticulously copied and finished for the 1786 bureau plat (b), but the 1880s version (c) is a mere pastiche with a rat-like tail.

C . A Bureau Plat

This 6ft 2½in (1.90m) wide desk was made for the *Cabinet Intérieur* at Versailles as a companion piece to the Bureau du Roi and delivered in December 1786. This bureau echoes the cylinder desk very faithfully, particularly in the meticulous copying of the mounts. Both desks were already out of vogue when they were made, but harmony of style was obviously considered more important than high fashion. The central drawer of the bureau plat does, however, tend more towards the restrained neo-classical taste of the 1780s in the simple rectangular beaded border around the marquetry panel. The drawer also projects slightly from the desk, whereas the one on the original is slightly inset. The decoration of the end panels of the bureau plat is worth noting. Gilt-bronze cornucopiae pour forth an abundance of marquetry fruit as on the Bureau du Roi, but the central medallions are inlaid with interlaced *LL* monogram. Evidently the monogram was made to match the ones later removed from the Bureau du Roi and replaced by porcelain plaques.

The bureau plat is well documented and the original costing of the job is recorded. Of the overall cost of 5716 livres, 25% went to Guillaume Beneman, the German cabinetmaker who replaced Riesener as court *ébéniste* in 1785, for the cabinetwork; 11% went on the marquetry, but by far the largest amount, 58%, was spent on the mounts, particularly the chasing and gilding. Making wax models of the original, locks and packing made up the other 6%. After the Revolution the bureau plat was sold at one of the many auctions of royal furniture for 5000 livres – less than cost price.

D . A Detail of the Back of the 19th-Century Copy

showing the central gilt-bronzed plaque with seven putti grouped around a portrait medallion of Minerva.

E . A Bureau à Cylindre, *c*1880

This was inspired the Bureau du Roi but differs in several important respects. The flamboyant mounts on the top part of the original desk – the twin-branch candelabra supporting a youth and a nymph, the clock with reclining putti, the urn finials – have here been omitted entirely, without spoiling the overall balance of the piece, and the slatted tambour of the 18th-century desk has been replaced by a solid cylinder which is more robust and less likely to jam. The overall shape and the ormulu mounts on the base of the desk are closely based on the original, although the lion pelt castings at the corners are noticeably less fine. Some of the marquetry panels also differ.

A

E

A . A Venetian *Lacca Povera* Bureau-Cabinet of the Mid-18th Century

It stands 8ft 7½in (2.63m) to the top of the cartouche. The mitre and cross-key cresting on the cartouche suggests that the original owner may have been a pope. The four figures have not been identified. It has a simply fitted writing compartment behind the fall-front, with cupboards, recesses and drawers in the two-door cabinet and a serpentine-fronted chest of drawers as a base, but its most striking feature is the landscape and figure decoration in brown, green and yellow on a bright red ground with gilt enrichments.

Venetian craftsmen specialized in producing highly-decorative pieces, and the theatrical effect was often heightened by the use of the *lacca povera* or *lacca contrafatta* technique, whereby prints were cut out and stuck to the surface before being varnished. This differed from other European imitations of Oriental lacquer in which the relief decoration was built up layer by layer.

B . A North Italian Walnut Bureau, 1730

The overall delicate inlay is of engraved bone. The main decorative motifs are flowerheads, joined by scrolling tendrils and interspersed with grotesque masks, strange winged beasts and other intriguing devices, including a pair of duelling dwarves at the centre of the shaped fall-front. Beneath the flap is a writing compartment fitted with drawers, and the main body, 3ft 9in (1.14m) wide, is fitted with long drawers shaped in the distinctive manner of South German and North Italian makers of the period.

A

B

C . A German Walnut Bureau-Cabinet

This 4ft 2in (1.27m)-wide piece was probably made in Wurzburg or Mainz c1740. It is made in two parts. The serpentine-fronted top section has a two-door cupboard, four small drawers down each of the shaped sides, and a narrow drawer in the pediment. There are two more small drawers in the sloped sections on either side of the slope-front writing compartment, and three long drawers in the ox-bow-fronted base. The rococo had a strong influence on German craftsmen and this fine-quality piece is embellished with carved rocaille work and scrolls and inlaid throughout with strapwork and asymmetrical motifs in walnut, pear and ebony. The sloping sections on either side of the fall and the multiplicity of small drawers are typical features of German writing furniture of the mid-18th century.

D . A Mid-18th Century South German Walnut Bureau

The strapwork veneer and other parquetry motifs decorate a ground of crossbanding and panels of burr walnut. The exaggerated shape of the three base drawers, canted outwards at the sides and echoed by the small drawers in the upper section, is a distinctive feature of this type of desk. The width is 4ft 2½in (1.28m).

1700-1800

A . An English George II Walnut Library Desk, *c* 1740

This is a small example of its kind, 4ft (1.22m) wide, with a leather inset top, cupboards on either side of the kneehole, one of which contains drawers, and a shallow drawer at each end of the frieze. The monumental treatment of this piece, with its scrolling monopodia topped by lion masks and terminating in claw feet, is typical of a lot of the furniture produced in England during the second quarter of the 18th century. The Palladian style, based on the work of the Italian architect Andrea Palladio (1508–80) had a second flowering during this period under the influence of the English architect William Kent, having first influenced British design in the early 17th century when it was introduced by Inigo Jones (1573–1652). The heavy, classically-inspired forms were very different from the dainty rococo experiments that were at the forefront of French design at the same time.

B . An English Mahogany Library Writing Table, *c*1758

This desk is characteristic of the mid-18th century Gothic Revival. It is now at Temple Newsam House, Leeds, but it was made for the Countess of Pomfret's house, Pomfret Castle in Arlington Street, apparently the only Gothic Revival house in central London (now demolished). The desk is 6ft 8in (2.03m) wide, with a leather-inset top supported on four pedestals decorated with medallions of applied Gothic tracery and with engaged cluster columns at the corners. There are three shallow drawers in the frieze down each of the long sides and each pedestal contains three drawers behind a door of solid mahogany. Most of the rest of the desk is of mahogany veneer on a pine carcase. The Gothic Revival affected the decoration of various types of furniture, but it was particularly well suited to library furniture; tall shelving and large, imposing desks like this one lent themselves to an architectural treatment.

C . An English Mahogany Library Desk, *c*1750

In Chippendale rococo style, this desk has a 5ft-(1.52m)-wide leather-lined top supported on serpentine-fronted pedestals with carved scrolling pilasters at the canted corners. The drawers, which are all fitted with brass handles in rococo style, are arranged in an interesting manner: each pedestal contains three drawers in one side and a cupboard in the other, but all the drawers in the frieze on the long sides are dummies. Each end, however, is fitted with a working drawer in the frieze, one of them fitted with an adjustable writing slope and a pair of retractable circular candle stands. This fine desk, which is very close to designs in Chippendale's *Director,* is a good example of the generally muted English approach to the rococo or 'French' style.

D . A Mid-18th-Century English Mahogany Kneehole Desk

2ft 6in (76cm) wide, this desk has a long frieze drawer and three small drawers in each pedestal. The shallow cupboard in the back of the kneehole is a distinctive feature of these desks, which were particularly popular in the first half of the 18th century.

D

A

C
B

A. An English George III Mahogany Architect's Table, c1765

The main features of this piece are a rising rectangular top adjustable on ratchets and square, chamfered legs with brass scroll brackets and brass castors. It has a frieze drawer fitted with a hinged writing surface and a concealed stationery drawer in the side. Pull-out slides, circular brass candlestands and gilt-metal carrying handles on each side add to the attractiveness of this practical little table, which is of a type produced in quantities too great to have been intended solely for architects, despite the popular name. This one is 2ft 8in (81cm) wide. They are often also referred to as artist's tables, and some are certainly fitted specifically for this purpose, but they are convenient for anyone working with large sheets of paper.

B. An Elaborate English Mahogany Bureau Dressing Chest, c1750

This extraordinary tour-de-force of English cabinetmaking, with its combination of inward and outward curves and heavy mounts, shows German influence but is thought to have been made by the Exeter-born craftsman John Channon. The chest is sophisticated not only in its rococo styling, but also in its design. There are five shaped drawers in the hooded central recess, flanked by two banks of four concave-fronted drawers. The whole of the frieze forms a single shaped drawer. This has a baize-lined slide over fitted compartments. When the drawer is pulled out for writing it is supported on the shaped canted corners which slide forward as an integral part of the drawer. The piece is 5ft 2in (1.58m) wide, and is inlaid with brass and mounted with gilt-brass.

Gilt mounts are rare on English furniture and rococo casting of this quality is rare indeed.

C. An English Mahogany Veneered Bureau Cabinet, c1755

This eccentric piece is also rather large, being 4ft 2½in wide by 7ft 10½in high (1.28 by 2.40m). The upper part is in the form of a four-sided pyramid, with six graduated shelves enclosed by a pair of doors adorned on the inside with mezzotints of great English poets. Beneath this is a fall-flap with a fitted interior behind. The base has eight shallow drawers above and below cupboards decorated on the inside with mezzo-tints of portrait busts of Ancient scholars. The poor quality of the workmanship in this distinctive but rather impractical desk would suggest that it was commissioned from a provincial cabinetmaker, but who dreamed up the design?

C

B
A

A . A French Louis XV Kingwood-Veneered Secrétaire-en-Pente
This piece, 4ft 6¾in (1.39m) wide, was built in two stages with two drawers over two cupboards in the base and a stepped interior of pigeonholes and drawers (one fitted for writing materials) behind a fall front which is supported on steel rods with brass knobs pulled out of the body. This is a high-quality piece with fine rococo mounts of gilt bronze, but its rather awkward two-part design, at variance with the sinuous curves of the applied decoration, suggests that this may be a very early example of the secrétaire-en-pente, which was only introduced to France in the 1730s. Like many early English examples it is fitted with a storage well with a sliding lid in the bottom of the writing compartment.

B . A large French Louis XV Tulipwood Parquetry Bureau en Pente
Stamped for Pierre Migeon (1701–1758), this desk is of the *galbé* (curved) form typical of French rococo slope-front desks, but is unusual for its size (5ft 1in (1.55m) wide) and for the arrangement of the drawers – there are two above the kneehole and three more on the lefthand side, but those on the right are dummies, with the three true drawers opening out of the side of the base. The flap itself is divided into two parts and encloses a *coffre fort* (strong box) along with three small drawers and shelves. The flat surface above the stepped top may have been intended to take a filing box or some other accessory.

C . A French Kingwood and Marquetry Bureau en Pente
3ft 9in (1.14m) wide, this desk of sinuous serpentine form with one long and two short drawers in the base, shows decoration which is typical of the *ébéniste*. The bombé sloping lid is inlaid, like the rest of the desk, with flower sprays on quartered grounds. It is stamped RVLC, the mark of Roger Vandercruse, who was also known as Lacroix, and tended to specialize in delicate marquetry work. He became *maître* in 1755, and died in 1799.

D . A French Louis XV Period Bonheur-du-Jour
Nearly all the surfaces of this desk are decorated with a marquetry of tulipwood, pear, satinwood and others, in imitation of oriental lacquer subjects. The central landscape panel is flanked by flower vases on the doors of the cupboards and there is a more extensive still life on the undertier, which is shaped at the front to make it easier to sit at the desk when it is in use. There are two cupboards and a drawer in the upper section and a single drawer in the frieze. The width of this desk is 2ft 7in (79cm).

E . A French Louis XV Bonheur-du-Jour
This is the work of Jean-Baptiste Vassou, who became a *maître ébéniste* in 1767. It is 2ft 11in (63cm) wide and made of tulipwood and amaranth decorated with trellis marquetry interspersed with flower sprays. The pierced superstructure has three small drawers across the bottom and the writing surface is lined with leather. The frieze drawer contains a series of compartments with flaps.

F . A French Louis XV Black-Lacquered Bonheur-du-Jour, *c*1766
This 2ft 2½in (67cm) wide desk is mounted with gilt bronze and with 17 shaped panels of Sèvres soft-paste porcelain painted with bouquets of flowers. The three-drawer *gradin* with three-quarter gallery is fixed to the body by dowels. The single frieze drawer is fitted with a writing surface that hinges back to reveal a storage compartment and a narrow compartment on the right for writing materials. This is one of about ten similar bonheurs-du-jour by the German-born Paris *ébéniste* Martin Carlin which can be dated by the marks on the porcelain to the 1760s. They are thought to have been commissioned by the influential *marchands-merciers* Simon-Philippe Poirier and Dominique Daguerre, who also bought various other small stands, desks and work tables with Sèvres plaques from Carlin

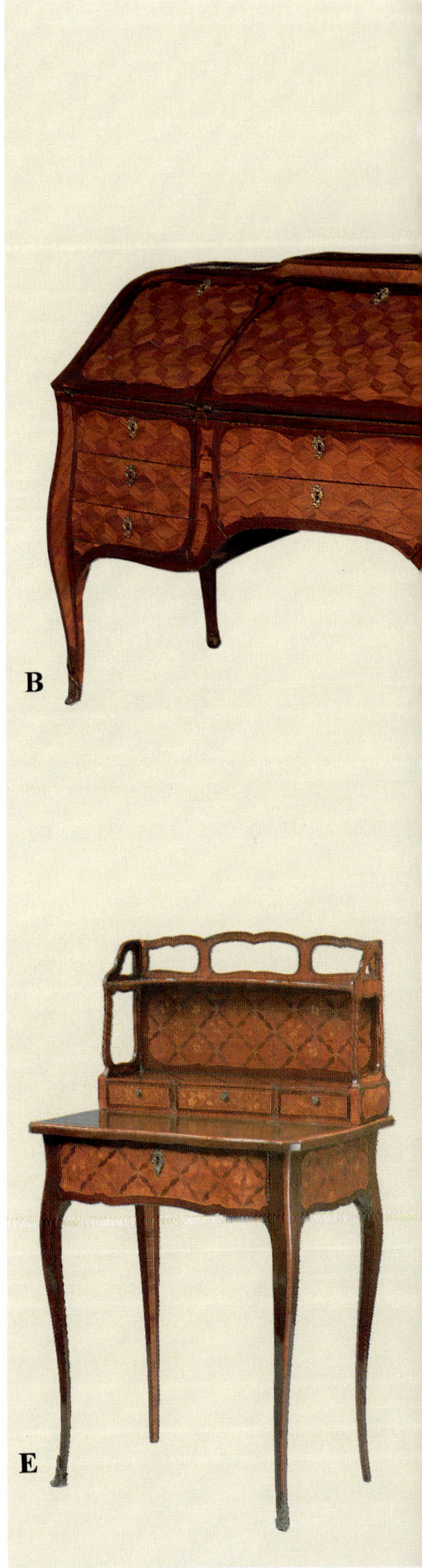

C

F

D

A

A. An American Chippendale Mahogany Kneehole Desk, *c*1760

This 3ft ½in (93cm) wide desk is known to have been made by John Townsend of Newport, Rhode Island. With the usual complement of long and short drawers around a kneehole cupboard, it is a fine example of the blockfront and shell furniture which was developed by the Townsend and Goddard families of cabinetmakers in the second half of the 18th century. The style later spread to Connecticut, Massachusetts and New York. Reflecting the overall blockfront form, the outer shells are convex and the two central ones are concave.

B. An American Chippendale Mahogany Slope-Front Desk, *c*1765–75

It has a fitted interior, four long block-fronted drawers and ball-and-claw feet. The blockfronts of Massachusetts pieces like this one tend to extend over all the drawers without any termination, unlike those on Connecticut and Rhode Island pieces which have large carved shell terminations at the top. This example is 3ft 3in (99cm) wide.

C. An American Chippendale Mahogany Slope-Front Desk, *c*1765–80

3ft 2in (97cm) wide, it is attributed to John Townsend of Newport, Rhode Island. It has a shell-carved blockfront interior of small drawers, pigeonholes and a cupboard. The substantial curved bracket feet are typical of the Townsend style, midway between the simple bracket feet of the Queen Anne period and the showy ball-and-claw feet which characterize the Chippendale period.

D. An American Chippendale Walnut Slope-Front Desk, 1779

This unusual desk has three graduated drawers between fluted quarter-columns at the corners, with a dummy drawer at the top disguising a storage space to which access is gained via a well in the elaborately fitted interior of pigeonholes and drawers. It is 3ft 5½in (1.05m) wide and stands on ogee bracket feet. It is from Pennsylvania and is inlaid with the name Abraham Grof and a date.

B

C

1700-1800

A. A French Louis XVI Period Bureau à Cylindre

This large desk, 4ft 10in (1.47m) wide, was made by Jean-François Leleu. It is of tulipwood, with restrained neo-classical ormolu mounts. As the leather-lined writing slide is pulled forward the solid cylinder front rolls back to reveal a fitted interior of small drawers. There are three further drawers in the frieze. Leleu became *maître* in 1764, having trained in the workshops of J-F Oeben, where he would have worked on the great Bureau du Roi. The flamboyance of that desk belonged to the earlier 18th century but it was one of the first to have the cylinder front, a feature fully developed here by Leleu in the sterner neo-classical style of the last quarter of the century.

B. A French Bureau à Cylindre of the Louis XVI period

The most immediately striking freature about this desk is the particularly rich ormolu decoration on the tulipwood in the form of entrelac, rosettes and stylized leaf borders and unusual ring handles. The solid cylinder front is panelled with a central parquetry medallion and conceals three drawers. Beneath it is a pull-out writing slide with ormolu knobs and three frieze drawers, one of which is reinforced as a *coffre fort* for the storage of valuables. Above the writing compartment is a marble-topped *gradin* of three drawers with a gallery. The desk is 3ft 2in (96.5cm) wide. Elegant cylinder desks of this type superseded the more basic slope-front desks in fashionable circles in the second half of the 18th century.

C. A late 18th-century Bureau à Cylindre

The desk, 3ft 2½in (98cm) wide, was reputedly made for Tsar Paul I of Russia by the German *ébéniste*, David Roentgen, but is now in Anglesey Abbey in Cambridgeshire. The inlaid Russian townscapes on the cylinder, drawer-fronts and side panels are typical of the high quality of marquetry work which helped to make Roentgen's workshops at Nieuwied famous all over Europe.

C

A
B

A . A French Amaranth, Tulipwood and Parquetry Bureau en Pente of the Early Louis XVI Period

It bears the stamp of Pierre Boichod, an *ébéniste* who became *maître* in 1769. Beneath the shallow slope-front, which is bordered with a wide gilt-bronze band cast with flowerheads, the interior is fitted with drawers and inlaid with sprays of flowers. There are no drawers in the urn-decorated frieze and access to the considerable storage space behind it is through a lidded well in the bottom of the writing compartment. Thus a single key secures the whole. Small bureaux of this kind (it is only 2ft 11in (64cm) wide) are often known as bureaux de dame, but slope-front examples are more common in Louis XV style.

B . A French Early Louis XVI Table à Écrire

Only 1ft 7in (48cm) wide, this little writing table is fitted with a frieze drawer containing a leather-lined flap and a pen tray. Beneath is a tambour slide concealing three more drawers. The overall decoration is trellis and Greek key parquetry, ormolu mounts and slender cabriole legs. It is stamped for Léonard Boudin, who became *maître* in 1761. The Greek key inlay and rather formal classically-inspired mounts would have been fashionable elements, married to the more sinuous lines of the rococo-inspired cabriole legs.

A

B

C

C. An Ebony Bureau de Dame by Adam Weisweiler

The gilt-bronze legs are in the form of caryatids with flower baskets on their heads and the interlaced stretcher, a typical feaure of Weisweiler's work, is mounted with a central gilt-bronze basket. It is only 1ft 6½in (47cm) wide, with an adjustable reading slope made from a panel of Japanese lacquer.

This is one of a group of similar pieces made by Weisweiler for the Château de Saint Cloud, just outside Paris, which was bought by Louis XVI from the Duc d'Orléans in 1785. The desk was installed in the private apartment of Queen Marie Antoinette, who, as the daugher of the Austrian Empress Maria Theresa, tended to favour *ébénistes* of Germanic origin like Riesener and Weisweiler. The latter began his career in the workshops of David Roentgen at Neuwied on the Rhine, and arrived in Paris at about the time that Louis XVI came to the throne in 1774. He became a *maître ébéniste* in 1778 and supplied a good deal of furniture to the royal palaces, including this desk, through the agency of the furniture dealer Dominique Daguerre.

The extensive gilt-bronze work on this desk has been attributed to Pierre Gouthière, the most celebrated *ciseleur* of the time.

A . An Unusual English Satinwood and Marquetry Half-Round Writing Commode in Adam style

This commode dates from the mid-1770s and *4ft 3in (1.30m) wide.* The central section, flanked by cupboards, contains three long drawers beneath a writing drawer which is concealed behind herringbone-veneered tambour slides. The writing compartment is fitted with an inkwell, small drawers and a central cupboard inset with a small clock.

The inclusion of a writing drawer in a commode of this type is rare, but the form and decoration of the piece are typical of the delicately neo-classical style that was very influential in England in the 1770s following the lead of Robert Adam and his brother James. Adam was an architect who aimed to create a harmonious relationship between furniture and the room that contained it; he was involved in the design of every detail of the house, from doorknobs to firegrates. His furniture was generally fairly severe in design but lightened by the use of delicate and airy classical motifs. The inlaid urns, honeysuckle, scrolls and trailing garryah flowers which adorn the drawer-fronts are typical.

Adam's neo-classical style was much spare and lighter than the Palladian style popularised by William Kent and others in the second quarter of the 18th century, and less seriously imitative than the classical revival inspired by Thomas Hope in the early 19th century.

B . An English Tulipwood Bonheur-du-Jour, *c*1775

The neo-classical marquetry decoration is in the Adam style. The upper section contains two small cupboards with oval paterae on the doors and a single shelf with a three-quarter brass gallery, while the serpentine main section is decorated around the frieze with stylised flowers and festoons and contains a single drawer. This piece is 2ft 11½in (90cm) wide.

The bonheur-du-jour began to appear in British homes after its great popularity in France.

C. An English George III Mahogany Tambour Desk and Bookcase, Late 18th Century

This is 3ft 7½in (1.10m) wide, with a base of four long graduated drawers on splayed or French feet, a fitted writing compartment with a slide and a bookrest, and a lancet-arch glazed bookcase. The tambour slide, formed from strips of wood with a canvas backing running in grooves, was a feature first introduced to Britain from France in the late 18th century and is illustrated in several of the pattern books of the 1780s and '90s. However, in his *Cabinet Dictionary* of 1803, Sheraton remarks that "The writing tambour tables are almost out of use at present, being both insecure, and very liable to injury". The tambour is certainly much more delicate than the simple fall-front, and also prone to jamming if not made to the highest standards. It is noticeable that makers almost invariably fitted two handles on tambour slides and even on solid cylinder fronts in an effort to encourage the user to open them with two hands and thus avoid undue pressure on one side.

D. An English George III Mahogany Tambour Desk

The whole desk is plain but for some geometric ebonised stringing. It is fitted with drawers and pigeonholes behind the shutter, which rolls back into the body of the desk. The pull-out slide incorporates a hinged bookrest with a baize lining and there is a pair of drawers below.

This light and elegant writing desk on slim tapering legs with spade feet is a good example of the more delicate style of furniture fashionable in England during the late 18th and early 19th centuries. It is very similar to a "Tambour Writing Table" illustrated in Hepplewhite's *The Cabinet-Maker and Upholster's Guide* published in 1788, but the stringing might suggest a later date. It is 3ft 7in (1.10m) wide.

A . An English Library Writing Table, c1771

This was made by Thomas Chippendale for Harewood House near Leeds.

The leather-lined top, 6ft 9½in (2.07m) wide, is supported on two massive pedestals, each with three graduated drawers behind a cupboard door on one side and a partitioned cupboard on the other. There are three drawers in the frieze on one side and a central dummy flanked by true drawers on the other. It is veneered in rosewood with engraved marquetry decoration in neo-classical style; the frieze with a band of linked rosette medallions, the four cupboard doors with vases topped by anthemion and festooned with husks. The insides of the drawers and doors are veneered in rosewood of a deep brown which would have originally matched the now faded exterior. Two hundred years ago the contrast between the light tones of the beech, tulipwood, satinwood, sycamore and holly marquetry and the darker tones of the main body would have been much more striking; nevertheless the desk, with its finely-made mounts of gilt bronze, remains a fine example of Chippendale's work under the influence of Robert Adam. It is important to realise that the rococo, gothic and Chinese styles usually associated with the name of Chippendale were a mid-century fashion. By the 1770s Chippendale's firm was supplying fashionable neo-classical furniture as part of his overall interior decoration service, and many of the finest and best-documented pieces are in this style.

B . An English George III Mahogany Breakfront Secretaire-Bookcase

This bookcase has four glazed bookcase doors in the upper section and three panelled cupboards in the base. The two doors at the ends enclose three drawers each, with a further deep drawer above to match the wide secretaire drawer in the centre which pulls out and has a fall-front for writing. Large library pieces fitted for writing like this one (8ft 9in (2.67m) wide) were very popular towards the end of the 18th century and were produced in large numbers.

C . An English Breakfront Secretaire-Bookcase of the 1780s or '90s

This beautiful piece is 4ft 4in (1.32m) wide and is veneered in satinwood with marquetry decoration in holly, harewood, tulipwood, ebony and pear, and with painted honeysuckle decoration along the scalloped cornice. Below the trellis-glazed cupboards are three deep drawers inlaid with a central patera and hanging garlands of flowers. The central drawer pulls out and is fitted with drawers and pigeonholes behind the green baize-lined fall front. Below are three long drawers, flanked by small cupboards with urn and swag inlay, and the bookcase stands on six tapered feet with simulated fluting. Elegant satinwood furniture of this kind has popularly been associated with Thomas Sheraton, but he made no specifically identifiable furniture and his *Drawing Book* of 1791 was really a reflection of the delicate neo-classical tastes of the time. As he wrote himself, his book was 'intended to exhibit the present taste of furniture, and at the same time to give the workman some assistance in the manufacturing part of it'.

D . An American Federal Period Mahogany-Veneered Secretary and Bookcase

Although this scroll-top writing desk owes a debt to the Chippendale style of pre-Revolutionary America, it also anticipates several features of the desks of the later Federal period. It was made in Salem, Massachusetts, during the last 20 years of the 18th century. The rosette-carved scroll pediment is a slimmed-down and elegant affair centred by a classical urn, and the relatively low upper section is a foretaste of the fashionable dwarf cabinets of the early 19th century. The top drawer of the serpentine four-drawer base is in fact a pull-out writing compartment with a fall-front, itself an innovation of the later 18th century. Inside it is fitted with small drawers, one carved with a fan, and a hidden compartment. Its width is 3ft 8½in (1.13m).

D

B

A

C

1700-1800

A . A Late-18th-Century English Mahogany and Satinwood Partners' Desk

Partners' desks are so called because they have drawers in both sides, the idea being that business partners could sit facing one another. This desk, 5ft 1in (1.55m), has three frieze drawers and six pedestals drawers in one side, with three frieze drawers and pedestal cupboards in the other. Whether they were used in the library, the study or in an office, they were intended to stand in the middle of the room rather than against a wall.

B . An English Harlequin Writing and Dressing Table of the 1790s

Shown open and closed.

Based fairly closely on designs published in the *Cabinet-Maker's London Book of Prices* in 1788, this table has a two-flap top which folds out to the sides to rest on supporting lopers. Underneath is a leather writing surface and a bank of drawers and pigeonholes which rises on two coil springs and can be fixed in position. It is 2ft 1in (64cm) wide when closed. Of the two drawers in the main body of the table the top one is a dummy and the second a dressing drawer fitted with an adjustable looking-glass. Below the drawers are double tambour slides made up of alternate strips of mahogany and harewood. This pattern continues around the base while the rest of the table is veneered in mahogany, crossbanded with tulipwood and with boxwood stringing.

C . A Writing Cabinet, *c*1800

This is a London-made multi-purpose piece of furniture, 3ft 4in (1.01m) wide, veneered in satinwood and sabicu with ebony stringing. It comprises a three-part glazed display case and a base with two long fitted drawers over a two-door cupboard. The lower of the two drawers, shown open here, is equipped for use when dressing, with a central adjustable mirror and, on either side, six wells with silver-topped bottles, three ivory boxes, a hairbrush, a pincushion and various other lidded compartments. Above this is a fall-front secretaire drawer with a leather writing surface and six small ivory-handled drawers, one of which holds a silver-mounted inkwell and a pounce pot. The shaped pediment incorporates a clock flanked by eight brass campana-shaped candleholders. The clock is inscribed *Week's Museum, Titchborne Street,* a reference to Thomas Weeks's museum of mechanical curiosities which opened at 3–4 Titchborne Street in the late 1790s. This seems to have been the source of the 20 or more cabinets of this type which are known to survive. The museum exhibited a variety of strange automata, including a 115-piece steel tarantula, and the spirit of the place is reflected in the fact that many of the cabinets were fitted with an automatic barrel organ in the base, connected to the striking mechanism of the clock and playing a variety of tunes. The maker of this cabinet is unknown, but the design owes a debt to Sheraton's *Drawing Book* of 1791, adapted to echo the façade of the museum itself.

C

B
A

1700-1800

A . An English Satinwood Work and Writing Table, *c*1795

A hinged leather-lined flap folds forward over the dummy drawer in the front and there is a sewing drawer in the side with a hanging bag for storing sewing materials. The book tray above has one long and two short drawers in the base. This piece is only 1ft 9in (54cm) wide. Such pieces often have a detachable book tray fitted with a large bow handle, and are then known as cheverets.

B . An English Mahogany Kidney Writing Table, *c*1800

Writing and sewing tables featuring the kidney or horseshoe shape first became popular around the middle of the 18th century, and examples are illustrated in cabinetmakers' pattern books from Chippendale onwards. This basic, practical shape, with sides curving around the writer, is often augmented by the provision of a writing slope and compartments in the drawer, or an adjustable slope rising from the centre of the table itself. This is a small example, 2ft 11½in (90cm) wide, with a leather-lined top and a single frieze drawer.

C . An Anglo-Indian Miniature Bureau Cabinet

This enchanting piece, with its veneer of intricately engraved ivory was made in the last quarter of the 18th century by Indian craftsmen for the British market. It is only *1ft 11½in (60cm) wide,* with a fitted interior behind the fall front and various lidded compartments and bottles in the large fitted drawer in the base. In the low superstructure above are further small drawers and two cupboards, all decorated like the base, with flowers, fruit and leaves in a continuous band.

D . An English George III Clerk's Desk in Mahogany

The leather-inlaid writing slope forms the hinged lid to a compartment containing two small drawers, and there is a full-width drawer and a shaped gallery in the base. Tall sloping desks of this kind, developments of the simple table desk of the 16th and 17th centuries, continued to be a standard design for clerks throughout the 19th century. Desks of similar design are still to be found in some schools today. This one is 1ft 11in (58cm) wide.

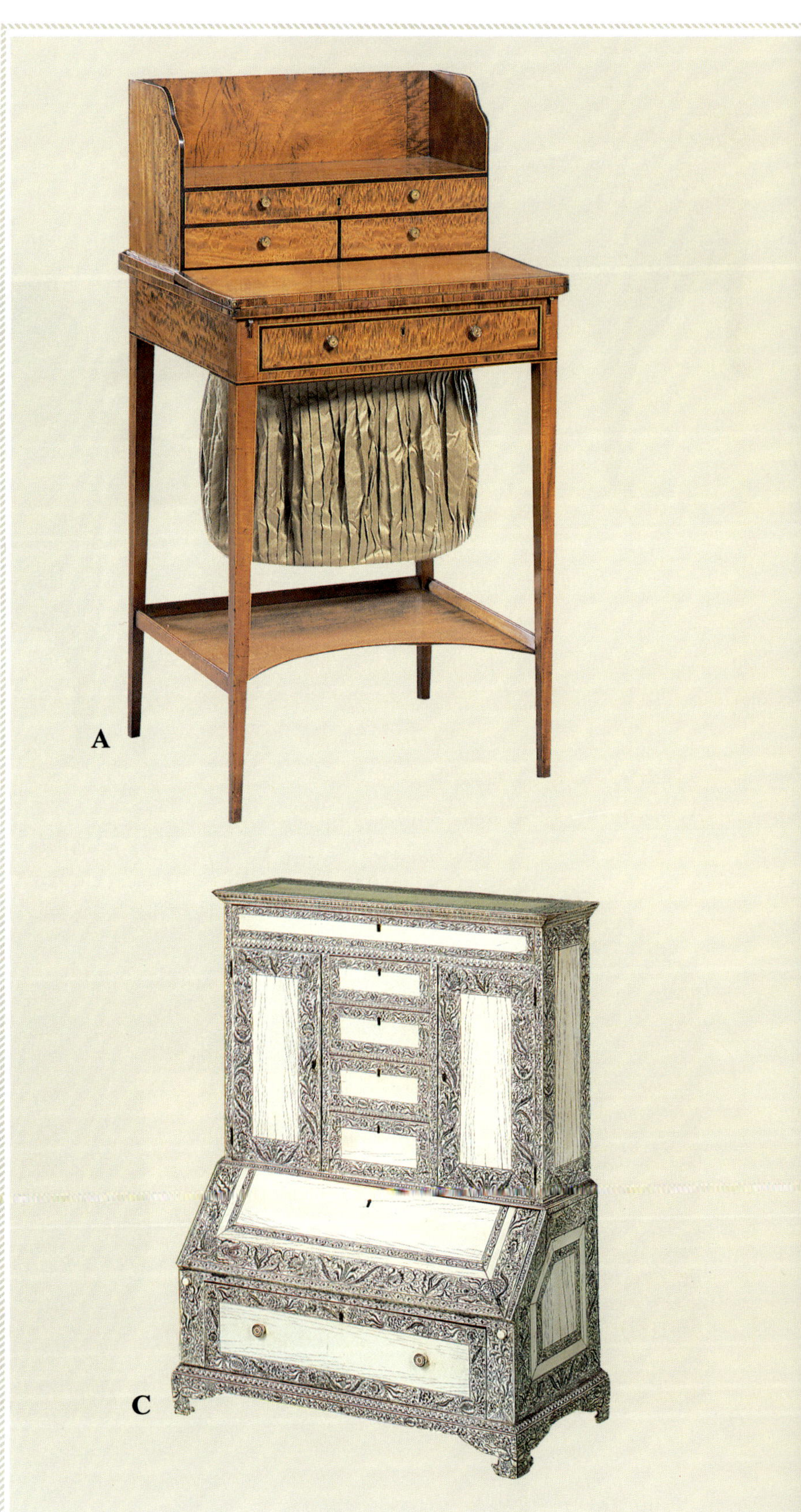

B

D

1800 *to* 1900

For the furniture historian, the 19th century is much more bewildering than the one which preceded it. It was a century when people were more conscious of fashion, and improvements in design and innovations reached a far wider public than had ever been the case before.

It did not, of course, escape without piling more than its fair share of 'overcharged magnificence' onto humble desks, cabinets and tables, but the simpler ornament that was characteristic of the first three decades of the century, was reflected in the Regency style in Britain, the Empire style in France and the Federal style in the newly independent United States. Furniture of this period tended to be more massive and more severely classical than the Adam and Sheraton styles which had preceded it in Britain of the Louis XVI style in France.

Chairs

Regency furniture in England took its name from the political Regency of the Prince of Wales from 1811–1820. Grecian influence in particular was fashionable (the 'Klismos' chair, which can be seen in London's Victoria & Albert Museum, was built from original drawings of ancient Greek seating), and much of the early work from this period was well proportioned and executed. However, in the main, mass production had a negative influence on fine craftsmanship as mechanized furniture manufacture increased to satisfy the demands of England's growing population. Comfort became a prime feature, assisted by the cheaper production of upholstered fabrics. Much of the design between the 1830s and 1890s was based on revivals of earlier styles, including Chippendale, Louis XVI and particularly lighter Rococo, which all finally contributed to an amorphous, often bulbous, look which could be loosely called Victorian.

Napoleonic France saw a decline of refinement in chair design from the time of the Empire (1800–1814) onwards. Imperial Rome was a key influence in Napoleon's reign, and Empire furniture was more for display than function – chairs were rigid and uncomfortable, becoming larger, deeper and more cubic, suggesting substance and grandeur – from the 1830s onwards, the effects of the Industrial Age crept in. As in England, a growing middle-class population provided an expanding market for furniture of all types, and machinery allowed the manufacture of far cheaper chairs. Revivals of Gothic, Renaissance, heavy Rococo, Louis XV and XVI styles followed. Even though talented cabinet-makers were still at work, craftsmanship declined, and most new chair designs borrowed much from earlier times: deep, buttoned and tasselled chairs were rife, as were heavily upholstered pouffes and stools. One exception to this, however, was in the work of the Austrian Thonet brothers. Their new techniques for bending wood allowed them to manufacture one of the most popular chairs of all time – the Bentwood chair.
Elsewhere in Europe, Empire furniture had its influence, but the revivals seen in France and England – and especially Gothic, Renaissance and Rococo – were also prevalent. Influences spread faster, thanks to the trend for international trade fairs, but national tastes continued to stamp revival furniture with individual marks; Italian decorative pictorial marquetry, for example, was copied by the English firm of Gillow.

America's Federal period also relied on classical influence, and the work of Duncan Phyfe, a cabinet-maker from New York, showed this at its best. Napoloeon's Empire style soon reached America, where it merged with native designs and styles. One notable exception to design trends was Shaker furniture, which retained simplicity and functionality.

American chairs of the Victorian period retained influence from Empire styles, but a curious mixture of manufactured and handmade components of pieces lost much of the original refinement of earlier revivals.

Sofas

As in the mixture of styles in chair design, 19th-century sofa design was characterized by experimentation, innovation and often cheap novelty. As new materials and working methods came into general use, manufacturers competed to produce the most arresting designs that would attract the buyers at the newly fashionable department stores and special exhibitions. The cool classicism of the early 1800s, achieved by individual craftsmen, was soon displaced by a miscellany of short-lived forms, ranging from the elegant 'Japaneseque' to the crude 'Adirondack Rustic' of American country retreats.

In 1828, the first patent for coiled wire springs heralded changes of basic form and structure that were to revolutionize the design of seat furniture. In order to accommodate the springs and cover them adequately with layers of stuffing, seats had to be much deeper, imparting a heavier, less-elegant effect. In some mid-19th century versions, there is no visible show-wood, and some frames were even made of iron. Such sofas are usually deep-buttoned and sometimes have additional springs at the back to give the High Victorian overstuffed effect.

One of the greatest influences on British and American design in the early 19th century was Thomas Hope (1769–1831), whose pattern book *Household Furniture and Interior Decoration*, published in 1807, popularized Egyptian and Greek forms which were based on his famed antiquities collection. In his Moorish-style drawing room, he used massive sofas that were continued around corners and finished with impressive sphinxes to emphasize the Eastern theme. A more formal sofa, with sabre legs, was finished off by a frieze containing the twelve great gods of the Greeks and Romans. Other sofa designs were copies of marble sarcophagi whose original austere effect disappeared under bright red, green or yellow upholstery and bronze Eastern of classical emblems that decorated the plainer mahogany. Hope's designs were imitated in a much simplified form by cabinetmakers, who sometimes superimposed his ornament on much cheaper structures to create a somewhat tawdry effect. In the 1830s, A W N Pugin led a Gothic Revival movement, away from ornamental classicism and back to what he believed were the only true styles, firmly rooted in ecclesiastical tradition. He also advocated the use of natural materials, a philosophy that was constantly expounded by John Ruskin (1819–1900).

As standards of living improved, craftsmen and factory workers also developed a pride and interest in their homes and purchased small sofas for their front parlours. To satisfy this mew mass market, a cheaper type of furniture began to appear. These sofas were produced by the busy furniture factories that gradually were replacing the small workshops in the old tradition. By 1900, this new industry was making thousands of identical couches, day-beds and suites. Such furniture was often flimsy and covered with cheap fabric that soon needed replacing.

The 19th century was also characterized by the rise of the big furniture warehouses and department stores where sofas were well displayed, sometimes in handsome settings. Indeed, shopping had become a more pleasurable occupation, and the displays encouraged people to take an interest in decoration, an interest that was fostered by the many magazines and books available on the subject. Many of the writers suggested the use of antique sofas, a taste that the factories satisfied with a proliferation of reproductions in the Queen Anne or Jacobean style.

In the United States, lavishly ornamented sofas in the Rococo Revival style were especial favourites, imparting as they did and atmosphere of great luxury. John Henry Belter, a German emigré working in New York, was to become the great commercial exploiter of the idiom. He combined technology with fanciful designs by patenting a method of laminating thin layers of wood so they could be steam-moulded. Working in a completely different style, Michael Thonet of Vienna also experimented with laminating techniques, producing some of the most progressive bentwood designs of the period for the mass market. Thonet chaises longues, two- and three-seater sofas in adult and child sizes, and hall and veranda settles all poured across the world, the lightness of their construction making them cheap and easy to transport.

Some of the most decorative Victorian sofas were

made by papier-mâché was already popular before its success at the Great Exhibition of 1851 in London. Made from pulped paper, glue and often sand that have been moulded and baked, Victorian papier-mache was painted, gilded and inlaid with mother-of-pearl on a rich, usually black, ground, thus providing a highly dramatic effect. As significant parts of their structures were fragile, relatively few papier-mache sofas have survived, so that any extant example in good condition attracts a high price, especially if its maker is known.

Such excesses of ornamentation and the increasing use of machine carving caused a number of craftsmen to revolt and start up various reform movements in Europe and North America. The best-known sofas in the idiom are the sturdy oak settles by Gustav Stickley's Craftsman Workshops in upstate New York and high-backed versions created by William Morris and his British followers, who also popularized 'Cosy Corners', sofas that were custom-made to fit the two sides of corners. Such pieces sometimes incorporated a high shelf for books or the display of china.

Fortunately, most 19th-century sofas were strongly made and a sufficient number appear on the market to give the buyer a wide choice. Most popular are the cabriole-legged chaise longue and the many variations on the double-ended spoon-back form with attractive show-wood. So popular are some of these mid-Victorian designs that they are being reproduced today. By 1900 a move towards simpler designs had begun. Most factories and cabinetmakers continued to produce heavily padded furniture alongside reproductions of 18th-century designs, so that furniture catalogues and magazines of the 1890s show sofas in a much wider assortment of styles that are available today.

Tables

As with sofas, 19th-century table design progressed from more lavish designs to simpler ones. At the outset of the 19th century, table designers were receiving their inspiration from two significant sources: forms and decoration newly imported from Egypt and the Middle East as a result of the Napoleonic wars there; and the same of Greece, due to recent excavations there (formerly only Roman ruins had been known). In addition, when the French royal furniture made before the Revolution was auctioned, literally millions of exotic pieces were sold cheaply all over Europe, which prompted a wide-ranging taste for imaginative work based on these elaborate, well-made 'prototypes'. Hybrid tables appeared in full force, sporting the likes of sphinx legs, massive hairy-paw feet and scrolling frieze decorations reminiscent of Arabic writing. In general, the output of this period was on a grand scale fitting for the emperor Napoleon's imperial interiors – and those of his relatives – throughout Europe. Early 1800s English Regency tables were as equally exotic as earlier Gallic Regency examples, and were adorned with animal heads and feet and bright wood grains such as black and yellow heads and feet and bright wood grains such as back and yellow striped calamander wood from the West Indies. Ivory inlay and veneer were popular on tables, and brass stringing and inlay often brightened plain woods.

The brilliance of the Empire period shone – and was celebrated – into the 1820s. Tables especially honoured the martial arts, with sabre legs curving outward like military swords, aprons studded with gilt stars on dramatically dark backgrounds akin to smart uniforms, and stretchers carved in rope-twist forms recalling the sea victories of Nelson.

The second quarter of the century, however, saw a return to relative mediocrity. After the fall of Napoleon, the homely Biedermeier style became popular on the Continent, chiefly in Germany and Austria. No-nonsense tables using native woods such as birch and ash appeared, undecorated on the tops and around the deep aprons. Known as *bois clairs*, the woods seemed dull compared with Empire veneers. Much Biedermeier furniture was usually quite ponderous, although good examples of tables were made throughout Europe (including Scandinavia and Russia), which were simple, yet elegant and nicely functional.

At this time, English designs became rather heavy, with dark, dull tops of every possible shape above deep aprons on thick, scrolling legs; in other words, tables thought of as typically Victorian. The 1840s and 1850s were also a period of revivals. Gilt Rococo tables appeared, as did neo-Gothic tables with arches and carved legs, and Tudor Revival oak refectory tables. Somewhat ironically, many of these historicizing designs were of better quality than the originals, mostly due to their having the Victorian advantage of new technologies and high-powered machines. Some of the tables illustrated in this section were included in the catalogue of the 1851 Crystal Palace Exhibition, an international trade fair held in London which presented a cross-section of tables: traditional, revival and innovative. Among the latter, papier mâché was a popular new material. Likewise, table legs took on exciting new looks – from Thonet's bentrosewood examples in Austria to American models featuring cast iron and unusual native-wood supports.

After the mid-century loss of direction, table design branched into the revivalist Arts & Crafts movement, whose primary exponents were critic John Ruskin and multi-talented designer/writer William Morris. Furniture workshops were set up which, according to the guidelines of Morris *et al*, ignored mechanization and modern factory methods and instead looked back idealistically to the medieval past.

In terms of shape and decoration, some Arts & Crafts tables overlapped with country furniture, which continued to coexist – as always – alongside the expensive pieces of furniture made for wealthy, discerning clients. These more rustic tables, such as those made by the so-called Cotswold school, were usually of excellent quality and classic design, but at times they could be mediocre models characterized not by a Georgian simplicity but by heavy stretchers and tops. The folk tradition is perhaps best shown by the works of the Shakers and other retrospective communities and groups in the United States who, rather than attempting to copy the past, simply continued the use of their ancestors' traditional skills and forms. The Arts & Crafts movement embodied the re-examination of style which gave tables a self-conscious look, and also paved the way for the rectilinear arm of *fin-de-siècle* style, which combined art and innovation to create distinctive tables and other items of furniture. Morris's and others' new way of looking at and making everyday objects was to have its effect c1900 on designers and craftsmen in areas as scattered as Glasgow, Vienna and Chicago, establishing the concepts of hand-crafted furniture which were to influence the work of Scandinavian and German designers at the start of the 20th century.

Desks

After the Directoire period in the 1790s, the Empire style of desk design lost some of its austerity but preserved a glossy appearance togehter with masculine, commanding forms suited to the new order. The new sleek styles depended on correct proportion for their effect and in France the *secrétaire à abbatant* usually took on an umcompromising architectural form with flanking columns and a simple pediment. The large area of the flap when closed in the vertical position contributed to the overall uncluttered effect. For the same reason the secretaire drawer or a fitted pull-out slide were favourite Regency solutions in Britain, being neat and unobtrusive when not in use.

On both sides of the Channel, dark and opulent veneers were fashionable, frequently set off by small amounts of bright metal-work – classically inspired gilt mounts beign the norm in France, brass inlay in Britain. In the United States, both Regency and Empire styles influenced fashionable cabinetmakers who found in the serious classical forms a suitable reflection of the aspirations of the new republic. A heavier, more classical style continued to be popular in America until the mid-century, but it had to compete with the influence of the host of revivalist styles which began to dominate European design after the 1820s.

1800-1900

A . A Pair of Regency Black Lacquer and Gilt Armchairs, *c*1800

This combination of black lacquer and gilt epitomizes Regency taste. Technically, the Regency period did not begin until 1811, but the term is used to describe furniture made between 1800 and 1820. The frame of these chairs is beech which has been ebonized to resemble oriental lacquer, although the manner in which the gilt is used is not at all to Eastern taste. The turned legs of gentle sabre form, and the scrolling horizontal arms, give a substantial, almost cubic, effect which characterizes armchairs of this period. The lion paw arm-supports and gilded acanthus scroll at the front of the arm are a simplified version of the exotic high-Regency style to come. These are, in fact, George III chairs made particularly attractive by the pictorial panels which form the back. These are painted in the *grisaille* palette (in tones of grey and black) which was first used to depict classical scenes on enamel and pottery in the late Middle Ages; typically revised and adapted, it works well here. The cane seats, covered with squab cushion, are broadened to accommodate the fashionable Beau Brummel coats of the period.

B . Two American Federal Dining Chairs, *c*1800

Whereas in England, furniture styles progressed smoothly through designers (Thomas Chippendale, then Robert Adam and the broadening influences of Thomas Sheraton, Hepplewhite and other pattern book designers), in America, the Revolution, which ended in 1783, caused major upheaval and a virtual end of new furniture imports until 1790. This limited the natural flowering of the Adam style, and many Federal chairs are based directly on, or closely inspired by, patterns from Sheraton and Hepplewhite, although the combination of decorative features is often unusual. The backs of these chairs, for example, are fundamentally simple square grids which have been embellished by vaguely Gothic panels and central satinwood inlaid panels. At a time when variations on established designs were the order of the day, any originality is greatly to be applauded. The chairs are almost certainly from New York, and are branded 'Anderson' beneath.

C . Two American Sheraton Chairs, *c*1805

American Regency at its best, these chairs are by a great chairmaker of the period, Duncan Phyfe, who worked in New York. The design is bold – drawn from 18th-century styles – yet innovative, combining turned columns, sabre legs and reeded rails on ormolu claw feet. The multiple, parallel carved lines give an almost Expressionist look to this sculptural furniture.

D . American Federal Chairs, *c*1805

These chairs (three of six) from the American Federal Period draws on various English prototypes and moulds them together into a unique American blend. The backs are shield or escutcheon-shaped, a design favoured by George Hepplewhite in his posthumous Pattern Book of the 1780s, while the inlay of husks and fan shapes is reminiscent of English Sheraton style as illustrated in Thomas Sheraton's Pattern Book. The tapered inlaid legs are also characteristic of English furniture from the turn of the century, although here it is mainly the use of inlay which gives the American flavour. The backs are unusual, with vertical, slender splats, and so is the position of the fan motif. English chairs would be more likely to be inlaid on the fronts of the legs; by English standards, these are a little top-heavy. They are the epitome of Federal elegance, the American equivalent of Regency.

E . Two American Sheraton Side Chairs, *c*1810

These chairs, with their extraordinary half-animal front legs are also possibly by Duncan Phyfe of New York. They epitomize American furniture of the time, very good quality English design with highly individual variations.

B

A

D

E

C

A . A Pair of Regency Simulated Rosewood Window Seats, *c*1805

By the beginning of the 19th century, chairs were sufficiently common to make stools redundant as seating in fashionable circles. This pair, however, are clearly fashionable stools and are very well built. They would probably have been placed beneath characteristically long, light, Georgian windows of the time. They have the typical Regency combination of dark wood and brightly-gilded, carved details; even the stretcher, which is almost invisible here, is beautifully finished. It is interesting that these are simulated, rather than solid, rosewood, which underlines the Regency approach that appearance was all, and fundamentals were less important. These stools are simply painted with a rosewood grain, a technique which was developed to a fine art, and it is often difficult to differentiate from the real thing. These stools also show the continuing presence of the X-frame from mediaeval times.

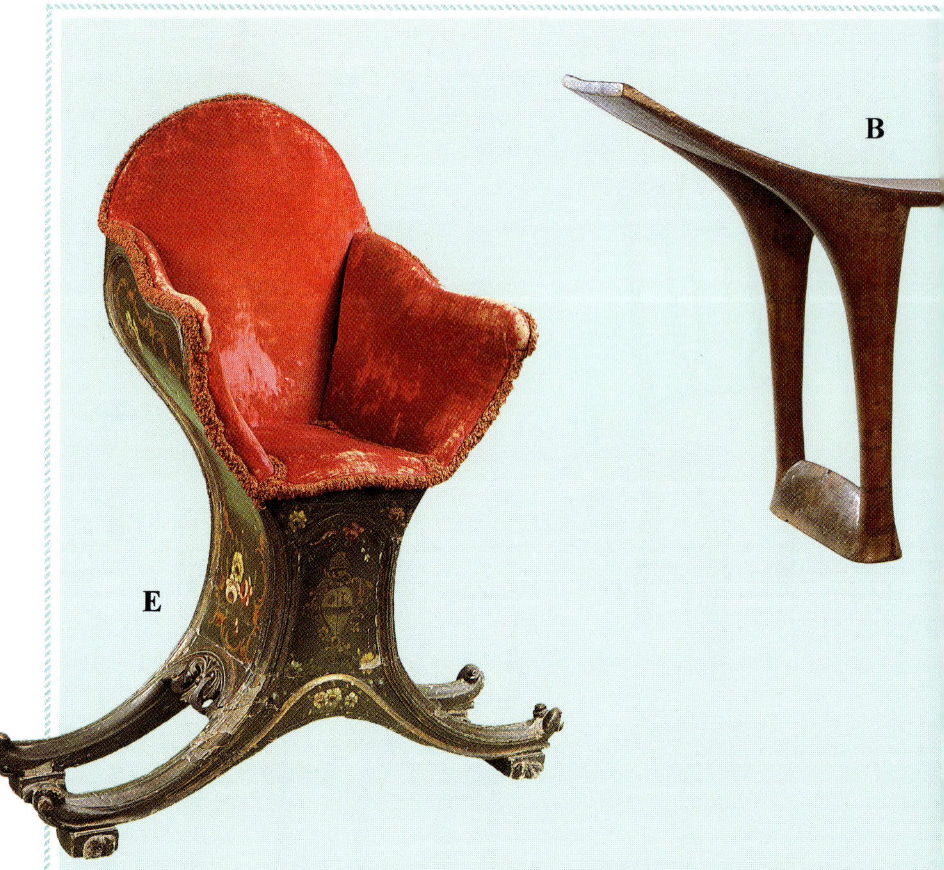

B . A Tahitian Wood Stool, *c*1800

If you were a member of the Iri or Nohara tribes, you may well have rested on one of these. It is, in fact, a rare example, as it is over a yard (3ft/1m) wide and carved from a single piece of breadfruit wood; this would have denoted the high status of its occupant. Primitive art, mainly Pacific and particularly African art, was extremely fashionable at the end of the 19th century, receiving greater exposure than before due to the French African colonies.

In the early 20th century, several painters, such as Pablo Picasso and Georges Braque, utilized primitive vigour as a source of inspiration, and so did Eileen Gray in her furniture for Madame Lévy's Paris apartment. Pierre Le Grain designed a variety of stools in both wood finish and sophisticated lacquer, such as the *Siège Curule*.

C . Two Silver-Mounted Anglo-Indian Chairs in Regency Style

These rather striking and elaborate chairs in Regency style show many signs of their Regency ancestors: the sabre legs, the reeded seat rail, and the rounded back with some organic decoration. It was not uncommon, as we have seen, for non-European craftsmen of the 17th and 18th centuries to produce copies either from a drawing, or from an actual European original; the effect was often charming although sometimes, as in this case, rather bizarre. The British severity of line is swamped here by the elaborately tooled and

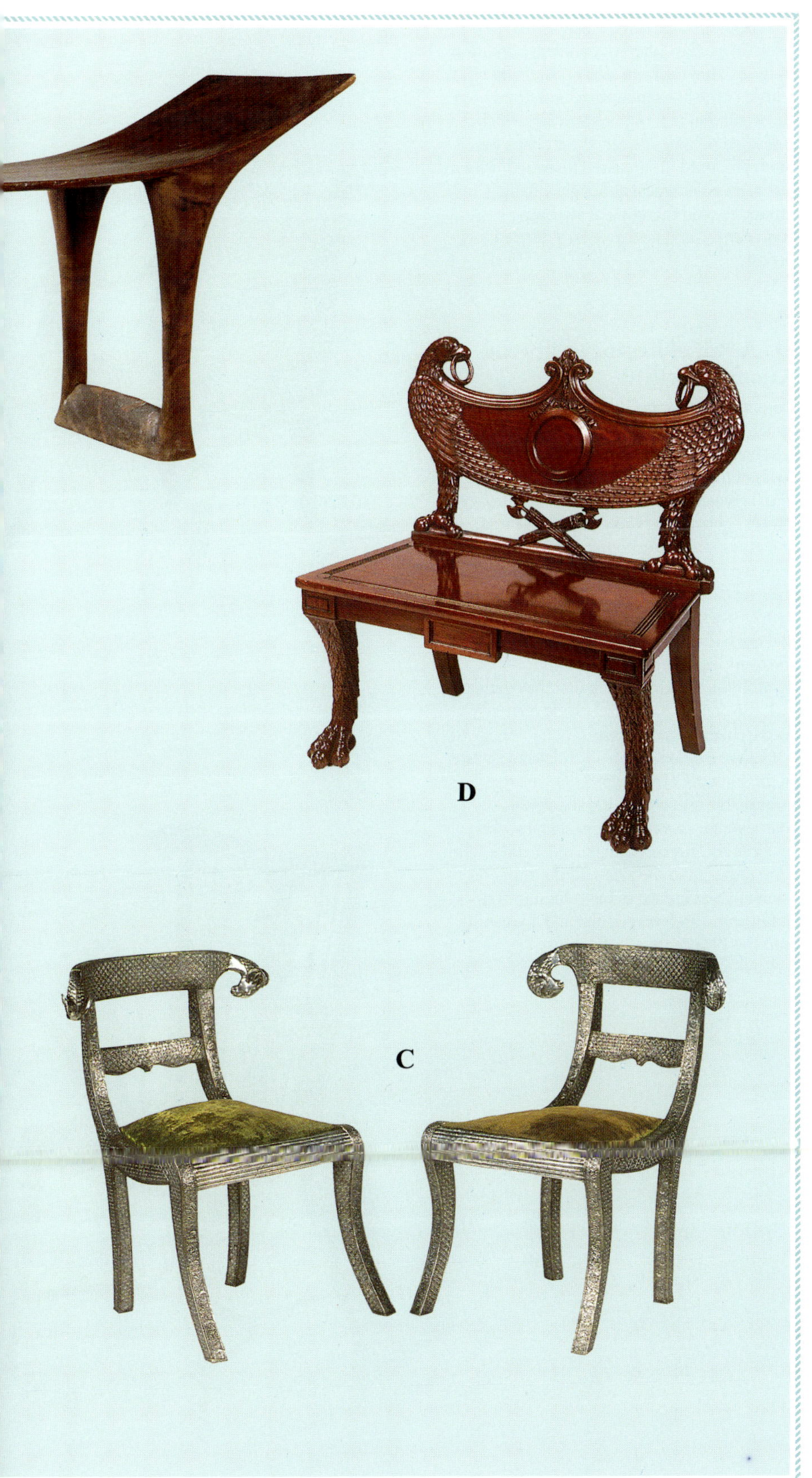

continuously decorated, thin-gauged Indian silver, and the chairs are not altogether successful. All these elements make these chairs extremely hard to date. Colonial pieces sometimes worked very well however, and often gave rise to a native export industry, such as the ivory artifacts of India and southern China. Although the English market does not always appreciate these hybrid pieces, the European Middle Eastern markets are often keen to acquire such goods.

D. A Regency Mahogany Bench, *c*1810

This is one of a pair of benches from Callaly Castle in Northumberland recently sold on the premises; the high price they reached is an indication of the taste of the 1980s. They are remarkable high Regency, a combination of organic forms (the back in the form of double eagles and the feathered paw feet on which the bench stands) and architectural ones (the rectangular seat with its reeded decoration and rectangular panels on the front). Also thrown in for good measure is a circular frame on the back, hung by ribbons, which was perhaps intended as a surround for a coat-of-arms, and a pair of battle-axes crossed in vaguely Imperial style. This is not so much a bench to sit on as a celebration of Regency quality and panache.

E. An Italian Gondola or Carriage Chair, *c*1800

This delightful Italian curiosity is more notable for its elegance than its practicality. As can be seen, it would not be very comfortable and was more of a ceremonial chair to be seen in rather than a chair to be sat on. Even its function is not clear, although it has been suggested that the outswept legs are especially broadened to sit on the edge of a gondola. It is known that these were certainly used in carriages of the time, perhaps in the same manner as a sedan chair. The decoration is principally rococo, flowering gilt all-encompassed by an asymmetric border; it shows how much more pervasive that highly decorative style was in Europe than in England.

1800-1900

A . A Regency Mahogany and Ormolu Armchair, *c*1810

This chair is very much in the manner of George Smith who published his book, *A Collection of Designs for Household Furniture*, in 1808. Curiously, on the underneath of one of the rails is written the name Smith, but while it is tempting to assume this was written by the man himself, there is no proof for this. All of Smith's favourite elements are there – the sabre legs, the scrolling arms and back, the generally cubic proportions (giving a massive look), and the dazzling contrast of gilded bronze on dark mahogany. This comes from the period when ormolu manufacture was at its height; on elaborate French furniture at the time, the gilded mounts chiselled by the *ciseleurs* often cost twice as much as the cabinet work itself. In England, Matthew Boulton founded his firm in the 18th century, which employed literally hundreds of craftsmen producing everything from solid silver to ormolu mounts for candle vases and furniture. There is little to surpass the quality of ormolu from this period.

B . A Regency Windsor Armchair, *c*1810

This is an excellent example of the traditional Windsor armchair form embellished with classic, crisp, elegant Regency decoration. All the uprights have finely-spaced spiral turning, the rails at the back and the splat have architectural decoration and fluting, and even the ordinary spindles have collars. Although the Windsor is thought of as being a country chair, it would have been expensive to buy new, and would generally have been found in a library or well-to-do home.

C . A Pair of Brass Inlaid Rosewood Dining Chairs, *c*1800

These chairs come from a set of eight chairs, comprised of six single chairs and two carvers. Made of rosewood with brass marquetry, they are absolutely typical of the good quality functional Regency furniture which was produced by many makers of the time, few of whom stamped their chairs or recorded their names. These two show many Regency features – the sabre legs, the bowed seat rails which are caned to take squab cushions, and the lines of brass inlay along the rails and legs. The inlaid panels are an English version of a Middle-Eastern or Arabesque design indicating a subdued interest in the exotic, and the back stretchers too, with their cross design and central anthemion, demonstrate a classic motif.

Sets such as these frequently appear in the salerooms today, often in excellent condition in spite of having been used on a regular basis; a little of the brass inlay may have lifted from the wood, but this can be easily remedied. As rosewood became scarcer, these chairs were often produced in simulated rosewood, which was more economical although equally attractive, and this popular style was consistently produced over an extended period.

D . A Pair of Regency Giltwood Armchairs, *c*1810

Compared with some Regency chairs, these armchairs in the style of Morel and Seddon are relatively restrained and owe much to the styles of the late 18th century. While their form is Regency in weight and bulk, they are almost cubic (being wide and deep-seated) and give a strong horizontal impression with their use of large, flat planes. Beneath the gilt they are carved with typical Regency motifs such as the feathering on the side and back and the bulbous architectural decorations on the front legs. Large, generous and comfortable-looking armchairs, they perhaps lack the organic forms and exotic references used in high Regency style.

George Seddon (1727–1801) became master of the Joiners Company in 1795, 'a large fashionable firm employing about 400 journeymen, carvers, gilders, metalworkers and joiners'. Representing mainstream English taste rather than the avant-garde, the company was known to have enormous stocks of furniture, and was popular and flourishing into the 19th century.

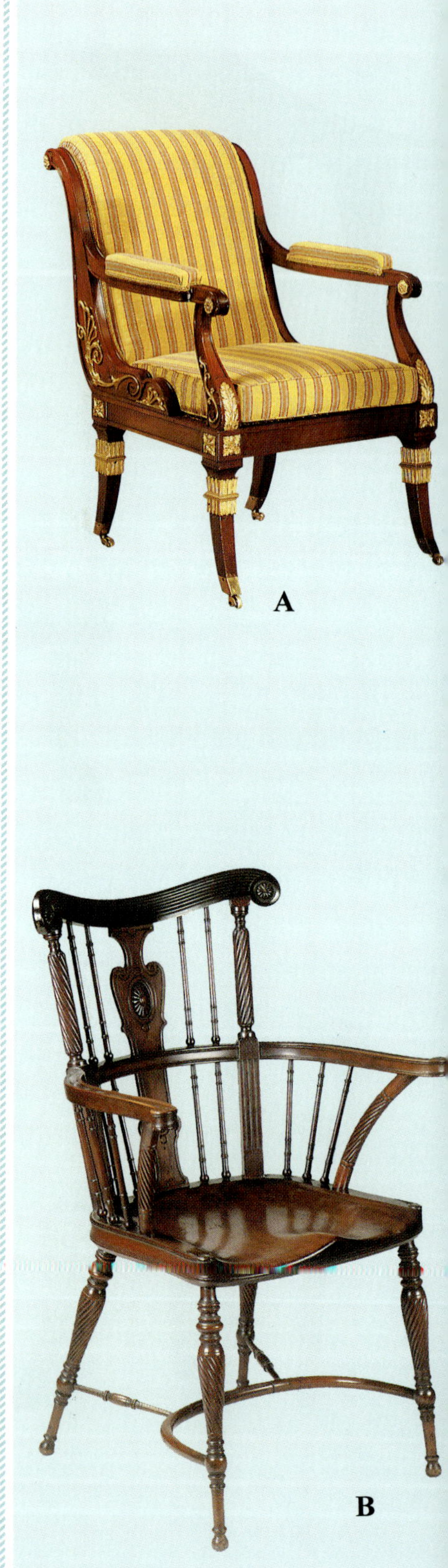

A

B

C
D

1800-1900

A . A Regency Green Painted and Parcel Gilt Bergère, *c*1810

This splendid chair is one of a pair from the collection of the late author, Dame Rebecca West, and bears all the hallmarks of lively and exuberant Regency design and colour schemes. It is very much in the spirit of George Smith and his designs published as *A Collection of Designs for Household Furniture* in 1808. True to the Regency spirit, it is a medley of features and styles, and the gilt lion masks on lion-foot supports typify the fashionable trend of sculptural and organic forms. The broad seat rail gives a monumental air, and the long curving back relieves the otherwise bulky feel. While it is lighter than many armchairs of the period, it nevertheless gives a substantial impression, retaining the roughly cubic proportion which lend it such confidence and presence.

B . A Regency Mahogany Sidechair, *c*1815

The most unusual pattern on the back of this chair actually incorporates a handle as an original fitment; the back itself is very small, encompassing the central anthemion with concave curves, and standing on a stout seat and legs. Here we can clearly see the influence of European styles; the decoration is limited in order to emphasize the flat planes of wood, and the outline, which in this case is unusual, is stressed more than the applied decoration. This chair came from Great Tew Park, in Oxfordshire, and is related to styles in Napoleonic France, and to the continental Biedermeier style, which has clear, simple lines.

C . An Oak and Holly Window Seat, *c*1815

At first sight, this seat by George Bullock does not appear to be a piece of revolutionary design, but in fact this is the beginning of a revival, inspired perhaps by a reaction against the elaborate designs of Thomas Hope & George Smith. Note the date, 1815, and the woods, oak and holly – both are British. Nor is the decoration typically Regency (no eagle's heads, lions' paws or trophies of war such as spears or helmets), there is no ormolu, and the legs are primarily turned horizontally rather than fluted vertically.

This piece and its pair were invoiced in 1817 as '2 oak window-seats inlaid French stuf'd and covered with green twilled calico welted with yellow velvet £23 2/-', and come from the library of Great Tew Park. The

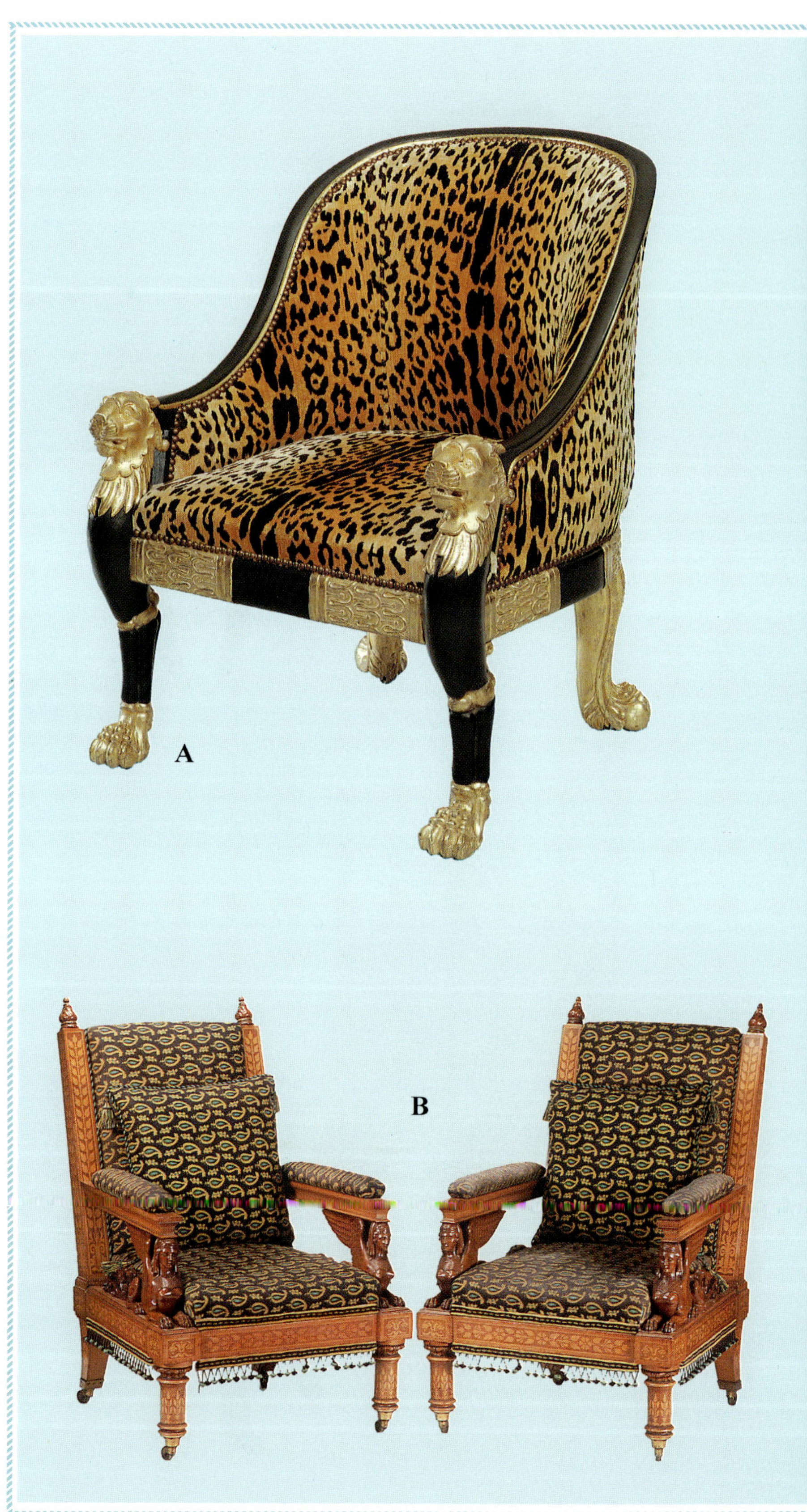

house was owned by Matthew Boulton, famous for his manufacture of Watt's steam engine and for his high-quality metal work in the late 18th century. The house is particularly interesting because it has remained virtually untouched from the time it was bought in 1815. The Boulton heirs were unwilling to modernize anything from the decorations to the electricity; consequently, much of the furniture mentioned on the original 42-page bill from Bullock to Boulton, dated 1817, remains. The library itself was designed by a Gloucester architect in the early 1830s, and is a fine example of the Gothic revival.

D . An Oak and Holly Sidechair, *c*1840

This side chair, executed by G J Morant, is also in oak and holly and probably dates from the 1840s. This is much more pronounced Gothic revival; the tapestry is probably original, with a Gothic design diluted only by a few central flowers, the back is a Gothic arch with carving above and the legs are turned in a vaguely columnar form.

E . A Pair of Early Victorian Armchairs, *c*1840

This pair of early Victorian chairs, again probably from the early 1840s, show an even more pronounced debt to Bullock. Also by G J Morant, they too use oak and holly, but the style of decoration is becoming much more Arts & Crafts, British woods with simple, unfussy British designs. The curious sphinx arm-supports are a retrospective Regency feature, and demonstrate how blurred changes in furniture styles can be. It would not be difficult to imagine that Morant's furniture, or the request for it, was inspired by the earlier, and therefore revolutionary, work of Bullock, who can be seen as a prophet of the Arts & Crafts movement to come.

A. A George IV 'Gothic' Window Seat, *c*1828

This is one of 28 oak window seats delivered to Windsor Castle in 1828 by Morel & Seddon, a leading firm of cabinet makers at the time. They were designed by Augustus Welby Pugin (1812–1852), who was the architect of the House of Commons and a major figure in 19th-century Gothic revival, a style which pervaded the second quarter of the century. Many of his chairs are in natural oak, and are almost invariably carved with the Gothic arch and a variety of tracery decoration. Colouring, another feature of Gothic revival, appears either in the painting of the furniture or the elaborate, sometimes garish, designs on the upholstery. Gothic is constantly revived in the history of applied art, whether by Walpole in the 18th century or by Pugin in the 19th century. The 19th century revival was partly underpinned by the ideas of the pre-Raphaelite brotherhood who felt the true nature of man, and therefore his art, had been reduced by the Renaissance; they logically therefore looked back to before the Renaissance, to the Gothic era.
Gothic was a very popular decorative scheme, used by architects such as Salvi to ornament the interiors and exteriors of buildings. Indeed, the style was so pervasive that it was popular well into the 20th century; the last great Gothic revival complex is the Wills Building in the heart of Bristol University. Finished in the 1920s, it looks like a ruined cathedral from the outside and a Victorian public school from within.

B. A William IV Throne, *c*1835

This William IV throne is exactly the kind of absurdly grand chair sometimes used to bolster a rather humble position. This throne has almost every Gothic motif, the arch, the quatrelobe circles beneath the arm, the mask heads, and the crested backs. It is not very much like a Gothic throne but it is wonderful nonsense.

C. A Pair of Rosewood Chairs, *c*1825

Gothic design extended to all types of buildings and furniture, including this pair of rosewood chairs. They are thought to have been supplied by Morel & Seddon, a name as much associated with cabinet making of this period as Pugin was with architecture and design. The proportions are cubic, with some upstanding Regency spirit fighting back, which was still the dominant style. The arm supports are fluted, with organic gilded carving below; the rails have typical Gothic arch panels; and the legs resemble the windows of Gothic churches. In all, a move away from elegant Regency and towards chunky Victoriana.

D. A George IV Painted Bergère, *c*1830

In this George IV painted Bergère we can see that the Gothic style was not the only one to be revived as Regency declines. The decorative rosettes on the front rails of this chair are in fact the Tudor Rose, and the unusual, swirling, conical legs also emulate the Tudor period. The Tudor Dynasty reigned throughout the 16th century in England (from Henry VII to Elizabeth I) and ended in 1603. The architectural designs of Elizabeth I's reign had as much impact on styles of the 19th and 20th centuries than perhaps even Gothic; while the Gothic style is reflected in noble houses and late Victorian workers' estates, Elizabethan and pseudo-Tudor development influenced everything from Liberty's current building in Regent Street, London, a symbol of the Arts & Crafts Movement, to vast estates of commercially-built houses in the south of England. Tudor revival furniture tends to be grouped with Gothic, but it is an important bridge to the Jacobean revival of 17th-century pierced and carved work.

A

C

B

D

A . A George IV or William IV Mahogany Armchair, *c*1830

It is difficult to precisely date this chair for it has many late Georgian characteristics. It is heavy, and is probably late Georgian or even from the 1830s. The upper half and splat are still reasonably elegant with scrolling arms on lion paw supports; it is certainly of Regency proportions, broad with a deep seat. But the front of this chair is almost grotesquely heavy with thick melon flutes and a pseudo-architectural scroll on the top of the legs. This could well have been the armchair to a suite of chairs and shows clearly how quality continues from the Georgian period throughout the 19th century, and how the large wooden armchair was a key piece in the Victorian move towards comfort.

B . 19th Century Giltwood Rococo Revival Chairs, *c*1830

These two chairs are from a set of 12 from Inveraray Castle, the home of the Dukes of Argyll – the suite was reupholstered in 1871 when the 9th Duke married one of Queen Victoria's daughters. Should the Royal family, on seeing the asymmetric forms, deep carving and c-scrolls on these chairs have thought to themselves, 'What an excellent rococo suite,' they would have been both right and wrong. Although these chairs have all the characteristics of those from the 1740s and 1750s, these are in fact rococo revival. After the exotic Regency period – itself often a revival of earlier forms – chair-making generally moved to reviving earlier styles, one of these being rococo. So what is the difference between genuine and revival rococo? Sometimes nothing, although the average rococo revival chair is probably a little heavier in design, perhaps more excessively ornamented, and sometimes slightly different in quality though not necessarily inferior. In practice, it is very difficult to see the difference on two chairs of the same design without physically turning them upside-down and looking at the quality of the wood they are made of. If it is an original, the construction of the frame and the preparation of the timbers is by 18th-century methods, which include hand-sawn rails, peg joints and properly aged wood. The 19th-century chairmaker would have more sophisticated machines at his disposal, and might well have produced a better quality product with less human irregularity. Although he would have copied directly from an 18th-century chair or pattern, his spirit would have been influenced by his own recent history (presumably heavy Regency), whereas the 18th-century craftsman may have felt something new, French and adventurous was being created.

C . A 'Georgian' Revival Mahogany Armchair, *c*1850

This unusual English armchair is a magnificent but heavy example of baroque run amok. It is a curious combination of decorative motifs, mostly bird-like. The straight lines of the upholstery indicate 1740 or 1750, but the arm supports (apparently cockerels' heads) are curiously carved at the front with classical floral swags. The broad seat rail has a running architectural design above a gadrooned edge, and the broad cabriole front legs have eagle heads on the top flanking a cabochon beneath the shell, all standing on feathered ball and claw feet. The carving is deep and of very good quality, but slightly incongruous. The curious back leg is clearly a later replacement, presumably of an early cabriole.

It is in fact a 19th-century revival, and a very good 'repro' at that. In spite of its oddities, it is a wonderful, and slightly mad-looking, chair.

D . A Shaker Rocking Chair, *c*1840

This chair is typical of the light, strong chairs produced by the Shakers in the area around New Lebanon, in the United States during the second half of the last century. The slat back, the mushroom finials on the arm ends, and the conical finials on the back are common to that area, although the plaited seat and the rocker form are general to Shaker chairs from their communities in New England and the Mid-West.

The Shaker sect spread to America from mid-18th century England in 1774 and flourished in the early 19th century. Their beliefs in the simple life, common property and self sufficiency determined the style of country furniture which developed in their closed communities, and was marketed (by catalogue) from the 1870s onwards. Their belief that 'utility is beauty' now seems familiar, perhaps because it was echoed by the values of the European Arts & Crafts movement of the 1870s, the latter produced similarly retrospective, or traditional, shapes with rustic grace. The earlier the chair, the better the quality, often made with posts of naturally-seasoned maple, fruitwoods or pine. The early examples were frequently dark red, painted, or stained in pale colours; toward the end of the century, however, their individuality declined and stains were used to simulate conventional hardwoods. The Shaker movement has declined in the 20th century, although two communities do exist today and are living museums of Shaker craftsmanship.

D

B
A
C

A . An English Satinwood Explorer's Chair, *c*1840

This delightful Victorian eccentricity is beautifully made of solid satinwood with brass and steel fittings. The maker's plaque is inscribed 'J Alderman Inventor Pattentee & Manufacturer, 16 Soho Square, London'. The extended handles, which are manufactured like the handles of surgical instruments of the period, were presumably for unhappy natives to carry the optimistic explorer through the relevant jungle. I have been assured that it also works well on the ground floor of a very well-known London furniture shop, given the right cooperation.

B . Two Chairs from a Suite of Spanish Furniture, *c*1840

We have seen how furniture in England and France lost its way in the 19th century after the tremendous creative surge of the first two decades. In Spain, the period of greatest affluence and Imperial expansionism was earlier, during the 17th and 18th centuries, and by 1800 it was in decline. This decline had a profound effect on the applied arts in Spain which tended to be dominated by the styles before 1750, especially baroque.

These chairs are a curious combination of the elaborate decoration associated with Italy and Spain, and the sculptural techniques of Andrea Brustolon and Antonio Corradini, 18th-century chair makers and sculptors, who had a lesser influence in England. The legs are astonishing rococo scrolls, upholstered in the characteristically Spanish painted leather often associated with Toledo. The overall effect is bizarre, although not altogether dissimilar to Antonio Gaudi's work of the late 19th century. Although much later, his work was also strongly influenced by Spanish tradition. One can see how the backs of these chairs are influenced by Imperial motifs similar to Regency and Empire, but the combination is pure fantasy.

C . Three Louis Philippe Giltwood Stools, *c*1840

Although French furniture became primarily revivalist in the mid 19th century, there were, as in England, occasional original and elegant creations such as these rope-twist stools associated with the work of Fournier. They bear little relation to anything that came before, apart perhaps from some elaborations of the rococo period, and are an amusing pun, reminiscent of the rustic furniture carved for The Great Exhibition of 1851 by Collinson from solid wood, which was intended to simulate natural tree branches with accompanying foliage. Here the result is elegant, French and amusing.

A

B

C

1800-1900

A . A Pair of Louis Philippe Boulle Armchairs, *c*1840

Louis Philippe reigned from 1830–1848, a period which roughly corresponded with a period of lack of direction in English furniture making; generally, English designers imitated earlier styles, such as Gothic and Jacobean. This particular pair of armchairs is very loosely based on the Louis XIV style, and in the manner of André Charles Boulle (1642–1732). He was a most celebrated *ébéniste* (cabinet maker) of the late 17th century and specialized in (and gave his name to), the technique of inlaying tortoise-shell with brass, or vice versa, for furniture which usually had elaborate ormolu mounts, like these chairs. Here, the high rounded backs and low seats are almost a caricature of the original styles, although the workmanship is still of good quality. European chairs and furniture have always tended to more elaborate decoration, and in France Boulle, as an elaborate style, continued well into the 20th century alongside Art Nouveau, as did Sheraton in England.

B . A Suite of Chinese Miniature Bamboo Furniture, *c*1850

This suite, measuring less than 1ft/30cms at its highest, was perhaps made as a toy for a child. It includes all the basic pieces of Chinese furniture: the altar table, which has miniature enamelled vessels on it, and is flanked by two large armchairs; a painting table in front (painting was a major Chinese scholastic pastime), flanked by a pair of slightly smaller chairs; and a side table for each one, with stretchers forming a 'cracked' pattern, emulating a desirable 'cracked' glaze on Chinese porcelain. The arrangement of pieces is formalized in this pattern for ceremonial purposes. It is interesting to see how real Chinese furniture relates to Chinese Chippendale; note particularly the aprons of these tables compared with 18th-century European fretwork.

C . A Windsor Chair, *c*1850

This good, if slightly late, example of an old friend, the Windsor Chair, perhaps represents the final stage in its development. Like most earlier models, the back is of yew and the seat of elm. The yoke, which forms the top of the back and the central splats, is fairly standard. It is interesting how the rest of the chair has been adapted to include the very Victorian habit of turning. Not only are the turned legs robust, but the central hoop which forms the arms is also on turned spindles, giving a sturdy and pleasing effect. The good colour of the wood and overall good condition makes this stout chair a worthy offspring of its British Windsor extended family: contrast this chair with its 18th-century predecessors, or the American Windsor. There is today a Windsor chair industry based in High Wycombe, traditionally founded because of a nearby supply of suitable forest. The modern versions are generally beech, which rarely achieves the fresh quality or mellow colour typical of earlier types.

D . A Morris & Co Adjustable Armchair, *c*1865

This homely chair by Phillip Webb was based on the sketch of an actual chair found in a Sussex carpenter's workshop. When William Morris, filled with pious enthusiasm, founded his influential Arts & Crafts factory in 1861, he engaged a number of important artists such as the painters Rossetti and Ford Maddox Brown. In practice, Phillip Webb, an architect, was the source of many of the earlier designs, such as this chair, until Georges Jacques succeeded him from 1890 onwards.

The principles of the Arts & Crafts Movement suggested a return to earlier methods of handmade production by people in small communities using good British materials; good functional furniture would be made to fill the homes of the populace at a popular price. The firm operated from 1861 to 1940 and did in general conform to the principles which William Morris had originally set out, 'to execute work in a thoroughly artistic and inexpensive manner'. Inevitably, ideals gave way to practicality and Morris found himself later with a distinction between necessary, 'work-a-day' furniture and 'state' furniture. One could be forgiven for summarizing their production by saying the 'work-a-day' furniture was plain and the 'state' furniture was expensive, elaborate and impractical.

At a time when Victorian elaboration was the norm, Morris & Co made an important contribution, especially in designing fabrics, producing wallpapers, stained glass and tapestries. Their overall interior designs, still on display in the Victoria & Albert Museum, London, represent the more acceptable face of Victorian design. Perhaps his greatest contribution was reviving the notion of the artist-designer, which had a major effect on furniture making during the 20th century and provided a link between the Victorians and Art Nouveau.

C

B

A
D

1800-1900

A. A European Throne Chair, c1880

This astonishing creation is almost neo-baroque in style but is loosely based on Regency ideas. It has a wide repertoire of classical motifs – a sphinx, urn and anthemion borders; the elaborate upholstery continues the decoration in what is almost a *trompe l'oeil* visual illusion. The key to its date are the grotesquely large scrolling legs, and general lack of proportion; it does not quite have the Regency crispness and is probably mid-European.

B. An 'Egyptian' Mahogany Armchair, c1880

This extraordinary chair has been inconclusively attributed to a design by Christopher Dresser (1834–1904), an important influence on design in England in the second half of the 19th century. He was more of a scientist than an artist, at a time when the two were not so mutually exclusive as they are today. He worked as a Professor of Botany for some years, and then as a professional designer, notably of domestic metalware such as the functional kettles and pottery of the Arts & Crafts Movement. One of his main influences was Japan, where he spent some time. He later worked as the editor of the *Furniture Gazette* in which he published his famous, anonymous credo contending that function and purpose, along with economy and proportion, should dominate ornamentation. As with many great theorists, the results were sometimes very successful but often were not: that is the case here. This armchair looks expensive, uncomfortable, probably delicate and perhaps unhealthy. It is, however, a vehicle for delightfully anglicized Egyptian motifs and is great fun, a consideration which Dresser did not include in his credo.

C. The 'Thebes' Stool by Liberty & Co, c1884

If the East India Company in the 17th century was one of the first importers of Oriental goods and furniture on a commercial basis, and Liberty's was probably one of the last to do so before the exotic appeal wore off. In addition to stocking Far Eastern goods, Liberty became renowned as an outlet for Arts & Crafts products, and for near-eastern artefacts which the company itself distributed all over Europe. It gave its name to the Italian version of Art Nouveau, 'Style Liberty'.

D

A

B

C

Although Liberty commissioned well-known designers, most of its stock was sold simply under the name of Liberty. This stool – a relatively early piece of Liberty furniture – was made of rosewood and mahogany inlaid and decorated with ivory, and has a leather seat. There are great similarities to a stool found in the tomb of the Egyptian Pharoah Tutankhamun; which suggests that Liberty had taken an authentic Middle-Eastern pattern, and designed and manufactured a good quality, well-marketed product from it. By the 1890s Liberty had its own workshop, which also made Tudor revival products by well-known craftsmen.

D. An Armchair by Antonio Gaudí, *c*1885

Antonio Gaudí (1852–1926) was primarily an architect and is best known for his wonderfully eccentric Cathedral of the Sagrada Familia in Barcelona, Spain. He studied and worked in Barcelona, the cultural capital of Catalonia, all his life. He enjoyed the patronage of several of the great Catalan families and built excessive private houses and designed several public projects, including the park. His chairs, like his architecture, were highly original and draw on many sources, including the standard Art Nouveau motifs. Swirling lines fluidly describe volumes and planes in the French style of Emile Gallé and details echo the more traditional Spanish sources such as Gothic and baroque.

This armchair, a relatively conventional piece for a man of Gaudí's imagination, clearly leans heavily on the baroque, with its elaborate gilt scrolls which are not dissimilar to the furniture of the 1720s. Even the exaggerated studs on the upholstery have a slightly mediaeval look about them. Gaudi, like other architect-designers, created furniture to fit the style of his interiors, and this chair, designed for the Palacio Guell, Barcelona best fits a heavy baroque interior. As one might expect, his furniture is extremely avant garde, perhaps no coincidence in a city that is also the home of Salvador Dali, the great Surrealist painter and sculptor.

A & B. A Set of Oak Dining Chairs and a Dining Table by Ernest Gimson, *c*1890

This classic English design (136a) could date from the 1950s or 1960s, although its roots in fact lie in the Arts & Crafts Movement. The chairs are ultra-traditional; if they were executed in mahogany, the plain rectilinear backs, chamfered legs, and simple arms sloping to the seat might easily be from the 1780s, a provincial version of Georgian seat furniture. Their strength lies less in what they are than in how they were made. Ernest Gimson (1864–1919) was greatly influenced by William Morris, and although he always worked as an architect, he founded a furniture workshop in Gloucestershire around the turn of the century. Although he made little furniture himself, his workers used traditional British production methods without machines, with one man performing all the steps from start to finish. Gimson solidly refused to mechanize his production, believing that he was working to provide affordable furniture for the ordinary man. In practice, he probably made little profit and his furniture was too inefficiently produced to be enjoyed by any but the well-to-do. Much of his output was even more traditional than these chairs, an example being the 18th-century ladder-back cottage chairs associated with the skills of one of his workers, Edward Gardiner. Although his furniture could scarcely be called exciting, he must be admired for his integrity.

The strength of the original Gimson design can be seen in these two chairs (136b) from a suite by Peter Van Der Waals, the Dutch craftsman who worked for Gimson as chief cabinet-maker for Kenton & Co from 1901 to 1904. He produced these chairs in walnut and rosewood, again leaning towards the plain and severe lines of George III mahogany furniture. This too could easily have been the work of a provincial Georgian cabinet worker, whose simplicity no doubt touched the puritan soul of the Dutch. Gimson was a typical founder member of the English Cotswold School, designers and manufacturers working in that area combined by William Morris' ethics.

C. An Ebonized Sidechair, *c*1890

This unusual Arts & Crafts chair is attributed to John Moyr Smith but shows similarities to the designs of the revolutionary architect and designer Edward Godwin. Although chairs and furniture of this period are often well documented and can often be attributed to a specific designer in many cases, the generic term 'Arts & Crafts' sometimes sums up all that can be said about them. This chair is an interesting amalgam of ideas: it is somewhat like the work of Carlo Bugatti, and even shows some Regency tendencies such as the animal front legs and hooves, or the simple gilt design on the black background. Godwin was one of the first to fully translate Japanese designs for English manufacture, and in spite of the turned stretchers and homely English look there is an austerity here which shows oriental influence.

D. A Secessionist Walnut Chair, *c*1895

There is a restful simplicity about this chair. It seems to fall exactly between the influence of organic, sinuous, floral Art Nouveau, and the harsh, straight lines associated with the Vienna Secession. It was designed by Joseph Olbrich (1867–1908), a founder-member of the Secession who designed the Secession Building in 1898. At the invitation of the Grand Duke of Hesse, he moved to Darmstadt to found the artists colony there, both literally – in the design of the buildings – and also through his own ideological influence. He died there at the age of 41 after a prolific career; his furniture was mostly for the houses he built, although perhaps because of his early departure from Vienna, it has a timeless, universally applicable restraint compared to the creation of his fellow Secessionists Josef Hoffmann, Otto Wagner and Joseph Urban.

B

D

C
A

1800-1900

A . American Art Nouveau Chairs, *c*1900

These are truly transitional chairs; a combination of swirling forms and outlines of Art Nouveau, heavily decorated rails not dissimilar to those of the baroque revival, and a massive frame, very wide and low, a little like Regency chairs. They are by Solomon Carpen Bros of Chicago, US, and were made around the turn of the century.

Art Nouveau was perhaps more of a European style, because of the turn of the century Paris exhibition. In Europe the organic forms and motifs of Art Nouveau had quickly taken root everywhere from the furniture to the architecture, whether by Antonio Gaudí in Spain or Victor Horta in Belgium. The United States, particularly the provincial states, focused more on geometric architectural style than difficult-to-produce, curvaceous, European forms.

B . Two Sidechairs by Carlo Bugatti, *c*1900

Carlo Bugatti's chairs and designs for interiors are wonderfully eccentric and difficult to categorize. They draw heavily on the Near East for inspiration (Syria and Egypt particularly) in their use of applied and worked metals, such as the copper on the left-hand chair, and the extensive inlay of many different materials – here, pewter, ivory and other woods. He had no fear of mixing different materials and methods; the seats on these chairs are made of vellum (fine skin normally used for writing), and hung with tassels.

Vellum became one of his trademarks, as did the circle or half-finished circle, and the chunky geometric look. At the 1902 Turin Exhibition in Italy, for example, the wood of some of his furniture was covered entirely in vellum, and sporadically decorated with abstract and naturalistic designs such as insects and birds. Bugatti originally trained as an architect before opening his first furniture workshop and outlet in Milan in the 1880s. He also produced silver jewellery and other goods. He is perhaps most famous for his sons, Rembrandt – who became best known for his impressionistic animal bronzes – and Ettore, the sports car designer.

B

A

1800-1900

A . An Italian Art Nouveau Suite, *c*1900

This combination of elegance and function typifies the work of Ernesto Basile and Vittorio Ducrot. It was designed by Basile, who was primarily an architect but in 1898 became chief designer for the Ducrot's firm, a sizeable interior design workshop in Palermo, Sicily. They designed extensively in the 'Liberty' style (the Italian version of Art Nouveau which took its name from Liberty's in London) as well as in more organic styles. They completed some prestigious projects and exhibited at Italian Fairs in the early years of the century, but overall, the firm's direction was more commercial, producing good quality, stylish furniture such as that of the Grand Hotel, Palermo, for general use.

B . An Art Nouveau Walnut Armchair, *c*1900

This classic Art Nouveau chair is attributed to, or designed by, Georges de Feure. It evokes the fluid, curvilinear, organic style of the turn of the century. It is not outrageous; indeed, it has the same fundamental structure as a restrained Louis XVI tub chair, and is a reminder that most Art Nouveau furniture was relatively normal and not necessarily innovative or bizarre. On this chair, the uprights are traced with lines in relief and have a suspiciously organic look, confirmed by the elaborate swirling pattern on the seat rail which joins the gently curving legs. De Feure was in fact capable of much more elaborate creations than this, and contributed to Samuel Bing's *Pavillon de l'Art Nouveau* at the Paris 1900 exhibition. He was not a furniture designer by trade, being primarily a painter and engraver; his designs for silver, ceramics and traditionally-influenced graphics won popularity and public acclaim in several European countries.

C & D . A Chair by Charles Rennie Mackintosh, *c*1897

Charles Rennie Mackintosh designed for the improbable setting of a Glasgow Tea Room (Miss Cranston's Tea Room in Argyle Street) a chair (143a) which is perhaps more famous than any other, and which was exhibited at the Vienna Secession in 1900. Mackintosh's personal philosophy was that chairs should fit their setting – in this case, to create an intimate space in which to converse over tea – and to phrase the room in the most appropriate terms. Mackintosh was a revolutionary figure with tremendous impact, particularly on the Vienna Secession (he spent some time in Vienna), and also on Frank Lloyd Wright who developed in a parallel fashion in the United States.

As an object, this chair is a highly original composition of geometric form which describes space in a very architectural way. Its proportions are perhaps closest to a throne, being over 4ft/122cms high, and with a broad splat at the back which gives it a massive appearance.

The same design was also executed in upholstered painted wood, for another Mackintosh Interior (143b). Mackintosh liberated design through his close links abroad, even though his personal architectural output was low. He is best remembered for the Glasgow School of Art building, which exhibits his changes in style (from organic to geometric) as building progressed, and as a source of inspiration for a group of radical Scottish architects called 'The Four'. After his stirring career, he gave up architecture in middle age and went to France to paint.

E . A French Pearwood Chair by Hector Guimard, *c*1900

Guimard was an influential Art Nouveau architect who introduced the work of Victor Horta to Paris, and this French chair has all the curvaceous lines and elegance of French Art Nouveau, a style which involved interior fittings and decorations, as well as the exteriors. He is famous for the characteristically sinuous entrances to the Paris metro.

This chair shows many hallmarks of the Nancy school of design, in northern France. Although the glass maker Emile Gallé was the first President of the 'Ecole de Nancy', founded in 1901 as a type of industrial design cooperative, it had several other important members who also made important contributions. Louis Majorelle, Eugène Vallin, Gallé and also the Frères Daum, produced both furniture and glassware. Their chairs are particularly noted for their classically Art Nouveau qualities of organic swirling loops with reeded detailing and stylized flowers. Gallé claimed that the new style referred only to decoration, and that his structures were fundamentally traditional. Nancy became almost a marketing operation, but the strength of image created constraints which the French designers Suë et Mare rejected in their manifesto.

D

B

A

A . An English Neo-Classical Sofa, designed by Thomas Hope, *c*1800

Thomas Hope (1769–1831) designed this sofa for his house in Duchess Street, London, which he acquired in 1789 and decorated in mainly Greek Classical style. The sofa was intended for the 'Lararium', one of the most curious rooms in the house, which contained Egyptian, Hindu and Chinese idols and curiosities and which was strewn with cotton drapery to give a tented effect. The sofa has a frieze that depicts the 12 great gods of the Greeks and Romans as represented in, in Hope' own words, 'The old stiff style of workmanship, round the Bocca di pozzo, in the Capitol'. Hope opened his Duchess Street house to the public and his designs were imitated widely, although in a much less ornamented and eccentric style. The design for the sofa was published in 1807.

B . A Russian Neo-Classical Mahogany Sofa, *c*1800

Little Russian furniture appears on the international market, mainly because the finest houses were decorated with French and Italian pieces. This example, made around 1800, is in the neo-Classical style and is brass-mounted. The lattice-panelled back gives the sofa an air of lightness and simplicity, characteristic of the early 19th-century interior. Made of mahogany, it stands on square, tapering legs, headed by roundels and joined by stretchers – the latter a necessary feature of such a delicate construction.

C . A French Consulate Mahogany Chaise Longue, attributed to Jacob Frères, *c*1800

Made *c*1800, this mahogany chaise longue is a superb example of the new classically styled furniture design that emerged after the French Revolution. Attributed to Jacob Frères, it was originally part of a salon suite and has shaped rectangular out-curved open sides with turned and tapered lotus-carved crest rails. The rectangular moulded splat is carved with a lozenge that encloses a central mask of Mercury and four paterae, each carved with a perched griffin and berried anthemion, one of the most popular early 19th-century motifs. It has a loose, rectangular cushion seat above a conforming seat rail, It is fitted with a panelled demilune, or half-moon, apron carved with a mask of Apollo. Dating from the Consulate period (1799–1804), the chaise longue stands on tensed animal legs with paw feet. The Jacob brothers made many of the pieces for the Empress Joséphine while she was furnishing Malmaison.

D . An American Early Federal Inlaid Mahogany Sofa, *c*1800

This inlaid mahogany sofa was made *c*1800 in New York. Pieces such as this in classical Federal style are highly coveted and command top prices. A most elegant piece, the sofa has an attractive, slightly bowed seat covered with a loose cushion. It stands on line- and bellflower-inlaid square, tapering legs, ending in cross-branded cuffs. The term 'Federal' is a chronological and not stylistic one, used for American furniture made between 1790 and 1830. It is so called because this was the period of Federalist-Party rule in Washington. The Federal style in American furniture is based mainly on late 18th-century European designs, although Federal pieces often have less ornamentation.

E . An American Early Federal Sofa, *c*1800

America's Federal Constitution, signed in 1787, fostered an even greater awareness of national pride and identity. The new nation favoured a Classicism that was restrained and very elegant, and any sofas in the style are now highly prized. The design of this piece, with its canework panels, is typical of the turn of the century, when the use of ornament was still firmly controlled. The shallow carving of the back rail is typical of the period, as is the use of unadorned but beautifully worked and finished wood.

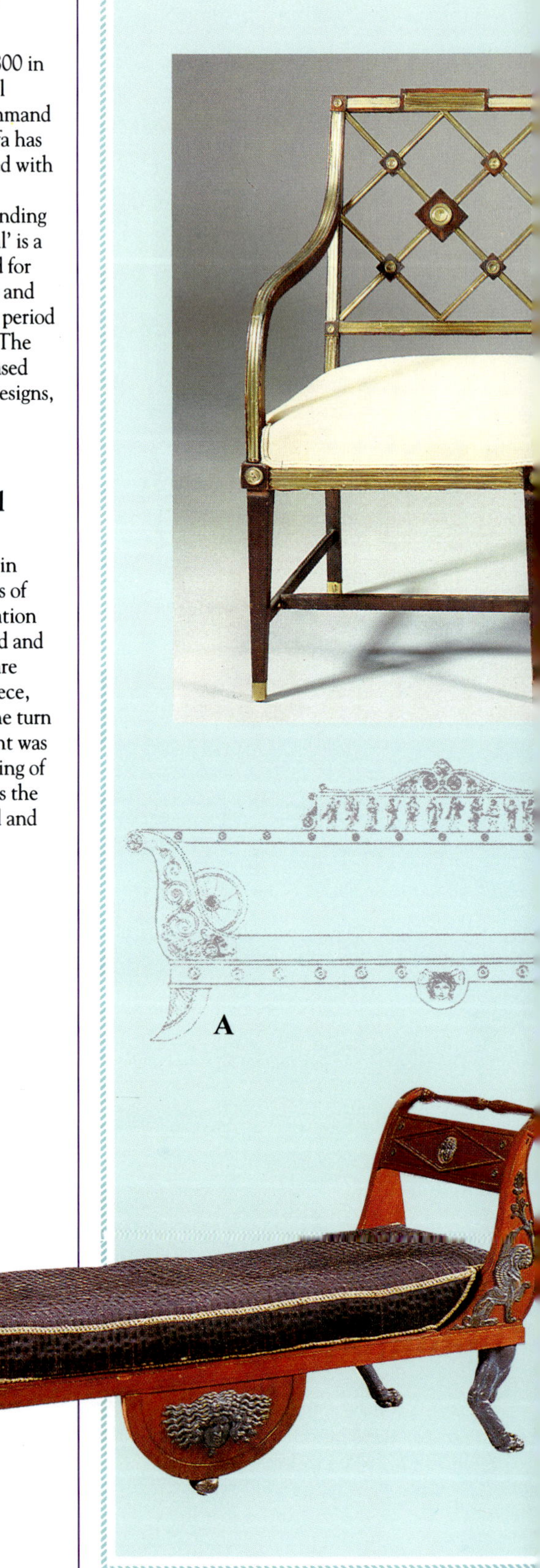

C

B
E
D

1800-1900

A. A French(?) Empire Walnut Day-Bed, after 1800

Day-beds of this type first became popular in France and were copied in other countries throughout the 19th century; they are still made today, although mainly for use in bedrooms. This walnut example has a prettily carved frame with the decorative addition of swags of carved leaves and flowers to the seat rail. Similar designs were produced in the last quarter of the 18th century, but the outward splay of the legs suggests a date after 1800. This type of day-bed was a progression from the separate armchair and matching stool of which Chippendale was so critical. More recent examples have sprung seats with a separate feather-filled squab cushion for added luxury.

B. An American Early Federal Mahogany Sofa, attributed to Samuel McIntire, *c*1805

This simple carved-mahogany sofa, was made in the United States *c*1805. The shaped back rail has carved and punch-work decoration comprising clustered fruit and flowers with swags centring four arrows. The arms are carved with acanthus, and the bowed seat is supported on square tapering legs. The carving is attributed to Samuel McIntire (1757–1811) of Salem, Massachusetts, as it has identical elements to the decoration on a documented McIntire piece in the Museum of Fine Arts, Boston.

C. A French(?) Ormolu and Mahogany Sofa, *c*1810

Ornately decorated with ormolu mounts, this small two-seater sofa is probably French, dating to *c*1810. It has a mahogany frame, and the seat rail features a rope-carved motif, centred with an ormolu pendant of leaf form. The back rail is also carved with linked flower forms, with an ormolu mount of crossed arrows in the middle. Acanthus-leaf ormolu mounts are featured, as well as bosses and ormolu on the legs. Such a piece, with its shallow buttoning and its rather over-fussy appearance, was popular with the new bourgeoisie of the First Empire.

B

A

D. An English Regency Gilt-Wood Sofa, *c*1810

In this Regency gilt-wood sofa, the severity of the rectangular back is broken by the curved sides. The arm supports, surmounted by animal heads and ending in paw feet, suggest a French influence. The sprung seat was a later addition. Originally the squab cushion would have rested on a padded surface. Styles from different countries were adopted much more quickly in the 19th century, with many European craftsmen taking their skills far afield.

E. An English Regency Quadruple Chair-Back Simulated-Bamboo Sofa, *c*1810

The ten legs of this English Regency-period four-seater or quadruple, chair-back sofa are united by plain and turned stretchers. An unusually complex piece, it is made of simulated bamboo. In 1803, Thomas Sheraton had described how beech was turned in imitation of bamboo, and the taste for such faux-bamboo was continued to some extent throughout the 19th century. It was a great favourite in Regency England, especially for the furnishing of interiors in the chinoiserie taste; such pieces were frequently painted or gilded.

1800-1900

A. An English Regency Parcel-Gilt and Oak Sofa, attributed to George Bullock, *c*1810

Deep fringes were often used in the early 19th century to decorate the lower edge of sofas, but were removed in the mid-20th century, when such ornament was felt to clutter the basic line of a piece. This oak and parcel-gilt example is of especially fine quality and is attributed to George Bullock (1777/8–1818), who worked out of Liverpool and London and furnished some of the most important houses of the period with his expensively constructed pieces. Some of Bullock's finest furniture was made of oak, and he was particularly fond of the use of inlays, roundels and turned, tapered legs. Bullock worked in the fashionable tastes of his time, including Gothic, but his most recognizable pieces are in the rectangular Regency style. Sofas of this quality were usually sold complete with loose protective covers of damask chintz or brown calico.

B. An English Regency Rosewood Sofa, *c*1810

The strong, rectangular shapes of English late 18th-century sofas were developed into a more pronounced and exaggerated form during the Regency period. Plain but highly polished back rails accentuated the line. The seat rail, often covered by the upholstery fabric in the previous century, was now revealed, again to emphasize the sofa's geometric structure. This rosewood version stands on fluted baluster legs, the show-wood continuing on the fronts of the arms. The slightly softer English approach can be seen in the rounded legs and the carving on the arms. Sofas of this type remained popular for use in libraries and other 'masculine' rooms until the 1870s.

C. An English Regency Triple Chair-Back Ebonized-Wood Sofa, *c*1815

A fine example of an early 19th-century English triple chair-back sofa, this piece stands on turned legs. The back rails have painted decoration and are separated by trellis-work back rests. The sofa has an ebonized finish and is very much in accord with the Regency taste for a variety of paint effects. Gold on ebony was a special favourite, particularly in the United States, where the combination was used on country-made pieces decorated by itinerant craftsmen.

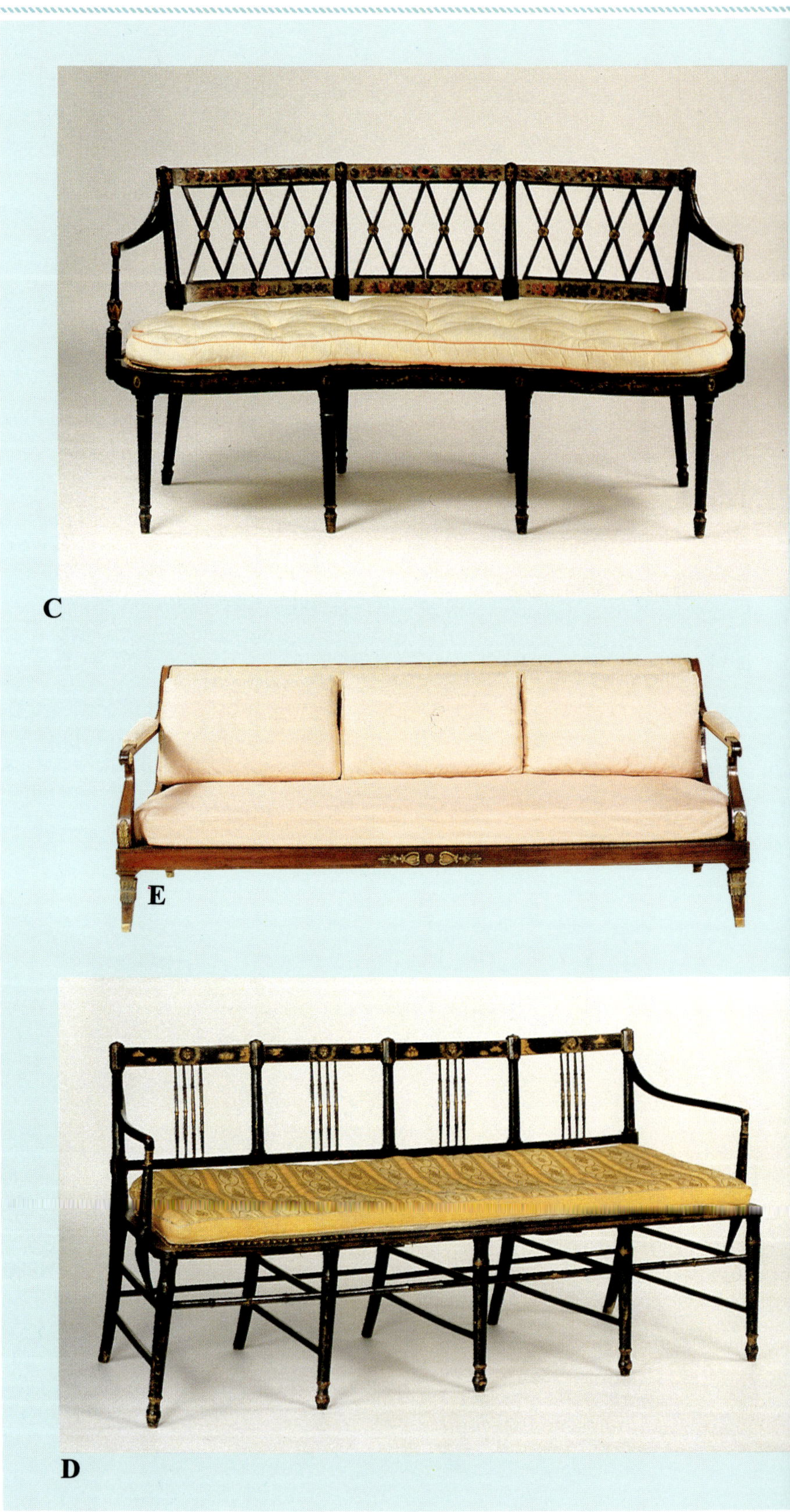

A

B

D. An English Regency Quadruple Chair-Back Parcel-Gilt and Ebonized-Wood Sofa, *c*1815

This simple version of a Regency-period quadruple chair-back sofa reveals the importance of turning in furniture that was being made in greater quantity for the rapidly expanding middle classes. The ebonized and parcel-gilt sofa has a particularly pleasing back rest, although the lower section is in part spoiled by the complexity of stretchers and legs that form the necessary support for this type of structure. The seats of such sofas were often caned, which made them a little more comfortable.

E. An English Regency Ormolu and Mahogany Low Sofa, *c*1815

The simplicity of some of the more progressive Regency designs suggests a much later period, so much so that this low sofa would fit equally well in a period or modern setting. Made of mahogany, the sofa features ormolu mounts, and the seat is centred with a delicate formal motif. The rich colour of mahogany provided an excellent foil for ormolu, while its strength allowed it to be inlaid and carved. Fairly low Regency sofas are popular for use in modern drawing rooms, where the higher, more Germanic versions appear much too formal.

1800-1900

A . An American Empire-Style Mahogany and Canework Sofa, *c*1815

The most progressive elements of European design were combined in New York to produce this mahogany sofa in a cool and reasoned interpretation of the Empire style. Made c1815, the back rail is carved in low relief to provide just enough ornamentation to soften the classical line. The method of constructing the leg supports is highly functional and made the piece of furniture very strong, despite its linear, quite delicate effect. The use of caned panels instead of upholstery contributes to the light but handsome styling. The addition of lion-paw feet is an acknowledgement of the European influences on American design and was added as a conventional rather than an intrinsic element.

B . An English Late Georgian Gilt-Wood Sofa, *c*1820

Although a number of such sofas were originally painted, relatively few have survived in good condition. The Prince Regent had made decorated furniture more acceptable in Britain by his interiors at the Royal Pavilion in Brighton, where paint and gilding were often combined. This elegant sofa, made *c*1820, reveals the lasting strength of the classical movement, especially in the shaping of the back rail. The low scrolled end is a particularly pleasing feature of this example. The carved headrest and the cabriole legs are gilded for greater effect. This piece is an unusual form of a basic design more commonly found in mahogany. Most sofas of this type are fitted with a mattress that is either tufted or buttoned. It is this type of 19th-century furniture which first became collectible, particularly in North America, where it began to be used in fashionable interiors in the 1930s.

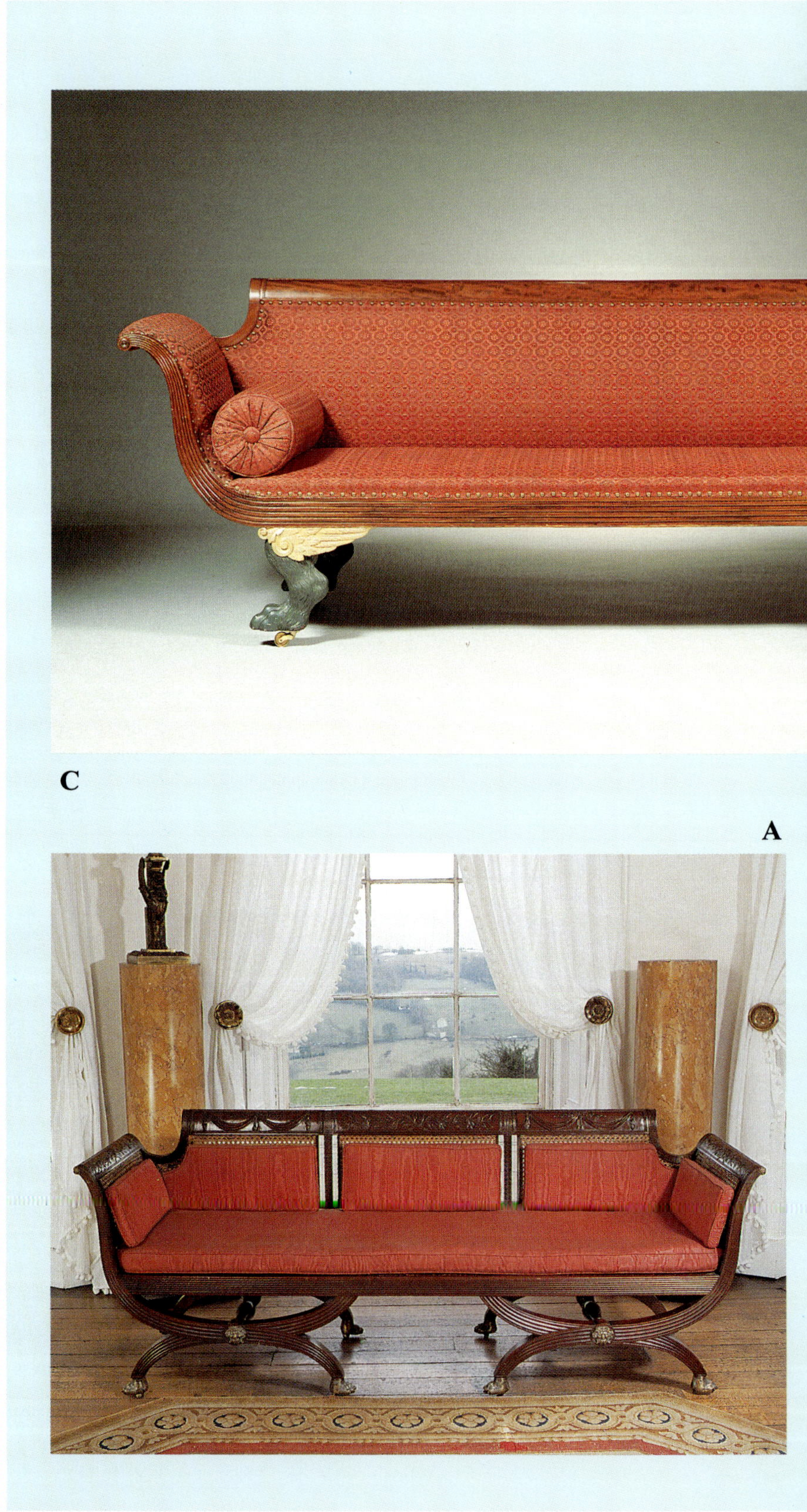
C

A

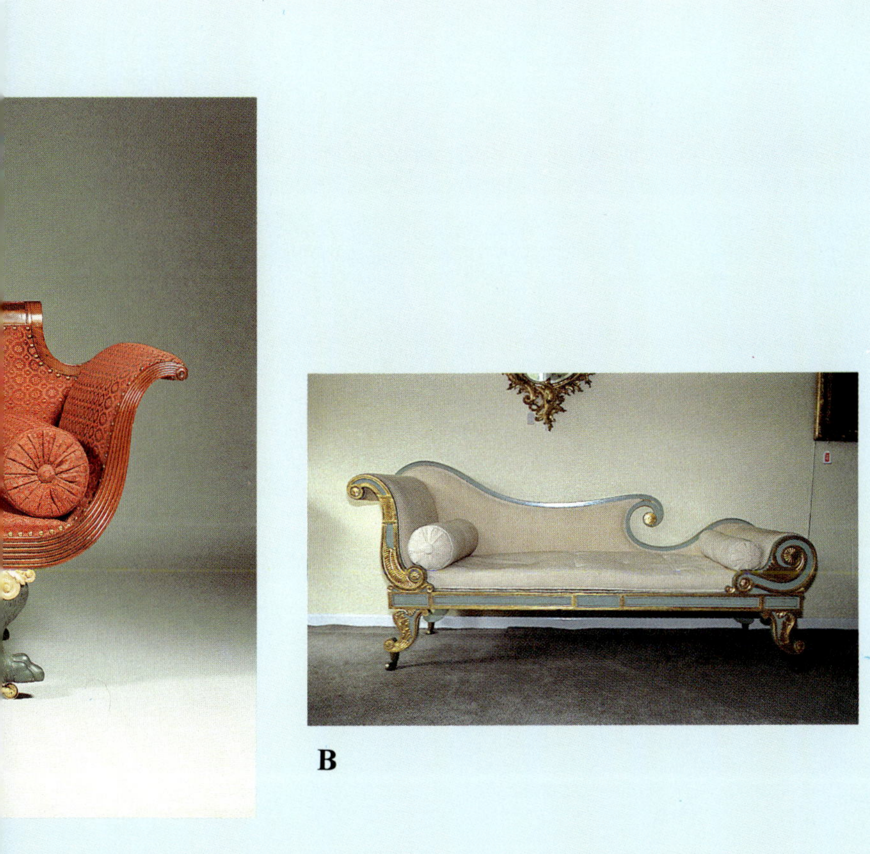

B

D

C. An American Neo-Classical Mahogany Sofa, attributed to Duncan Phyfe, *c*1820

This fine neo-Classical mahogany sofa has been attributed to Duncan Phyfe (1768–1854) and was made c1820. Phyfe, Scottish by birth, was listed in New York City directories from 1792. The line of this sofa is not as pleasing as his best work, although the use of classical motifs on the legs is typical of the fashion for Greek- and Roman-inspired devices, especially popular in New York between 1805 and 1825. Phyfe specialized in light, very elegant seat furniture, usually made of mahogany, a wood that was strong but had a good, rich colour. In Phyfe's workshops different craftsmen were responsible for various aspects of a piece's construction and assembly, a prototype of sorts of later factory methods. The moulding on the front rail is typical of the personal style Phyfe developed from English Regency designs.

D. An English Regency White-Painted and Gilt-Wood Sofa, 1820–30

This sofa is typically 19th century in construction, but was made very much in the grand manner of the early 1700s as part of a suite for an important house. Dating to the reign of George IV (1820–30), the low, rectangular padded back supports three cushions. The seat rail is continued upwards to the outward-splayed arms, which hold the long squab mattress in position. The heavy spiral-turned legs are an unusual feature. The structure is painted white and gilded, and the seat rail is decorated with gilded flower motifs.

A . An English Gothic-Revival Rosewood Sofa, *c*1825

In High Gothic style, this sofa, with its dangerous-looking pinnacles, is the type of structure that was often criticized by the high priest of the taste, architect AWN Pugin. The aim of many furniture makers who worked in the style was to create pieces that resembled the more ornate early Gothic buildings, admired because of their ecclesiastical grandeur. Made during the reign of George IV and dating to *c*1825, this triple chair-back version is made of rosewood inlaid with satinwood stringing. The ogee-arched backs are bordered with pierced strapwork and the fluted pinnacle supports are also pierced. The padded arms are decorated with a carved foliate scroll, and the concave-shaped apron is decorated with unusual tracery. The structure stands on tapered legs ending in square feet.

B . An English(?) Late Regency Rosewood Sofa, *c*1825–35

Rosewood was very popular in the second quarter of the 19th century, especially for the show-wood on drawing-room and parlour sofas. The very simple square lines of this sofa are somewhat in the Beidermeier idiom, although the piece is probably English, as indicated by the carving of the show-wood and the baluster-turned legs. Intended to stand against a wall, this type of sofa was suited to the more formal social uses of the late Regency period. The back has shallow buttoning, and the arms are upholstered in a manner suggesting the styles of the Victorian period.

C . An English Regency Parcel-Gilt and Simulated-Rosewood Sofa, *c*1830–37

Large suites of furniture in much lighter construction were popular in the drawing rooms of the Regency period. Such furniture was designed to display the simple grace of the occupant and the cool elegance of the fashionable interior, rather than for comfort. This sofa, in parcel gilt and simulated rosewood, comes from a suite comprising a sofa and six open armchairs. The quadruple back provided useful seating for a number of people in the much smaller reception rooms of town houses of the period. Caned seats made it possible to move the furniture much more easily, at the same time contributing to the then fashionable light and delicate effect. The trellis-work back and the turning of the front legs show a slight influence of the chinoiserie taste.

B

C

A

1800-1900

A . An English Regency Rosewood Chaise Longue with Brass Inlay, *c*1830–37

A nicely proportioned classical example of the Regency period, this chaise longue is made of rosewood, one of the most popular woods of the time, and is inlaid with brass, another highly favoured form of decoration. The inlay on the seat rail is generously detailed, and there is additional ornamentation on the outward-curving legs. These comfortable day-beds were intended to be moved about the room, for example, from fireside to window, and usually have castors. Although used in the 18th century, castors are much more common on 19th-century sofas. In this instance the metal mounts on the feet are original and contribute to the classically inspired effect. The original upholstery was probably silk or damask, although most sofas of this period have been reupholstered a number of times.

B . A German Biedermeier Maple Sofa

A classic and very fine example of the Biedermeier style, this maple sofa is one of a pair. The term 'Biedermeier' derives from the German word *bieder*, meaning plain and unpretentious, and it was a style with its roots in middle-class taste. The sofa was one of the most important items of furniture in the German house, and a sofa of this superb quality, made of very expensive wood, would have been made for wealthy people. The shaping of the arms is both unusual and skilful, as the round bolster fits within the curve. The use of inlay is characteristically delicate and was intended not to intrude on the simplicity of the basic design.

C . An English Late Regency Mahogany Sofa, *c*1835

Exhibiting a strong German influence, this sofa, made *c*1835, shows some lingering elements of the Germanic Biedermeier style, especially in the flat arm fronts and the geometric shaping of the seat. The purity of the German styling of the sofa, which was in fact made in Britain during the reign of William IV, is submerged in ornament, in order to create a more impressive piece of furniture for homes where wealth had to be displayed. The detachable back has pierced foliate cresting centred by a scallop shell. The vase-shaped arm facings are decorated with foliate scrolls, and the apron is carved with anthemia. The mahogany sofa stands on carved, shaped feet.

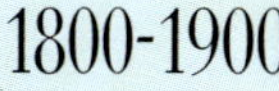

E

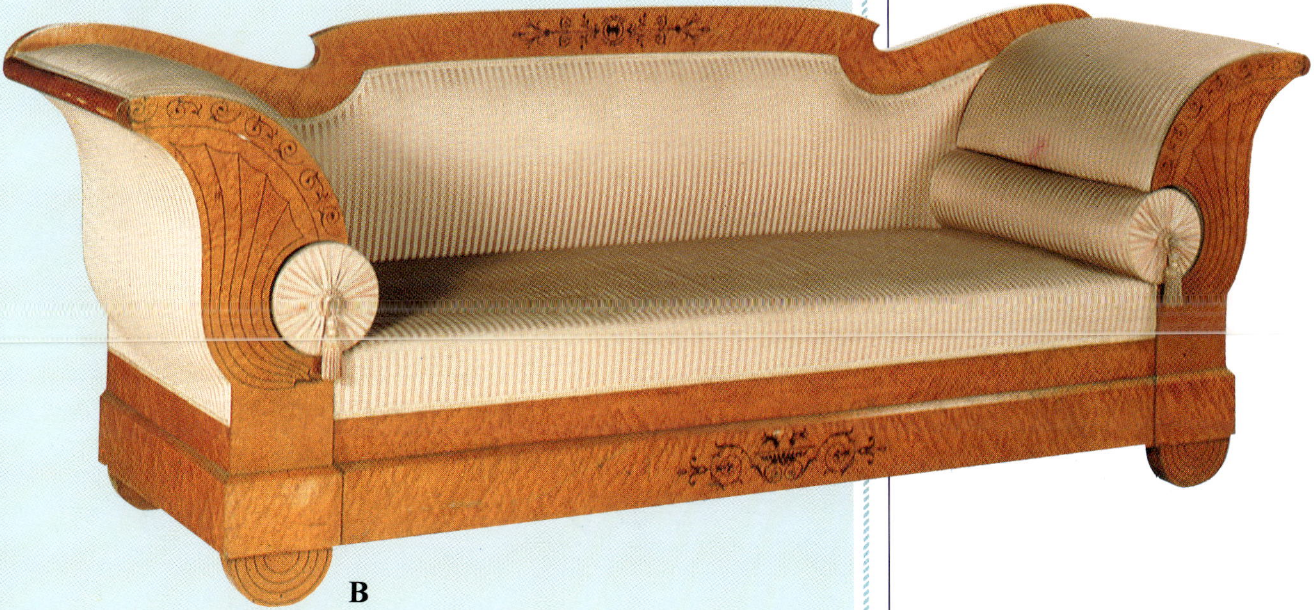

B

D. A French Mahogany Day-Bed, *c*1840

A nicely shaped *meridienne*, or day-bed, this mahogany sofa dates to c1840. Such pieces first became popular in France during the Napoleonic period. This version has a shaped padded back and scroll arms within a plain frame showing a strong Biedermeier influence. The scrolled arms are in the softer style that generally became popular in the second quarter of the 19th century. The moulded arms and the deep apron are decorated with applied gilt-metal leaves and swags. The *meridienne* stands on well-shaped scroll feet. The foot of such a day-bed can sometimes be lowered to give added length, although in this example the section is fixed in position,.

E. An English Victorian Rosewood Sofa, *c*1840–50

This massive and ornate early Victorian sofa is now reupholstered in red brocade. Made of rosewood, it stands on heavily carved cabriole legs ending in realistic ball-and-claw feet. The simplicity of the seat and back rail shows the ongoing influence of early 19th-century forms, although, in this instance, the styles look satisfactory together. The curved wooden arms reveal a more progressive influence. One of a pair, the sofa was probably made for a ballroom or a very large drawing room. Originally, there were probably some matching armchairs.

1800-1900

A . An English Victorian Georgian-Revival Sofa, *c*1840s

A mid-19th-century English-made sofa, this example is in the impressive, somewhat heavy style especially preferred for use in dining rooms and libraries. The shaped back can be taken off, thus allowing the piece to be moved more easily. The short, sturdy cabriole legs and the deep carving of the apron below the seat rail make the design typical of the 1840s, when flat shapes or massive turned legs were more common. Variations on this heavy style of English furniture continued to be made until the 1920s in Eastern countries such as China and India.

B . A French 19th-Century Gilt-Wood Sofa in Louis XV Style

French furniture makers have always had a fondness for sofas with padded oval backs. In this 19th-century gilt-wood version in Louis XV style, the oval is part of the back rail, which has a moulded leaf-carved frame with beaded edging. The scroll arms are leaf-carved and have small, padded armrests. The sofa stands on spirally fluted, leaf-carved turned legs. There is a separate padded cushion. The sofa is from a salon suite that also includes six matching armchairs.

C . A French Louis XVI-Revival Sofa, *c*1850

During the 19th century French furniture makers constantly produced retrospective designs. This piece was in the style of the 1780s, although it was constructed *c*1850. Standing on tapered legs, the gilded sofa has a moulded frame and upholstered arm supports. When reupholstered in a sympathetic fabric or in one of the French machine-made tapestries popular for such revivalist pieces, the structure would have much greater appeal. Similar designs have been produced in France throughout this century and can often only be precisely dated when the original covering is intact.

C

D . An English Mid-Victorian Upholstered Chaise Longue/Settee, 1850s

Some sofas were a combination of a chaise longue and a double-ended settee. Two people were able to sit comfortably on this overstuffed version. The inward curve of the seat is especially attractive, as are the boldly shaped feet. Such designs, whose upholstery was fixed to a wood or even metal framework, were much more economical to produce than those with an abundance of carving or inlay. The introduction of coiled springs made seats much more comfortable and it is this aspect of many 1850s sofas that gives them so much appeal today. This example was reupholstered in the 1930s in an unsympathetic patterned moquette. When re-covered in a more suitable fabric, it will be an attractive

E . A German Rosewood Suite, *c*1850–60

German furniture, although heavily influenced by French designs, was more restrained in effect. This mid-19th-century suite of neat furniture is made of rosewood and is now upholstered in brocade. The complete suite also included eight side chairs and would have furnished a complete room. The sofa stands on rather poorly formed cabriole legs, but has an attractively constructed seat with a treble curve reflecting the shape of the armchair fronts. The three sections of the apron are carved with the same foliate design that is used for the cresting of the back rail.

1800-1900

A & B. Two English Victorian Renaissance-Revival Sofas, *c*1853

Most mid-19th-century sofas of this type have the backs separately fixed, usually with some form of metal bolt. These designs, first published in 1853 in the *Victorian Cabinetmaker's Assistant*, are in the highly ornamented Victorian Renaissance style with impressive crests on the back rails and pendant carving on the scrolled arms. Detail such as the hanging decoration was dowelled in place. These designs could be made of rosewood or mahogany; where rosewood was used, the veneer was applied more thinly and the recessed and delicate parts of the carving could be hatched in gold or gilt. In the top design, the centre of the back, extending to the curve of the moulding beyond the leafage, is made from one solid piece of wood that was 3 in (76 mm) thick. The ring surrounding the head could be turned and later fixed in place and the ornaments on its edge could be shaped on the lathe and then profiled. The head was separately carved and screwed on from behind.

C. An English Victorian Walnut Chaise Longue, *c*1855

An attractively shaped piece, this chaise longue dates to the mid-19th century. It is made of carved walnut and stands on cabriole legs. In the French style, the sofa is from a salon suite comprising a low-seated armchair, an occasional chair, six salon chairs and a pair of footstools. The design of the chaise longue relies completely on the use of curved, organic forms, a style much admired throughout Europe by 1850. The undulating back rail is headed by a carved central motif that is reflected in the decoration of the curved seat rail. In France, similar suites were often gilded, a taste that was never very popular in Britain and North America, where polished walnut or mahogany was preferred.

D. An English Victorian Rosewood Sofa, *c*1855

A good-quality Victorian sofa, from c1855, its serpentine back is framed in rosewood. The scroll-end arms have upholstered rests, and the cabriole supports have scroll feet. There is foliate carving on both the arm fronts and the centre of the back rest. It is reupholstered in a striped brocade which, unfortunately, detracts from the attractive shaping of the piece. However, the show-wood on this example has remained in surprisingly perfect condition and adds considerably to its appeal and value.

E. An English Mid-Victorian Walnut Chaise Longue, *c*1855

An attractive Victorian chaise longue of *c*1855, this walnut example stands on very cursive cabriole legs. The seat rail is centred with a carved device, the scrolled front arm is also carved and the back rest is deep-buttoned. Now upholstered in moss-green velvet, the piece would originally have been used in a parlour or a very formal bedroom or boudoir.

F. A French Ormolu-Mounted Chaise Longue, *c*1852–70

At its most ostentatious, some French mid-19th-century furniture seems to have been designed more for a stage set than domestic use. This regal piece was made during the reign of Napoleon III (1852–70), a period characterized by the lavish display of dress and furnishing encouraged by the court. This chaise longue has a rectangular out-scrolled back and a deep, well-padded seat. The sides are decorated with ormolu mounts representing flower- and fruit-filled cornucopias. These are surmounted with a profile of a classical woman and end in rams' heads. The base is centrally mounted with a rectangular plaque depicting various Muses and decorated with scrolling foliage flanked by centaurs and putti. The foot is mounted with a figure of a swan amid scrolling laurel. The chaise longue stands on winged-lion monopodia.

1800-1900

A . A French Boulle Revivalist Sofa, *c*1860

The seat of this *c*1860 French sofa has a deep shaped apron front, and its top rail has decoration at the centre. Its appeal, however, lies in its boulle finish. Boulle is an inlay of tortoiseshell, wood and brass that was used by André-Charles Boulle (1642–1732), who was *ébéniste* to Louis XIV. Various methods of laying the thin tortoiseshell and brass on to the wooden carcase were employed . Sometimes the brass, laid on a ground of shell, was engraved or combined with other materials – such as pewter or mother-of-pearl – to create very rich patterns. Boulle marquetry was usually applied over oak or deal, and the parts not decorated with inlay were veneered in a complementary shade of wood. Although the method went out of fashion after the reign of Louis XVI, some pieces continued to be made afterwards, producing an effect both rich and eye-catching.

B . A French Ebonized-Wood and Ormolu-Mounted Sofa, *c*1860

Dating to *c*1860, this French sofa is ebonized and decorated with ormolu mounts. Standing on four front and three back legs, the design is unusual in its asymmetry. The high back is also exceptional for the period, and either refers back to 18th-century designs or looks forward to later Art Nouveau. Such a piece would have been made for a very fashion-conscious customer. The use of ormolu was particularly popular with French furniture makers, who embellished their better examples with mounts carved mainly with foliate forms. Although now upholstered with a rather unsympathetic fabric, it would find a ready buyer because of its unusual shape and good general quality.

C . An English Victorian Walnut Sofa, *c*1860

This Victorian sofa is supplied with scrolls and curves in such abundance that it would satisfy the most ardent lovers of the ornate style. The padded, triple-seat back is set within a pierced, moulded scroll frame that separates to form unusual inverted-heart shapes. The carved apron is centred by a feather motif repeated in a simplified form between the three back supports. It stands on moulded scrolled, curvilinear supports. Made of walnut, the piece was constructed *c*1860 and would have been used in a formal drawing room, probably along with matching armchairs. Reception-room furniture of this kind was upholstered in velvet, brocade, silk or black horsehair and edged with gimp.

D

C

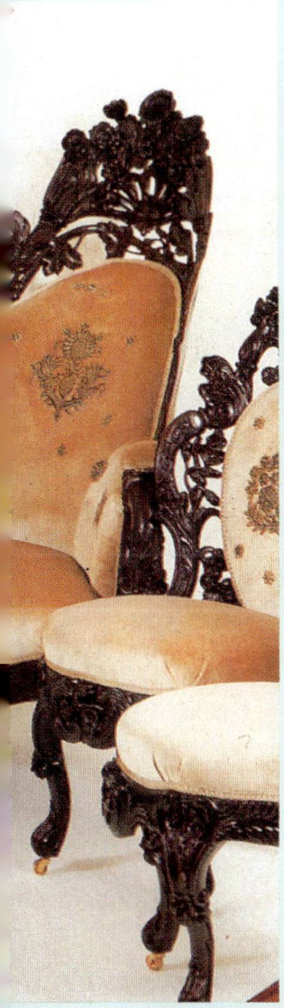

A

B

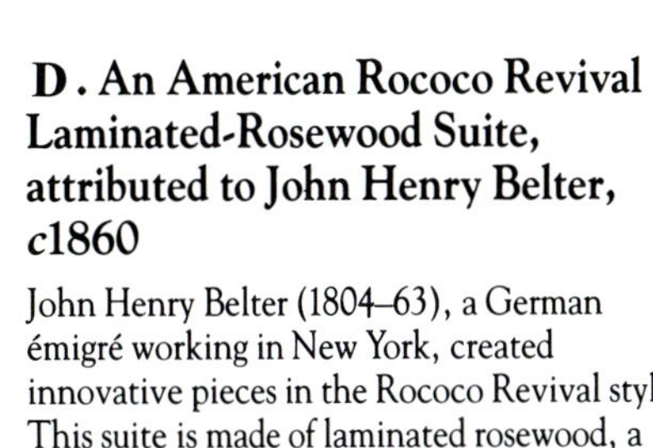

D. An American Rococo Revival Laminated-Rosewood Suite, attributed to John Henry Belter, c1860

John Henry Belter (1804–63), a German émigré working in New York, created innovative pieces in the Rococo Revival style. This suite is made of laminated rosewood, a process he patented. His third patent, registered in 1858, related to seat furniture. Thin layers of wood were glued together and bent under steam pressure in moulds. The resulting thin, curved pieces could then be carved or pierced. He sold his 'Parlour Sofas' in 1855 for $350. This sofa is typical of his work, with its lavish use of scrolls and pierced work in the bold, robust form that was his hallmark. Belter had served his apprenticeship in Germany and the European influence is apparent in his work, although the finished designs are completely idiosyncratic with their hand-carved ornamentation and complex shapes.

1800-1900

A . An American Rococo Revival Laminated-Wood Love Seat, attributed to John Henry Belter, *c*1860

The love seat – intended, of course, for two – was especially popular in the United States, with variations produced by many factories. This fine example is attributed to John Henry Belter, although it should be noted that, to date, no piece of seat furniture bearing his label has been found and there were no pattern-books issued by his firm to help in identification. The love seat has his characteristic cabriole legs and a serpentine front to the seat. The use of laminated wood with pierced work and hand carving is also typical of his finest work. Belter Rococo Revival furniture again became popular in the 1920s, and his pieces are today great favourites in salerooms because of the current preference for High Victorian styles. Love seats are especially favoured because they are small enough to be used in a bedroom or a hall.

B . An English Mid-Victorian Carved and Upholstered Sofa, 1860s

This very elaborate sofa exhibits all the features that were scorned in the middle years of the 20th century. Today such pieces are highly desirable and command good prices – despite the very high cost to reupholster them in the original manner. Such designs were most popular in the 1860s when they were covered in richly coloured silks and velvets. In this version, the front of the seat is left plain and edged with cord and gimp. The oval section at the back has a different edging. Such designs required very highly skilled upholsterers, as the shell-like effect of the overstuffed arms would be a problem to all but the most experienced worker. This sofa is especially attractive because of the pierced-work carving on the back and on the seat rail.

C . An English Victorian Sofa, *c*1860–70

This sofa is a mid-Victorian British interpretation of an earlier French design. The advent of the coiled spring meant that seat furniture could be much more comfortable and they were used even in designs where they were not appropriate, such as this one. The squared seat edged with cord was a popular upholstery of the period, but is only occasionally re-created today when re-covering Victorian furniture because of the additional expense. This type of sofa is very popular, since it combines comfort with a High Victorian effect.

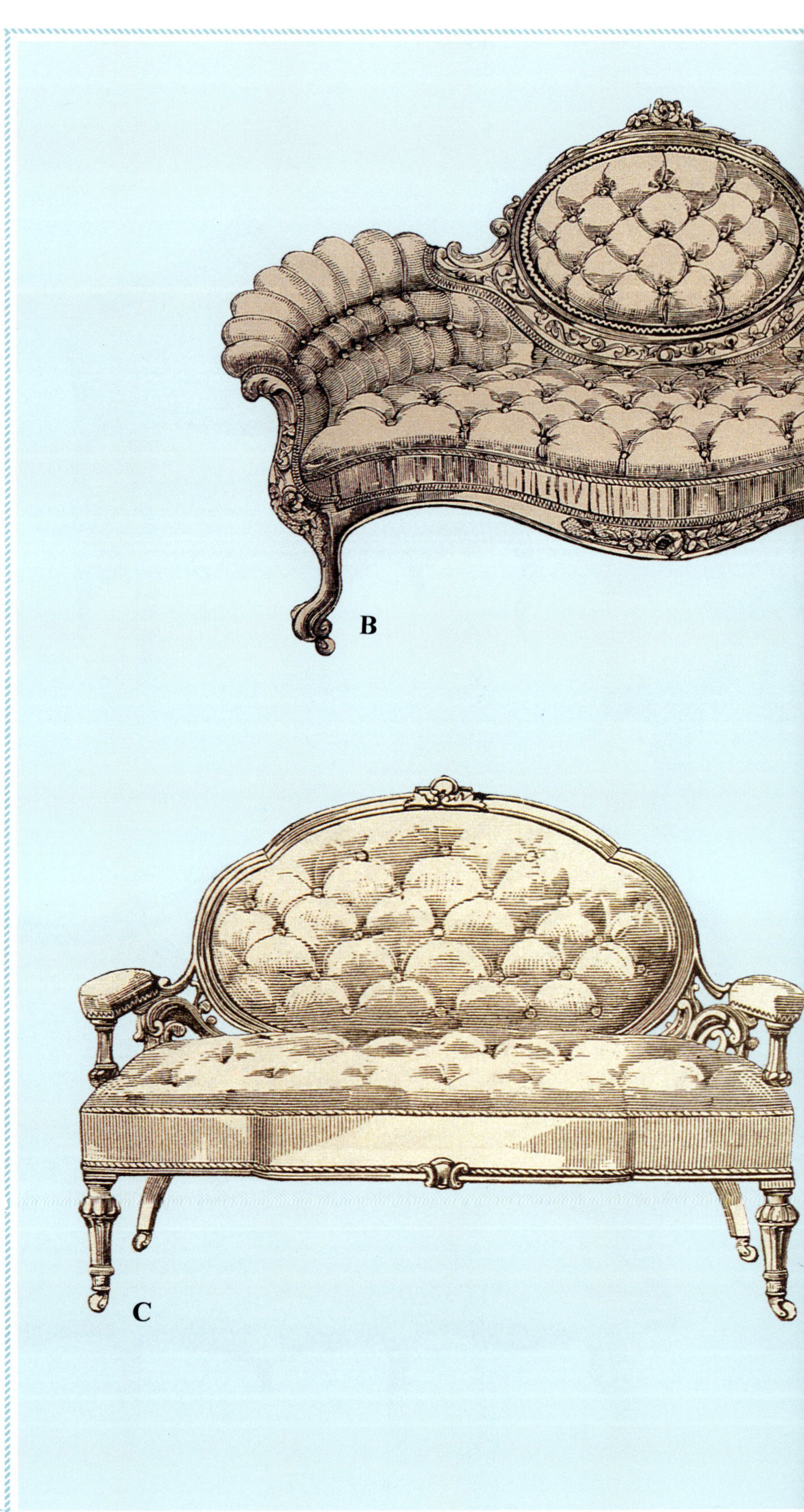

A

1800-1900

A. An English Arts & Crafts Sussex-Type Settle by Morris & Co, after 1865

The most famous of all the furniture produced by William Morris and his associates was the Sussex type of rush-seated chairs and sofas. Such items were sold by Morris & Co from 1865 until the early years of the 20th century, and they became very fashionable among followers of the Arts & Crafts Movement, as well as those decorating in the Aesthetic taste. The somewhat fragile construction was usually ebonized, but examples were also made in walnut and mahogany. Similar settles were made by several other firms, as they could be produced cheaply enough to supply all sections of the market. Despite the fact that they were not comfortable, these settles were originally intended for use in the drawing room, sometimes accompanied by occasional chairs and armchairs. Today they are more often found in dining rooms or halls.

B. An English Mid-Victorian Walnut Sofa, *c*1865–75

The attractive shaping of the back of this walnut sofa makes it desirable to anyone furnishing a room in the mid-Victorian manner. Though primarily intended for one person to recline on in the parlour or drawing room, provision was made to seat a second person by rounding and padding the foot. Standing on cabriole legs that continue into scrolled arms, the piece typifies the most decorative furniture of the period made in Britain for middle-class homes.

C. An English George II-Style Walnut Sofa with Needlepoint Upholstery, probably 19th century

As 18th-century sofas in fairly simple styles have been favourites with interior decorators for such a long time, there are many examples extant that have been much restored or slightly adapted. This colourful model, in George II style, is partially composed of 18th-century elements. The walnut cabriole legs have conventional shell carving on the knees and end in ball-and-claw feet. The serpentine cresting above the padded back sweeps to the less satisfactory padded out-scrolled sides. The gros- and petit-point needlework is an especially attractive feature and depicts on several panels a series of figures in Arcadian dress in romantic landscapes. The upholstery is finished with braid and close nailing.

D. An English George II-Style Mahogany and Parcel-Gilt Day-Bed

This day-bed, in George II style, is made of mahogany and parcel-gilt. It has a pierced and carved apron below the gilt Greek key pattern of the seat rail. The cabriole legs end in lion-paw feet, Benjamin Goodison (d.1767) supplied two day-beds of this design for the picture gallery at Longford Castle in Wiltshire in 1740, although these were equipped with a graduated pile of cushions at the head and foot. Fine 18th-century designs have never gone out of fashion completely, and many superb copies were made in the 19th century, when the quality of craftsmanship was still attainable and the knowledge of old working methods still at hand.

E. A French Boulle and Ormolu Revivalist Sofa, *c*1870

This French-made sofa dates to around 1870, but is made in the style of the late 18th century. Such an impressive revivalist piece reveals the skill of the *ébéniste* to full advantage and would have been very expensive when made, as its surface was finished with boulle marquetry. As boulle was, by nature, fragile, it was usually fitted with ormolu mounts which, besides being decorative, protected the corners and more exposed sections of a piece. The application of ormolu often became an end in itself, with fully gilt sections frequently used for their decorative value rather than practical necessity.

A

B

E
D
C

A . An English Victorian Curved Sofa by Hampton & Sons, *c*1870

A much more lavish interpretation of a High Victorian curved sofa; such a piece was popular for use in a bay window. Some very large half-round versions were especially made to fit inside windows of that type. The deep buttoning, fringe and ornamental tassels of the overstuffed back all contribute to a piece of furniture that would have been relatively expensive when first produced. Hamptons, established in 1830, included this design in their catalogue of 'Cabinet Furniture', which also stated that their upholstery department was 'composed of English, French and German cutters-out and stuffers, therefore they are enabled for style and taste to compete with any house in the trade'.

B . A French 19th-Century Gilt-Wood Sofa in Louis XVI Style, *c*1870

This gilt-wood sofa is from a French Louis XVI-style suite constructed in the 19th century. The acanthus-carved arms, with padded rests, continue to the delicate stop-fluted legs. The sofa retains its original Aubusson tapestry, which depicts two animal scenes with dogs, birds and serpents set within double borders. The manufacture of tapestry at Aubusson was helped during the reign of Louis XV, when pastoral scenes and landscapes were most popular. In the 19th century, coverings for sofas were produced in quantity, although pieces in good condition are in short supply today. Aubusson tapestry was made for a wide, middle-class market rather than for palaces, and the subjects have a restrained, though charming, quality.

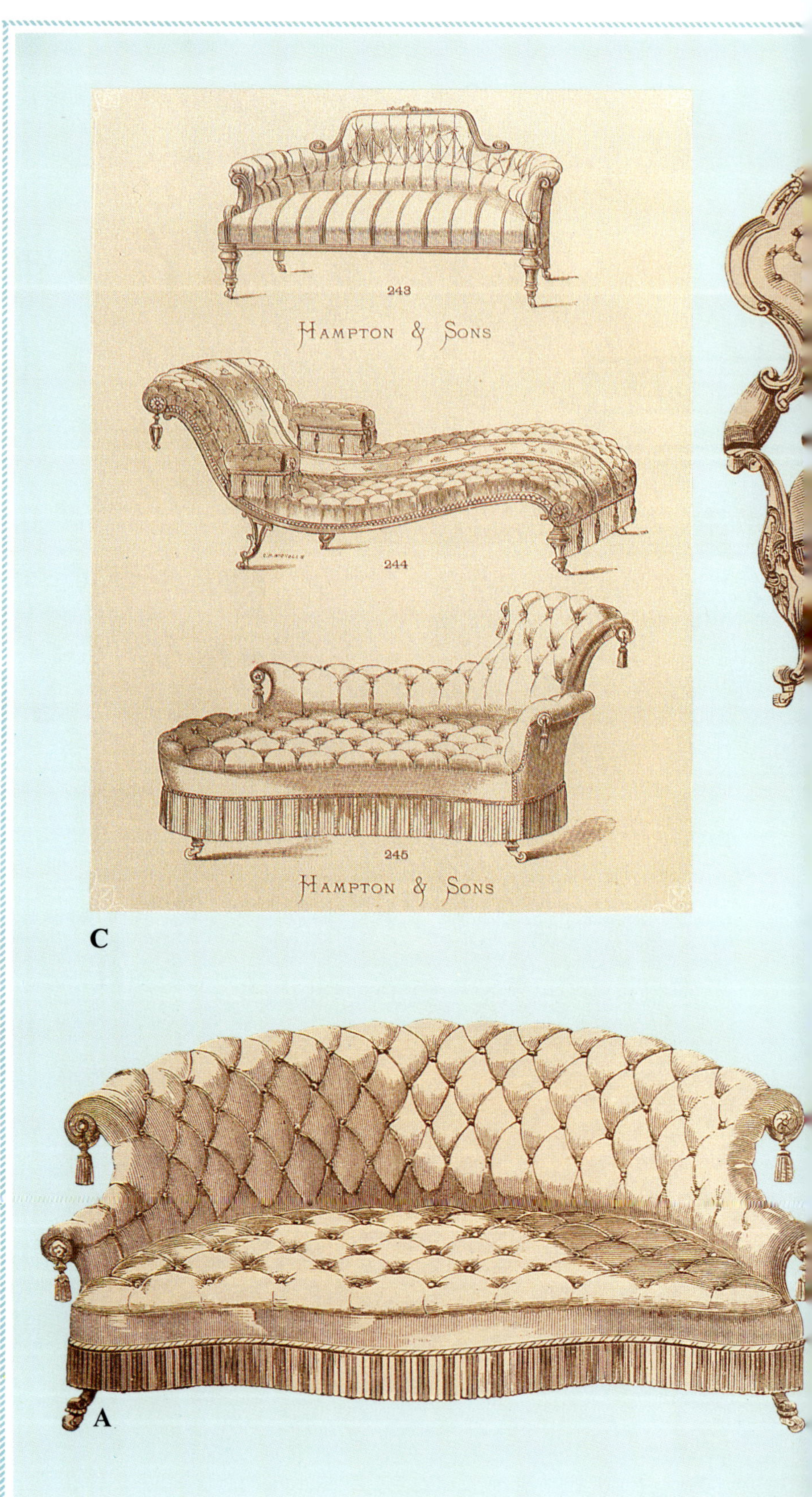

C

A

C. Three English Victorian Upholstered Sofas by Hampton & Sons, *c*1870

It is only in catalogue drawings or contemporary paintings that the complexity of Victorian upholstery can be fully appreciated. The chaise longue in the centre of this page, from the catalogue of Hampton & Sons, London, reveals the craft at its most extreme. The wooden-framed sofa, standing on both turned and cabriole legs, was embellished with a deep fringe terminating in silk drops. As though the back rest was not sufficiently complex, a large wood silk-wound drop gave the finishing touch. The central plain panel, running the length of the chaise longue, was edged with braid and contrasted with the deep-buttoning of the remainder of the seat and the arms. A wider braid was used above the seat rail. Such work was very labour-intensive and obviously expensive but, unfortunately, such pieces have rarely survived intact. The top sofa is of a much more conventional form, although few modern upholsterers would consider deep-butttoning a striped fabric, which is a highly specialized skill whose final result must be perfect. The other example illustrated, a deeply sprung chaise longue, was upholstered in plain velvet or silk and edged with a very deep fringe that concealed its turned legs. Large tassels hang from roundels on its sides and back.

D. An English Victorian Sofa by Hampton & Sons, *c*1870

This is one of the most ornate – and impractical – forms created by the Victorians; the fragility inherent in such a design has meant that few examples have survived. The deep-buttoned upholstered chair backs are joined by a pierced and carved section which gave the piece a charming delicacy but must have been extremely uncomfortable. The complexity of the ornamentation on the back is complemented by the plainly upholstered seat and armrests. An armchair and an occasional chair were made to match this piece, although all were sold separately by London's Hampton & Sons around 1870.

1800-1900

A. An English Victorian Sofa by Hampton & Sons, *c*1870

A somewhat cumbersome Victorian design, this piece of furniture seems to present an excuse for the extremes of the upholsterer's craft. Offered for sale by London's Hampton & Sons c1870, the sofa has a shaped wooden back rail and a wooden centrepiece on the overstuffed back rest. It stands on cabriole legs and has a slightly curved seat rail. The customer was able to select the wood for the construction, although stock lines were usually of mahogany or walnut. The cost would have depended mainly on the quality of the covering fabric.

B. Three English Victorian Upholstered Sofas by Hampton & Sons, *c*1870

This trio of sofas was offered by Hampton & Sons of Pall Mall East, London, c1870. All rely on the luxurious effect of deep-buttoning and stand on heavy turned legs fitted with castors. The first two designs are typical of the mid-19th century, but the straight-backed settee shows the prevailing influence of Regency-period styles. The central sofa is a curious combination of a settee and a chaise longue, although it would only have seated one person comfortably. Manufacturers such as Hamptons strove to provide the novelty-seeking public with endless variations of the fashionable shapes of the period, adding scrolls, tassels and deep-buttoning to catch the attention of even the most jaded eye.

C. An English Victorian Sofa, *c*1870

An almost monumental sofa, this English-manufactured piece dates to 1870. Many curious designs, which seem to owe as much to the builder as to the carpenter, were made after the 1851 Great Exhibition. Most of the decorative woodwork on this sofa was machine-made, but nonetheless it combines to create a very impressive effect. The contrast of the deep-buttoned and plain upholstery is also striking. A matching armchair and an occasional chair were also available. Today, the cost of upholstering such a sofa in the original manner would be close to prohibitive, so when they appear on the market they are usually plainly covered in velvet, with not even the deep-buttoning reproduced. To result in an effective look, however, the extravagant use of fabric and actual craftsmanship should be copied, thus giving an authentic period atmosphere to a piece.

B

A
C

A . An English Victorian Sofa by Hampton & Sons, *c*1870

This was one of the most economical styles of sofa offered by Hampton & Sons, London, c1870. It is only the elegant carving of the front of the back rest that separates this design from the thousands that were made for use in working-class homes. The style of the upholstery was very simple and could be replaced by any local handyman. This up-market version relies on beaded mouldings and fluted turned rails for its effect. It was available with an armchair and an occasional chair; such suites were sometimes found in the dining room or study.

B . Three English Victorian 'Conversation' Sofas by Hampton & Sons, *c*1870

Sofas of the 'conversation' or 'sociable' type were ideal centrepieces in large halls or ballrooms, as well as in the drawing room. In the lower versions shown, no show-wood was visible and the pieces are very much in the manner of Eastern ottomans made without back rests. Such designs relied on the quality of the upholstery fabric, usually silk or velvet, for their effect. In order to give a more luxurious effect, the legs were covered with a rich, deep fringe. The top design was very adaptable although, unfortunately, the occasional chairs and sofas have often been separated over the years and the design of the chairs is not at all satisfactory in isolation. This form of 'sociable' was preferred in France and gilded versions are found more frequently than walnut or mahogany examples. The illustration is from Hampton & Sons' catalogue, c1870.

C. Three English Victorian Sofas by Hampton & Sons, *c*1870

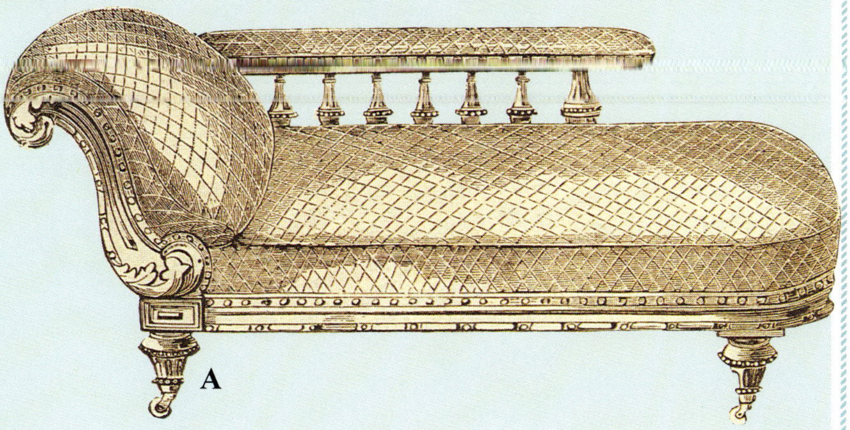

Because of their large size and the high cost of reupholstering, many sofas of this type did not survive the 1930s and 1940s, when they were scorned as examples of the worst excesses of Victorian taste. As relatively few now come on the market, they are much sought after and command good prices. These three models, advertised by Hampton & Sons, London, *c*1870, show how the structures could be arranged to sit three or four people. The top version is the most extreme; its upholstered armrests on shaped wooden supports would have suffered damage very quickly. This type of upholstery also necessitated custom-woven fabric that would have added to the expense. To give an even greater air of extravagance, deep fringing was used both on the armrests and on the seat. The centre 'conversation' is completely upholstered and deep-buttoned, possibly over an iron frame; it stands on turned wooden legs. The cabriole-legged design is also deep-buttoned, but the structure relies on the show-wood for its effect, making this type of sofa the most desirable – and expensive – today.

D. An English Mid-Victorian Upholstered Sofa, 1870s

It is often only in contemporary line drawings that the finishing detail of upholstery can be seen. This straight-backed sofa, dating to the 1870s, was finished at the lower edge of the seat with a thick cord. A finer version was used to accentuate the square side of the seat, a feature that contrasted well with the deep-buttoning. The construction depends on the use of turned legs and supports, which are also used as part of the decoration. The shaped back rail is centred with a floral crest. The sofa formed part of a suite, along with a matching armchair and so-called 'lady chair' or 'sewing chair', made without arms.

1800-1900

A . An English Victorian Gilt-Wood Sofa, 1870s

One of a pair of English gilt-wood sofas, this example was made in the French manner and dates to the 1870s. Standing on foliate-carved cabriole legs, the sofa has a front seat rail that is centred with a shell. The back is divided into three sections so that the necessary supports form part of the decoration; these supports extend down to form the back legs. The top rail is crested with foliate carving.

B . An English Victorian Mahogany Two-Seater Sofa, 1880s

An almost severely plain English mahogany sofa, this two-seater dates to the 1880s. The simple square lines of the piece are relieved only by a slight curve to the seat. The show-wood around the back and the seat are carved with foliate forms, and the arm supports continue down to simple turned legs. Such pieces, originally designed for more occasional use (such as in a music room), were intended to be placed against a wall, and the backs were therefore very plain. The upholstery, which has been replaced, originally would have been in a similar silk brocade, to further add to the impression of lightness.

C . A French Gilt-Wood Suite in Louis XV Style, 1880s

The furniture styles made popular during the reign of Louis XV have frequently been reproduced. This gilt-wood salon suite from the 1880s is upholstered in brocade of a retrospective style; it is composed of a sofa and four armchairs. The sofa has a padded back set within a shaped moulded frame that is carved with a floral cresting. Its seat and elbow rests are padded, its arms moulded and its shaped apron is carved with flowerheads and leaves. The sofa stands on moulded curvilinear supports with scroll feet. Although such sofas are not very comfortable, they are nonetheless liked because of their versatility: they look effective in a hall, bedroom or drawing room.

B

A

C

A . A Late 19th-century English Victorian Gilt-Wood Sofa

The best 18th-century designs continued to be reproduced throughout the 19th century, and indeed some are still made today. This gilt-wooden version has a shaped padded back set within a moulded frame, and its border pattern is interspersed with scrolled and foliate devices. The back is surmounted with a very Victorian-style flower and scroll crest. The armrests and the apron of the treble-curved seat front are similarly decorated with moulding. Reupholstered in cut velvet, the sofa also has padded armrests. Traditionally, this type of furniture has not appealed much to British and American buyers, although the market is now widening because of the interest in interior decoration.

B . A French Gilt-Wood Sofa with Tapestry Upholstery in Louis XVI Style, *c*1880–90

Louix XVI-style salon suites have remained favourites up to the present day and are frequently reproduced. This late 19th-century version, with turned and fluted legs, was probably once part of a suite. The moulded frame is carved with ribbon banding and flowerheads to give the feminine, delicate effect that is typical of the genre. The division of the back into three sections, separated by gilt-wood supports, adds to the light effect of the sofa. During the late 19th century, many reproduction suites of this kind were upholstered with specially woven tapestry panels, often in the 18th-century manner. Also, good-quality silk continued to be used in France for a much longer period than in Great Britain or North America; thus, it can give late sofas a deceptively early appearance.

C . An English Late-Victorian Pub Settle, *c*1880–90

This late Victorian settle was originally made for a public house in Whitechapel, London. The heavy construction made it ideal for use in an area where the furniture was subject to considerable wear. With its turned legs and rather stiff arms, the piece reveals how traditional designs were perpetuated. Some pub settles have polished wooden seats but others were upholstered in leather or deep plush. Despite their large size, old benches usually sell quickly, as they are preferred for use in hotels. Even in recent years, publicans in London were able to order similarly made pieces from East End craftsmen.

C

B
A

A . An English Victorian Gilt-Wood Sofa in 18th-Century French Style, *c*1880–90

This late 19th-century reproduction of a French 18th-century sofa is now upholstered in flowered cut velvet. The moulded frame has foliate decoration on the back rail, centred with a carved flower device, a design repeated on the two sections of the seat rail. The arms are fitted with padded elbow rests. Gilded French-style furniture of this type has remained popular to the present time and modern reproductions are still made. Victorian versions are favoured because of their high quality.

B . An English Victorian Sofa in William & Mary Style, *c*1885

The popularity of early English furniture is long established and many well-made copies and reproductions of 17th- and 18th-century pieces are now so old that they have a value of their own. Many Victorian-era copies are now appreciated for the quality of their workmanship and, more especially, for the good tapestry, usually French-made, used for their upholstery. As Victorian women also worked on sets of needlework covers for antique-style sofas, it is possible to create a William & Mary-style interior from later, but nonetheless, fine-quality copies. This sofa has well-carved stretchers made of walnut and is decorated with a deep fringe in the late 17th-century manner.

C . An English Arts & Crafts Sofa by Morris & Co, *c*1889

William Morris (1834–96) opened his establishment for the manufacture and sale of household furnishings in 1863. He believed in a return to medieval-style craftsmanship and in making products that should be available to all sections of society; in fact, his creations remained too expensive for the majority. This settle, whose design is attributed to George Jack, was custom-made by Morris & Co for Stanmore Hall in Middlesex; it was one of four intended for the vestibule. Morris & Co was commissioned by William Knox d'Arcy to redecorate and furnish the Hall, to which WR Lethaby also contributed designs. The sofa has a rectangular buttoned back and a fringed padded seat. Its three front legs are spirally fluted and joined by moulded stretchers. The visible wood is mahogany, and the settle is covered with a Morris fabric known as 'Flower Garden'.

D . A Scottish Art Nouveau Settle and Armchair, by Graham Morton, *c*1895–1900

This small high-backed settle and matching armchair were made in a restrained Art Nouveau style in the late 1890s by Graham Morton of Stirling. Light furniture with a limited use of upholstery was preferred by progressive decorators who were reacting against overstuffed Victorian suites. Like the furniture made by Morton's compatriot, Charles Rennie Mackintosh, sofas with such elongated straight backs were not comfortable; thus clients furnishing in the style were generally more concerned with line and fashionable elegance. The craftsmen-made piece is beautifully balanced and ornamented but much cheaper versions in simplified forms were produced at the time by factories. For a sofa in this manner to be valuable, it would need to be attributable to a known maker or a particular school or studio workshop.

C

B

A

D

1800-1900

A. A Portuguese Card Table, *c*1800

It is the tortoiseshell veneer that gives this piece its striking appearance, although structurally it is a standard D-shaped card table. Portuguese colonies in the West Indies and Central America allowed the indulgence of a taste for exotic veneer, and it is fairly common to come across 18th-century furniture and precious cabinets treated in this way.

Tortoiseshell decoration took two main forms. The first used clear shell through which colour from the wood could be viewed, and the second, seen here, employed various shades of the shell – blond (light) and dark – for contrast. In fact, the fan inlay on the table top and the panels around the frieze are reminiscent of Northern European satinwood and mahogany equivalents, but tortoiseshell pieces are far rarer.

B. A French Directoire Mahogany *Tric-trac* Table, *c*1800

The lid of this mahogany games table lifts off to reveal a sunken backgammon board, and its drawers would have contained the pieces required for playing. The game *tric-trac* was an early form of backgammon and was played all over Europe (in England it was known as 'trick-track'); its name derives from the sound of pieces hitting the board.

A typical piece of Directoire furniture – so-called after the post-Revolution French government of 1795–99, and referring to late 18th- and very early 19th-century furniture – it shows clear George III Regency influences in its fluted legs, echoed on the corners of the table itself. The carved decoration and gilded brass details help to lighten the piece somewhat.

C. An English Regency Games Table, *c*1800

This versatile games table with concealed chess-board top, sliding flap for candlesticks and a drawer which turns into a writing surface with inkwell and pen tray shows all the signs of Georgian preoccupation with gadgetry. Small, well-proportioned and neat, it was probably for occasional use, and may once have had a well for sewing. The piece's straight lines indicate influence from the late George III period, as typified by Sheraton and Hepplewhite. The use of rosewood on the top and the turned stretchers that are both round- and square-sectioned give it a Regency flavour.

C

A
B

1800-1900

A . An English Library or Writing Table, *c*1800

This curious table seems unusually proportioned, and on closer inspection it is clear that its legs have been cut down, perhaps due to damage. This leaves an impression of a low and very wide table, and the eight legs give it a feeling of grandeur. It has drawers on both its sides and ends – although those on the ends are dummies – and the small centre frieze drawer is fitted with compartments for writing equipment. The drawer outlines and line decoration may seem slightly unrealistic and excessive, but may well have been added at a later date; it was quite common for changes in taste to lead to a change in veneer in this way.

B . A French Empire *Guéridon*, *c*1800

This *guéridon*, with its small circular top, clearly performs the same function of the original *guéridon* – that of candlestand. It shows traces of the Louis XVI style, ie, the marble top with brass gallery, which sits on a straight neo-classical central column ending in three hipped cabriole feet. Overall, it is severe, the only decoration being a bit of ormolu. As such, it reflects the attitude of Republican France (at which time it was made), whose people were trying to emulate Roman nobility in terms of furniture making, as well as other arts.

C . An American Federal Dining Table, *c*1805

This remarkable table is nearly 17ft (5.2m) long and 5ft (1.5m) wide. It has two end sections with leaves above a cock-beaded frieze, tripods at the ends and three double scrolled supports. These end in brass animal paw feet and castors. The six mahogany and four poplar leaves are an unusual combination, based on a patent by Gillow's of London and Lancaster, and referred to today as having an accordion action.

In the United States, this type of mechanism was mostly used in New York, although this table was made in Philadelphia and was supposedly the property of Thomas Jefferson, President of the United States from 1801 to 1809. Jefferson spent some time in Europe, and his Virginia house, Monticello, which he personally designed along the lines of Italian-revival architectural principles, contained much European, or American European, furniture. This table was given to the Maryland Historical Society in 1924.

E

C

D . A Regency English Calamander Sofa Table, *c*1805

The most striking feature of this stunning sofa table is its unusual wood. Calamander was imported from Ceylon and has contrasting patterns (brown, mottled and streaked) of dark brown or black on a paler background. A fine-grained hardwood, it became popular for veneering and cross-banding over a period of 50 years or so from 1780.

The wood is strongly associated with the Regency period and the table shows many other classic Regency features. The brass strung border to the table top is studded with stars (known as a stella border), and the legs are also brass strung, with brass cappings cast with a leafy decoration. This table amply demonstrates the Regency interest in a variety of patterns, in contrasting colours and in brass inlay.

Sofa tables were made to accompany sofas, and not settees. Settees generally had a hardwood (often mahogany) frame and were designed for halls. On the whole, they were less comfortable and certainly less fashionable than Regency sofas, which were lavishly upholstered and typically accompanied by a matching table.

E . An American Federal Work Table, *c*1805

It is likely that this carved mahogany work table is by Duncan Phyfe (1768–1854), or from his New York workshop. The beginnings of the style for heavy carving that arrived in the early 19th century can clearly be seen here.

The top part of the round section is plain, with finely figured veneer, but the bottom half shows a reeded 'tambour' (sliding door) made of vertical slats which slide into the side panels. The amount of texture indicates that the style for plain wood has gone, and the deep top section gives the table a heavier feel. The elegant, sweeping legs are both reeded and carved.

A . An American Federal Dressing Bureau, *c*1805

This American dressing table was probably made by John and Thomas Seymour of Boston, Massachusetts, and is clearly influenced by European Sheraton furniture. Light and elegant, it has square, tapering legs and contrasting inlay of mahogany and bird's-eye maple. The long, shallow drawers emphasize the horizontal feel, and the elongated mirror is supported by curving brackets – the only part of the piece which is not a straight line.

The term 'Federal' refers to furniture made towards the end of the 18th century and the beginning of the 19th, broadly corresponding to English late Georgian or Regency taste. As with many other American designs, basic English styles were adapted with regional variations.

John Seymour (c1738–1818) was a major figure in Massachusetts furniture circles. British born, he emigrated to America with his son, Thomas, arriving in Maine in 1785 and settling in Boston in 1794. They worked for a wealthy clientele, producing high-quality work – contrasting woods were one of their specialities, and their output was much influenced by Thomas Sheraton and George Hepplewhite.

B . An American Federal Dining Table, *c*1805

This table has a hinged section in the middle which can be used as a separate table. The two serpentine-ended external tables can also double as sideboards. With the intermediate flaps, the whole table stretches to amost 14ft (1.7m) in length.

It was probably made in the workshop of Duncan Phyfe (1768–1854), the best-known and probably most influential New York Federal cabinetmaker. His work related closely to that of the English Regency style. Phyfe's family emigrated from Scotland to Albany, New York, in the 1780s. Young Phyfe then worked as a joiner in New York City, where he had a shop from 1795 to 1847. This sold a large number of his original variations on European styles, which often included references to Greek and Roman design and featured his strange animal feet which extended up the leg.

Before Independence, New York had been secondary in furniture making, but after 1780 it grew rapidly and soon had the largest group of cabinetmakers in the nation. Generally, Hepplewhite and Sheraton designs were followed, interpreted by makers such as Michael Allison and Elbert Anderson.

A

C. An Empire *Guéridon, c*1805

In its role as a small occasional table for domestic use, the *guéridon* reached its peak of popularity in the early 19th century. Essentially the same form as the earlier Louis XVI version, the decoration and style on this table are pure neo-classical.

The table is made of mahogany, a favourite wood of the Empire period, and one that was increasingly scarce; its shortage was due to the English blockade of French ports, thus raising its price and leading to an increased use of indigenous woods such as oak, elm, ash, maple and beech in France. The table's top is a plain grained granite surrounded by an ormolu rim, which had by this time taken the place of a gallery. The sabre-shaped supports end in a Greek key pattern (a classical motif very popular in the Napoleonic era) and sit on a concave tripod base. The tripod frieze itself has typical classical architectural panels.

During the Consulate and Empire periods in French history (1799–1804 and 1804–15, respectively), furniture production recommenced after the upheavals of the Revolution. Although less refined than during the eras of Louis XIV, XV and XVI, the industry still employed over 10,000 workers in more than 100 workshops. One leading manufacturer alone, Jacob-Desmalter, employed over 400 men and exported one-third of its output.

1800-1900

A. An English Regency Mahogany Serving Table, *c*1807

One of the most influential designers in the Regency taste (known formally as English Empire) was Dutch-born Thomas Hope (1769–1831); this monumental, chunky serving table of his stands at over 6ft (1.8m) wide. When not used for serving, it would have been decorated with silverware and ceramics of the time, including such objects as centrepieces and knife urns, which opened to reveal stands for cutlery.

The piece shows a clear departure from the prevailing George III furniture styles – generally thought to end around 1800 – and the influences of its dominant designers, Adam, Hepplewhite and Sheraton. Not light, flowered, nor detailed, the table reflects Hope's interest in the antiquities of Greece, Egypt and the Middle East, and, as with many of his works, is a combination of several styles, borrowing a leg here, a stone frieze there.

Hope himself was a friend of the French architect/designer, Charles Percier (1764–1838), renowned for his severity of style and his quote: 'I scarcely was able to hold a pencil when instead of flowers, landscapes and other familiar objects, I began dealing in those straight lines which seem so little attractive to the greatest number'. Often twinned with George Smith as a provider of avant-garde designs, Hope in fact, like Smith, was absorbing ideas which were current in Europe and presenting them in a coherent form.

B. A German Neo-Classical Writing Table, *c*1810

Traditional German furniture had a history of carved decoration and dark woods which stretched back to the 16th century. Court furniture, however, was largely influenced by French design, although several renowned cabinet-makers were at work, including the brothers David (1743–1807) and Abraham Roentgen (1711–93).

This desk is typical of early 19th-century neo-classical work throughout Europe, combining elements of English and French style from the end of the 18th century. The pierced brass gallery on both tiers is a classic Louis XVI feature, as are the ormolu appliqués. The overall shape of the desk is very similar to Regency writing desks, and the fluted legs seem to anticipate William IV style.

This type of furniture was also very popular in Austria. Vienna was the centre of the Austro-Hungarian Empire, and pieces such as this were used to furnish official state rooms such as those of the Wüzburg Residenz, refurbished by Johann Valentin Raab in the early 19th century.

C. A Regency Mahogany Writing Table, *c*1810

This small writing table is interesting for its unusual mechanism, which allows the table to be adjusted. When used as a writing desk, the central leather-tooled surface lies flat; when employed for reading or drawing, it can be tipped to the angle required.

The table stands on unusual twin trestle ends which finish in splayed sabre legs. The reeded decoration and panelling of the frieze drawers, which are fitted with compartments, are typical of the Regency period, as is the preoccupation with gadgetry.

D. A Regency Writing Table, *c*1810

At the end of the 1700s, before the Empire styles of the early 19th century, furniture design lost some of its nationalist tendencies (Louis XV, George III, etc) and became more international. This was an obvious product of a world with better communications, coming at a time when British design was very popular in mainland Europe, and French and Italian design was influential in England.

This table shows two contrasting influences, an English Regency severity of line, and a French Louis XVI passion for gilt mounts. The latter is seen also in the pierced brass gallery around the back of the table top, in the gilt beading of the drawers and legs, and in the central ormolu mask. However, the mixture of styles works well, and this functional table exhibits a fine balance of decoration and line.

B

C
D
A

A . An American Federal Carved Mahogany Work Table, *c*1810

This small, distinctive work table stands 29in (73.5cm) high and is probably the work of Henry Connelly, the Philadelphia cabinetmaker whose furniture is often associated with that of his contemporary, Ephraim Haines. It was bought from Henry Connelly by the great-grandmother of the present owner.

Although not beautiful, it is a striking piece, with highly original applied decoration on each corner which comes as a complete contrast to the finely carved column and quadruped base. The table was made during a period in American history when native styles began to depart drastically from European traditions; here, for instance, the base is very European, while the top is a product of the maker's imagination.

A city with a strong neo-classical tradition, Philadelphia boasted over 100 cabinetmakers at this time. The screw-thread decoration on the top is a version of the original idea of flanking classical columns, although the rather busy threads give a less tranquil effect.

B . A Federal Mahogany Card Table, *c*1810

This card table was probably made in New York. The plain faces of the top and geometric line show an interest in the quality of the veneer rather than the decoration, and give the table a similarity to the Biedermeier furniture of Europe between 1820 and 1840. The supports of this table are four slender carved columns with splayed feet, and overall the table is beautifully proportioned. The visual weight of the top is almost exactly equal to that of the base.

It is an original and elegant piece, and although unattributed, it was obviously made by a cabinetmaker of considerable distinction.

A

B

C . A French Empire Gilt Wood Console Table, *c*1810

The period after the French Revolution of 1793 saw a succession of short governments in France. These included the Directoire (1795–99), the Consulat (1799–1804) and the Empire (1804–15). All three are terms loosely applied to the characteristic furniture of their respective periods, but they all reject the typically ornate, gilt-encrusted French furniture styles of the 18th century.

Exotic influences, and particularly Egyptian ones, are most associated with the Empire period. After Napoleon I's victory at the Battle of the Pyramids in 1800, both the French and English plundered considerable amounts of Egyptian artefacts, and shipped them to Europe. This created a distinct impact on decorative artists and cabinetmakers, and was supported by the book of engravings *Voyage dans la Basse- et Haute-Egypte,* by French architect/engraver, Dominique Vivant Denon (published in 1802). This brought the exotic to the notice of domestic designers such as the Jacobs in France and Thomas Sheraton in England.

D . A Russian Mahogany Console Table and Pier Glass, *c*1810

The beauty of this piece lies in its purity of line and sparseness of decoration. The combination of mahogany and ormolu decoration is clearly influenced by French Empire – the clear grain markings of the 'flame' mahogany are featured around the mirror frame – and so too are the delicate winged-sphinx legs. The format of a pier glass above a console table was first perfected in the Palais de Versailles. The term 'pier' refers to the wall space between tall windows, and tables were designed to fill the gap.

Such clear French influence on Russian work is quite typical. Generally, furniture is only classified as Russian if documents still exist to prove Russian manufacture, as many pieces were made in France specifically for the Russian market during the 18th and early 19th centuries. After Napoloen's defeat by the armies of Tsar Alexander I (1801–25) in 1812, the threat of foreign invasion was lifted from Russia's shoulders. The Tsar sought to rebuild Russia's native furniture industry, and imported many foreign architects and designers to help. This led to a style which combined Empire and Biedermeier, of which The Palace of Pavlovsk near Leningrad is one of the best examples. By the mid 19th century, the quality of workmanship was declining all over Europe; Russia was no exception and it saw a brief Arts & Crafts revival as a reaction to lowering standards.

A. An English Regency Console Table, *c*1810

This is one of a pair of tables in the English Empire style, so called as it reflects the grandeur of that time. It is often sculptural, heavy and dark, although some pieces which are influenced by wider European taste have considerable gilt scrolling.

The table is in the manner of Thomas Hope (1769–1831), an unusual and original man who was the son of a banker in Amsterdam. His family emigrated to Scotland at the end of the 18th century, and he later moved to London, where he displayed his collection of antiquities gathered on a Grand Tour of Europe and the Middle East between 1787 and 1795.

Hope was a scholar and an architect, and his Greek, Roman and Egyptian artefacts were placed in a house which was furnished to his own designs with pieces such as this. His furnishings were often decorated with winged lions and masks to match the antiquities themselves.

In 1807 Hope published his ideas and designs in *Household Furniture and Decoration* which, along with George Smith's *A Collection of Designs for Household Furniture and Interior Decorating,* influenced high Regency design well into the 19th century. It contrasted sharply with Robert Adam's neo-classical work, which had been so popular since the 1770s. On his death in 1831, Hope was buried in a mausoleum he himself designed at his country home of Deepdene in Surrey.

B. An Unusual English Regency Mahogany Library Table, *c*1810

The feature which distinguishes a library table from the often-similar centre table is its functional design. Drum library tables, for example, consist of a swivelling top which allows the reader to rotate it in search of a particular book, and generally library tables had drawers along both sides and at both ends.

The unusual feature of this library table is that it has no drawers whatsoever, although the sides are panelled as if to simulate them. However, the top of this table consists of two hinged lids which, when opened, reveal undivided compartments clearly designed to hold folios of papers, such as maps, accounts or prints. (Bound into enormous books, architectural prints were very popular at this time, with artists such as Giovanni Battista Piranesi producing drawings of Italian villas or architectural details.) The reeded, splayed quadruped base of this piece is typical Regency, as is the cross-banded rosewood decoration.

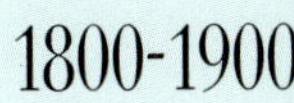

D

A

B

C . An English Regency Marble-topped Table on a Gilt Wood Base, *c*1810

The Regency era's preoccupation with exotic colours and materials is nowhere more clearly illustrated than in 'specimen' marble-topped tables such as this. Invariably Italian-made, such circular pieces contained up to 200 different varieties of marble, in this case including *portoro, broccatello, verde antico, breccia, siena, rance* and many others.

The vogue for using different marbles began with 17th-century *pietra dura* work, a form of marble inlay fashioned in Baroque styles. These marble tops were expensive at the time, despite being produced in fairly large numbers, and were almost exclusively from Rome or Florence – the Carrara quarries north of Florence produce marble to this day.

The base of this piece is typical of these tables – the tops were so heavy that the support needed to be extremely sturdy. Here, this original period base consists of a stylized lotus pedestal ending in a trefoil platform on bun feet. It is unusual to find the original top with its base, as seen here, and in fact many of these tops were bought separately from the base at the time.

D . An Early 19th-century Mahogany Centre Table, *c*1810

The origin of this handsome table is unknown, although it is almost certainly European and probably French, English or Italian. Placed in a formal setting, a centre table such as this is more likely to have been used for display than as a functional dining or side table.

It is typical of the French Empire style (roughly equivalent to English Regency style, 1800–20), which was consistently revived in mainland Europe. Although this piece is dated *c*1810, it could have been made as a revival piece as late as 1860 or 1880. The brass edge to its top and brass stringing along the edge link it to the Regency period.

Two clues to its neo-classical influences are seen in the ormolu laurel-leaf decoration on the legs, and its cross-shaped trestles; the latter were used by both the Greeks and Romans in their furniture, as can be seen in surviving wall-paintings and decorated vases.

A . An American Federal Serving Table, *c*1810

A fine mahogany serpentine-fronted serving table, this piece was produced during a period in American Federal furniture history which corresponds to the English Regency. It was probably made in Salem, Massachusetts, by Samuel McIntire (1757–1811). He and John Seymour, a British cabinetmaker who emigrated in 1785, were dominant forces in Massachusetts furniture production at the end of the 18th century. They used excellent veneers, as seen here, and turned out beautifully finished pieces. As links with England weakened into the 19th century, their personal styles were more apparent in their furniture.

This table is elegant, with naturalistic carving on the flanking columns which sit above fluted legs. Carving such as this appears on other McIntire pieces, some of which may be seen in the Museum of Fine Arts in Boston. This American adaptation of architectural motifs retains much of a Regency, or Federal, feel, however, which is not surprising for a table from the English-orientated New England area. Salem contained a number of distinguished cabinetmakers at the beginning of the 19th century, including William Hook, Nehemiah Adams and the Sandersons.

B . An English Regency Rosewood Sofa Table, *c*1810

With the arrival of sofas in the drawing room during the Regency era, its 18th-century ancestor – the mahogany settee – was relegated to the hall, for some time its traditional location, where it was used by waiting guests. Along with the sofa came the accompanying sofa table, in this case made of the popular rosewood. Already strongly grained, the top is also cross-banded with satinwood and coromandel, and when highly polished would present a dazzling contrast. The frieze drawers, which are real on one side and blank on the other, are edged with stringing and have scrolling motifs which are echoed on both the ends and splayed legs of the table.

The clarity and simplicity of the line decoration prevent the table from seeming excessive. This type of ornament was recommended in Thomas Hope's *Household Furniture,* published in 1807, and other pattern-books of the time.

A

B

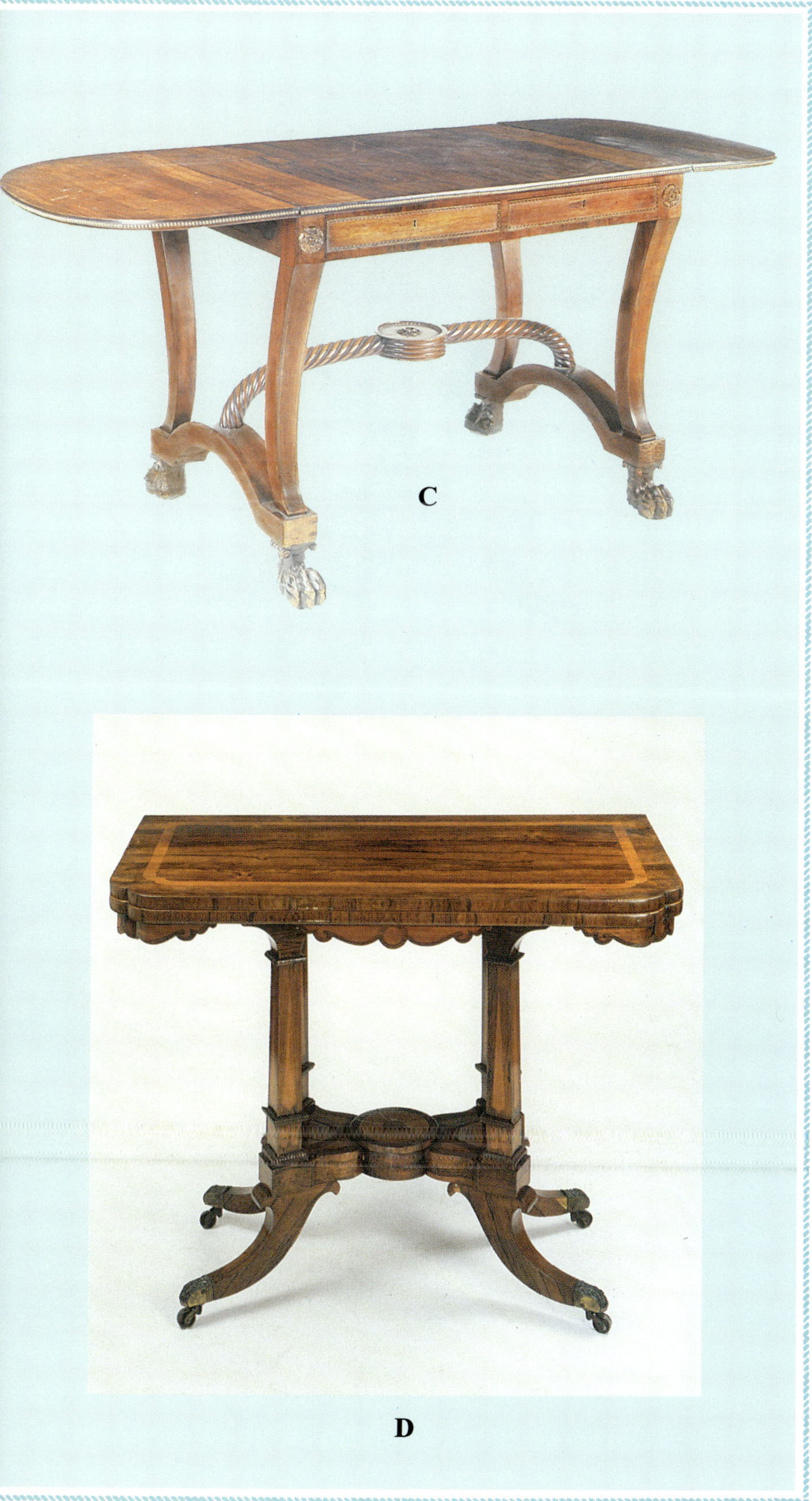

C. An English Regency Rosewood Sofa Table, *c*1815

This table is interesting for the unusual construction of its legs. At each end, two outward-curving sabre legs are joined by an arched stretcher and rest on substantial lion-paw feet. The two end stretchers are joined by a central rope-twist stretcher.

The rope-twist form of carving first appeared after Nelson's Battle of Trafalgar in 1805, during the Napoleonic wars with France ending at Waterloo in 1815. The motif became very popular, and was sometimes used on all the rails of a piece of furniture.

D. An English Regency Rosewood Card Table, *c*1815

Card tables use a number of different mechanisms to support their folding leaves – a concertina action, gate legs, swivel tops, envelope leaves, etc – but this table uses a unusual clock-like hinge. The two back legs swing out around a circular hinge (like the hands of a clock), which is hidden in a central capstan between the four legs, forming a cross shape. In fact, a join can be seen between the stable top half of the capstan, and the lower section, which hinges. The card table then folds out as normal.

Overall the piece is heavy, which dates it to late Regency. The top has a scrolled apron and is joined to the platform by four stout legs, supported in turn by four splayed legs. The legs are designed as columns, with capitals and pediments, and elsewhere there are traces of architectural details, with some naturalistic inlay.

A. An American Federal Work Table, Boston, Massachusetts, c1815

This elegant work table is attributed to the influential Massachusetts cabinetmakers, John and Thomas Seymour. Their work shows a preference for contrasting woods (in this case, mahogany, bird's-eye maple and flame birch); the piece is typically of high quality and neat proportions, and includes characteristic fluted legs and an emphasis on straight lines. The table is a combination of Georgian and Regency design, using elegant Hepplewhite inlay and broad neo-classical panels of colour. It is petite and very elegant, with fine deep carving of the mahogany.

The partnership was noted for inventive adaptations of European designs; the Winterthur Museum in Delaware has a famous desk which is labelled 'John Seymour and Son, Creek Lane, Boston' and dates from c1800. This is also based on a Hepplewhite design, and has a hybrid American use of inlay. It too has unusual neo-classical characteristics which might be considered slightly misplaced by English standards.

B. An English Regency Mahogany Drop-flap Work Table, c1815

This small sewing table shows all the Regency attributes which might be expected of this date. Decorated with dot-and-line brass inlay and its top cross-banded in rosewood, this practical table was fully equipped for its purpose: its main draw was sectioned into a sewing box, with compartments for cottons, needles, scissors and such like, and the 'sliding well' drawer made of fabric that hangs beneath would have held balls of wool, crocheting needles and other bulkier items.

Measuring only 18in (46cm) square, this diminutive table, with its carved and scrolled support and elaborate sabre inlaid legs, has less appeal nowadays as sewing skills decline.

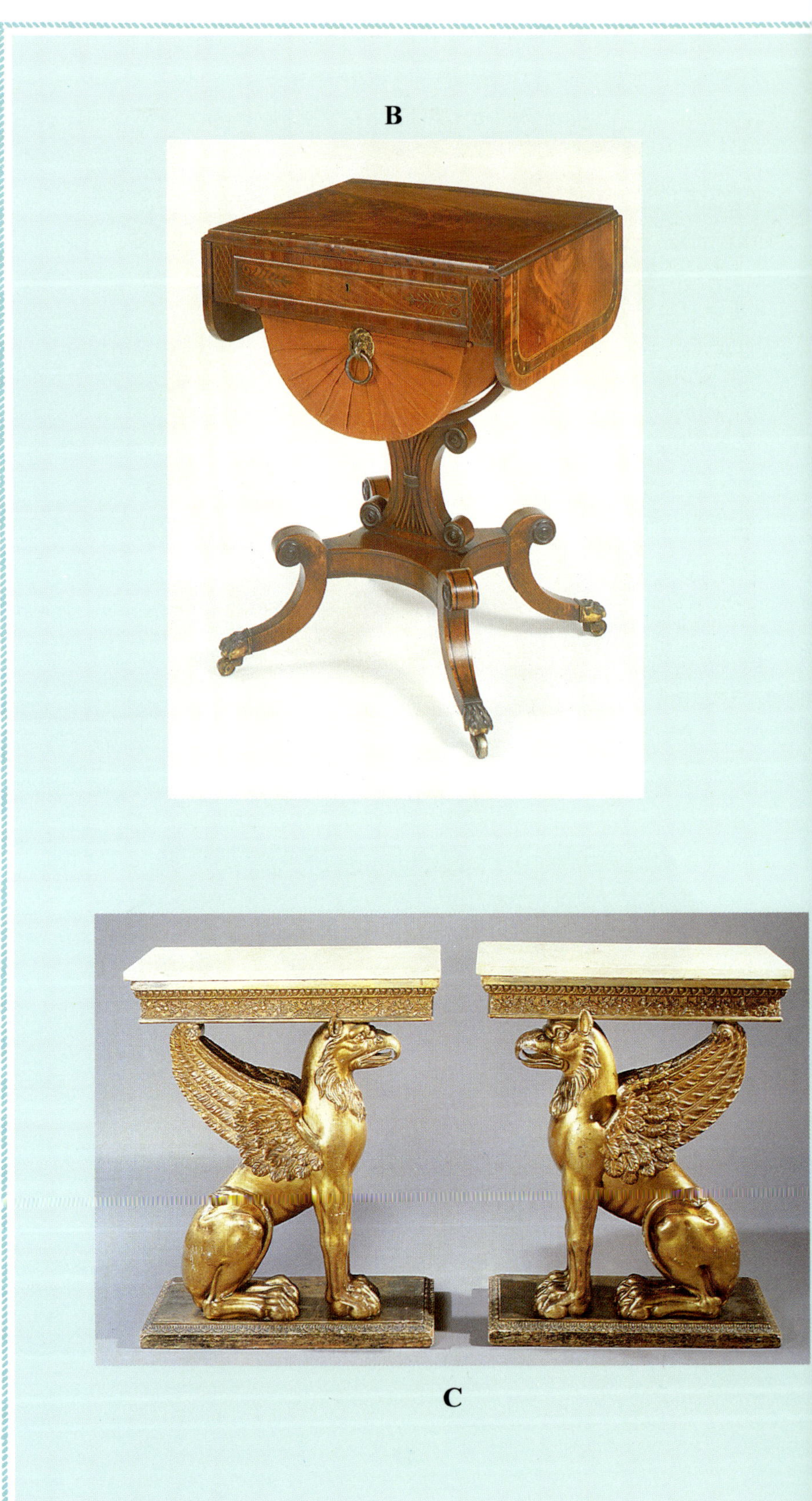

B

C

D

A

C. A Pair of English Regency Gilt Wood Console Tables, *c*1815

Purely decorative, console tables were designed to sit against a wall, often between windows, and as such became part of the room fittings rather than standing as individual pieces of furniture. Often large brackets with no other support, many had large mirrors above, filling wall space, and lent themselves to excessive ornamentation.

The use of the griffin (a winged lion with a bird's head) as a table support is typical of designers Thomas Hope and George Smith, and has become synonymous with Georgian excess. They are ideally adapted here as supports for their marble tops, which were a feature of the original console (or 'clap') tables of the early 18th century. Based on Italian prototypes, those early examples were often carved by Italian journeymen (travelling craftsmen) and were highly fashionable. Louis XVI's Palais de Versailles, the height of late 17th-century furniture styles, contains many examples of the marble-topped console table. They are an integral part of the decorative scheme, dividing the wall vertically into windows and mirrors in the *Galerie des Glaces*, (Gallery of Mirrors).

D. An Italian Empire Console Table, *c*1815

Many of the characteristic features of the Empire style seen here – the laurel leaves on the frieze, the heavy lion-paw feet, and the ornate horn-like fruiting legs – were in fact found in Italy before the end of the 18th century. However, it was not until the French Empire style of Napoleon's reign became popular that Italian workmen employed these features in a coherent way. The resulting style is known as Italian Empire.

The Bonaparte family were installed in force in Italy during Napoleon's reign. His brother, Joseph, became King of Naples, another brother, Lucien, was appointed Prince of Canino, and his sisters, Elisa, Caroline and Pauline, all married into leading families, the first two in Tuscany and Naples, respectively, and Pauline into the Roman Borghese family. Not only did this ensure the Bonapartes' power base, but it also spread the Napoleonic 'Empire' style to some impressive interiors. Elisa, for example, was responsible for importing French workmen to decorate several magnificent rooms in the Pitti Palace in Florence.

1800-1900

A. A French Empire Dining Table, *c*1815

A dining table such as this, designed to fold away when not in use, underlines the change in circumstance of the well-off in France after the Revolution. The Parisian bourgeois lived in much smaller homes than 50 years previously, partly due to a lack of space in Paris (where the French court had moved to from Versailles), partly to redistribution of aristocratic wealth, and so required furniture on an appropriate scale.

The ten legs of this table allow it to open out with a concertina action. The extending leaves – normally three but sometimes five – are supported by the central legs, both of which extend on a diamond-shaped frame. Typically Empire, the table is very plain, the top geometric, and the decoration on the frieze is restricted to finely figured wood. The legs are turned at the knee to create a 'knop' (collar) above the brass castors below.

Mahogany was the favoured wood of the Empire period (1804–15), despite the fact that a severe shortage made it extremely expensive. It was generally imported from mainland America and the West Indies, but the Continental Blockade imposed against the French in 1806 (when the English refused to export it from the territories they occupied) meant very little mahogany reached France.

B. An English Regency Sofa Table Attributed to George Bullock, *c*1815

This sofa table in the English Regency style is more substantial and impressive than its 18th-century predecessors. The influences of George Smith and Thomas Hope both can be seen here, the former in the chunky lion-paw feet and substantial pedestal, the latter in the brass inlay of exotic architectural patterns made so popular by Hope. This table top is squarer than earlier examples, which gives the piece weight, but it is lightened by the linear central column and ormolu mounts.

It is attributed to George Bullock (active between 1800 and 1820), who originally worked in Liverpool and Birmingham before setting up in London in 1815. Although much of Bullock's work was for the mass market, he also produced a large body of avant-garde designs, and is often thought of as an architect of the English Renaissance in the 19th century. His style became fully accepted in the 1930s and 1940s, but one of his major commissions was for the house of the metalworker, Matthew Boulton, at Great Tew in Oxfordshire. So many pieces were delivered to Boulton in 1817 that Bullock's bill ran to 42 pages.

C. A Pair of English Regency Mahogany Card Tables, *c*1815

Although it is difficult to date this pair precisely – they could have been manufactured any time between 1795 and 1815 – it seems likely from the turned legs that they were made after the turn of the century (square-sectioned legs and flat sides would indicate an earlier date).

During Regency times card tables started to appear in pairs, in fours and occasionally in larger sets. Generally made of mahogany, sometimes of satinwood, and others again in a combination of the two, card tables were occasionally made in woods such as oak, by provincial manufacturers.

These tables are of excellent quality, as well as being utilitarian and discreet – all the desirable qualities of so-called 'brown' furniture, which was made of mahogany and dated from the Georgian period, ending with the reign of George IV.

D. A French Empire Mahogany *Guéridon*, *c*1815

The *guéridon* in its original 17th-century form was a candlestick holder with a carved support; *guéridon* was the name given to young black pages at the courts of the time, and a common form of candleholder was the carved and painted form of a black page, many of whom were brought from the Moorish African coast for this purpose. During the 18th century the term expanded to include candlestands or small round tables (at this time the carving had disappeared), and by the end of the 1700s the table usually had two tiers. By this date, however, *guéridon* was used to refer to any round table.

This table is 4ft 3in (1.3m) across, and has a leather top for writing on. The drawers in its vertical, handsome frieze suggest that it might have been a library table. It is strikingly plain, but quite smart, and shows very little decoration apart from the gilt drawer knobs and the three 'hipped' cabriole legs ('hipped' refers to the sharp turning just above the knee).

The use of beautifully figured mahogany and the imposing effect of this table are reflections of the increased confidence and wealth of Napoleonic France. Interestingly, although France and England were at war at this time, the two leaders of furniture making were developing along very similar lines – this could almost be a Regency library table.

A

C

D

B

A . A Swedish Empire Console Table, *c*1815

The second half of the 18th century saw a long period of peace and prosperity in Scandinavia which was to be shattered by the Napoleonic wars. Sweden found itself caught between loyalties to France and England. The Bernadotte Dynasty, which still rules in Sweden today, descends from a marshal of Napoleon's who was invited to take the throne in the early 19th century; the destruction of the Danish fleet and half of Copenhagen by the English in 1801, however, was more than enough to persuade the Swedes to declare allegiance to England.

One effect of this was the development of a native furniture industry which took elements of design from both England and France; encouraged by interruption of sea traffic during the wars, Sweden had to rely more on its own production, and also saw considerable imports overland of furniture from Germany. The industry was helped by large quantities of high-quality native pine, which also gilt well; the small Scandinavian furniture-making industry which developed initially produced foreign designs, such as this one.

B . An English Late Regency or George IV Library Table, *c*1820

This library table has the distinguishing marks of a revolving top, and drawers on both sides. Many features of late Regency design are here, including the single turned column support, a platform leading to four sabre legs, and a fairly small base compared to the table top.

The use of rosewood and brass inlay can be seen on the strung drawers, and elsewhere on the form. The anthemion (or honeysuckle) decorative motif was popularized by Robert Adam, who originally took it from Roman architectural friezes, and revived by Thomas Hope in the early 18th century.

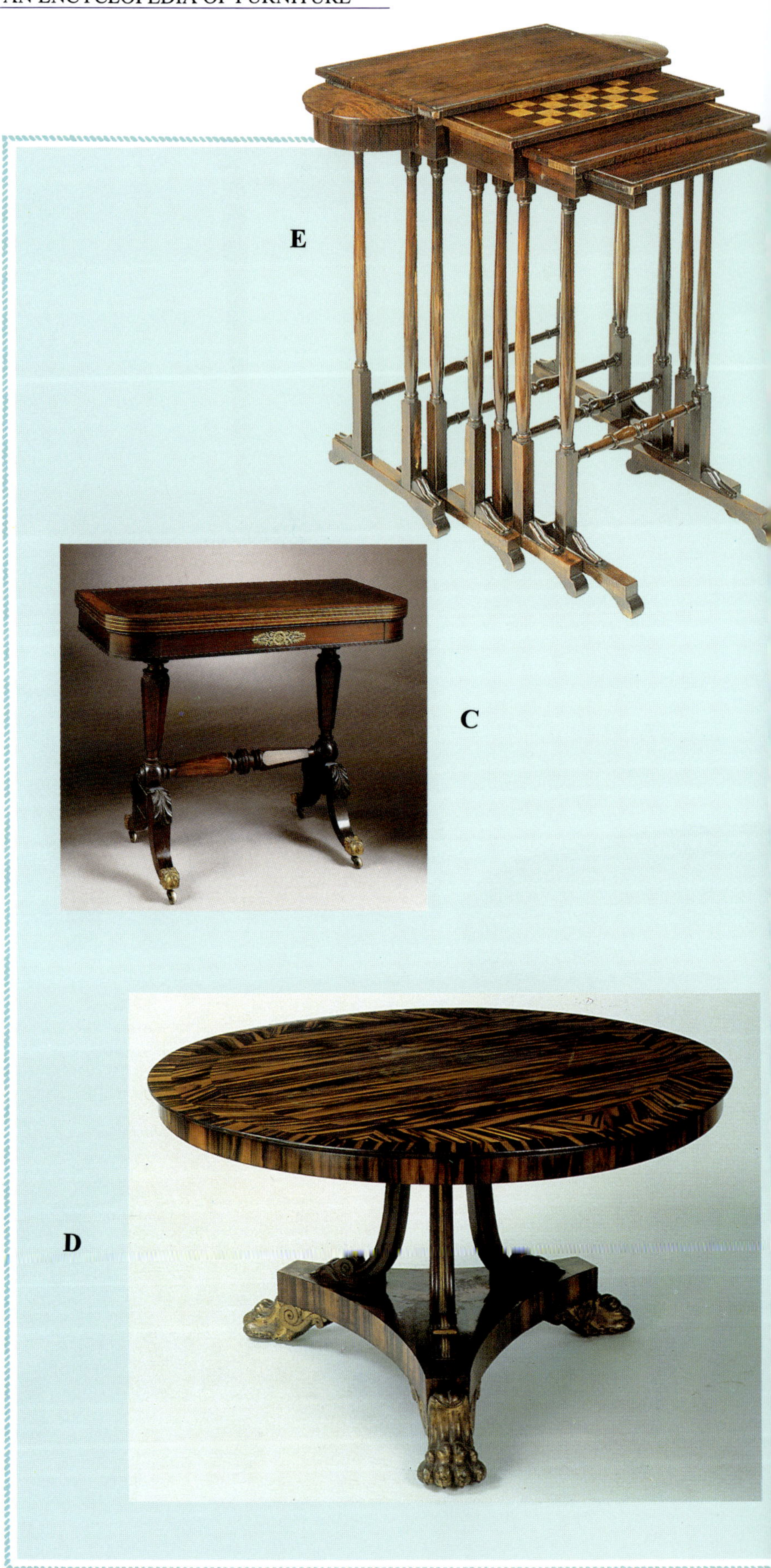

A

B

C. An American Card Table, c1820

This D-shaped card table is of high quality, and is made of rosewood and mahogany. The gilt-metal decoration, in strung lines at the top, appliqué on the sides and on the castors, is an unusual contrast to the wood. A well is revealed by lifting the hinged lid; inside, the original marbleized paper lining has the maker's label in the centre:

'D. PHYFE'S CABINET WAREHOUSE,
NO 170
Fulton Street New York
N.B. CURLED HAIR MATRASSES
CHAIR AND SOFA CUSHIONS,
AUGUST 1820'

The trestles of this table are tapering faceted columns, as is the stretcher, and there is heavy carving on the knee. The elegant styles of the Regency period are here being succeeded by George IV's more decadent branch of Regency styles.

D. An English Regency Zebrawood Centre Table, c1820

The dazzling zig-zag effect of the zebrawood veneer on the top of this centre table overshadows its slightly unorthodox construction. Most late Regency pieces would usually have a single pedestal or four supports to a quatrefoil base, rather than the three outward scrolling legs seen here. These join a trefoil base, which in turn is resting on three massive gilt lion-paw feet.

Imported from the colony of British Guiana in South America, zebrawood consists of a brown background streaked with darker brown stripes. This very rare table heightens the effect of the grain by being double cross-banded, giving a most unusual, almost herringbone pattern.

E. A Set of English Regency Quartetto Tables, c1820

In late Georgian and Regency times, it was fashionable to have a variety of tables scattered around a drawing room. These could have been sofa tables, Pembrokes, or trios or quartettos – sets of three and four, respectively.

Although this quartetto lacks true George III elegance, it is still well made and has the unusual feature of a chess-board on one table, and half-round hinged compartments for playing pieces on another. In this photograph they appear half-stacked, but in fact they are all quite separate, and would have been placed around the room.

A . An Early 19th-century Danish Mahogany Dressing Table, *c*1820

This unusual neo-classical table shows many typical signs of Scandinavian or mid-European furniture – its disproportion gives it a sense of bulkiness, and its plain surfaces and cubic feel are reminiscent of the Austrian Biedermeier furniture made between 1820 and 1840.

The deep drawer in the frieze gives the table a slightly top-heavy feel, particularly as it is placed on such slender legs – the legs themselves, with their in-and-out curves, are not a traditional form such as cabriole or sabre. The stretcher supporting the whole piece bows in from the front and back, creating an undertier that might have been used to hold a jug and bowl.

The piece shows several well-executed neo-classical details, including the ormolu vases on the top of the two classical columns flanking the mirror; the swing mirror's arch pediment decorated with fan-shaped inlay; the pierced bronze applied decoration on the drawers, including the caduceus (Mercury's symbol) on the corners; and the table's lion-paw feet, although these are slightly weak.

When opened, the drawer displays several compartments of differing sizes, some open, some with lids of ash. The use of ash rather than the more common oak, mahogany or deal is a hallmark of Scandinavian and mid-European work.

B . An English Regency Mahogany Breakfront Side Table, *c*1820

The six legs of this side table accentuate its depth, as does the broken line of the front. It is in the manner of Gillow's, an English cabinetmaking firm founded by Lancastrian Robert Gillow (1703–73), and which still exists today as Waring & Gillow. The very successful firm opened a branch of its business in London's Oxford Street in 1770, and from around the 1820s onward stamped its work with the mark 'Gillow's' or 'Gillow's, Lancaster'. The firm's cost books from the late 18th century still survive, providing a fascinating insight into the cabinetmaking business at the time.

This table is decorated on thee sides only, as it was designed to stand against a wall; a recognized form since the 16th century, the side table became more fixed as furniture styles became heavier, and by this date would generally have been used as a serving piece. Although similar in function to a sideboard, this table is 3ft 6in (1m) wide, whereas a sideboard would be approximately twice that length.

B

D

C. An English Regency Sofa Table, *c*1820

Toward the end of the Regency period, increasing emphasis was laid on table feet, and bases spread upward and outward in many different forms. This reflected the move toward more sculptural furniture of the Victorian era – the standard form of sofa table followed this trend, which placed less emphasis on veneer. Mahogany and other veneers of the 18th century were being exhausted by this date, as many of the mature forests of the West Indies and Central America had been cut down.

The rosewood top with boxwood stringing seems a little large for the single pedestal supporting the table, whose flaps extend on outstretched brackets. When closed, the table top would be approximately the same width as the four strong, splayed sabre legs ornamented with scrolls which come from the quatrefoil base.

D. A Finnish Pine Table, *c*1825

This interior of a chimneyless hut of the early 19th century was originally from the village of Jaakuna, and is now in the National Museum of Finland. It is very primitive, showing clearly how traditional furniture design can remain almost static through time, in contrast to court or up-market designs which, thanks to available wealth, changed rapidly with fashion. Traditionally, tools were scarce, and most items would have been made by those who used them. Tables such as this were little more than an adzed plank supported on two sections of trunk, as were the benches by its side.

This table is reminiscent of medieval furniture from Central Europe, which was probably made in the same way. It is still in its original setting, and so can be dated with some accuracy, although we know similar tables are many centuries old. While not highly finished, the table follows the natural contours of the wood, a concern which was revived in the early 20th century in Europe and was always central to Oriental work.

A. An English George IV Mahogany Games Table, *c*1825

This table is interesting for its variation on the unfolding mechanism, or action. Whereas on an average four-legged card table the back legs would swing out to provide support for the table top when unfolded, here the table rests on two turned columns. The elegant solution is for the top to swivel through 90 degrees, and then to open out over the frieze. The frieze itself contains a baize-lined compartment to hold playing cards and pieces.

Because the Regency period was such an experimental one, it can be difficult to date pieces such as this. Although the table top and splayed feet could easily be Regency, the bulbous turned baluster supports suggest a slightly later date.

B. A Restauration Table, *c*1830

The French Restauration period lasted from 1815 to 1848, and refers to the brief restoration of the Bourbon dynasty – the descendants of Louis XVI – to the throne. Traditional furniture had in fact continued through the lean early years of the century, and this piece does show Empire characteristics – the anthemion decoration on its claw feet and its heavy architectural structure, for example. But both France and England also saw revival movements during this time; in France, Gothic styles made their reappearance, with furniture carved with Gothic tracery known as *à la cathédrale.* The Restauration period has a number of similarities to German Biedermeier furniture – plain lines, a lack of decoration and an interest in native woods – and in fact the two styles developed along parallel lines.

It is the light wood that makes the piece so strikingly different from Empire furniture. A fashion for *bois clair* (literally, pale wood) led to a move away from bronze appliqués; inlays, such as ebony, pewter and plain brass, were used as contrast to the wood. From this date on, less emphasis was laid on architectural design (furniture from the beginning of the century was dominated by the designs of the architects, Fontaine and Percier), and more importance was given to ornament. This was reinforced by the success of new pattern books such as that of Michel Jansen, published in 1835.

The popularity of *bois clair* was aided by the move toward mechanization around this time. The Industrial Revolution replaced human workers with economical machines. These produced smooth, regular veneers, which brought out the best even in European woods, and allowed for new manufacturing techniques to be developed with less emphasis on hand finishing.

A

B

C

D

C. An English George IV Rosewood Games Table, *c*1830

In comparison with earlier games tables, this piece appears much heavier. This is partly due to the use of unrelieved rosewood – a dark wood when on its own – and also because of the departure from earlier neatness of line. The bulging compartment at one end of the table would have contained pieces for both backgammon and chess. The legs are no longer 'standard' Regency (splayed from one main column at each end) but stand separate, filled with delicately turned spindles, similar to designs produced by Gillow.

Two unusual features for a piece of this date are the gadrooned bottom of the games board section and the chunky paw feet with scrolling behind them. More at home on a piece of George II furniture, they are clues to the beginning of a revival of early Georgian styles.

D. An Ash Biedermeier Folding Breakfast Table, *c*1835

Probably Austrian or German, this table is typical of the Biedermeier style which was so popular in Europe (and particularly Austria, Germany and Eastern Europe) during the first half of the 19th century. The Biedermeier movement took its name from a fictional character who represented the typical German Philistine – which indicates the style's reaction against the 'aristocratic' past.

The lines in Biedermeier pieces are always clear and simple, and concentrate on the vertical and horizontal. This often gives a feeling of neo-classical simplicity, but sometimes leads to heaviness. With this table, the deep frieze and weight of the table top are balanced by the massive cubic feet on which the plain column legs are sitting.

Although Biedermeier can be thought of as an artistic movement (its most famous exponent being the self-taught artist, Carl Spitzweg, 1808–85), it mirrored a tendency throughout Europe to return to an uncluttered but dignified form. The combination of elements from English Regency, French Louis XVI and neo-classical styles led to a form that seemed to herald the Art Deco concentration on line.

A . An English William IV, or Victorian, Games and Work Table, *c*1840

This curious variant on the Georgian sewing table is made of walnut, a popular Victorian wood which came back into fashion in the mid 19th century. The top box held playing pieces for the board, and the well was for sewing equipment. On a Georgian piece, the well would have been a sliding drawer, but here it forms part of the central column, which rests on a squat, fluted baluster ending in three scrolling supports.

The piece is over-decorated compared to its Georgian equivalents – each black square on the board is decorated with geometric marquetry – and gives an overall bulbous impression.

B . An English William IV Pollard Oak Library Table, *c*1840

This table is a reminder of how fashions change – until the 1970s, heavy Victoriana such as this would have been quickly dismissed. But despite its lack of a named designer or cabinetmaker, which inevitably makes it less popular than other attributed pieces, furniture in this vein is becoming more desirable as earlier work becomes rarer.

Although this table was probably made during William IV's reign, it is difficult to date with accuracy. The beautiful pollard oak veneer reflects the Arts & Crafts Movement's revival of interest in native woods (oak being indigenous to Great Britain), and the flat table top with deep undecorated frieze has the flavour of German Biedermeier furniture of the 1820s, which encouraged bold, undecorated shapes. It is the trestle ends, carved, fluted, splayed feet, and baluster-turned stretchers which are an exaggeration of George IV or heavy Regency styles and give the piece its heavy look.

C

D

C. An English Victorian Papier Mâché Table, *c*1845

Papier mâché had been used in Persia (Iran) and the East for centuries before it was introduced to Europe in the 17th century. Made by moulding pressed paper or wood pulp mixed with glue and chalk, it was lightly polished once dry. The resulting dense and shiny surface took oil paint very easily. It is a similar finish to japanning, and sometimes hard to distinguish from lacquer; the main disadvantage to papier mâché is the difficulty in repairing furniture when chipped or otherwise damaged.

In 1772, Henry Clay of Birmingham, England, patented a form of the process, popularizing the little-known product in England. He produced numerous high-quality pieces, including a writing desk of 1784 found in Horace Walpole's London house in Strawberry Hill. The Birmingham company of Jennens and Bettridge, established in the late 18th century, became the most prolific producers of 19th-century papier mâché work, and this table is typical of their output. Furniture pieces included suites, settees, beds, pier tables and occasional tables such as this, and always carried their stamp. The firm employed many well-known artists of the day to paint scenes such as this on their work, among them John Frederick Herring (1795–1865), the celebrated sporting painter.

D. An Italian Renaissance Revival Writing Desk and Chair, *c*1850

After the fall of Napoleon Bonaparte in 1815, the Empire style continued to be popular in Italy, although it became diluted by various revivalist movements. One of these was the Renaissance revival, popular just before the *Risorgimento* (or unification of Italy) in the mid 19th century. In a sense, the Renaissance revival reflected a mood in Italy which was looking back to its 'finest hour' in design; in the same way, the Renaissance itself had revived the supremacy of Roman times.

In fact, this table is based on a Roman design (seen in wall-paintings made of marble) but its shape and decoration are taken from a Renaissance table style popular in the mid 16th century. The grotesque, swelling pedestals and loose cross-framed design reflect the Mannerist influences of the late Renaissance, and the supports are decorated just below the top with broad melon fluting which was much used on Renaissance chests. The overall effect, however, is clearly 19th century. The chair is late Empire style, and both pieces are lightened with floral marquetry characteristic of 19th-century Italian work.

1800-1900

A . A Mid 19th-century Florentine Black Marble Table on Gilt Wood Stand, *c*1850

Justly famous for its marble work since the 16th century, Italy was still considered a leader of art and learning in the middle of the 19th century. The precise craftsmanship shown in the micro-mosaic decoration here was admired throughout Europe, and this type of work was widely exported. Using hundreds of pieces of chipped marble and glass per square inch, the inlaid ovals depict various well-known Roman ruins and surround a familiar classical picture of doves drinking from a fountain, known as 'Pliny's Doves'. The table is edged with a band of malachite, a green mineral (sometimes used to veneer table tops) which takes its colour from copper traces.

The large gilt stand supporting the marble top has a structural, slightly Baroque feel to it; in fact, it could almost be 17th-century Venetian, and demonstrates that while furniture styles have changed considerably over the centuries, national characteristics endure. Several such tables were exhibited at the Great Exhibition of 1851 held at London's Crystal Palace and are recorded in the official catalogue.

B . An English Victorian Sutherland Table, *c*1850

Gate-leg tables had been made from the 16th century onward, and this six-legged form was established by the 17th century. Generally, the legs supported a round oak top, although this sophisticated version shows late Regency or Georgian influence in its rectangular leaves. The table has a surprisingly light feel to it, particularly as rosewood tables can be dull. It has a slender undercarriage and legs, both with fine turning, and the two centre legs are curiously joined by a horseshoe stretcher. This table is a specifically Victorian style which probably takes its name from the family which popularized it.

A

C. A 19th-century Scandinavian Pine Chamber Table, *c*1850

After Scandinavia's severe decline in power during the 18th and early 19th centuries, it became isolated, both geographically and in terms of trade, fashion, wealth and style. This meant that furniture designs remained fairly conservative, dominated either by European Empire styles or by the Scandinavian folk tradition; examples echoing the latter are often difficult to date.

This chamber table is of a characteristically simple construction; it has a functional drawer in the frieze, the legs are turned and the stretchers are heavy, much in the manner of a 17th-century English joint stool. The painting of the wood-grain effect on the drawer is typically German or Scandinavian, but was transferred to the United States, where it still survives, by that country's Central European immigrants. Nineteenth-century pine was of much better quality than today's, as the trees were older and more mature; thus furniture of this period endured well.

The Crystal Palace Exhibition, London, 1851

In England in 1851, largely thanks to the efforts of Prince Albert, Queen Victoria's husband, an exhibition of products from all over the world was organized at Crystal Palace. Furniture designs and other decorative objects in a variety of styles from the mid 19th century were extensively exhibited. The massive display was housed in the especially built Crystal Palace, an elaborate and revolutionary structure erected in London's Hyde Park and made of glass panels on a steel frame. Its arched roof stood more than three storeys high, and it contained fountains, sculpture, trees and pavilions on different themes from different countries. The catalogue of the Exhibition produced by *The Art-Journal* – more than 300 pages long and containing over 1,000 illustrations – provides an intriguing commentary on Victorian taste. Ralph Wornum (1812–77) wrote an editorial essay in the catalogue discussing style, decoration and excess which is still relevant today. He was critical of excessive ornament and of the naturalist school (which used design motifs taken from nature), and dismissive of the revival movements (such as Rococo and Gothic), which presented some exceedingly heavy compositions.

'Ornament run riot' can certainly be seen in these catalogue entries. But arguments against natural motifs, central to 19th-century design, were sometimes contrived; arguing that nature should not change the structure of a piece perhaps simply shows a preference for neo-Classicism. At least, however, design has moved away from Empire styles worldwide. The Victorian style, which these prints illustrate, seems to be distinct from the past, albeit heavy, and perhaps it can be said to have paved the way for Art Nouveau.

A. Table by J & W Hilton of Montreal, *c*1851

'Amongst the contributions of our fellow subjects in Canada,' reads the catalogue, 'there are some specimens highly creditable to her manufacturers.' These included an elegant fire engine, a sleigh and this table. It comes from French-speaking Canada and accurately reflects Central European tastes of the time. There are few straight lines, the legs are scrolled, the top is irregular and carved with foliage, etc, and the stretchers meet in a pseudo-classical urn. It is made of 'boldly carved' black walnut.

B. An English Console Table and Frame for Mirror with Bracket, *c*1851

These were made by the Gutta Percha Company, which was set up in London to manufacture objects made of the new composition, gutta percha. This 'natural plastic' was derived from the juice of Malayan trees, which provided an amorphous white substance that could be moulded into various shapes. In this case, it has been moulded onto a wire armature to form an extravagantly Victorian example of a Rococo console table and mirror above. It is exactly the style of furniture that Ralph Wornum so objected to in his commentary on the exhibits at the Great Exhibition, its decoration being both excessive and rather improbable.

C. An Ebony Table by Doe Hazelton & Co of Boston, Massachusetts, *c*1851

This table draws upon a number of different sources. The front legs are reminiscent of furniture by William Kent, the early 18th-century English designer, who commonly used herm figures (half-human, half-architectural) such as these. The scrolling stretchers which support a vase of flowers have a Rococo feel, as does the apron's central cartouche, with its mask head. Circling the apron is a naturalistic ornament of a flowering vine, and the top is typically Victorian with its irregular shape. It is carved in ebony, the darkness of which would increase the heavy effect. Eighteenth-century American furniture drew heavily on European styles, a trend which continued into the 19th century, as an international style evolved.

D. The Crusader Chess Table from Ireland, *c*1851

This table is the work of a Mr Graydon of Dublin, and is historical revivalism at its most extreme. Its extraordinary shape has four lobes surrounding the central square and bowing sides. It is decorated with relief work such as that found on the Parthenon, but here showing the medieval Crusaders in their battle against Islam. The legs – or corner pillars – each stand on four columns directly taken from Romanesque architecture, which was popular in Europe during the 11th century. Plucking decorative motifs from many different centuries and countries, this table is enthusiastic, if not tasteful.

A
C
D

A . An 'Elizabethan' Table and Stool, *c*1851

This ensemble was made by the Englishman, C J Richardson, who according to the Great Exhibition catalogue was 'known by his excellent work on Elizabethan ornament and furniture, in which he has with much perseverance and ability pointed out the peculiarities and rich fantasies visible in this school of design. He has now practically realised his knowledge . . . ' Fully fledged Renaissance Revival, this table is probably most closely based on a combination of 1550s Italian design and English styles of fifty to a hundred years later; the mask head and decoration on the trestle ends are similar to a chair in the Victoria & Albert Museum, London, designed by a Frenchman in the 1640s. Typically Victorian, this bears little resemblance to any work from the reign of Elizabeth I (which ended in 1603) or immediately after, but draws on an impressive medley of sources and styles.

B . An Italian Table Made for the King of Sardinia, *c*1851

This table was made by G Capello of Turin and is basically Empire-style. It is based on classical ideals – a square shape, simple dignified decoration on its top and neo-Classical pedestal with anthemion motif. Italy generally is thought of as excessive in its decoration, but these pieces are fairly restrained in terms of ornament.

C . A 19th-century Table by Michael Thonet of Vienna, *c*1851 and

D . A Neo-Rococo Austrian Table by Carl Leistler, *c*1851

The table by Michael Thonet (1796–1871) has an unusual construction: it is made of bent rosewood, which is shaped so that the grain of the wood follows the line of curve required; rather than relying on mortice-and-tenon joints or screws and nails, it concentrates on the elasticity of the wood (which was bent under intense steam to allow it to be manipulated in this way). Thonet was famous for his bentwood chairs, made in the millions and still manufactured today.

The bentwood table is in complete contrast to the more conventional table by Leistler, manufacturer of furniture in the 'later Venetian taste', which uses some of the Baroque decoration of the late 17th and 18th centuries – elaborate scrolling, loose natural forms and heavy construction. Interestingly, Thonet and Leistler were at one time business partners: in the 1840s they supplied furniture

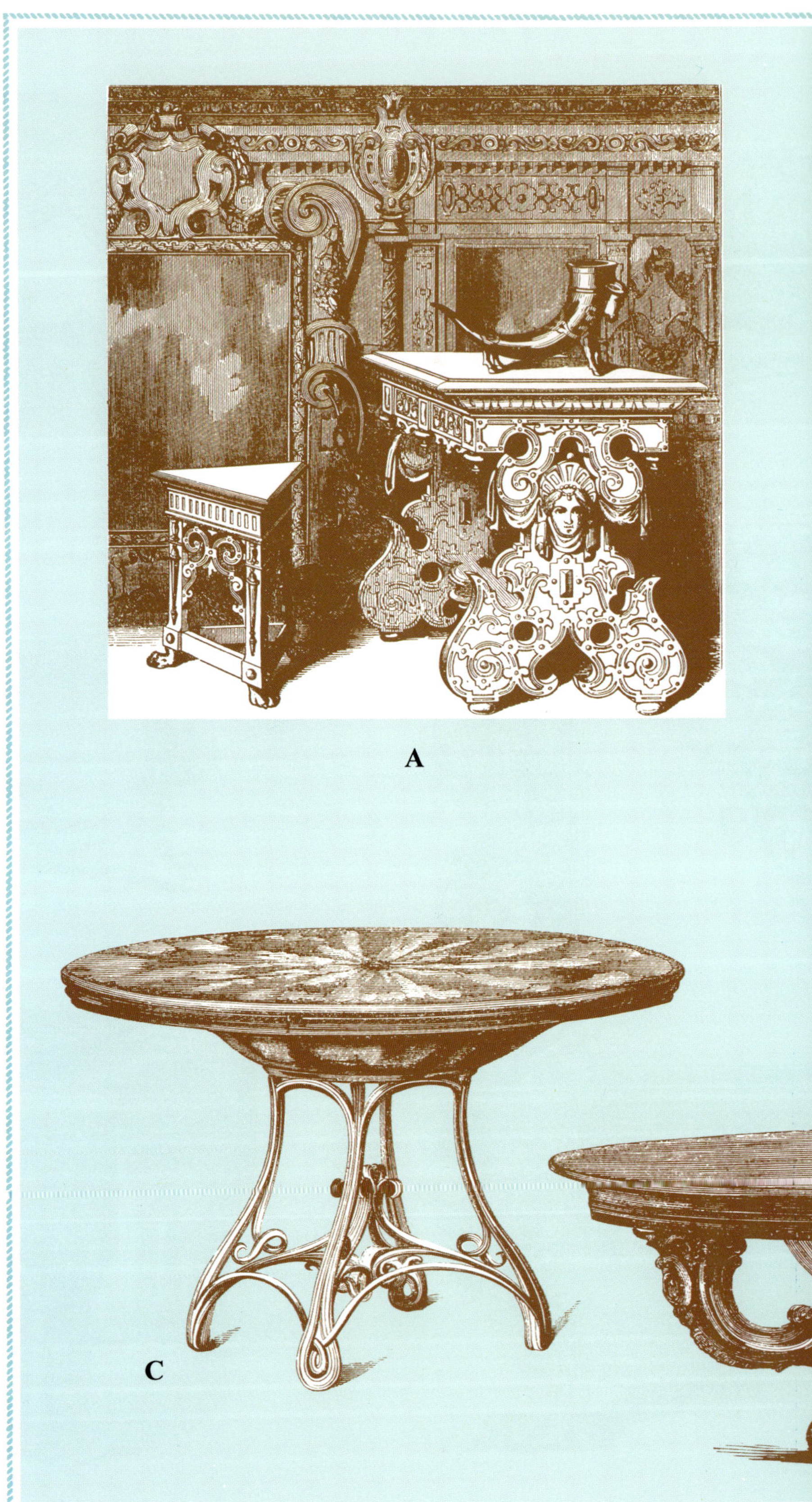

A

C

to Prince Liechtenstein.

These two tables are from exactly the same date, but whereas Leistler's looks backward for inspiration, Thonet's looks toward the 20th century.

E . An English Cast-iron Deerhound Table, *c*1855

This cast-iron table was made by the Coalbrookdale Company, which was established in the 18th century by Abraham Darby. It produced many notable works during the Industrial Revolution, including the Severn Gorge Bridge of 1779, and continued well into the 19th century, producing both industrial pieces and even domestic bronze sculpture. In the second half of the 19th century, the company reproduced a large variety of French bronze animal sculpture, made by Coalbrookdale in cast iron which was patinated to simulate the original. Such experience provided the necessary skills to make this astonishing ensemble.

This table, exhibited at the *Exposition Universelle* in Paris in 1855, was designed by John Bell, who was influenced by the English Victorian sculptors, John Flaxman and Francis Chantrey. A student at the Royal Academy, Bell exhibited there until 1879 and produced some fairly well-known sculptures, such as *The Eagle Slayer.* The arms on the dogs' collars here are of the Hargreaves family in Lancashire, for whom the table was made; it was probably the property of Colonel John Hargreaves of Whalley Abbey.

Coalbrookdale produced catalogues of their wares, and this table appeared in the 1860 edition, listed at a price of £80. It may well be unique, as no others are known; it is now in the Ironbridge Gorge Museum in Shropshire.

1800-1900

A . A 19th-century Dutch Marble-inlaid Table, *c*1860

This 19th-century revival of a Rococo table (originally produced in the first half of the 18th century) makes the most of the Dutch passion for ebony or ebonized furniture. (Ebonized furniture consisted of black lacquer-painted furniture, made to look like ebony.) Exotic materials such as tortoiseshell, ivory and marble were extracted from countries occupied by the Dutch during the 17th century, and were often combined with ebony to produce a lighter finish overall.

The sculptural effect and apron carving of this table were very much to Victorian taste, and a number of these were exported around Europe. The style of the cabriole legs and pierced stretcher dates from c1720, and the top shows a variety of marble *pietra dura* work, almost always imported from Italy. By the mid 19th century, however, many of the fine stones found in early *pietra dura* mosaic had been exhausted, and the marble inlay here is distinctly dull in comparison with earlier work. Around this time, many marble pictures were mass-produced, and were generally of a lower quality.

B . A 19th-century Austrian Porcelain *Guéridon, c*1860

The fashion for porcelain furniture was inspired by the 19th-century passion for decoration. This piece is made with porcelain from the Vienna factory, and is decorated with gilt scrolls and precisely modelled fruiting vines on its stem.

Porcelain furniture had a great advantage over wood in both carving and gilt work. Its harder surface could be modelled with far more detail, and gilt – and other bright fired-on glazes – could be applied directly to its surface. (Gesso has to be applied to wood before the gilt, or else the polychrome is absorbed.) Porcelain was obviously more fragile, though, and pieces such as this were often held together with internal metal rods and brackets.

Austria at this time was at the centre of the Austro-Hungarian Empire, which covered much of the Northern Mediterranean. The hand-painted decoration on the table top shows rustic scenes from the more exotic corners of the Empire, including Hungary and Dalmatia. Labelled with the name of each area they represent, they are extremely precise in their detail.

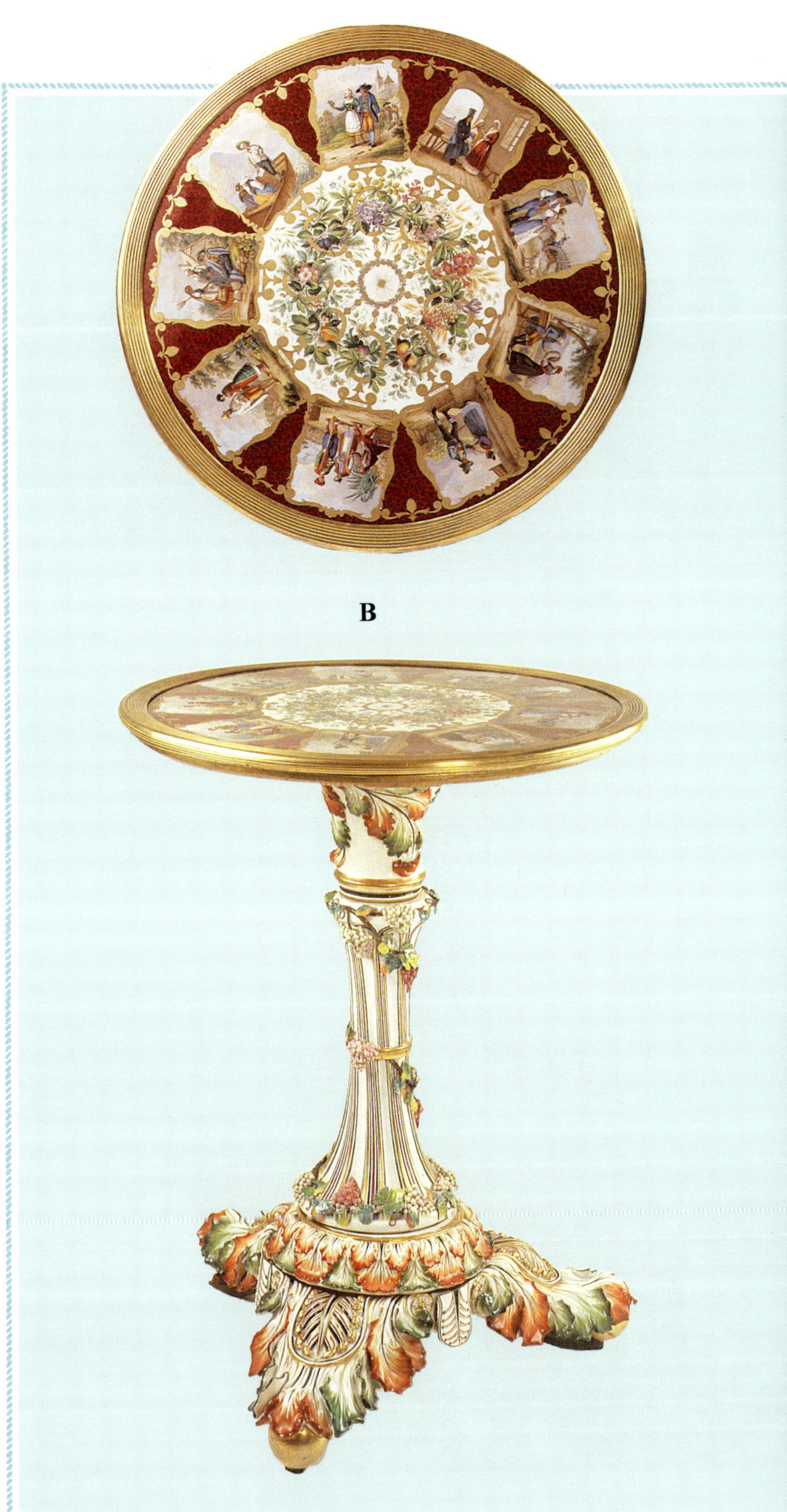

B

C. An English Victorian Burr Walnut Centre Table, *c*1860

Despite the first impression this table gives of being heavy and dull, it has a top made of intricate burr walnut. Like pollard oak, burr walnut was a specially chosen cross-section used for veneer because of its attractive pattern. If it was highly polished, the effect of this table would be very different, drawing attention away from the bulbous legs and toward the fine grain of the wood and the carved ivy border along the table's shaped edge.

The unusual angle of this photograph emphasizes what Eero Saarinen (the Finnish-American 20th-century architect) called 'a slum of legs'. The table's four scrolled legs and supports surround a central turned finial sitting on an octopus-like platform. The whole of the bottom half of the table is covered with scrolling, possibly a precursor of organic Art Nouveau decoration.

Although it is difficult to imagine why such heavy styles were ever ordered or made, this table was based on past design (the carving could be seen as the death throes of George IV or Chippendale decoration); and popular taste, then as now, often preferred safer, established designs to more recent developments.

D. A French Tulipwood and Porcelain Mounted Writing Table, *c*1860

This writing table in the style of Louis XVI, popular a hundred years earlier, shows the characteristic combination from that time of tulipwood and porcelain plaques. Originally these plaques came from the newly established Sèvres porcelain factory (*c*1750). They were decorative, rectangular set pieces of a floral or rustic peasant-in-a-landscape pattern on white, surrounded with a gilt border and on an overall background colour, such as the green used here.

Simon-Philippe Poirier and Dominique Daguerre, two Parisian furniture dealers, specialized in producing pieces exactly like this in the mid 18th century, employing many known craftsmen such as Martin Carlin (d.1785), who excelled in this style. Many of the pieces were dated, and this table is typical of those produced *c*1765.

The table's only concession to its real date of *c*1860 is the fact that its size and proportions have been reduced to accommodate 19th-century living styles.

1800-1900

A . A 19th-century Italian Marquetry Breakfast Table, *c*1865

This spectacular table is inlaid with various woods on an ebony background. The central floral pattern is surrounded by strapwork, embellished with scrolls and trailing flowers. Italy had a long history of high-quality marquetry which dated back to the 16th century. This form shows certain similarities with *pietra dura* (stone inlay) work for which both Florence and Rome were renowned, and the decoration is based on many of the same motifs.

The edge of the table is finished with a gadrooned brass band, and the whole top sits on a single column with a trefoil base. It tips on its side for storage, as all breakfast tables do, and probably also to display its distinctive design.

B . An English Victorian Inlaid Dining Table, *c*1867

Although this table is sturdy compared to Georgian pieces, it shows the beginnings of a movement to abandon the excessive scrolling and clumsiness of earlier Victorian tables. The top is made of amboyna, a light wood, and is bordered with fine-quality marquetry. The legs and support are neatened with straight edges, and the central column uses parallel lines to suggest fluting. The ebony stringing of the edges, both on the top and the undercarriage, gives the table a smarter, lighter feel.

The undercarriage, with its square-sectioned members, is slightly reminiscent of late 17th-century design, although the oval top is a typical 19th-century shape. The marquetry on the top shows the monogram 'AM', of the original owner, displayed in four cartouches around the table edge. It was made for Alfred Morrison and displayed at the Paris Exposition of 1867.

C . A 19th-century Louis XV-style Writing Table, *c*1870

The mid 19th century saw a vogue throughout Europe for revivals of all dates. One of the favourites was Louis XV, and despite being made up of curious parts, this table is very much in the spirit of mid 18th-century designs. It has a tulipwood background, it is decorated with marquetry and the top is edged in brass. However, the stretcher and stand supporting the legs at each end are clumsier than those elements on the elegant writing tables of the 18th century.

The table is stamped with the name of its 19th-century maker, Gardiennet, and is well made. Many revival pieces were direct copies, taken from actual pieces or pattern-books, but some makers found it impossible to resist making 'improvements'.

D. An English Victorian Mahogany Writing Table, *c*1880

This quality reproduction of a Louis XVI writing desk bears the stamp of Edwards & Roberts of Broadmoor St., London. Working toward the end of the 19th century, the company specialized in manufacturing several revival styles, such as the piece here and Edwardian breakfront bookcases. The original Louis XVI style, which flourished roughly a hundred years earlier, was a plainer reaction to elaborate Rococo designs, and was influenced by English taste of the time. In many cases, Edwards & Roberts would follow the original drawings and produce virtually identical reproductions of a piece, but in this case there are obvious adaptations to suit Victorian tastes.

The use of ormolu to emphasize the fluting on the legs and the edge of the table top are typical of the original style. But the lack of expensive, high-quality veneer in the Victorian era accounts for the use of lighter woods, giving a lighter feel to the piece. The dark wood used here is mahogany, the lighter, amboyna – a West Indian wood with a tight, swirling grain. As on authentic Louis XVI pieces, the table's sides are decorated with banding, but the scrolling marquetry on the top is Victorian. Although the piece is well made, it misses the feel of true Louis XVI furniture.

E. A 19th-century Writing Table, *c*1890

This is a clear copy of the Louis XVI style of a century before, popular in France in the 1770s and 1780s, the last two decades before the Revolution. Probably made in France or England, it also could have originated in Italy or Germany, which also had long traditions of fine marquetry and cabinetmaking.

The tulipwood cross-banding and trellis-and-dot veneer on the table top and sides are typical late 18th-century French decoration, but on close inspection adjustments have been made to the original style. It is slightly smaller than a similar piece from a century earlier, probably because late 19th-century homes were not as palatial as the châteaux for which an original would have been destined. The inlaid leather top tends to be a later feature, and the brass fittings seen here would have been fire-gilded ormolu work. This complex process involves applying melted gold to bronze; lethal fumes are given off, but the technique results in a truly gilt effect, one which is then hand-finished. In the 19th century, it was replaced by a cheaper electrical process, similar to silver-plating, which never really achieves the same result.

1800-1900

A . An Early 19th-Century Gilt Bronze Mounted Mahogany Table à la Tronchin

This desk is obviously French in style but is in fact probably of Scandinavian or German origin. The baize-lined top is adjustable to any angle and can be raised to a convenient height on the four corner supports, which slide down into the legs as the top is lowered. There are two drawers and two slides in the frieze. The table is named after Théodore Tronchin (1709–81), a Swiss doctor who was a strong advocate of fresh air and exercise, good posture and loose-fitting clothes. In the 1770s he ordered an adjustable table of the type illustrated here, apparently because he felt it was more natural to read and write in a standing position. His desk was raised and lowered by means of a handle at the side and this system is seen on many example. Although the table has taken his name he did not invent it, and in Britain such pieces are generally known as architect's tables.

B . A French Empire Mahogany Secrétaire à Abattant

The black marble top, 3ft 2in (96cm) wide, is a large fall-front with a fitted interior behind and a pair of cupboard doors in the base. The bold square lines of the secrétaire à abattant were well suited to the aspirations of Napoleon's years of success, and this is a good example of the use of large expanses of veneer with fine figure, set off by small and often highly-classical mounts in gilt bronze. Here the escutcheon on the drawer is flanked by a pair of winged angels in loose drapes and stylised torches are placed either side of the main desk. The influence of the French Empire spread this style right across Europe, from Italy to Scandinavia.

D

B

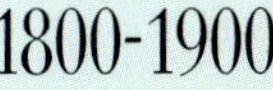

C

A

C. An Early 19th-Century Secrétaire à Abattant

The fall-front writing compartment has one drawer above and three below, and the whole is flanked by reeded columns with gilt capitals, bases and bands. The spectacularly colourful flower decoration is formed from pieces of plain and stained mother-of-pearl set in black lacquer, a technique known as *lac burgauté,* and the desk probably originates from one of the Dutch Far Eastern colonies. It is 3ft 6in (1.07m) wide.

D. An Early 19th-Century Russian Writing Cabinet

This remarkable piece is only 3ft 1in (94cm) wide but 9ft 2in (2.80m) high to the top of the double bird's head finial on the dome. Conceived in neo-classical vein, it is veneered in Karelian birch and poplar, woods generally found only on Russian pieces. Beneath a clock in the upper section is a cupboard with a classical figure in gilt bronze in a niche on the door. The cupboard is flanked by two pairs of white marble and gilt bronze columns, and beneath is a drawer with a fold-down front. Behind the leather-lined fall-front the writing compartment is fitted with small drawers and pigeonholes built in the same style as the exterior, with white marble columns flanking a mirror-backed central niche over an area of simulated brickwork. The base is a simple two-door cupboard.

1800-1900

A. An English Regency Carlton House Desk

This mahogany desk, 5ft 1½in (1.61m) wide, is on ribbed tapering legs with castors at the feet and carved paterae at the heads. There is a brass gallery around the top, and the gilt bail handles are in the form of looped drapery. This example has a bank of six drawers in the superstructure, with two cupboards (one with a slot for posting letters in the top, probably for incoming mail) and two more drawers in the curved sloping wings, but many variations of this distinctive and practical design are to be found. In some cases the wings are stepped rather than sloping and in others they continue round at the same height as the back. An adjustable slope for writing is also a common feature.

The type first appeared in the late 18th century and continued to be popular during the Regency period. Edwardian examples in the same style are also found.

B. An English Regency Mahogany Carlton House Desk

This is a good example of the influence of Greek, Roman and Egyptian antiquity on furniture design during the early years of the 19th century. The leather-lined writing slope is flanked by small drawers with gilt-bronze lion's head handles, the frieze is inset with Sphinx busts, and the moulding of the legs, which rest on brass paw feet, derives from a classical motif of a bundle of reeds. The whole desk is 3ft 7in (1.89m) wide.

C. An English Regency Carlton House Desk

The distinctive D-shape of this writing table puts it firmly in the Carlton House family, but the massive flanking pillars in the form of fasces are most unusual; they stand on ebonised feet carved with two tiers of lotuses and serve as cupboards, secured, like all the drawers, with Bramah locks. The circular tops are inlaid with compass medallions.

Maritime decorative motifs, like the dolphin handles on the main drawers, became popular after Nelson's naval victory at Trafalgar in 1805. This desk is made of mahogany with gilt edging and handles, 4ft 9in (1.45m) wide.

A

D

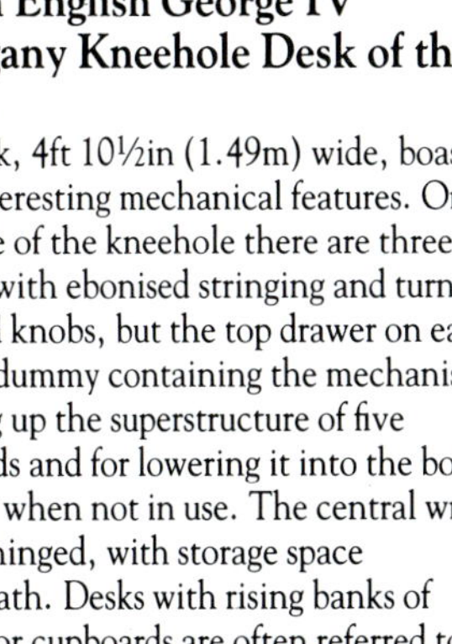

B

C

D. An English George IV Mahogany Kneehole Desk of the 1820s

This desk, 4ft 10½in (1.49m) wide, boasts some interesting mechanical features. On each side of the kneehole there are three drawers with ebonised stringing and turned ebonised knobs, but the top drawer on each side is a dummy containing the mechanism for cranking up the superstructure of five cupboards and for lowering it into the body of the desk when not in use. The central writing slope is hinged, with storage space underneath. Desks with rising banks of drawers or cupboards are often referred to as 'harlequins', perhaps because the superstructure springs up like a harlequin, or because it disappears like a harlequin.

A . An Early-19th-Century English Regency Secretaire-Cabinet

The main decoration on this piece (2ft 6in (76cm) wide) is satinwood stringing. It has a fitted fall-front writing drawer over a cupboard with brass grille doors in the base. The low glazed cupboard in the superstructure, without the architectural pediment and cornice which had been a normal feature during the previous century, is typical of the smaller cabinets that became fashionable during the Regency period. The use of latticework backed by fabric is also characteristic of the lighter approach of the period.

B . One of a Pair of English Regency Rosewood Secretaires

The open shelving rests on turned gilt-bronze supports with X-shaped inserts. The base is 3ft 1½in (96cm) wide with a deep writing drawer over a two-door cupboard with metal grille fronts, backed with fabric.

The use of exotic, deeply-figured veneers outlined by gilt-bronze beading was much favoured during the Regency period, and small secretaires or cylinder desks were generally preferred to the more imposing slope-front bureau-bookcases which continued to be made by country craftsmen. It is unusual to find desks made in pairs from any period.

C . An English Regency Rosewood Lady's Writing and Sewing Table

The body rests on ring-turned taper legs with castors. It has an adjustable reading stand hinged along the front edge, a pull-out writing slide above a dummy drawer in the front, and a drawer at the side fitted for writing accessories. The pleated bag underneath is for storing sewing materials and the matching screen at the back slides up and down so that the desk can be placed close to the fire while the woman's complexion is protected from the heat.

D . A Small Regency Mahogany Writing Table, *c*1815

This writing table was made in the manner of Thomas Hope, and has a drawer fitted with an adjustable writing slope, a pen tray and compartments. The lion's head and ring handles, the brass paw feet and the delicately shaped and reeded legs are all typical of the austere classical style which Hope introduced with the publication of his *Household Furniture and Interior Decoration* of 1807.

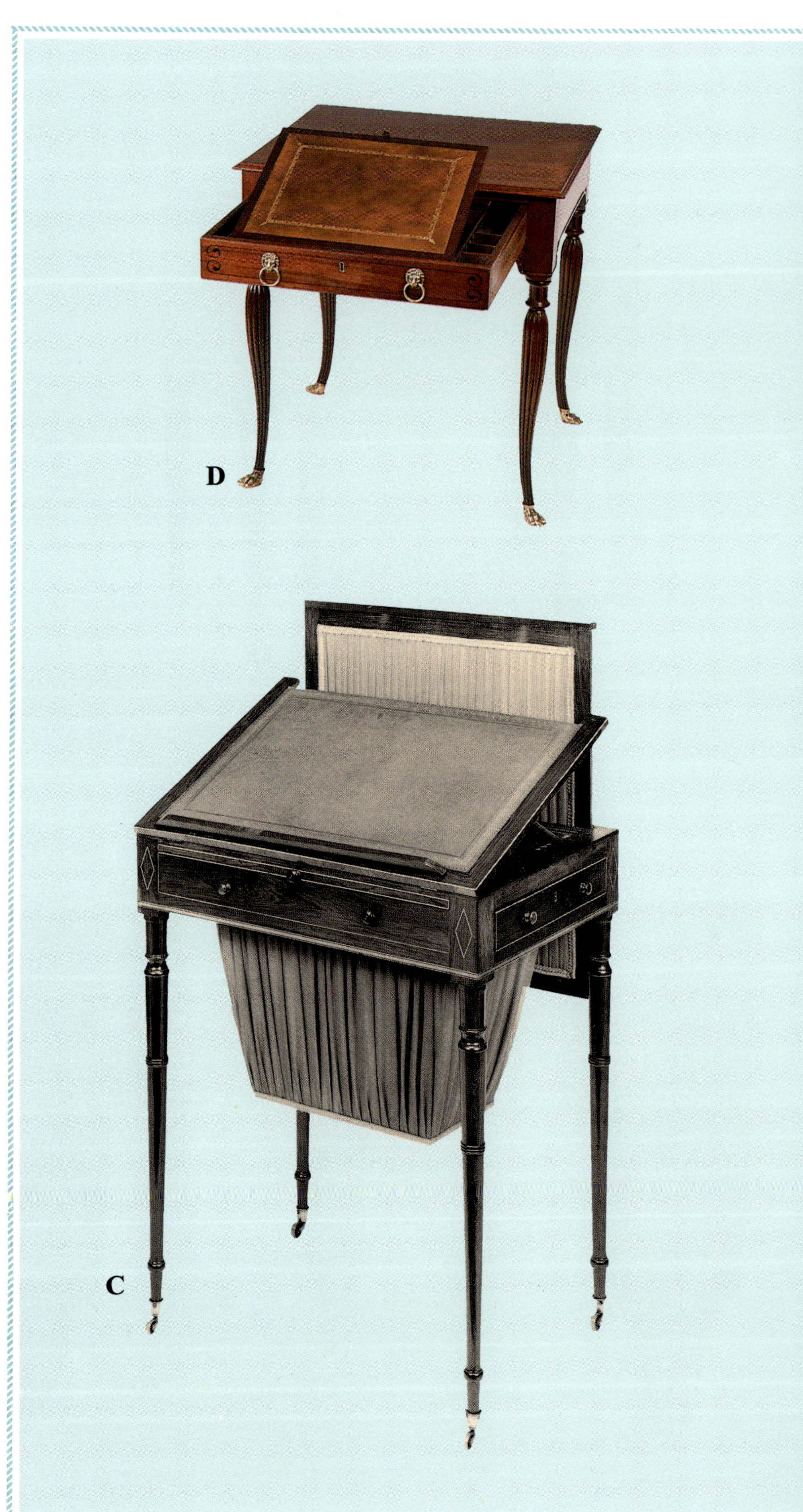

A

B

1800-1900

A. An English Regency Mahogany Library Desk

This piece (4ft 7in (1.04m) wide) is conceived in French Empire taste with plain panels at the ends centred by gilt-bronze Bacchic masks and flanked by free-standing reeded columns at the corners. It has open folio racks below a green leather-lined top with a matching slide.

B. An English Regency Mahogany Library Table

This large writing desk (6ft 3½in (1.12m) across), with three drawers in each side of the frieze, is designed to stand in the centre of a library. It is banded with satinwood and boxwood stringing and supported on four ring-turned tapering legs with brass castors. Its unadorned elegance is a good example of the sterner side of Regency design, ideally suited to the library and very different from some of the exotic creations of the period commissioned by the Regent himself for the Brighton Pavilion representing the other extreme.

C. An English Regency Mahogany Library Writing table

This typical Regency design, similar to the sofa table but without its drop end-flaps, is strung with boxwood and ebony. The lionhead and ring handles and heavy scrolled supports acknowledge the severe Greek taste made popular by the pattern books of Thomas Hope and George Smith. The main body is on end-supports joined by a single stretcher and is 4ft (1.22m) wide.

D. An English Regency Mahogany Writing Table

This is known to have been one of a pair supplied in 1811 by Gillows of Lancaster and described as 'mahogany chamber writing tables, reeded legs and rails beaded as common'. They were intended for bedrooms and are typical of the standard Regency output of this firm, who were the leading cabinetmakers outside London in the 18th and 19th centuries and among the first to regularly stamp their furniture. This desk is 3ft (91cm) wide, with two frieze drawers and a lidded well containing a pen tray and bottle holders in the top.

C

A

1800-1900

A . An American Federal Period Mahogany Tambour Desk
This desk is 3ft 1½in (95cm) wide, and was probably made in New Hampshire in the late 18th or early 19th century. The upper section is delicately inlaid with chequered lining and contains a central cupboard with two inner drawers, flanked by sliding tambour shutters. In front of this is a hinged flap which folds out to form a writing surface supported on lopers and there are four long graduated drawers in the base.

The low superstructure of this piece reflects the European fashion for smaller, more elegant desks during the same period, but the combination of tambour shutters and a fold-out writing surface on a chest of drawers is one of the most distinctive original forms of the Federal period.

B . An American Federal Mahogany Secretary and bookcase
This is known to have been made by Ebenezer Eustis of Salem, Massachusetts and dated 1808. Of imposing proportions, 5ft 4in (1.62cm) wide, it comprises drawers, cupboards and a central desk drawer in the lower section, upon which rests the glazed bookcase. The bookcase top is slightly receded from the unit below – a characteristic Sheraton feature – and the flat surfaces, delicate line inlays and peg-top feet all reflect the English style of the period. The pediment with its brass eagle and urn finials is an American touch. Sometimes known as Salem secretaries, large Sheraton-style pieces of this type are one of the distinctive forms of the Federal period.

C

D

A

B

C. An American Federal Mahogany Butler's Desk, *c*1810

This desk is 3ft 11in (1.20m) wide, and was probably made in Philadelphia or New York. The two curved sides each contain a two-handled drawer over a cupboard, while the breakfront centre section holds a shallow drawer over a pull-out writing drawer and a two-door cupboard. The writing comparment is fitted with three satinwood drawers.

D. An American Pine Slant-Front Desk

This simple four-drawer desk, hand-painted with brightly-coloured birds, flowers, hearts and other traditional motifs as well as paterae and stars in imitation of more sophisticated pieces, is a reminder that by no means all 19th-century furniture was produced in mainstream styles.

It was made in Mahantango Valley, Schuylkill County, Pennsylvania, 3ft 6¾in (1.09m) wide. Expatriate communities, isolated by terrain or by choice, continued to produce their own distinctive forms, sometimes long after they had become old-fashioned in their countries of origin. The painted decoration here continues the traditions of the Pennsylvanian Germans (sometimes known as Pennsylvanian Dutch) who settled in large numbers in the South East of the state.

1800-1900

A . A Viennese Mahogany Secrétaire à Abattant, *c*1820

The inverted pear-shaped body, 3ft 7in (1.09m) wide, is fitted with a semi-circular drawer at the top with a fan-carved fall front. Below it is another shallow drawer and there are two more drawers below the main flap as well as one in the low platform. The whole desk is gilded and supported on massive lion-paw feet. The writing compartment, concealed behind a shaped fall, contains an architectural arrangement of drawers around a mirrored temple interior with secret drawers.

Elaborate and eccentrically shaped secrétaires such as this example were based on French Empire style, but they were an Austrian and German speciality. Plainer examples in Biedermeier style often have a surprisingly modern, almost Art Deco look, but the use of classical acanthus and egg-and-dart moulding ties this piece to the early 19th century.

B . A North German Secretaire in Biedermeier style, *c*1820

The exterior of this desk is birch-veneered with a fitted interior in contrasting dark mahogany veneer. It is of typical architectural form and shown here as it was intended to be seen, the focal point of a domestic interior. Like the other pieces in the room it is characterized by strong form, light colour and minimal applied ornament.

C . A mid-19th Century French Walnut Bureau à Cylindre of the Louis Philippe period

This bureau is 4ft 11in (1.50m) wide, with a solid cylinder front which rolls back to reveal a fitted interior and a leather-lined writing slide. This solid and heavy reinterpretation of the Louis XVI cylinder bureau has three drawers above the desk and nine drawers below, including three in the frieze.

1800-1900

A . A French Mid-19th-Century Bonheur-du-Jour
This fine quality piece is of ebony decorated with lacquer, gilt metal mounts and pewter stringing in the manner of the late 18th-century *ébéniste* Adam Weisweiler. It is mounted with Japanese lacquer panels, having shelved cupboards in the superstructure and a secretaire drawer in the base fitted with a leather-lined writing surface and four small compartments, and measures 2ft 7in (79cm) wide. It bears the mark of Prosper Guillaume Durand, who, with his father, made furniture for various royal palaces in the 1830s and became *ébéniste du roi* under Louis Philippe in 1839. His business flourished until the 1860s, producing *meubles de luxe* in Louis XVI style.

B . A French Kingwood Veneered Secrétaire à Abattant of the 1860s
This secretaire is 2ft 8in (43cm) wide, with a fall-front writing compartment decorated with a black and gilt lacquered chinoiserie scene and a two-door cupboard decorated with a pair of painted ribbon-tied bouquets. It bears the burnt-in mark of Alfred Beurdeley, the last principal of a family firm that specialised in producing high-quality furniture in 18th-century styles, following the Parisian taste for the many 'Louis Revivals' of the 19th century. This rather stolid-looking desk draws on the late Louis XV period for inspiration only, but the Beurdeley workshops, like many leading Paris cabinetmakers of the time, also produced excellent copies of 18th century pieces.

C . A Mid-19th-Century French Bonheur-du-Jour
The galleried superstructure of serpentine shelves flanking a cupboard are decorated with marquetry birds on an ebony ground. There are three serpentine-fronted drawers below, one of which contains an inkstand. The shaped stand contains a single drawer and a slide and is similarly decorated with flower marquetry on an ebony ground. It measures 2ft 9in (84cm) across. This is a typically eclectic 19th-century product displaying elements from several different 18th-century styles. The bonheur-du-jour is essentially a post-1750 form but it is seen here in an exaggerated rococo style with heavy mounts and elaborate marquetry cartouches of leafy scrolls.

D . A French Bureau à Gradin, *c*1860

Profusely mounted with gilt bronzes of the highest quality and inset with black and gold chinoiserie lacquer panels, this 19th-century creation was inspired by the rococo masterpieces of over a century before. Few 18th-century pieces, however, achieved the easy opulence seen here. It is but a short step from these sinuous leafy mounts stretching up from the legs and terminating in double candleholders, to the wholly organic treatment of desks by the Art Nouveau craftsmen of the last quarter of the century. The natural sweep of the *gradin* itself is also forward-looking, but the central clock with its bronze putti supporters is pure 18th-century rococo. It is 5ft 3in (1.60m) wide, with six small shaped drawers in the gradin and two larger drawers in the frieze.

A. A French Napoleon III Kingwood, Tulipwood and Marquetry Bonheur-du-Jour of the Mid-19th Century

The superstructure consists of a two-door cupboard and two drawers topped by a gilt-brass gallery and a frieze drawer fitted with a velvet-lined slide. Almost every surface of this Louis XV revival desk is decorated with a pattern of continuous floral scrolls of rather uninspired form, but there are two 'show panels' of high-quality marquetry in the shaped ebonised reserves on the cupboard doors. Like much of the 18th century style furniture which filled wealthy French homes in the 19th century, this desk shows an enthusiasm for the decorative quality of the rococo but does not quite recapture the poise and balance of the earlier age. It is 2ft 7½in (79cm) wide. The best 19th-century French reproduction furniture is very hard to distinguish from 18th century originals, however.

B. A Secretaire-Cabinet, 1860s

Shown open and closed.

This remarkable piece was presumably made for the French market, but is mounted inside and out with Dresden painted porcelain plaques. Most of the plaques show lovers in landscapes painted in the manner of Watteau, but at the centre of the swan neck pediment at the top is a small oval portrait of Marie-Amelie, the wife of Louis-Philippe of France. When the doors of the cabinet are opened, her portrait appears superimposed on a large circular portrait of the emperor himself in a full-bottomed wig and armour. The interior of the cabinet is fitted with numerous porcelain-mounted drawers grouped around a central cupboard, and below this is a fall-front writing drawer with chequerboard inlay. In the base is a serpentine-fronted cupboard with two doors. The whole piece is 4ft 3in (1.30m) wide and 7ft 9in (2.27m) high.

C. An English Mechanical Writing Desk

This extraordinary desk, 3ft 5½in (1.05m) wide, was presented to Princess Alexandra of Denmark by the people of Bath in 1870. It was intended to mark her marriage to the Prince of Wales in 1863, but the sheer complexity of the design and the difficulty in obtaining the materials caused considerable delay. Like many of the presentation and exhibition pieces of the Victorian period it is a virtuoso display of ingenuity and fine workmanship in exotic woods, but typically the overall effect is less than graceful. The four legs are in the form of peacocks carved from solid rosewood, attended by pairs of cherubs carved from limewood. Each bears a different coat-of-arms, for England, Wales, Scotland and Ireland. The sides and the back are mounted with Royal Worcester plaques depicting various episodes in the history of Bath with royal connections. The two shelves in the superstructure are of ivory, supported on ivory columns with ormolu capitals. From the centre of the leather-lined writing surface a counterbalanced ivory stationery compartment rises at the turn of a key to form a slope. Inside it is fitted for letter-writing, with lidded boxes for stamps and an oval looking-glass mounted in the hinged lid.

D. A Mid-19th-Century English Papier Mâché Table Desk

This English piece, 1ft 3in (38cm) wide, is inlaid with mother-of-pearl and decorated with sprigs of flowers and views of castles. The domed lid and double doors of the upper part open to reveal a stationery rack and the shaped front folds forward to become a writing slope.

E. An English Victorian Camphorwood Travelling Secretaire Chest, *c*1870

Built in two parts, each 2ft 6in (99cm) wide, this desk has flush brass mounts to reinforce the corners and flush brass handles on all the drawers. Chests of this kind, also known as campaign or military chests, were produced in great numbers during the 19th century for soldiers and administrators bound for the colonies. The two box-like sections would probably have been packed into protective pine cases whilst in transit, with the four turned feet unscrewed and stored in one of the drawers.

B

C

Davenports

The davenport was one of the most distinctive types of small desk found in the 19th-century English home. It began as a plain and neat slope-front desk right at the end of the 18th century and survived in a variety of guises, some highly ornate, right up to the end of the 19th century. Several of the variations of the standard form are illustrated here.

A. An English Regency Burr Elm Davenport

This is a slightly ornamented version of the earliest style of plain rectangular davenport which first appeared in the late 18th century. Like them it has a sloping desk top which slides forward when in use to give knee-room, and is quite small, 1ft 8in (51cm) wide, on lobed bun feet and with a turned spindle gallery around the top. It has three drawers with turned ebonised handles on the righthand side and three dummy drawers on the other, with pull-out slides on each side. On the righthand side there is also a small pen drawer.

B. A Satinwood Davenport of the Mid-1820s

This elegant desk retains the little pen drawer in the side found on earlier models; however, the fluted columns with leafy capitals supporting the hinged slope-front make it easier for the writer to sit at the desk and there is no need for a sliding top section. There are four drawers down the righthand side behind a panelled door and the width of this desk is 1ft 8in (51cm).

C. A Rosewood Davenport, Mid-1830s

This example has a sliding top, but the slight overhang of the front and the carved scroll supports hint at the fully detached cabriole supports of the later piano-front davenports.

It is 1ft 11½in (60cm) wide, with four drawers in the side and a hinged leather-lined slope over a satinwood-veneered interior of small drawers

D. A Typical Victorian Walnut Piano-Front Davenport, *c*1850

It has leaf-carved scroll supports at the front, four drawers down one side and four dummy drawers down the other and a stationery compartment beneath a hinged top with a fretwork gallery. The hinged piano front folds back to reveal a pull-out writing slide and small drawers. Davenports of this type were made in very large numbers in the mid-Victorian period. This one is 1ft 10in (57cm) wide.

B

D

A . An English Victorian Papier Mâché Davenport

Because it was light, strong and cheap to produce, papier mâché offered Victorian furniture-makers a free hand in the mass manufacture of highly-decorated pieces. The main centre of production was in the Midlands around Birmingham, where Jennens & Bettridge were the most important firm. Tea trays, small boxes, screens and tables are the most common papier mâché survivors, but larger reminders of this once-thriving industry are more rare.

This example, 2ft 3in (68.5cm) wide, is black japanned and decorated with gilding and mother-of-pearl. The piano-fronted flap is hinged in two places and folds back to reveal a velvet-lined writing slope with drawers and pigeonholes. On the righthand side a small pen drawer can be seen above a cupboard containing two drawers and an arched recess.

B . A Victorian Ebonised Davenport

This compact little desk, 1ft 10in (58cm) wide, is one of many variations on the highly popular davenport pattern, having a two-door cabinet superstructure in the manner of a bonheur-du-jour. The exterior is inset with panels of burr walnut veneer, inlaid with boxwood stringing and mounted with a brass gallery and strips of brass beading along some edges. Here the cabinet is shown opened to reveal the boldly striped veneer of the backs of the doors, the pair of matching drawers with inset handles and the stepped interior of pierced fretwork letter racks. The writing drawer, which contains two brass-topped glass ink bottles and a pen tray, is also open to show the adjustable leather-lined slope. The base contains four drawers down the righthand side, with four matching drawers on the left.

C . A Walnut Davenport of the 1890s

This unusual piece has a square flat top surrounded by a wooden gallery on three sides and supported on a central pedestal. The frieze at the front of the top drops down to reveal a pull-out writing slope in bird's eye maple, fitted with small drawers and a pen tray. The ends of the pedestal are fitted with pierce-carved panels of interlaced ribbon design backed with silk, one of which forms a door which conceals four mahogany-fronted drawers.

A

A . A Superior Grade Example of Wooton's Patent Desk

In the picture, the desk, 4ft (1.22m) wide, is shown closed to display the richness of its architectural ornament and open to reveal the complexity of the storage compartments inside.

This type of desk was manufactured at William S. Wooton's factory at Indianapolis in the late 19th century and was very popular with businessmen. It was available in four grades (this example is particularly heavily ornamented) but each grade worked on the same basic principle. The front is divided vertically into two sections, one fitted with a letterbox for messages when the desk is closed. These sections swing out on castors, so that anyone sitting at the fold-down writing surface is effectively surrounded by pigeonholes and drawers of every shape and size. As a practical work-centre the Wooton Patent Desk is unrivalled, even by the most lavishly fitted bureau-cabinets of the early 18th century. It is also a supreme example of Victorian igenuity and eclectic ornamentation.

B . An American Late-19th Century Extra Grade Walnut Cylinder Desk.

This is another type of desk patented by Wooton, less well-known than the larger double-doored examples but made with characteristic attention to detail. It is fitted with a pull-out writing slide and the base pedestals contain drawers which swing open to reveal the extensive filing compartments.

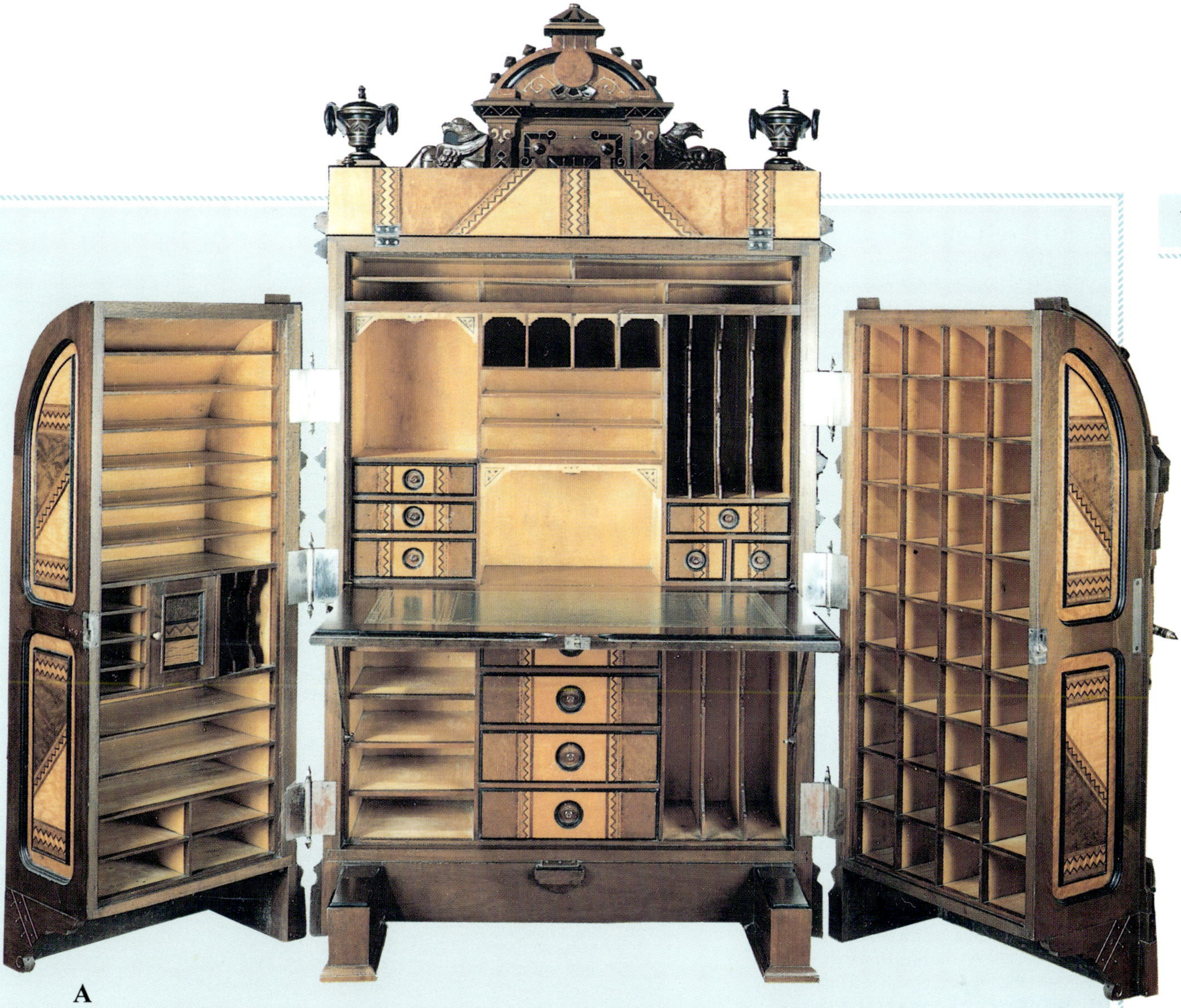

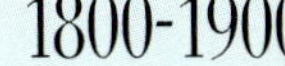

A

B

1800-1900

A . An American Victorian Painted Pine 'Cottage' Desk-and-Bookcase, *c*1860

The piece is in three sections, comprising a glazed bookcase with a wide, overhanging cornice, a slope-front writing compartment fitted with drawers and pigeonholes, and one long drawer overhanging a base of three graduated drawers. "Cottage" furniture was a mid-19th century fashion in the USA; it was cheaply constructed in factories but could be richly painted to brighten even the humblest home. This desk was manufactured by the Heywood Brothers of Gardner, Massachusetts, and is a very superior example of the type, and is thought to have been decorated by Edward and Thomas Hill, two English brothers who later gained fame as landscape painters. Their work is evident here in the landscape vignettes on the slope front, the sides and the bottom drawer.

B & C . Two Examples of the Revival of Sheraton style

This revival took place in England at the end of the 19th century. The 4ft (1.22m)-wide Carlton House desk, which is of satinwood inlaid throughout with delicate neo-classical ornament, is a faithful echo of similar desks made a century before. This tiny sycamore slope-front lady's desk, which is only 1ft 5in (43cm) wide, follows the Sheraton style with its delicate tapering legs, boxwood stringing and inlaid roundel, but it is not of a design so often associated with the Sheraton period. The top is hinged and inside there is a velvet writing slope with bottle wells and a pen tray, while the frieze holds a single drawer.

A

B

C

1800-1900

A . An English Oak Cabinet and Desk, 1862

This massive piece of furniture was decorated by the architect John Pollard Seddon and decorated by Morris, Marshall, Faulkner & Co in 1862. The central sloping section lifts and tilts on a double ratchet in the same way as the top of an architect's table and beneath it are small shelves and drawers for storing papers. The paintings on the main panels represent an allegory of the arts, symbolised by episodes from the honeymoon of René of Anjoy, and were executed by Ford Madox Brown, Danté Gabriel Rossetti and Edward Burne-Jones, all of whom were members of the firm founded by William Morris in an attempt to restore Medieval values to the applied arts. Morris, the founding father of the Arts and Crafts movement, was reacting against the mass-production of furnishings in the Victorian period and advocated honest craftsmanship, carried out by a contented craftsman for the use and pleasure of the community. This consciously Medieval desk illustrates the two contradictory sides of the movement: simple, undisguised construction (which was to influence 20th century designers) is combined with a chivalric idealism. Morris's furniture was always a luxury product, way beyond the means of the ordinary people he wished to serve.

B . An American Sycamore Writing Cabinet on Stand

This was designed by George Jack for Morris & Co in 1893. Jack was an American-born architect who joined Morris as chief furniture designer, giving an 18th century feel to many of the pieces produced in the 1890s. This writing cabinet, which has a central fall front flanked by cupboards, is very different in style from the painstakingly Gothic furniture produced by Morris and his associates in the infancy of the Arts and Crafts Movement. It is 4ft 7½in (1.41m) wide, decorated with a marquetry design of oak and ash leaves, thistles and other stylised foliage.

C

A

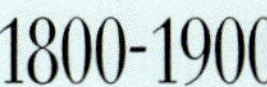

B

D

C . A Late-19th Century English Oak Writing Desk

This desk was designed by the leading English architect and designer Charles Voysey. It has a single cupboard in the upper section with decorative copper hinges and a simple fold-out writing surface. Voysey was influenced by William Morris but he developed a personal style in furniture design, frequently incorporating pierce-decorated hinges, as here. He influenced the designs of Charles Rennie Mackintosh and was one of the first to appreciate the importance of functional industrial design.

D . An English Oak Writing Desk Designed by Arthur Heygate Mackmurdo and made by the Century Guild, *c*1886

The first successful craft co-operative, the Century Guild was set up by Mackmurdo in 1882 with the aim of rendering 'all branches of art the sphere no longer of the tradesman but of the artist'. Mackmurdo was an architect by training but, having come under the influence of John Ruskin, he proved better than Ruskin at putting ideals of co-operative craftsmanship into practice. He succeeded in uniting artists from the traditionally separate disciplines of architecture, interior design and decoration, and the guild flourished until 1888.

A . A Late 19th-or Early 20th-Century Marquetry Cylinder Bureau

A high-quality reproduction after a Riesener original of the late 18th century, it has a fitted interior beneath the cylinder and a pull-out writing slide with a leather lining, over three frieze drawers. It is 3ft 8½in (1.13m) wide. There is an oval flower marquetry panel at the centre of the cover and the mounts are of a good standard. This elegant and practical writing desk is of a pattern particularly favoured by Paris *ébénistes* during the late 19th century.

B . 'La Forêt Lorraine', 1889

This carved walnut bureau was made in Emile Gallé's factory at Nancy in the west of France and exhibited at the *Exposition Universelle* in Paris.

Although he was a leading figure in the Art Nouveau movement, Gallé tended to avoid the extremes of organic form in his furniture design, and this little desk is wholly traditional in its basic shape. Gallé revitalised the craft of marquetry, using a wide variety of fruitwoods and exotic woods to create beautiful, intricate inlays. The inspiration for these marquetry designs came from the countryside of Lorraine. Gallé was a knowledgeable botanist, and his favourite themes were local plants including cow-parsley, water lilies, orchids and irises, with insects such as dragonflies and butterflies. There was a strong link between the decorative arts and literature at this time, and Gallé often inscribed his furniture with quotations from Hugo, Verlaine and other contemporary poets in order to endow the work with greater significance. He sometimes also gave names to his pieces, in the manner of paintings or music, this desk being an example.

D

A

C

B

C. A French Mahogany, Oak and Walnut Writing Desk, *c*1900
This desk was made at Louis Marjorelle's factory in Nancy. It has a central letter rack flanked by small drawers and an undertier shaped at the front to accommodate the writer's legs.

Majorelle trained as a painter but then concentrated on running his father's furniture business in Nancy, making 18th-century reproduction furniture. During the 1890s, he began to emulate the organic, sinuous forms of the Art Nouveau furniture produced by Emile Gallé's factory, which was also in Nancy. By the time this desk was made, Majorelle was the biggest supplier of Art Nouveau furniture in France, making use of mechanized workshops to turn out high-quality pieces of good design.

D. A North Italian Bureau-Cabinet, *c*1900
The decoration on this desk is a combination of neo-rococo and Japanese-inspired elements, painted over in cream and gold. The upper doors are decorated with a crane, ducks and reeds, and the base doors with Japanese figures dancing and playing music in a landscape. Between the two is a shaped-front secretaire drawer. The whole piece is 3ft 9in (1.20m) wide.

1900

to

1999

Throughout the 19th century, communications had improved, and the large international fairs of Paris, London, Philadelphia and Chicago had meant more sharing of ideas was possible than ever before. New marerials, such as plastics, plywood and tubular metal, were introduced, and two main directions appeared; the Arts & Crafts Movement's interest in line was developed in England and America, then elsewhere in Europe there was a move towards the decorative swirls, of Art Nouveau. The successors of these two were encompassed in the eclectic Art Deco era which peaked in 1925 and was later replaced by post-war functionalism, moving on through the 20th century into increasingly streamlined, mimimal designs.

Chairs

The most dominant trend in 20th-century chair design was that of the northern Europeans – the Scandinavians and Germans. One of the first to design attractive functional furniture for mass-production was the German architect, Richard Riemershchmid. His chairs were specifically designed for factory production, and consisted of several elements produced separately and then nailed together. This radical approach was mirrored by the Dutchman Gerrit Rietveld, a founder member of the De Stilj group of artist-designers. Their belief in using only primary colours and rectangular forms, and a commitment to the Machine Age, led to their continuing influence on modern chair construction through simplicity and lightness.

In 1903, the Vienna Secession, under the leadership of architect Josef Hoffmann, transformed itself into the Wiener Werkstatte (Vienna Workshop) whose studios manufactured Werkstatte's typical grid-like designs, mainly in black and white. In Scotland, Charles Rennie Mackintosh abandonded Art Nouveau curves and founded the Glasgow School, which concentrated on line and geometric patterns. In Germany, the Bauhaus movement blossomed within a decade into a force that still influences design today. Originally headed by Walter Gropius, who later moved to the United States, it encouraged its participants to seek new design answers to problems of material and function. This is exemplified in the work of Marcel Breuer, which also shows the link between the Dutch De Stilj movement and the Bauhaus. Brauer's early experimentation with tubular chrome chairs led to countless derivations; Mies van der Rohe, for example, exhibited his Barcelona chair at the Paris *Exposition Internationale des Arts Decoratifs et Industriels Modernes* of 1925, the showcase of the Art Deco movement.

Art Deco threw up a host of talented and innovative designers in all spheres of the arts, including chair design. Working in France in the 1920s, Le Corbusier redefined furniture into three categories – chairs, tables and shelves – and designed standard pieces for the interiors of his buildings accordingly. Although individual, his chairs show the desire for anonymous design that pervades the second half of the 20th century – equipment, rather than art. In the United States, Frank Lloyd Wright was also designing pieces for his own interiors, and the chairs show he designed for his own house were clearly indebted to the Arts & Crafts movement. In England, designers were less innovative, tending to react to these movements as they arrived from Europe and the United States, although the design firm of the PEL (Practical Equipment Limited) were soon using metal tube and plywood in their chair designs.

The suppression of artistic expression in Germany of the 1930s changed this northern European domination. Both between and after the wars, Dutch craftsmen continued to work in the handmade vein to great effect, but mass-production supremacy moved over seas. In Finland, Alvar Aalto – one of the most prolific designers of modern times – played an interesting role, falling between the traditional craft approach of Scandinavia and the new forms developing in central Europe. His bentwood forms echo those of the Thonet brothers in 19th-century France, but belong unmistakably to the 20th century.

After the Second World War, American design flourished with an influx of talented craftsmen and designers such as Walter Gropius and Eliel Saarinen before and during the two World Wars. Saarinen's son, Eero, and Charles Eames worked with plastics, fibre-glass, and moulds which have been imitated and adapted worldwide since that time.

Plastic has become a commonplace material for furniture in the second half of this century. Its effects on design were crucial, moving the emphasis away from decoration and back to fluidity of line. More recent developments show a growing division between designer chairs for the collector and the development of the mass market.

SOFAS

The same division between designer-made and mass-produced pieces exists in sofa design; but it is the industrialization of design which has remained the pre-dominant force in popular sofa design of this century. Despite the speed of change, there is a parallel with the development of sofas in the 1800s. Simplicity characterized fashionable pieces in the early years, to be followed by a passion for new materials and methods that were forgotten at the end of the century, when more ornamental seat furniture, often in antique styles, became the vogue. Today, the most expensive sofas have feather-filled cushions and sprung constructions. Synthetic upholstery fabrics, plastic preformed cushions and laminated woods are now mainly reserved for cheap mass-produced sofas. The transition from button-backed sofas with turned legs found in every parlour before World War I, to the Space Age attenuated steel or chrome sculptural works of the 1950s and 1960s, is a reflection of the radical changes and advances in manufacturing methods. Today we have true mass-production with preformed foam padding and simple upholstery that is frequently fixed in position with metal staples. While such production methods have meant that comfortable seat furniture is available to people of all income levels, craftmanship and the quality of design have suffered, often resulting in dull uniformity. A few exclusive firms do produce finer work, but they often concentrate on traditional styles of reproductions, with exciting sofas seen only in (mostly trade) exhibitions or in the studios of a few innovative craftsmen. The most desirable 20th-century sofas are made by the well-known progressive designers, whose work set trends that were often modified for the popular market. In the early years, British firms like Heal & Son in London worked very much in the tradition of C F A Voysey and Mackay Hugh Baillie Scott to supply fashionable people with well-made furniture that looked effective in the new-style interiors from which Victorian clutter was banished. Upholstery colours, again in reaction to the dark richness of Victorian rooms, was much lighter, their patterns simpler. Pale greens, cool pinks and fresh lilacs formed a good background for furniture in the high-backed idiom of Scotsman Chales Rennie Mackintosh or the sinuous curves of late Art Nouveau.

Alongside early 20th-century designer furniture, which attracted only a small segment of the market, there were many reproductions of 18th-century designs some of which were made to such high standards that they now command good prices. Favourites too were sofas with loose chintz covers, a type that was especially popular for use in the fashionable cottage-style homes that were built in the suburbs as well as the country. Because of its adaptability, chintz-covered seat furniture has never gone completely out of fashion.

World War I inhibited the development of European furniture design, but across the Atlantic styles were much livelier. There was a vogue for pale silk-upholstered sofas in plain, rather square designs, a perfect complement for the cigarette-smoking, gramophone-playing fashionables of the early 1920s. Europe caught up with American ideas in the 1920s, and strident colours, such as green and red, or orange and black, were used for upholstery. Geometric appliqué, tassels and various metallic effects were also appleid in the Jazz Age, when the sofa became the centre of a new extravagant lifestyle. Animal-skin covers gave a striking, primitive look to the new metal-framed sofas, while velvet was printed in zebra or leopard patterns.

By the late 1930s, upholstery colours had also become simpler, with creams and brown shades predominating, although abstract patterns, especially wavy lines and triangles, often cut moquette, were very popular.

The last quarter of this century has seen great contrasts of style, ranging from sculptural constructions of artist-craftsmen to pairs of traditionally styled sofas that belong to no particular period; many of the best designs being directed at the office and contract-furnishing trades.

Tables

Since 1900, explosive changes in fashion and art have produced a wide and confusing range of tables, varying from revived antique styles in the Chippendale vein to modernist towers of plate glass. A simple way of placing a table within a sensible context is by asking the question: 'Is this table made up mostly of clean, straight lines, or is it curved and decorated with rich patterns, exotic wood grain and carving?'. These two types of tables swing in and out of favour over the first half of the century, and indeed afterwards. The Arts & Crafts firms of the 19th century influenced the 'straight clean line' table makers of the early 20th century. These included the Charles Rennie Mackintosh's tables with plain lacquered or painted finishes, a minimum of decoration and often of a size rather grand and unfriendly, as well as Frank Lloyd Wright in America and Josef Hoffmann in Vienna. Hoffmann and his colleague Koloman Moser produced designer tables of black, white and metal grids during the first 20 years of the century. The students from that workshop carried the gospel of the straight line all over Europe.

In 1915 in the Netherlands the De Stijl movement applied the affection for rectilinearity, primary colours and flat surfaces to furniture making; Gerrit Rietveld (1888–1964) made geometric shaped tables which even today seem revolutionary. In Germany, Bauhaus students concentrated on new materials and techniques, creating Machine-Age tables of tubular steel, with glass tops and often no decoration save a chrome finish to the metal. Likewise, in Finland Alvar Aalto experimented with novel uses for plywood, perfecting this material with new woods and glues and producing moulded tables and trolleys from one or very few parts. Crucial advances were being made using this and other new materials and methods, and the increasing use of plastics also led to a preponderance of synthetic tables. The other branch of Art Nouveau was French in origin, its two design centres being Paris and Nancy, where Emile Gallé (1846–1904) produced handsome tables, chairs and case pieces with sensuous curves and ornate-inspired embellishments. The flat tops of his tables were of irregular shapes, often inlaid with landscapes, blossoms and twisting stems; their legs likewise were rarely straight but instead were carved, in some cases like spreading vines, in others as massive dragonflies. Parisian Hector Gimard (1867–1942) designed tables with undulating curves, very much akin to his ornate wrought-iron Belgian architect, designed curving, looping tables for is similarly decorated buildings, as did Antonio Gaudi (1852–1926) of Barcelona, whose amorphous, anthropomorphic shapes feature knobby knees and crooked elbows, sometimes with wrought-iron supports.

The distinction between tables with straight lines and those with curves and decoration adapted from nature extended into the Art Deco period, although the later elements become much more stylized and less organic in the 1920s.

Designers turned to rich materials, both traditional and exotic, including lacquer, snakeskin, marble and sharkskin. Jacques-Henri Lartigue, for instance, supported a table on a striking sphere of marble, and Rose Adler inlaid a black-lacquer table with *coquille d'oeuf* (crushed eggshell, an oriental innovation). Such Parisian furniture tended to use conventional materials and be based on styles from Louis XV to tribal African. But there was still competition, in the form of tubular metal, Machine Age furniture, and popular antique reproduction styles. In the post-war period, Milan took on increasing importance, as designers such as Carlo Mollino (1905–1973) produced light-hearted ecomonical tables. The use of plywood increased, alone or combined with other materials, such as Formica (a laminated plastic). The Milan designers developed an optimistic style whose tables featured light constructions and bright colours. Throughout the 1960s and up to the present day, Italy had produced not only functional but also visually exciting tables, the designs of Ettore Sottsass (b.1917) for the Memphis group foremost among them.

With their built-in strength, plastic and fibreglass allowed new furniture shapes to be moulded. Charles Eames, one of the most influential American furniture designers of the century, experimented with plywood dring World War II, and afterwards produced a monochromatic, single-pedestal table, all made of glass-reinforced polyester – a truly novel creation. Great Britain also produced good-quality tables, especially in the no-frills, traditional vein, such as those by Gordon Russell (1892–1980), whose sturdy forms looked back to 19th-century Arts & Crafts furniture. The Swinging Sixties, on the other hand, gave birth to bizarre Pop Art tables, such as Allen Jones' *Table Sculpture*, whose base is a crouching, sado-masochistic woman; this is a good example of how new materials (painted glass fibre and resin) allowed the return of tables based on shapes and curves.

In the 1980s there are two main streams: tables made for use such as may be bought in any large store and are relatively inexpensive to make, utilizing new materials and methods; and tables made for art's sake – Danny Lane creates his from stacks of glass, not intending them to be functional, but 'sculptural'.

Desks

At the beginning of this century, the writing desk, now an essential part of a well-appointed home, was found in many different guises, but the well-tried solutions of the past – fall-fronts, fitted drawers and pull-out slides – were generally retained even when the overall style was avant-garde.

Throughout this century, writing desks have continued to be made in antique styles. Such imitation can be seen as an endorsement of the functional designs of earlier craftsmen, but it is also a reflection on the status of the writing desk as an accepted, even though increasingly old-fashioned item of furniture, for it is the novelties of an age – radios and refrigerators being 20th-century examples – that tend to attract the most distinctive and progressive styling.

The Second World War set in its own limitations on furniture design just as World War I had done, and in Britain it led to government intervention in the furniture industry, so that only approved designs could be manufactured between 1943 and 1952. The 'Utility' furniture that resulted – plain, unpretentious, but of guaranteed minimum quality – was intended to help the re-furnishing of bombed-out homes, but also helped to establish the idea that utility and good design were not mutually exclusive.

Generally, though, it was not the home that was most affected, but the office, itself an increasingly important aspect of modern life, complicated by the advent of teleprinter, telephone and typewriter.

Frank Lloyd Wright's sheet-metal desks designed for the Larkin Building in Buffalo, New York, in 1904 were an early intimation of the shape of things to come, just as his more aesthetically pleasing wood and tubular steel desks designed for the Johnson Wax office in Wisconsin in the late 1930s pre-figured the post-World War II designer-desk systems.

In Europe, design standards were adapted to machine production and spawned a generation of utilitarian office furniture that was very obviously modern. The need for utilitarian furniture has further increased in the last quarter of the century with the growing importance of computers. Apart from the need to house and use the machines themselves, the new technology has also posed problems in the management of electrical cables on a large scale.

Faced with the welter of cables and the loom of the visual display unit, the traditional desk has retreated – but only as far as the offices of senior management, where a large and imposing antique desk has always added respectability to power.

A & B . Oak Spindle Chairs by Frank Lloyd Wright, *c*1901

These chairs, typical of Wright's furniture, clearly owe a great debt to Mackintosh. Wright first designed similar chairs for his own dining room, which was very geometric, stark and fundamentally based on a grid. Linked with developments in the Glasgow School and in the Vienna Secession, this chair is tall and linear (about 5ft/1m 52cms high) and its undecorated austerity is akin to Japanese design.

Frank Lloyd Wright (1867–1959), born in the United States a year before Charles Rennie Mackintosh was born in Scotland, had a profound influence on American design, living through all the major styles from the Arts & Crafts Movement through to the 1950s. He subscribed to the holistic approach to design, which suggested that furniture in the many houses he designed should reflect the shape and spirit of the space which it occupied. He practised this to an almost excessive degree, producing a sparse style that architects and designers loved, but which was not particularly practical. Although Wright designed some economy furniture for ordinary use, it is obvious that this chair uses a vast amount of timber, would be expensive to produce and, as can be seen, when gathered around a table would effortlessly congest any normal-size environment. In spite of this, Frank Lloyd Wright was certainly one of the United States' most important 20th-century architect-designers, not least for his early treatment of the relationship between furniture and its surroundings.

C , D & E . An Oak Sidechair by Frank Lloyd Wright, *c*1920

This chair (146a) in Wright's familiar materials, oak and leather, was designed for the Imperial Hotel in Tokyo, Japan. Again, it is minimalist and geometric in line, based on the hexagon and the octagon, and is another example of Wright's desire to fit the movable furniture to the spirit of the immovable space in which it is contained. He insisted on designing everything for the hotel, including fabric and carpets. The structure itself was built of concrete and so survived the disastrous earthquakes of the 20s, before falling prey to property developers in 1968.

Frank Lloyd Wright's influence can be seen on furniture executed by George M Neidecken, c1910, for the E P Irving House in Decatur, Illinois, US (146b and 146c).

F. An Office Chair by Frank Lloyd Wright, *c*1904

This early example of adjustable office furniture was made for the completely fire-proof building of brown-painted steel of the Larkin Company in Buffalo, New York. It is a strange combination of Secessionist design, with its geometric lines and grid decoration, and a functional modernity.

G. An American Sidechair by Frank Lloyd Wright, *c*1950

Designed for the Trier House, this chair combines Wright's main ideals; that furniture should be sympathetic to its surroundings, and that it should be accessible to all, the plywood construction being cheap to manufacture.

H – M. Chairs by Josef Hoffmann, *c*1905

This is a good example of Josef Hoffmann's bentwood designs, executed by the specialist factory of Kohn & Kohn (**H**). Hoffmann was an influential architect, closely associated with the Vienna Secession and later to be a founder of the *Wiener Werkstätte* (literally, the Vienna Workshop) in 1903. Although he was radical in his designs, being much influenced by Mackintosh, he was also highly respected, and taught at the Vienna School of Arts & Crafts for over 30 years.

One of the signatures of his chair designs are the curious lobes or spheres which support the joints on the front legs. The backs of these chairs are a pastiche of a Sheraton tea tray, decorated with an inlaid fan in the centre. Hoffmann also designed furniture with sharp, geometric motifs, often decorated with grid-like patterns, and sometimes studded leather with brass caps to the legs.

The other two chairs pictured here (**I**) are from a set of six, and show the emphasis placed on simplicity and respect for tradition. Although many of his clients were extremely affluent bourgeois Austrians, Hoffmann also published furniture designs under the title *Simple Furniture*, which he considered to be an aspect of good design.

Hoffmann was a prolific designer of chairs, some of which are faithfully reproduced today by Franz Wittmann. This, the *Biach* chair (**J**) shows Hoffmann's command of the bentwood medium, as produced by his own factory. Characteristically using geometric shapes, simple straight lines, and spherical supports at the joints through which screws join seat to leg, the design was light, economical to produce, yet sturdy and stylish.

This dining chair c1908, the *Armlöffel* or Arm Spoon (**K**), clearly shows the original spirit of the Secession: austere and angular, it is decorated with the grid pattern only, one of Hoffmann's strongest trademarks. He included this chair in several of the interiors he designed, the only departure from sharp, straight lines being the spoon-like arm rests which give the chair its name.

This later chair (**L**) was designed for the Haus Koller in 1911, and shows the impact of the Art Deco movement on Hoffmann's designs. The Haus Koller was a more sumptuous and luxurious enterprise than his turn-of-the-century interiors and this chair shows nothing of the straight, geometric lines or purist look seen earlier. Its chic, sculptural forms are soft and welcoming, altogether more organic with the edges highlighted with another of Hoffmann's trademarks: the tape with alternating black and white design. The long, straight, upright curves show how Hoffmann was not insensitive to the Art Deco style of the 1930s; this could almost be by the famous Deco *ensemblier* (interior designer) Emile-Jacques Ruhlmann.

This *Kubus* armchair (**M**), designed in 1910, could easily be the product of Bauhaus in 1930. Its name derives from the cubes which make up the upholstery, although in fact every part of the chair is a pure geometric shape; even the castors are hemispheres. The resemblance to Bauhaus comes in its large, flat planes which are not dissimilar to the work of Walter Gropius or even some of Marcel Breuer's early works, such as his easy chair of 1923. The proportions are similar to those of a Regency chair.

K

L

M

N. An American Art Nouveau Armchair by Greene & Greene, *c*1908

Without knowing its origin, first sight of this chair suggests many sources. Its form is that of the caqueteuse, with the high back and splayed arms of the 16th century; the starkness and decoration suggests something of Japan; and the splat and emphasis on the grain of the wood could almost be Morris or Mackintosh. It is in fact American, designed by Greene & Greene for the Blacker House, and like all their chairs, was commissioned by clients for their architectural projects.

The brothers worked mostly in California, and greatly admired the work of Gustav Stickley, using some of his furniture in their first houses. Interestingly, they originally attended the St Louis Manual Training High School, which, as its name suggests, laid great emphasis on manual skills; perhaps this gave them their love for wood, which was

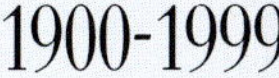

N

O

extensively worked to reveal the grain rather than simply varnished. Both were trained as architects, and though Henry continued, Charles gave up architecture to explore his ideas that art consisted in making the everyday beautiful, and that form would emerge from the medium itself. Of the two brothers, Charles probably designed most of the furniture; he visited England in 1901, and had the same admiration for Japanese taste as the English Arts & Crafts makers. Greene & Greene were enthusiastically received in Europe, and were perhaps the most English of the American Arts & Crafts designers.

O. Norwegian Painted Chairs by Gerhard Munthe, *c*1911

A crucial aspect of the tremendous changes in the perception of design represented by Art Nouveau (and Art Deco) was the wide scope for *individual* development that they afforded: despite the attempts by many scholars and critics to categorize Art Nouveau works as, say, 'organic' or 'linear'.

The delightful fantasy chairs by the Norwegian Munthe are a perfect example. These are simply a virtuoso indulgence of decoration; the sculptural, carved mask heads clearly come from Scandinavian folkloric tradition, and likewise the interlacing strapwork has a Gaelic look to it. The naïvely carved scene on the back panel doubtless depicts a fairy-tale episode. The chair absorbs many different styles from arabesque to Regency, all converted into this burst of colour. Here, the new stylistic freedom is productive rather than limiting.

A – H . Chairs by Gerrit Rietveld, c1917

Gerrit Rietveld (1888–1964) was a natural designer, trained in cabinet-making, jewellery, and then finally architecture. This chair (**A**) demonstrates immediately that something dramatic has happened in the development of furniture. 1917 marked the transition between the organic, curving Art Nouveau style and crisp, chic Art Deco. Here there are suddenly straight lines and complex shapes formed out of the most simple techniques coupled with striking colours. It can be argued that Rietveld certainly marked, if not began, a revolution which in a sense continues today.

The dramatic interplay of straight lines to form patterns was not a wholly new idea – in the 1860s Godwin, greatly inspired by oriental design, produced geometric household furniture. Similarly, Mackintosh, Lloyd Wright and the Viennese designers such as Hoffmann used lines to produce shape. Here, the lines produce form by enclosing space; the structure has very simple components, and the chair's colour is reminiscent of the geometric painting of Mondrian, whose famous squares of colour are concerned with proportion. The link with art was no coincidence since Rietveld formally joined the Dutch De Stijl movement around this time, a movement which promoted simple form and primary colours. This chair was a complete original, unlike anything made before, and represented an absolute departure from traditional structure. It removed the remaining design rules.

Rietveld's second great chair (**B**) was the Berlin Chair, designed for the Dutch Pavilion at the Berlin Exhibition in 1923. In some ways, it is an even more exaggerated demonstration of belief in the principles of De Stijl; it is much simpler, and uses only tones of black and white. Although much less famous, it is in some ways more pleasing and is truly sculptural in the way it encloses space and portrays mass. It is free from the excesses of previous decorative styles, such as Gaudí's neo-baroque or even earlier 18th-century designs; in this chair, everything is totally functional. If compared with the Schroder House in Utrecht, which Rietveld designed in 1924, it can be seen that both have the same stark, functional construction, creating form by placing similarly-shaped slabs in different planes.

To show his command of diverse materials, in 1927 Rietveld designed the Beugel Fauteuil (**C**); it may look like the Red-Blue chair in plywood and tube, but in fact it takes its strength from all the integral triangles from which it is formed. Rietveld's chairs were never merely artworks. He founded his own

E

H

B

A
G
C
F
D

workshop and retailers in 1911; many of his original designs were produced by G A Van Der Groenekan, and this chair was mass-produced by Metz & Co in the late 1920s – such is the revival of interest in the De Stijl movement that recently even the paper bags designed by Metz & Co and printed labels used by Rietveld as a trademark on his Red-Blue chairs have become collectable items; some were recently auctioned in Amsterdam.

Rietveld's imagination was inexhaustible. He produced many single chairs, side chairs and low chairs, such as the Military chair (**D**), 1923, an unapologetically functional object made of very simple joints and inexpensive materials which dismantles completely. The Piano chair (**E**) was a rather more design-conscious piece of domestic furniture made of mahogany billets joined with wooden dowels, and with simple leather fabric. Clearly a continuation of the line construction of the Red-Blue chair, it has a dramatically different effect. Rietveld also produced chairs in other media (examples are rattan or wickerwork), some of which proved to be less successful. His zig-zag chair (**F**) was another striking departure from tradition and he made the prototype himself in 1934. Later produced by Van Der Groenekan, it is of a design so simple that one wonders why it had never been done before; although the joints on the Z had to be extra strong, this was achieved by simply bolting the two parts around a dove-tailed joint. Typically, the materials were very simple and it could be produced cheaply, a continuing theme in his work. In 1934, he produced the Crate desk, a desk that could be made with no more material than would normally be used to make a packing case. In the same year Metz & Co produced the Crate chair in red spruce, a design which has been revived and is in production today.

Another of Rietveld's truly original ideas were the chairs sculpted from a single sheet of fabric, showing his concern for the method as well as the result of design. The Birza chair (**G**), designed in 1927, was in theory cut from one piece of fibre which was then folded and fixed into a rigid shape. It was designed for the Birza Room, an interior which took the name of its patron, Dr W Birza. The overall effect shows similarities to the work of Frenchman Emile-Jacques Ruhlmann in the shape and the sabre legs, and echoes the achievements of the Bauhaus and Scandinavian designers in plywood. Unhappily, technology had not quite caught up with Rietveld, and Van Der Groenekan allegedly refused to make others by the designer, because of the trouble he had had with the first. The same theme recurs in a remarkable aluminium chair (152h), designed during the Second World War, made from a single piece of aluminium stamped with holes and held together with riveted buttresses. Although it looks like a space-age fantasy, to the designer it was an exercise in economy of material, combined with structural strength to give interesting form. He designed most of his chairs by actually emphasizing the material used rather than the original idea.

A . The Napoleon Chair by Edwin Lutyens, c1919

This unusual, asymmetric chair was designed by the famous architect Edwin Lutyens for his own use. It is called the Napoleon chair because he had seen a painting of Napoleon sitting on a similar piece of furniture.
The piece has never been traced. Lutyens had a pair of these chairs built for his own fireside in Mansfield Street, London, appropriately a large house designed by Adam. He had such affection for them that he even had a pair made for the miniature library in Queen Mary's Doll's House, which he finished in 1924. This example is in fact c1988, since the design is being commercially reproduced by Lutyens' grand-daughter, and is based on the example in the Victoria & Albert Musuem, London. So, this is a 1980s revival of an Edwardian revival of a Napoleonic chair.

B . A Set of Chairs and a Games Table by Emile-Jacques Ruhlmann, c1920

If one thinks of Art Deco furniture as being chic, then Emile-Jacques Ruhlmann (1879–1933) is surely the most typical Deco designer. Even in his day he was hailed as the successor of the great 18th-century French cabinet-makers, and in the design of these chairs there are striking similarities. The elegant tapering legs with the brass caps, very characteristic of Ruhlmann's work, are similar to the stylized French and English chairs of 1800–1820. Although the upholstery here is fairly restrained, Ruhlmann often used exotic fabrics such as leopard skin with coloured woods and lacquering. After tentatively exhibiting his work before the First World War, he came to dominate French interior design in the 1920s. His devotion to the excesses and the virtues of elitism could not be further from the ideals of the English Arts & Crafts movement, or the soon-to-dominate German Bauhaus.

D

B

C & D. A Dining Chair and an Armchair by Robert Mallet-Stevens, *c*1920

Robert Mallet-Stevens (1886–1945) was a French architect-designer, and most of his chairs were made to fit his interior schemes. They were primarily of tubular construction, placing great emphasis on simplicity and plain design which could be economically produced, rather as Hoffmann had done at the turn of the century. France, through the work of designers such as Emile-Jacques Ruhlmann, had formally led the way in design with high quality, sumptuous and expensive craftsmanship. Combatting the increasing competition from cheap and functional Dutch and German imports became one of Mallet-Stevens' concerns, and one which he championed as a member of the Establishment in the 1930s, moving his own design away from lush Deco style.

A . Lloyd Loom Chairs by W. Lusty & Sons, *c*1925

Although primarily thought of as being garden furniture, and advertised in 1922 as being 'ideal for the garden room or sun parlour', Lloyd loom furniture has achieved classic and popular status. It was born out of a mechanical innovation by Marshall B. Lloyd, a pram manufacturer from Menominee, Michigan. His wicker prams, highly fashionable with the Victorians, were made by weaving split-wood cane or rattan by hand, much as they had been since the 17th century. Traditionally, the warp was fixed to a frame and the weft inserted over and under alternately. After several attempts at mechanization, in 1917 Lloyd devised a machine which would weave fabric in a similar way, but at 30 times the speed.

The wicker that Lloyd wove was primarily fabric, but in England production was by W. Lusty & Sons of Ruskin Works, Bromley by Bow, London. The Lustys' version was described as having a 'heart of steel', an 18g steel wire in every upright wrapped in coiled paper. The manufacturing process was relatively complex. The new woven fibre was moulded around a frame, generally of beech but sometimes metal after 1956, and the parts were then joined together while the wicker was still soft. It was then sized and baked to make it rigid. Steam-cleaned in caustic soda, spray painted and baked again, this gave a smoothly-woven, evenly-painted look with a glossy finish. All Lusty Lloyd loom had a metal trade label and was stamped with the date and year of manufacture. There were literally dozens of different models. More flexible than wood, it was perhaps more like plastic than the original wicker. There were wing chairs, sidechairs, dining chairs, occasional tables, linen baskets and pedestal cupboards on anything from bracket feet to cabriole. The seats were of three grades, one stuffed with wire wool, another simply plywood, and for the greatest luxury rubberized foam on Hessian fully-sprung (on which I am now sitting as I type).

The early pieces were the most adventurous, with the designs coming from the United States, and at one time Lusty created a development department for innovation. A family partner tellingly observed that 'he got it all wrong. What it needed was a technician, not an artist. In the end everyone experimented with designs which had to be sculpted and sometimes a good one turned out.' While this philosophy was in sharp distinction to the ideas of other designers of the time, there is no doubt about the popularity of what it produced. In the firm's heyday, paint was mixed in quantities of 10,000 gallons a time. In an edition of *The Cabinet Maker*, 1930, the editor stated: 'Such perfection of weaving and comfortable springing is now found in this woven fibre furniture that it is in the most constant use in the most fashionable households, liners, cinemas, lounges and dance halls.' These enduring designs were competitively priced to allow use by all. Lusty Lloyd loom are shortly to recommence manufacture, a pointer to the quality of their original design.

B & C . An Asprey Dining Set, *c*1925

These throne-like Art Deco chairs were commissioned by an Indian Maharajah from Asprey of Bond Street, London, to accompany the glass-and-chrome illuminated dining table. The table is inlaid with panels by René Lalique of France, whose firm is best known for its decorative tableware, and art glass. Combining these delicate panels, depicting birds among foliage, with heavy square-sectioned legs, has a monumentally impressive effect. The chair is stylish and unique.

D & E . Art Deco Salon Suites, *c*1925

This suite (**D**) was designed by Louis Süe and André Mare who in 1919 founded the Paris interior decorating firm, the Compagnie Des Arts Français which did much to popularize Art Deco. Their declared aim was to allow a cohesive style to develop without the suffocating singularity of Art Nouveau, in its French form dominated by waving organic stems and budding flowers. Süe et Mare were architect and painter respectively who combined with various other craftsmen working in fabric, wood and even glass, to produce some prestigious interiors. This suite was for the famous Exposition des Arts Décoratifs held in Paris in 1925. Although their work was prestigious and exclusive, they favoured the use of traditional skills and artists to create a more sober, though still sophisticated, look in the increasingly bizarre world of Paris in the 1920s.

The suite is based on a Louis Philippe prototype. Louis Philippe (basically French 1840s) drew heavily on the designs of the Louis XV and XVI periods a century before. If this suite was upholstered in traditional cloth and some of the sharp Art Deco corners were softened, it could be seen to be very much in an 18th-century style. The use of the Beauvais tapestry is itself retrospective, similar to the tapestry workshops set up by the Arts & Crafts movement in England at Windsor, to emulate the work of the Mortlake workshops of the 17th century. This suite in a style revived twice over still has an essence of Frenchness

C

E

B

A

D

about it, the product of a national concern for style which has developed its own identity over the centuries.

The second suite (**E**) by Maurice Dufresne uses straight vertical lines contrasting with gentle horizontal curves, which are echoed in the seat rails and set off the tapestry; the result is not excessive, but still chic.

A. The Wassilly Chair by Marcel Breuer, *c*1925

This chair, perhaps one of the most famous of all 20th-century designs, later took its name from the artist Wassilly Kandinsky for whose studio it was made at the Bauhaus. Breuer (1902–1981) left Hungary to study painting in Vienna and in 1924 took charge of the Bauhaus workshop concerned with interior design. He encouraged the students to produce in simple media, in keeping with the broad principles of originality and function. The stylish Wassilly chair has been in continual production since 1925, and its historical importance in generating the designs of Mart Stam, and Mies van der Rohe is undeniable.

As political difficulties dogged the Bauhaus, Breuer moved to England where he helped the firm Isokon to develop designs using sculptured plywood, which again sparked off an entirely new generation of furniture. Remarkably, he was considered much more important as an architect and was invited by Walter Gropius, former head of the Bauhaus, to teach at Harvard University in the United States in 1921. He continued his impressive, celebrated career in the United States, and in the end, in spite of the grandeur of his buildings, it is his chairs which arguably have had the greatest impact.

B. The Transat Chair by Eileen Gray, *c*1927

Eileen Gray has become one of the best known individualists in 20th-century design, and this is perhaps her most famous chair, originally made for a house she built at Roque Brune in France, on Corbusier's recommendation. She was born in Ireland in 1879, trained at the Slade School of Art in London before 1900 and then became an apprentice at a lacquer workshop. She worked all over Europe during the next 30 years with many of the great names of the 20th century; as can be seen from this chair, she took elements from each. It is elegantly simple, punctuated with germanic brass fittings, has a French look, and yet leans toward Mies van der Rohe. Like Frank Lloyd Wright, her long life saw many styles come and go, and her interior designs particularly survive them all.

C & D. Chairs by Mies van der Rohe, *c*1929

Ludwig Mies van der Rohe (1886–1969) was another architect-designer from the influential German Bauhaus of the late 1920s; his two main designs – the Barcelona (**C**) and the M R (**D**) chairs – had tremendous impact on subsequent 20th-century furniture. Mies van der Rohe was born the son of a German stone-cutter and was apprenticed to a furniture designer and architect, Peter Behrens. He started working for himself in 1912. The Barcelona chair takes its name from the Barcelona International Exhibition for which it was designed, with accompanying ottoman or footstool. Although swiftly conceived, the modernist German pavillon at the exhibition, with straight lines and minimal encumbrance, was a great success, as were the chairs, produced in Berlin and still made by Knoll International today.

Although a director of Bauhaus from 1930–1933, his furniture designs disregard economy and concentrate on opulence. The flattened steel frame of the Barcelona is in fact quite complex and relatively expensive to produce. He was most famous, however, for his furniture made from tubular steel, generally chromed and close to an original design by Mart Stam which consisted of a continual tube bent to form base, legs, seat and back. Mies van der Rohe was first to patent the idea, although he claimed that it worked on a different principle to Stam's original. This became the basis for the M R range, designed in 1931, with comfort depending on the springing in the tubular frame and the luxurious leather upholsteries. The simple appearance is deceptive; more for aesthetic reasons than structural ones – his famous maxim was that 'God is in the details' – the chair was very carefully designed to give this air of simplicity. Before the Second World War he fled from the Nazis to the United States, where he was for many years the director of the Illinois Institute, Chicago. Able to develop many of the ideas he had formed as a young man in Germany, he produced some dramatic works such as the Lake Shore Drive apartments in Chicago in the 1940s, and the Seagram Office building in the 1950s.

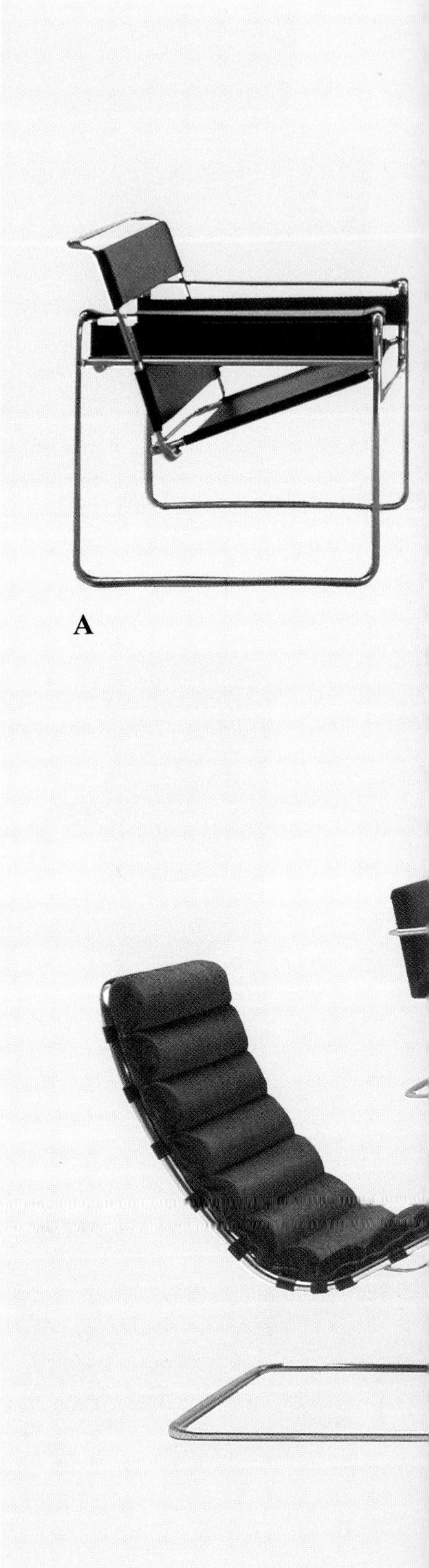

A

C

B

D

1900-1999

A . A French Chair by René Herbst, *c*1930

René Herbst (1891–1982) lived in Paris and produced a variety of minimalist designs, including a series of chairs based on chrome stretched with expandable elastic. This chair was one of a series, which included armchairs and chaises longues, with a classic simplicity and function. They are reproduced by Écart today. Herbst claimed that the two necessary conditions of modern art was the rejection of ornamentation, and purity of line. The result is French Bauhaus, with the addition of a little chic.

B . A Suite of Wrought-Iron Art Deco Furniture by Raymond Subes, *c*1935

If the straight lines and elongated forms of this suite clearly belong to the Art Deco movement, the style of the chairs perhaps best indicates its source – revivalist. If one were to change the proportions by flattening and widening the chairs, they would have an oval back, a broad seat, the gilt details and dignified drapes more familiar from the state chairs of the Napoleonic era. Even the marble table underlines the analysis; wrought-iron supports of a U-shape are not unfamiliar beneath the brightly patterned marble of Napoleonic console tables. The furniture certainly borders on the kitsch, and may be more at home in the wrought-iron tradition of Mediterranean furniture.

C – G . Chairs and Stool by Alvar Aalto, *c*1937

This chair (**C**) is one of an original series of laminated wood furniture, the Scandinavian equivalent of Bauhaus tubular steel. Alvar Aalto (1898–1976) was a major Finnish architect of the Modernist movement, concerned not only with the spaces in the buildings in which people lived, but the furniture which occupied those spaces. His belief that the fitments should be as human as the people in them led him to reject metal in favour of organic, or natural, products. Aalto's early designs were exhibited at Helsinki in 1931 showing unusual shapes which were the results of his experiments with wood in the 1920s using some tubular support.

When designing the Paimio Sanatorium during the early 1930s, the first project that brought him international attention, he wanted to get away from tubular metal for the furniture. He therefore devised the Paimio chair on a laminated frame with a veneer seat

G

A

B

C
F
E
D

(**D**). Friendlier than other chairs, it also has a delightfully bizarre shape, as unusual as anything from the rest of Europe and self-sprung on the natural flexibility of the wood. The easy chair is covered with a lattice of webbing, and when fully reclined resembles a chaise longue. The design cleverly reduces the need for complex techniques in production; there are few corners to be joined or joints to be made, the wood is virtually continuous and the linear appearance pleasing. Aalto founded a firm known as Artek which still produces his furniture today. It is not all exotic; the stacking stools designed around 1930 for the Viipuri Library (**E**) were simple, functional and space-saving, an idea which he continued with a similar chair of simpler design, without the laminated springy legs made of several leaves of wood (**F**). By 1933, he had designed a broad range of extremely variable furniture including his high-backed armchair, not dissimilar to a traditional 18th-century English Wing Chair (**G**).

Comparisons have been drawn between Aalto's laminated birch furniture and moulded plywood furniture produced in the 1930s by, for example, Summers and Eames; the fundamental difference is that Aalto makes the structure work in the design, producing an integrated whole which is also elegant. His designs have a classic appeal which remains popular today.

H . A Pair of Laminated Birch Sidechairs by Gerald Summers, *c*1938

With the influence of design exhibitions, which were now plentiful in most European capitals, and an influx of European designers such as Marcel Breuer, the Modernist style gradually filtered into England. Although this ultra-modern furniture was associateed with the design firm PEL (Practical Equipment Limited, a branch of the artistic Isokon Group), there were also self-styled craftsmen working with the new techniques. Gerald Summers, who designed for the firm Makers of Simple Furniture, created some highly original models. This elegant design is delightfully simple and economical; it is simply a cut-out of wood which is bent round and held together by the seat rails, a little like folded paper. The result is pleasing to look at as well as being cheap and practical. The same principle was used in his more famous plywood armchair, which again was cut out of a single sheet of material, the arms being bent upwards and the legs being bent downwards. It is surprising that such an innovative idea did not achieve greater acclaim or commercial success.

I & J . An Italian Plywood Chair by Carlo Mollino, *c*1945

This unusual variant (**B**) on the plywood chair is by Carlo Mollino of the Milan School of Designers; Milan had become an important design centre between the two World Wars, and home of the Triennale exhibitions. Mollino is perhaps the best-known name from this period. His most famous design is the unusual reclining chair of 1949. The more conventional chair is not dissimilar to the work of Gerald Summers and has the sophistication of being sprung by the tensioning bars between the legs. It was manufactured by Apelli and Varesio. The Milan School's designs are exciting, especially when compared with much of the post-war British Utility furniture.

Most of Mollino's designs in plywood use the natural tension of the bentwood in the same way as Aalto and Summers: this prototype (**C**) is also moulded to give added shape.

K . LCW ('Lounge Chair Wood') by Charles Eames, *c*1946

Charles Eames is perhaps the most famous of modern chair designers, and is certainly the most collected. He is rightly applauded for two notable achievements: for using plywood which could be permanently moulded in two planes rather than in one, as Gerald Summers and Alvar Aalto had done; and secondly, as a designer of truly sculptural chairs, partially the result of this technique of exploiting complete freedom in three dimensions. The joy of really pliable plywood was that the seat and back could be moulded exactly to the human form, dispensing with the need for upholstery. After the Second World War there emerged a new generation of chairs based on this principle, partly devised in collaboration with Eero Saarinen, using plywood glass fibre and then plastic on a variety of supports. His designs were recognized in the Second World War, were exhibited in the Museum of Modern Art in New York, and in 1948 won a prize in an international competition for low cost furniture design, appropriately combining cheap and easy production with design elegance.

L . An Oak Dining Suite by Gordon Russell, *c*1950

Immediate similarity can be seen between this suite and the suite pictured earlier by Ernest Gimson, and establishes Gordon Russell as having inherited the best aspects of the 19th-century Arts & Crafts movement, as seen in

I

L

H
K
J

the work of the so-called Cotswold School. Russell was slightly less anti-mechanist than Gimson; indeed, he became a specialist in industrial production and during the Second World War designed for the British 'Utility furniture' scheme, which concentrated Great Britain's resources on making only one type of furniture as cheaply as possible.

The design of these chairs is retrospective, and almost identical to English Farthingale armchairs of the mid-17th century. Similarly, the table is based on a heavy, rustic, distinctly non-technical design. The quality of the furniture is discreet but excellent. In *Design Magazine* in 1951, Russell wrote that the 'tradition of pioneering should prove to be a decisive influence when a survey of the situation in AD2051 comes to be written'. While this may be the case, it may be thanks to the innovative work of designers such as Race rather than to the retrospective work of Russell & Sons, Broadway, Worcestershire.

A . Chairs by Harry Bertoia, c1952

Although Harry Bertoia's most famous chair, the wire-grid backed dining chair, became a lasting image of the 1960s, it was in fact designed in the early 1950s. Bertoia was an immigrant from northern Italy, where he grew up surrounded by Milan School chairs which clearly influenced him greatly; in the United States, he became a metalworker and a student sculptor. He met Eero Saarinen and Florence Knoll, and worked for some years with Charles Eames who is now considered the most important 20th-century American designer. His work with Eames after the Second World War on plywood and metal designs clearly influenced his own development; in this range of wire-structured chairs, some of them support sculptured seats in manmade fibre reminiscent of Eames' work of this period. Bertoia described them as being 'mainly made of air, like sculpture. Space passes through them.' He spent much of his life working for Knoll International (who still produce the chairs shown), producing designs directly for their factory and also fulfilling architectural commissions of sculptural kinds. These amorphous shapes and bold colours have come to symbolise the United States' West Coast of the 1960s.

B . A Pair of Black Lacquer Chairs, c1952

These chairs by Isola and Gabetti, with their unusual stretchers joining the legs in an interesting (but uneconomical) way, have a sculptural quality not dissimilar to the works of Carlo Mollino. They share with his work the acceptance of a notion of upholstery versus structure, and achieve impact with their bright colours.

C . Chairs by Eero Saarinen, c1955

With the exception of tubular steel furniture and some bentwood designs, almost all the chairs in this book have four legs, which come independently from the seat. Saarinen said of his pedestal design that 'the underside of typical chairs and tables makes a confusing and restless world . . . I wanted to clear up the slum of legs'. It is hardly surprising that he worked closely with Charles Eames: the fruits of their partnership formed at the Cranbrook Academy of Art, Michigan, US, (of which Saarinen's father was director and architect) are easy to see in his soft-outlined, sculptural seats.

Saarinen was born in Finland in 1916 where his father was a major architect. He grew up, however, in Chicago where his father designed the 40 buildings of the Cranbrook Academy of Art in Michigan, and for one of which Eero designed the furniture. In 1940, he designed with Eames a range of furniture based on plywood shell which was featured in a competition for organic design in home furnishings, organized by New York's Museum of Modern Art. There is something very European about the outline of these pedestal chairs, a design which was also present in his collaboration with Eames and which perhaps goes back to his European origins, even though most of his life was spent in the United States. Like Harry Bertoia, his chairs have become one of the lasting images of the 1960s, the Tulip chair appearing in the first English Habitat catalogue of 1971.

B

C

A

A . The Coconut Chair by George Nelson, *c*1956

Although this chair appears to be soft and sculptural, it is in fact supported both by steel legs and by a metal shell which keeps the fabric upholstery in shape, hence the name Coconut. They were commercially produced by the Herman Miller Furniture Company. The chair shows the strong influence of Charles Eames and Eero Saarinen, paves the way for greater design freedom in the 1960s, and was exploited on a large scale by European designers. The metal shell eventually gave way to fibreglass and other modern materials, truly popularizing this style.

B . A Fibreglass Desk Chair by Jean Lele, *c*1969

Although this looks as dated now as it was outrageous at the time, it in fact represents a coming-together of three distinct trends. First, it owes a debt of origin to Charles Eames, Eero Saarinen and even Harry Bertoia who exploited and explored the use of new materials in a soft, sculptural way. Second, it fully exploits the possibility of fibreglass, its great strength and ease of construction, and creates an integral sculptural environment for the user – this idea was not a novelty, many people have sat at Victorian desks with folding bench seats – but what is new is the harmony of line in this extravagance. Third, it marks the outer boundary of the avant garde as allowed by the new materials (just as it could be said that the English Habitat designs of moulded-fibre furniture were the inner boundary). A brief look at the 1980s shows a regression from this degree of innovation, or at least a return to more traditional forms.

C , D & E . The First Habitat Range of Chairs, c1971

War-time shortages in Europe had seen a new generation of designers and therefore designs emerge. By the 1960s the main technological changes, the use of plastics and new materials, had given new freedom to structures, and designers such as Charles Eames or Vico Magistretti were not slow to exploit the possibilities. The 1960s also saw a marketing revolution as represented, if not begun, by Englishman Terence Conran with his Habitat shop. The notion of selling furniture in kit form to be assembled at home was not a new one; Gerrit Rietveld and Bauhaus designers had used this technique 50 years before with some success. Mass production was not new either; Giles Grendey and Thomas Chippendale, for example, employed vast workshops in the 18th century, and the Thonets produced many millions of bentwood chairs in the 19th century. However, the Conran combination of high-volume production sold in kit form via catalogue soon became tremendously popular.

The first catalogue of 1971, from which these three illustrations are chosen, combined Habitat-designed wares with other designers' work including that of Eero Saarinen and Harry Bertoia. The mass production kept prices down, and imaginative room settings in the catalogue promoted the idea of more stylish households; easy access by post or by visiting the rapidly-growing chain of stores ensured Habitat's success. There is little in the first catalogue of enormous originality, as can be seen from this selection, centred on practical 1960s clean lines, with bright colours and some up-market modern furniture classics, including Conran's own design line. The Habitat range created a demand for bourgeois style which it then exploited with a chain of stores somehow very different from the traditional British quality stores, such as Heal's or Waring & Gillows. Interestingly, the largest single feature in the catalogue on chairs is taken up by photographs of Thonet's bentwood chair, 'no 14', designed in 1859.

F . Two Boxing Glove Chaises Longues by De Sede, *c*1978

These chairs, or arguably sofas, are nearly 3ft/91 cms high and 5ft/152 cms long, and are magnificent for their wit. It is surprising that such a delightful and sensuous form had not been thought of before. There is, however, more to it than mere novelty; it belongs to a branch of art which is the descendant of Surrealism, or even of visual illusions as enjoyed by baroque painters. In the 1930s, Dali thought that chairs were taken too seriously and devised one that constantly fell over and even spilt drinks! These chairs are not dangerously challenging or disturbing, and in this sense they are not surreal: they are a gentle joke at the expense of design pretension. They do not try to 'break the monopoly upon that which is real' (Ehrenzweig). After all, they really are quite comfortable to sit in, and 'comfortable' is not a word normally associated with Surrealism!

B

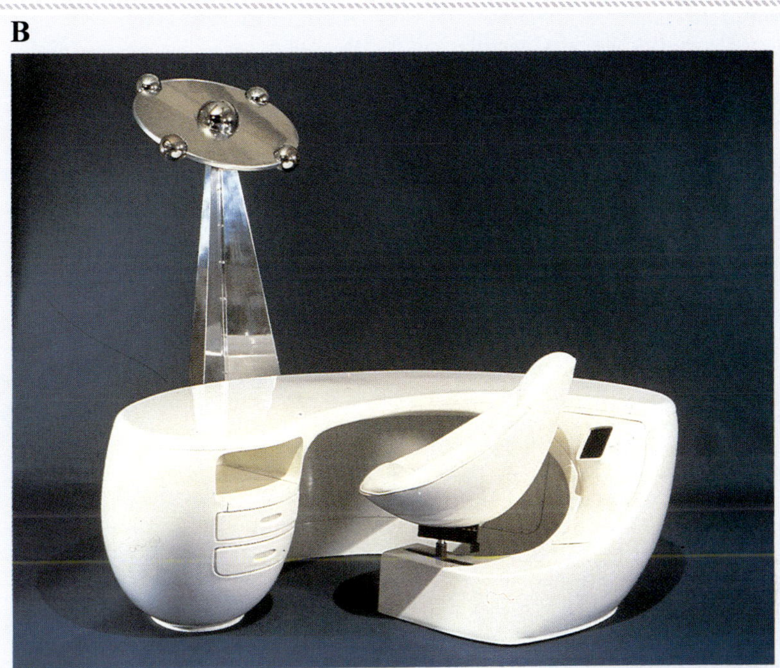

D

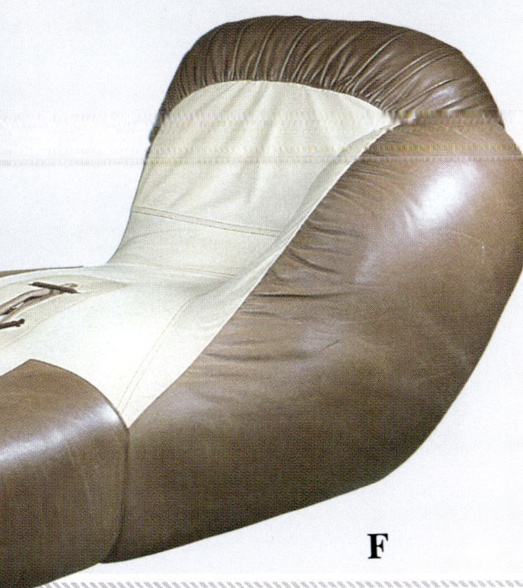

C

F

The following ten chairs (176–185) have been selected by the British Crafts Council as being of exceptional merit. They differ from most other contemporary chairs in that they are generally made in small numbers, in contrast to international firms. Each chair has been subject to rigorous examination by master craftsmen and is therefore fundamentally sound.

A. A Glass Chair by Danny Lane, 1980s

Pundits claim that Lane has already become a classic, the sort of comment one is bound to get when dealing with contemporary art. However, the chair is certainly dramatic. It is the sort of glistening apparition which the 17th or 18th centuries would have greatly appreciated. Glass chairs are extremely scarce, although some were produced in the 19th century in formal, throne-like, precisely-cut material. Made of dozens of individual slices of float glass which are held together by rods in columns, it is only just a practical chair, being extremely heavy and not very comfortable; and the accompanying chaise-longue is even worse. But it is exciting and amusing, epithets which could equally have been applied to elaborate rococo or more bizarre Regency designs. This chair has a sculptural quality of which Gaudi or even Bugatti would have been proud.

B. A Bench by Andrew Holmes

Initially, Andrew Holmes' furniture has a slightly off-beat 1960s look, perhaps because it is primarily made from materials from demolished houses. Holmes is a sculptor by training and views his furniture as functional – a popular 18th century notion – and indeed this bench shows similarities to Gothic box chairs, with the same homely air. He argues that muted colours are reassuring – a latter day Alvar Aalto?

C. A Steel-Framed Chair by Eric de Graaff

The first impression of this opportunely photographed chair is its emphasis on structure, underlined by the use of colour quite separate to the 'upholstery'. The sharp geometric lines forming squares and rectangles owe a clear debt to Gerrit Rietveld, also to Josef Hoffmann and the Vienna Secession, or even Charles Rennie Mackintosh. An appealing feature of this chair is the way the lines which form the frame not only support the body but also enclose and define space, which is in turn punctuated by the flat planes forming the seat and the back. It works well in that it is beautiful and reasonably comfortable.

D. A Chair by Fred Baier

Fred Baier produces furniture in a variety of styles, and recently completed a large commission with another graduate from the Royal College of Art, London, for a celebrated circular Art Deco mansion in Surrey, which included a circular double bed. Fitting the form of the furniture to the form of the house has echoes of Frank Lloyd Wright, although this particular chair in stained sycamore with leather and horse-hair upholstery has a quasi-Italian look about it, vaguely reminiscent of Carlo Mollino. Whether or not academic exposure to a history of style is always beneficial, Baier chairs are well-crafted, imaginative and generally sensible.

E. A Caterpillar Rocker by Jeremy Broun

This chair is visually stunning, a good combination of colour, structure and practicality. The frame is of stained birch plywood, the slats are red-black mahogany. It has the advantage of being a truly original idea: just as Saarinen and his pedestal chairs converted four chair legs into one, so this chair seems to be altering the design of the rocking chair. Not simply concentrating on structure and colour, it is fundamentally changing traditional designs in a move towards simplicity. Broun is first a craftsman, second a designer and this is perhaps the most avant garde of his work. He is quoted as saying he 'likes to take a risk with material' and to 'exploit its character'; it is an achievement to do this without losing direction.

C

D

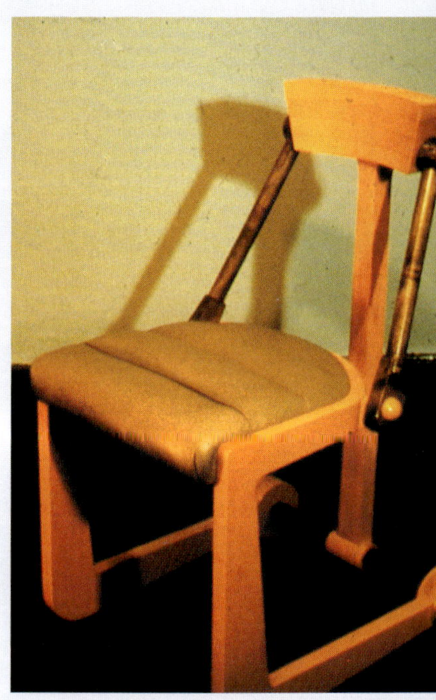

E

A

B

1900-1999

A. A Sidechair in Beech by Richard la Trobe Bateman

There is more than a hint of Gerrit Rietveld about these very straight lines, geommetric patterns and simple joints. Richard la Trobe Bateman considers that economy of means, clarity of technique and practicality are important principles, a view which Rietveld would no doubt have applauded. They are good-looking chairs made with interesting techniques, such as the splitting of green timber. They have been called Constructivist, which apparently means they show a serious concern for disciplined, logical form. However, they suffer perhaps from Rietveld's problem of beauty without comfort.

B. A Folding Chair by David Colwell

This is a true craft chair, based on a traditional design and executed in traditional fashion: the timber has been bent by steam while still green and then left to season. It was made in a workshop in Wales by a small team in the Morris-style Arts & Crafts fashion, and the X-frame is one of the earliest forms of European chair dating from the Middle Ages. It is appropriate that it should be revived in this more modern folding form.

C. A Set of Dining Chairs by Rodney Wales

These simple chairs are an interesting combination of many different styles. The caqueteuse, a 16th-century form, had a very slim back and a hemispherical seat like these, although here the backs have been stylized into almost Mackintosh proportions and have reminiscently square-silhouetted designs, not unlike Secession design. Wales has won awards for a combination of good design and potential for mass production. The simplicity of the chair suggests that the potential popularisation is great as it takes design away from the rarified elite and places it in the home.

D. A Chair in Cherry Wood by Rupert Williamson

One can instantly see from the complex structure of this chair that it requires cabinet-making skills worthy of any good 18th-century craftsman. There is much 18th century Chinese Chippendale chair in the design, although there is no carving (a practice which is almost defunct in modern design, presumably because of cost rather than taste). It has a great sculptural quality about it, the back forming a splendid almost Gothic arch

C

F

E

D
B
A

above a long sweeping down-turned arm, reminiscent of Hepplewhite. One of Williamson's chairs is in the Victoria & Albert Museum, London, which perhaps suggests that these are modern chairs for the antique lover.

E . A Chair by John Coleman

This elegant design by John Coleman has the regrettably rare quality of being the right shape for the body. This important criterion seems to have escaped the majority of chair designers from all periods. The angled back clearly gives plenty of lumbar support, allowing the lower back to curve in its natural direction – forwards rather than in an injury-prone backwards.

This chair has clean lines, and is practical. It is primarily of ash, and is made-to-order, reviving the close link between maker and customer which is often now long and strained. It is homely but not dull.

F . The Oil Rig Desk and Chair, by Stephen Owen

Salvador Dali, the Surrealist painter, claimed that chair design was taken far too seriously; Stephen Owen has effectively avoided that pitfall. This design based on an oil rig in Art Deco revival style utilises straight lines and geometric patterns to give it a lively effect which punctuated with the bright colours contrasting with the black. It is an amusing example of novelty furniture made acceptable by wit.

A. A Folding Chair by Phillippe Starcke

Phillippe Starcke is something of a 1980s cult designer with an impressive track record: he designed the French presidential apartment at the Elysée Palace, the night club *Les Bains Douches*, as well as several American hotel chains. The appealing thing about this chair is its simplicity, practicality, and elegance of line. It clearly looks back to PEL, or perhaps the Bauhaus and Gerrit Rietveld for its roots. It has the very real advantage of being practical for modern living and not expensive to produce.

B. 'Mister Bliss', a Chair by Phillippe Starcke

Characteristically linear, this is a surprisingly rare attempt to design a chair on which to kneel, a far healthier posture than sitting. It is extraordinary that new designs shows such little regard for comfort and health, preferring an impressive look. This chair is based on the principle of increasing the angle made by the body and legs to more than 90°, which allows the lower back to curve inwards in a natural way; most chairs have the opposite effect.

C. The Spaghetti Chair by Gian Dominico Belotti

Gian Dominico Belotti, born in 1922, is from the pre-Second World War generation of Italian designers. He originally studied sculpture and later followed an architectural training in Milan where he was more concerned with ideological considerations than commercial ones. This chair, designed in the late 1970s, showed an interest in materials and a simplicity belonging to the Marcel Breuer tradition, which continued after the Second World War.

D. A Chair by Carlo Forcolini, 'Signorina Chan'

This striking, contemporary chair contrasts the sculptural element of the triple-curving back with the linear element of the straight, stark tubular frames, and the two strong colours, contrasts which perhaps pervade the decade. It is no surprise that Forcolini was a pupil of Vico Magistretti; indeed they have worked closely together producing 1980s designs which tend toward richness and indulgence, far removed from the simplicity of the Minimalists.

C

D

A . 'Quarta', a Chair by Mario Botta

Mario Botta trained at the Milan School of Fine Arts in the early 1960s, did some practical work in the studio of Le Corbusier, and now works as an architect in Lugano, Italy. This chair, the fourth of an interesting series, combines linear elements (each surface being made of slats) in a sculptural way. Although the image is exciting, the planes formed are very hard. This would not perhaps win an award for comfort, but it has the visual impact which Italian design frequently does, and several of Botta's designs are in the study collection at the Museum of Modern Art in New York.

B . A Chair by Vico Magistretti

This is a classic Milanese chair, relying on simple elements and yet having a sculptural quality. Vico Magistretti graduated in 1945 and began to design in the period of post-war rehabilitation, following the original pioneers such as Terragni and Carlo Mollino, whose work this in some ways resembles. Magistretti exhibited and won awards at numerous Triennales, and his work in the Milan movement, which has become an originator of international style, can be found not only in the first Habitat Catalogue, but in New York's Museum of Modern Art.

C . 'West Side,' a Chair by Ettore Sottsass, *c*1980

This striking chair is by Ettore Sottsass who was one of the organizers of the radical Memphis Collection, an exhibition of 1981. He has been described as a metaphoric designer, the object itself being of little importance, but the conflict between colour, shape and structure is exploited to amuse and upset the eye. Sottsass was born in Austria in 1917, has worked extensively in Italy as consultant designer to Olivetti, and also studied at the Royal College of Art.

A

C

B

1900-1999

A. An Italian Art Nouveau Banquette by Carlo Bugatti, *c*1900

Part of a wonderfully exotic drawing-room suite, this is one of the most arresting sofas ever designed. Created by Carlo Bugatti (1855–1940), it combines metallic insets with light and dark woods in a curious Italian interpretation of the Art Nouveau style. Bugatti created a sensation with his eccentric furniture at the Turin Exhibition in 1902. Moorish and Far Eastern influences are often predominant in his designs, and he was willing to combine various materials and techniques in order to create a special effect: polished metals, silks, carved wood and paint, for instance, could be contained in a single piece. This sofa is a superb example of his creative genius at its most extreme, revealing his passion for suspended circles, thonging and massive silk tassels.

B. An English Late Victorian/ Early Edwardian Yew and Elm Sofa in the Windsor Style, *c*1900

Made *c*1900, this triple chair-back settle reflects the popularity of antique furniture at the turn of the century. The classic Windsor-style sofa is made of yew and elm woods and has lancet backs with pierced splats. The shaped, solid seat is set on unusual pierced cabriole legs, and the crinoline stretchers are also quite decorative. The Gothic shaping of this George III-style settle makes it especially attractive, particularly in combination with the fine workmanship that it exhibits. Despite being a reproduction, the settle sold at auction for several thousand pounds, revealing the strength of well-made Edwardian reproductions. The term 'Windsor' is used for stick-back chairs with turned legs, solid seats and arms, which were mainly produced in the High Wycombe area of Buckinghamshire from the late 17th century. American Windsors are more usually painted, although those made in Britain and intended for use in the garden were also coloured. They are differentiated by the shaping of the back and can have fan, hoop or comb backs.

C. An English Edwardian Chesterfield Sofa, *c*1901–10

An Edwardian version of the Victorian Chesterfield, this sofa is now upholstered in Italian damask. In most designs of this type, the arm can be lowered, enabling the user to recline on the sofa. Because of the seat springing and the overstuffed arms, seating of this type was extremely comfortable. Layers of straw, horsehair and padding combined to make furniture that relied for its effect on the quality of the upholstery fabric.

C

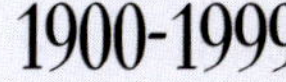

A

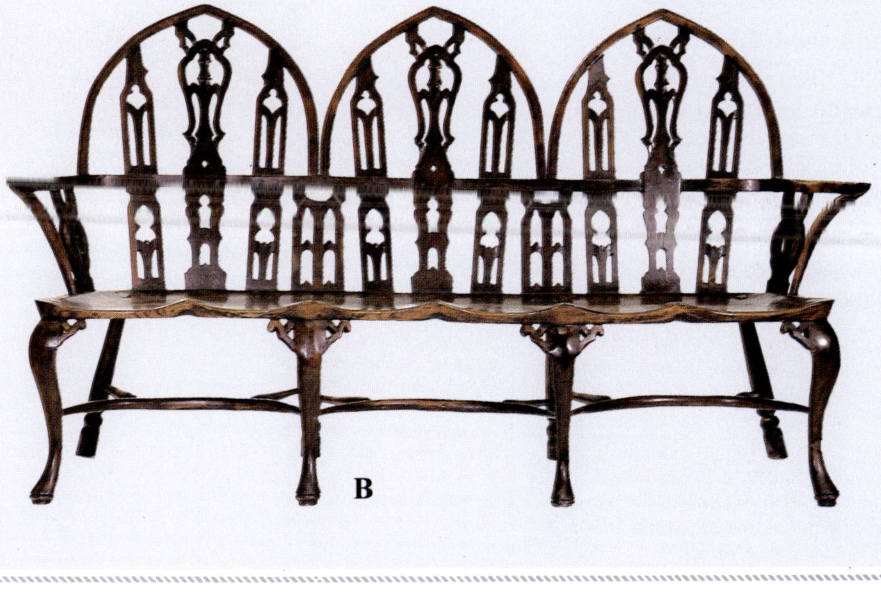

B

1900-1999

A . A Scottish Art Nouveau Built-In Sofa by Charles Rennie Mackintosh, *c*1902–04

This built-in sofa at Hill House, Dunbartonshire, Scotland, was designed by Charles Rennie Mackintosh (1868–1928), who was also the architect of Hill House. His early work was much influenced by CFA Voysey, but by 1900 his own elongated, dramatically simple styles were well established. As he was primarily an architect, he was mainly interested in furniture that contributed to the totality of a house or room. His built-in seating set new trends which were to have a considerable influence on the development of German commercial furniture. This example is one of his simplest constructions, relying on upholstery for its effect. Much more typical of his work are the decorated cupboard fronts and the high backed occasional chairs. The simplicity of such interiors appealed to the more artistic sections of society and the work of Mackintosh and his Glasgow followers was featured in the leading journals on the Continent.

B . An English Edwardian Chesterfield Sofa, *c*1905

The Victorian Chesterfield-type sofa was updated in the Edwardian period by the addition of a high back, which gave it added comfort. Although the proportions of the Chesterfields were more pleasing to the eye, this new design gave the user more support for his or her back. Standing on solid, turned legs, the sofa had adjustable arms at either end. It was upholstered in a fashionably patterned tapestry.

C . An English Edwardian Sofa in 'Queen Anne' Style, *c*1905

The Edwardian passion for furniture made in 'Queen Anne' style is evident in this high-backed example, which stands on rather long cabriole legs. It is upholstered in Morocco leather and has a sprung seat stuffed with hair. Although such atavistic designs were admired, the comfort of coiled springs was not abandoned in the interest of authenticity.

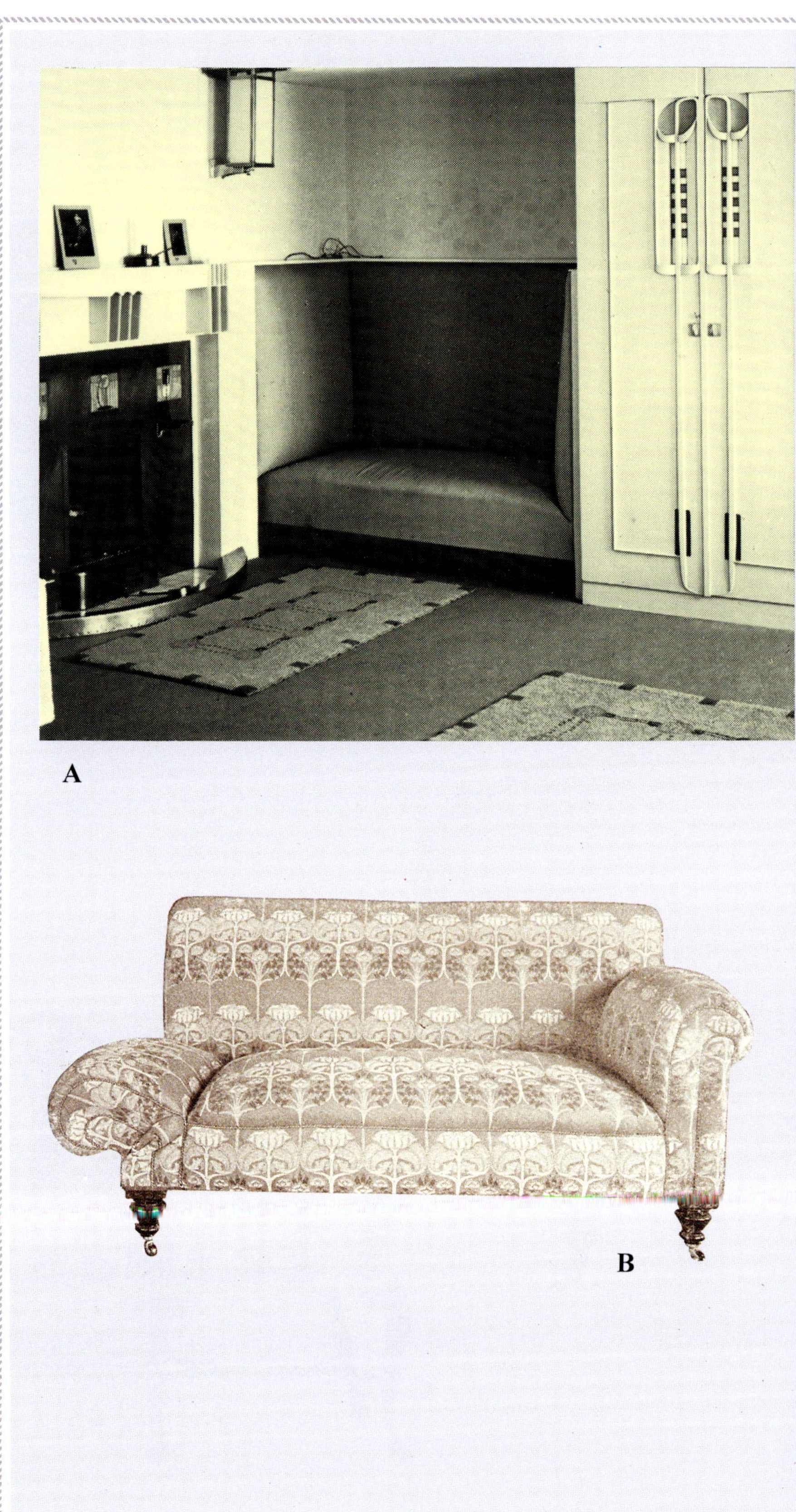

A

B

C

D

E

D . An English Edwardian Mahogany and Upholstered Sofa, *c*1905

A simple Edwardian sofa made in Britain around 1905, this stands on sturdy turned legs and features a back rest decorated with machine carving. The sprung seat and heavily padded back rest made the piece quite comfortable and, happily, they have survived in some number. In this example, the show wood is mahogany, but cheaper versions were made on which a heavy stain was used to disguise the construction.

E . An English Edwardian Walnut Suite in 'Queen Anne' Style, *c*1905–10

By 1910, it had become fashionable to furnish with antiques, although everything made after 1800 was largely ignored. Good 18th-century furniture was scarce, so high-quality copies were produced. Some of these are so good that they now attract very high prices when they appear in the salerooms. This chair-backed sofa, part of an early 20th-century reproduction of a 'Queen Anne' suite, was produced in figured English walnut. Its makers claimed it was a copy of an original at the Victoria and Albert Museum, and it was suggested as furniture for a dining room in the traditional style. The complete suite originally cost £35.

1900-1999

A. An Italian Art Nouveau Sofa, by Ernesto Basile, *c*1900

This sofa, part of a suite, was designed by the Italian architect Ernesto Basile, who was appointed as chief designer at Vittorio Ducrot's interior design workshop based in Palermo, Sicily, in 1898. Basile's design output for Ducrot was largely in the 'Stile Liberty' (the Italian term for Art Nouveau, coined in tribute to the London department store), combining elegance and function, although he also produced pieces employing the more overt organic forms usually associated with Art Nouveau. Ducrot's firm was on a solid commercial footing, producing quality furniture for hotels and private homes, although some prestigious projects were also commissioned.

B. An American Arts & Crafts Teak Settle, by Charles and Henry Greene, 1906

This teak storage bench was designed by Charles and Henry Greene for the Blacker House in Pasadena, California, in 1906. The two Greene brothers were primarily architects who, upholding the traditions of the Arts & Crafts Movement, believed that the furniture and fittings of a house should be in perfect accord. Like Gustav Stickley, in New York State, they drew on traditional American styles but were prepared to accept modern construction methods much more readily than their British counterparts, they were also influenced by Japanese design. This teak settle, with a carefully constructed but deceptively simple back rest, derives from the functional pieces owned by the early settlers. The seat lifts in two sections for access to the storage space below. In rural homes, this would have been used for linen or blankets, but in the elegant houses of the avant-garde, who commissioned most of the Arts & Crafts work both in the United States and Great Britain, it was more likely to have been used for travelling rugs or the storage of decorative textiles.

D

A

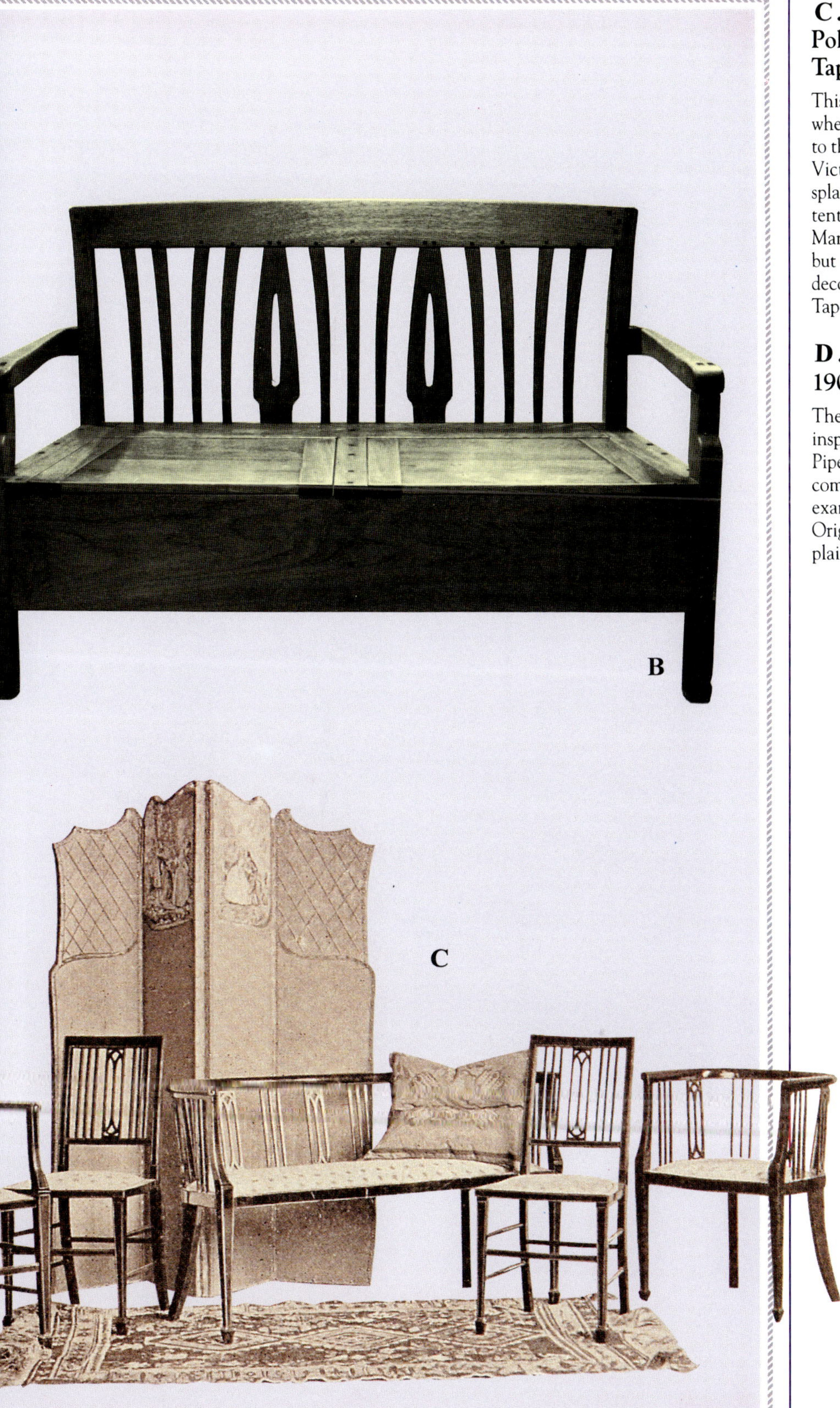

C. An English Edwardian Polished-Mahogany Suite with Tapestry Upholstery, 1909

This type of suite was high fashion in 1909, when very light furniture was used in reaction to the deep-buttoned heavy products the Victorians had loved. The pierced centre splats of the chair and sofa backs show a tentative influence of the Glasgow School. Many painted suites of this design were made, but in this instance polished mahogany, decorated with an inlay, was employed. Tapestry was used for the upholstery.

D. An English Edwardian Sofa, 1909

The Edwardian affection for lighter furniture inspired some designs that now look skimpy. Piped cushions and upholstery became more commonplace after 1920, making this 1909 example progressive, if hardly attractive. Originally it would have been upholstered in plain, ribbed tapestry.

1900-1999

A. An American Arts & Crafts Oak Hall Bench, *c*1910

Gustav Stickley (1857–1946) was a follower of the writings of William Morris and believed that the design of furniture should evolve in a natural way from the traditions of its country of origin. Working in northern New York State, he was also heavily influenced by the somewhat austere style of Shaker furniture, from which all ornament was banished. He described the pieces he made as 'Structural'. This *c*1910 oak hall bench is typical of his work, for which locally available woods were used in order to make it cheap enough for middle-class Americans to own. Stickley believed that art should be brought into the homes of ordinary people and that by using well-designed objects in daily life they would be encouraged to adopt a plain-living, high-thinking philosophy. The products of Stickley's Craftsman Workshops enjoyed great popularity in the early years of the 20th century, as did his monthly journal, the *Craftsman*. Examples in the early tradition, such as this settle, are very popular, as they typify the American Arts & Crafts movement.

B. An English Arts & Crafts Living Room with Built-in Sofa, designed by M H Baillie Scott, 1911

The influence of William Morris extended into the 20th century because of the strength of the various designers that perpetuated his Arts & Crafts ideals. In this living room, designed by M H Baillie Scott (1865–1945), the sofa is built into an alcove with shelves for the storage of books and ornamental pieces. Created in 1911, this room represents a lighter interpretation of the Arts & Crafts tradition. Baillie Scott favoured painted interiors, wherein furniture and wall decoration combined to give a somewhat medieval atmosphere. Most of his furniture was made of oak or mahogany by JP White of Bedford. Since Baillie Scott's individual furniture pieces were not highly original designs their impact can only be appreciated fully in the designer's drawings, which combine his furniture with carefully selected rugs, murals and fittings.

C

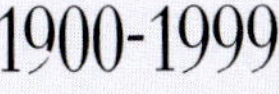

A

B

C. An English Sitting Room with German-Style Sofa by Heal & Son, *c*1918

Heal & Son furnished this fashionable sitting room for a town flat around 1918. The sofa is in the simple German style and composed of plain, flat shapes that were ideal for mass-production; it stands on wooden legs. For its effect it depends on the use of a contrasting fabric that accentuates the angular line. Heals, based in Tottenham Court Road, London, aimed at producing simple but good-quality furniture in which both traditional and modern influences were apparent. Ambrose Heal Jr (1872–1959), joined the family business in 1893 and by 1901, at the Glasgow Exhibition, was well-known for his simple furniture with its reticent use of ornament. Many Heal designs were trendsetters for later mass-producers of furniture. The use of brightly coloured cushions in abstract patterns was to be a common feature of sofas in the 1920s.

1900-1999

A . An English Upholstered Sofa, 1920s

The elegant lines of this sofa are obviously derived from the 18th century, but the lack of any visible show-wood and the fact that the seat continues down to floor level make its 1920s origin perfectly clear. Well constructed and featuring feather-filled cushions, it was marketed as a quality piece in its time. Today it would no doubt find a ready buyer, someone who wishes to obtain classical, well-made and comfortable seat furniture.

B . An English Early 20th-Century Knole Sofa, 1920s

Dating to the 1920s, this is a curious variation on the traditional Knole sofa. In this design the two high sides can be lowered, but the padded arms remain static. As in a genuine Knole, the sides are held in place with ornamental tasselled ropes which are looped around the back projections. The high sides of a Knole made the design especially suitable for use in draughty, cold rooms, while the depth of the seats made it possible to use the structure as an occasional bed. Until recently, such 20th-century examples were almost unsaleable but the current interest in curious, decorative furniture has made them more popular.

C . A French 20th-Century Gilt-Wood Sofa in Louis XV Style

This sofa, upholstered in brocaded silk, is a good 20th-century reproduction of a Louis XV-style piece. The padded back is set within a moulded frame with a foliate scroll carved cresting. The apron is also decorated with a foliate scroll at the front centre and there is further carving on the cabriole legs as well as the arm and back supports. The sofa comes from a five-piece salon suite also comprising two armchairs and two side chairs. Gilt-wood furniture of this type, although constructed comparatively recently, sells for good prices because of the high quality of the workmanship.

A

D

B

C

D . An English Sitting Room with Chesterfield Sofa by Heal & Son, 1920s

A simplification of the Victorian Chesterfield sofa, this example stands on square, tapering feet and is upholstered in the plain fabric that was so fashionable in the early 20th-century. The ruched cushion, seen on the floor, was a type that became very popular in the 1930s and was often found on sofas and armchairs. This sitting room was designed by Ambrose Heal of Heal & Son; the illustration, by Palmer-Jones, is from a contemporary magazine. The stark simplicity of the light fitting and general décor contrasts with the antique-style pie-crust occasional table and the lamp table. The growth of decorating magazines in the 1920s and 1930s made the general public more aware of design trends, with fashions changing at an accelerating rate during these decades.

1900-1999

A. An English Two-Seater Sofa, 1920s

This typical 1920s two-seater sofa has matching cushions on the seat and at the back. Boldly patterned upholstery fabrics, which were in vogue during this period, have again come into fashion. The feather-filled cushions make this design even more luxurious. Cheaper versions were supplied with fillings of cotton waste or even straw.

B. An English Three-Piece Suite, including a Chesterfield Sofa, 1920s

By the mid 1920s, the matching 'Three-piece Suite' was an essential part of every British middle- and working-class home. This type of sofa structure, with comfortable springing and a high back, continued to be made until the 1950s. The maker described this sofa, rather confusingly, as a 'Chesterfield'; the term is now used only for a sofa whose padded back and arms end at one level. This suite was constructed with hardwood frames, and extra-long, steel-coppered springs were said to be used. The pieces stand on round, turned feet. The double-boarded front, emphasized by the use of cord trimming, was a popular design feature of the period.

C. An English Cretonne-Covered Chesterfield Sofa, 1920s

In the 1920s, ordinary working people were able to buy new furniture for their homes. As many of these had small sitting rooms traditional designs, such as the Chesterfield, were adapted for such interiors. This version was deeply padded and well sprung, making it extremely comfortable. One arm could be dropped, so that, despite its length, the sofa could be used for reclining. The basic version was sold covered in plain cotton upholstery. The illustrated model has a loose cretonne cover.

D. An English Oak Convertible Sofa, 1920s

The concept of a sofa that converts into an occasional bed has great practical appeal, and examples from the 18th and early 19th centuries occasionally appear on the market. This advertisement for 'A real friend in need' appeared in the 1920s. Made of turned wood, the sofa was 45 in (115 cm) wide and pulled down to form a full-length bed. The finish was described as 'Jacobean Oak'. It was fitted with corduroy cushions available in four colours. At just under £3, it must have been one of the cheapest pieces of furniture on the market. For an extra 10 shillings a full double-bed width was available.

B

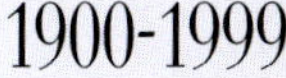

A

C

A real Friend in Need!

—and a very versatile friend too—just the right Settee Bed for every home. A really handsome piece of furniture. A deep, comfortable settee, a cosy lounge, and a serviceable bed all in one. Soundly constructed of highly polished Jacobean oak.

"WONDER" SETTEE BED

Fitted with three cushions, [illegible] in Brown, Red, Green, [illegible] Corduroy. 3 ft. 9 ins. wide, and Extending Full Bed Length. Can be had 6 ins. wider for 10/- extra. Carriage Paid England and Wales. Scotland 5/-, Ireland 7/6 extra. *Post Orders:*

ALFRED A. JACOBS,
(Dept. G.H.), Elm Grove, Southsea.

London Showrooms for Callers:
Evelyn House,
62, Oxford St., London, W.1

69/6

D

1900-1999

A . An English Built-In Sofa, in Cottage Tudor Style, featured in 1922 advertisement

In the early 20th century, the window-seat sofa became a great favourite for the country cottage-type suburban house, often in the Tudor style that was sprouting throughout Britain. Functional wooden frames were produced, which could be extended to fit a bay of almost any length. The effect depended completely upon the attractiveness of the upholstery fabric. This advertisement for 'art furnishing' dates from 1922, but the style had been used by artistic people before 1900. As sofas of this type were built-in, very few have survived intact.

B . An English Carved-Rosewood Settle in Chinese Style, 1924

The current passion for decorative furniture has popularized 19th- and early 20th-century Oriental furniture, which formerly was extremely difficult to sell. An example such as this would always have attracted some attention, as it is both cleverly made and has a known provenance. It is marked with two metal and enamel commemorative medallion insets, surmounted by flags and bearing the inscription: 'British Empire Exhibition 1924, Chinese Restaurant'. The pierced and carved back is ornamented with a fruiting-vine motif and has a central upholstered splat. Made of 'Huang hua-li' wood, a Southeast Asian rosewood, the settle's panelled seat has scrolled ends, made more comfortable with a squab cushion. The settle has a pierced and carved ornamental apron at the seat front and stands on cabriole legs. Pieces made for the great international exhibitions were always of good quality, as they functioned as advertisements for the products of the various countries.

D

A

C . A French Art Deco Lacquered Chaise Longue by Pierre Legrain, 1925

One of the most famous 20th-century sofas is this chaise longue designed by Pierre Legrain (1889–1929) in 1925. Legrain was typical of several versatile Art Deco designers in Paris who could create almost any object from a chair to a scent bottle. Like Carlo Bugatti in Milan, he was fascinated by exotic materials and forms. The chaise longue reveals his quirky, capricious approach, as the 'zebra' skin in fact is made of soft printed velvet and the armrest, usually placed against a wall (and consequently invisible) is beautifully decorated with mother-of-pearl. There is a small shelf at the front of the armrest, perhaps for an elegant cigarette holder or a slim volume of avant-garde poetry. Although its structure looks very simple, almost crude, the sofa is beautifully finished, making it an exotic and expensive fancy.

D . A French Art Deco Smoking Room by Jean Dunand, featuring a Lacquered Settle, 1925

In this smoking room with lacquered walls, ceilings and fittings, a modern sofa is seen at its most basic. Designed by Jean Dunand, who was especially fond of lacquered effects, this bench-type settle was made for the Pavillon d'un Ambassadeur, exhibited at the 1925 Paris Exposition. It depends for its effect on the abstract upholstery fabric, although the basic construction is extremely simple. Such completely functional pieces of French Art Deco furniture contrast with the highly decorated pieces which designers like Dunand, Marcel Coard and Pierre Legrain also made. For collectors of vintage furniture, the period is especially interesting as, even in the work of one designer, the contradictory influences of northern Europe, Japan and Hollywood can be seen.

A . A French Art Deco Gilt-Wood Suite by Louis Süe and André Mare of the Compagnie des Arts Français, *c*1925

This sofa, with its matching armchairs and footstools, is part of a seven-piece suite designed by Louis Süe (1875–1968) and André Mare (1885–1932), which was especially made for the 1925 *Exposition Internationale des Arts Décoratifs et Industriels Modernes* in Paris. The tapestry upholstery is after Charles Dufresne. The gilt-wood sofa, with its drop-in squab cushion, is deliberately atavistic in style, and is well served by the traditionalism of the tapestry covering. In fact, Süe and Mare often looked to much classic 18th-century French furniture design for their inspiration. Indeed, luxury and comfort were the two most important elements in the design of traditional-style French sofas shown at the Exposition, yet, alongside such suites, pieces in the decidedly progressive Moderne idiom were also displayed.

B . A French Art Deco Gilt-Wood Suite by Maurice Dufrêne, *c*1925

The strong colours, exotic costumes and opulent stage sets of Diaghilev's Ballets Russes influenced all spheres of French design after the company's triumphal Paris debut in 1909. In this salon suite, the Beauvais-tapestry upholstery has been woven in a painterly, Fauvist style that can almost be considered a distinct homage to the Russian impresario. Its designer, Maurice Dufrêne (1876–1955), worked for the Parisian department store, Galeries Lafayette, which set up La Maîtrise in the 1920s, an atelier for the design and production of furniture and other decorative arts. This gilt-wood sofa is a superb example of a carefully planned, progressively designed piece of decorative furniture relying more on visual impact than function.

C

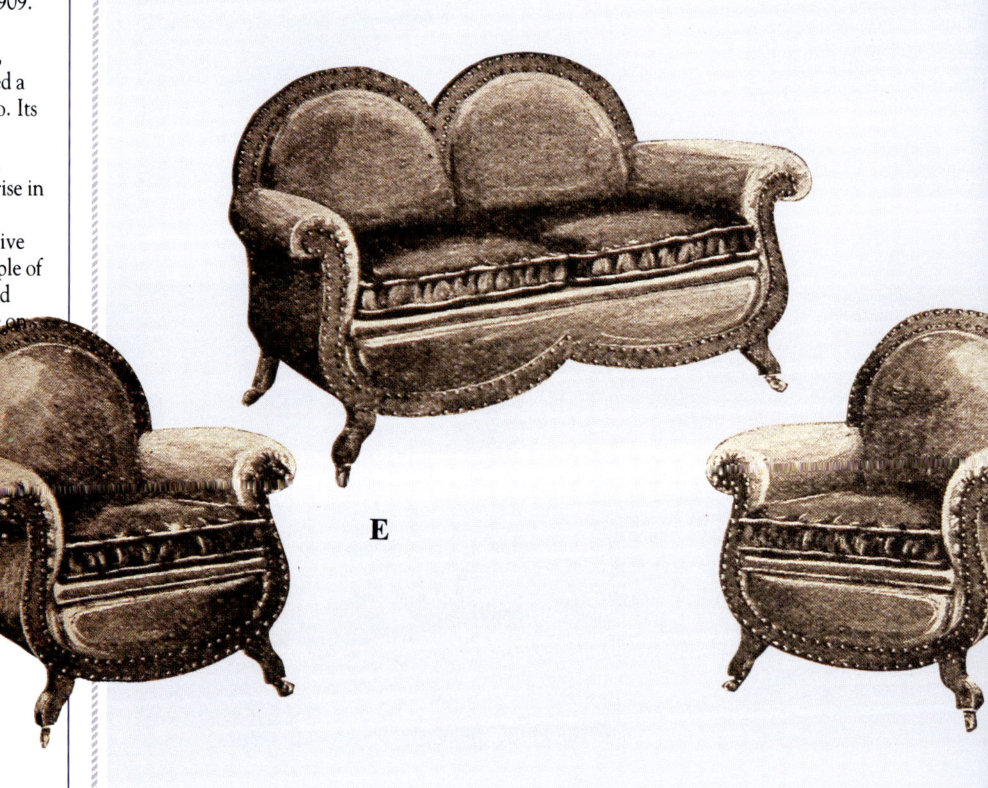

C. A French Art Deco Gilt-Wood Sofa with Tapestry Upholstery, designed by Paul Follot, 1920–25

Much French Art Deco furniture was superbly crafted of often-lavish materials and decorated with a traditional Gallic attention to detail that distinguished it all the more. This sofa, part of a suite of furniture, was designed by Paul Follot (1877–1941), whose influence on the development of French interior decoration between the wars was considerable. The gilt-wood sofa shows a tentative updating of the 19th-century design, and is used in combination with a strikingly modern tapestry upholstery.

D. A French Gilt-Wood Sofa in the Empire Style, *c*1926

The French love of gilded furniture continued into the 20th century. In this fashionable flat, photographed in 1926, the very tentative influence of the Art Deco style can be seen in the furnishings. The design of the three-seater sofa was described as 'Empire Style'. The dark brown velvet upholstery was chosen to blend with the purple, gold and grey of the other furnishings.

E. An English Moderne-Style Suite, late 1920s

Most mass-produced English furniture of the late 1920s attracts little interest, but this suite, whose forms somewhat relate to the French Art Deco style, is a good example of down-market Moderne. Although the style is at odds with the close nailing of the upholstery, it is sufficiently pronounced to give a good period feel to a decorative scheme. The sofa was upholstered in 'antique' brown Pexine or Pegamoid and fitted with brown velvet cushions. It was sold by the Midland Furniture Galleries, Southampton Row, London.

1900-1999

A . Reproduction of an English Sofa by Sir Edwin Lutyens, 1929

Despite the general decline in craftsmanship after World War II, it was still sometimes possible to obtain work made to very high specifications. This is a recently made sofa constructed from a design by Sir Edwin Lutyens (1869–1944), known as 'the society architect'. This sofa was originally designed for Government House, New Delhi, in 1929 and is a good example of the careful elegance that was a feature of all his work. In the tradition of great architects, Lutyens designed a great deal of furniture to complement his houses.

B . An English Art Deco Chaise Longue by Betty Joel, *c*1930

The manufacturers of foam-filled furniture embraced the styles of designers such as Betty Joel (b.1896) to create seating where comfort was paramount. This progressive chaise longue was created by Joel *c*1930. Betty Joel Ltd produced some of the most progressive British furniture of the 1930s and 1940s, making use of steel and laminated wood. In this sofa, padding gives a feeling of luxury to a simple curved shape, making it a desirable item for an interior in the Art Deco style. To some extent, the progressiveness of this structure is lost because of many modern interpretations.

C . An English Two-Seater Sofa by the City Cabinet Works, *c*1930

During the 1920s and 1930s most ordinary British families owned a sitting-room sofa of this or very similar type. This version, made by the City Cabinet Works in Moorgate, London, was one of the more expensive designs and was upholstered in French damask. A three-seater, 6–ft (1.8–m) version was also available. The sofa had a birchwood frame and coppered steel springs, and a mixture of hair and fibre was used for stuffing the cushions. Like many other sofas of the period, it was available in a fixed or drop-end style.

B

A

C

1900-1999

A . An English Modernist Laminated-Beech and -Plywood Chaise Longue, by Marcel Breuer for Isokon, 1935

Laminated wood was creating considerable interest among furniture makers by the late 1920s, and Marcel Breuer had produced a cantilevered chair in 1925. This chaise longue, in laminated beech and plywood, was designed by Breuer in 1935 for the Isokon furniture company of London. Breuer designed his furniture both in steel and woods, to provide maximum comfort with a minimum use of material and labour. The chaise longue reveals how modern furniture-making methods can be used to create a structure in which perfection of form is still paramount. Breuer had left his native Germany in the early 1930s to work in Great Britain. He perpetuated many of the ideals of the Bauhaus philosophy, using great economy combined with the most up-to-date methods of construction to create highly sculptural, modernist furniture. This chaise longue was originally fitted with a continuous cushion that did not detract from the concept of unity.

B . An English Painted and Upholstered Sofa by Duncan Grant and Vanessa Bell, mid-1930s

Custom-designed for a music room, this sofa was created by Duncan Grant and Vanessa Bell in the mid-1930s. Its fabric was especially printed to complement the painted murals in its setting, where the furniture was intended not to intrude but to form part of a complete harmony. The painted furniture and the rugs were also designed by these Bloomsbury Group artists. This upholstered, very simple sofa illustrates the very different approach of the artistic avant-garde in the 1930s and 1940s in comparison to the austere work of the leading German designers, who were banishing all superfluous decoration from their creations.

C . 'Mae West Hot Lips Sofa', based on a painting by Salvador Dali, 1936 37

The 'Mae West Hot Lips' sofa designed in 1936–37 by Salvador Dali (1904–89), is a classic example of the way a piece of furniture can be used to express an artistic concept more dramatically than a purely decorative object. The nonpareil 'Cupid's bow' lip shape, popularized by the 1920s and 1930s actresses, offered the artist an organic and highly sexual outline, ideal for a display piece. Upholstered in vibrant red, with the lips slightly parting as the sofa was sat upon, the sexuality of the object is positive and aggressive.

D . An American Model Room containing Plexiglas Furniture by Lorin Jackson, *c*1940

By 1940, manmade plastics were becoming an important material for furniture making. In this contemporary photograph, the transparent plastic called Plexiglas was used for most of the objects. The substance was mady by Rohm & Haas Co Inc and was used for the chairs, side tables and picture frame, as well as the sofa's arms and legs. The furniture in the room was designed by Lorin Jackson and was exhibited at Grosfield House in New York in 1940, at the annual exhibition of decorators' interiors. Furniture of the type was still very expensive, and it was not until the 1950s that plastic became cheap and widely used. This early use of plastic is interesting, as it shows a sofa made in a progressive material for the luxury trade.

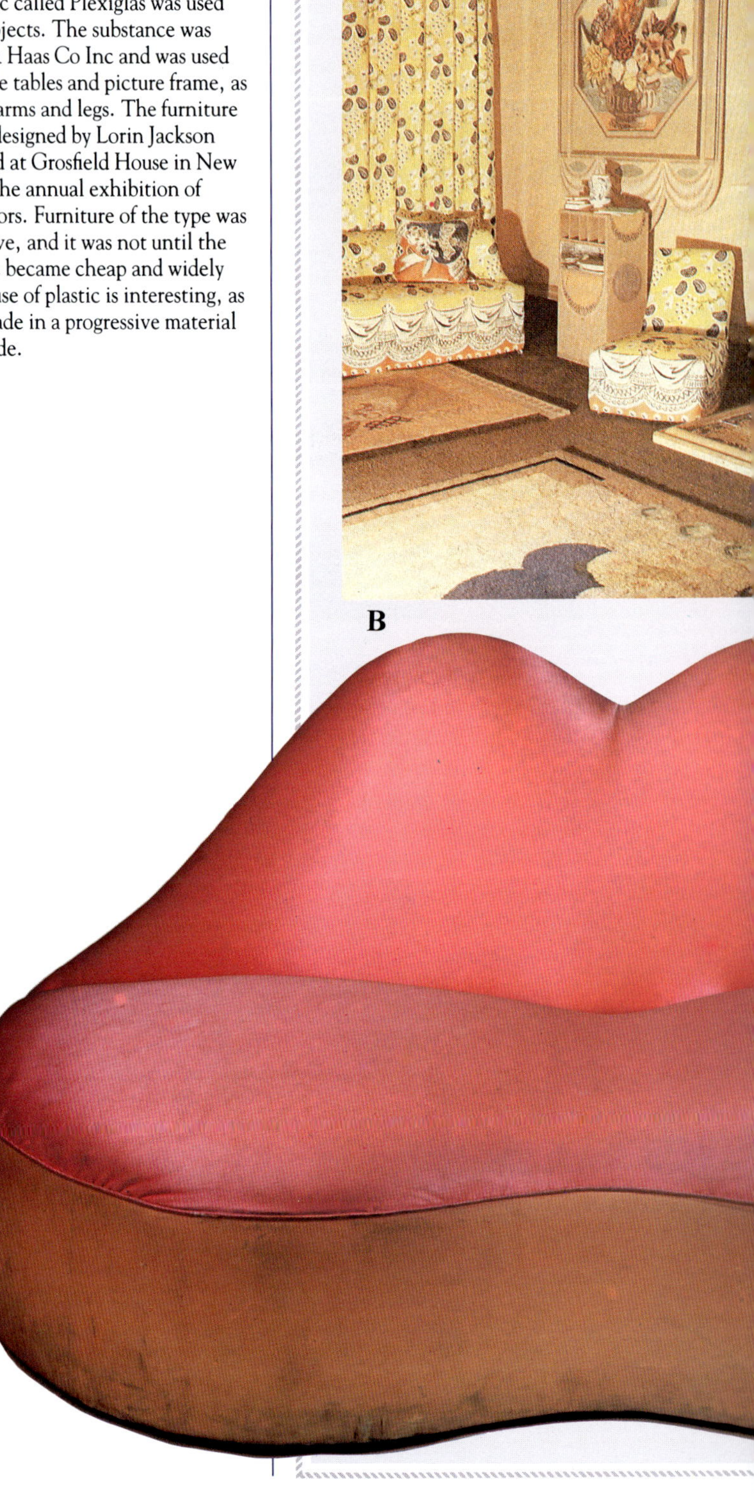

B

A
C
D

A. An American Interior containing an Upholstered-Wood Sofa, 1940s

American designers led the world in the 1940s, as furniture making in Europe was restricted to pieces in the most economical styles. The sofa is composed of the rectangular shapes that were later to form the basis of many mass-produced pieces in the 1970s; it is upholstered in a blue-green textured fabric. At the fireplace side there is only a soft cushion, but the other arm is upholstered over wood to form a support for the integral shelves that acts as an occasional table. In this Los Angeles interior, the movement away from the suites of seat furniture that were favoured in the 1930s can be seen, as the chairs were upholstered in contrasting colours.

B. An American 'Marshmallow' Sofa by George Nelson for Herman Miller, Inc, 1956

The amusing 'Marshmallow' sofa, dating to 1956, suggests the atmosphere of the period – rock 'n' roll, wasp waists and a passion for wire framework in everything from underwear to furniture. This sofa, with its spindly legs and geometric shapes, heralds the 'Op Art' styles of the early 1960s. Its designer, George Nelson (b.1908), design director of the trendsetting American firm Herman Miller, Inc, from 1947 to 1965, created furniture for the open-plan type of interior that was popular in that period. Tin-lined furniture of this type, with molecular shapes, sometimes in different colours, produces a Sputnik-like effect.

C. An English Pop Art Sofa, 1950s(?)

A Pop Art sofa made in the deliberately bad taste known as 'kitsch', its designer is not known (perhaps by choice!). An Edwardian couch, with machine decoration and standing on turned legs, has been transformed into a work of art by the witty addition of a reclining lady, her breasts forming additional cushions on the back-rest. The sofa is upholstered in gold satin to form the lady's evening dress, and the incised and machine-carved decoration has been highlighted in gold to give further richness. Parts from a shop-window display figure have been adapted to form the 'human' head, arms and feet. Such pieces by known artists are now heavily collected by enthusiasts who specialize in these amusing creations of the 1950s and 1960s. During the latter decade, many curious sofas were made for shops such as Mr Freedom in London, which sold one sofa made as a set of huge false teeth.

A

C

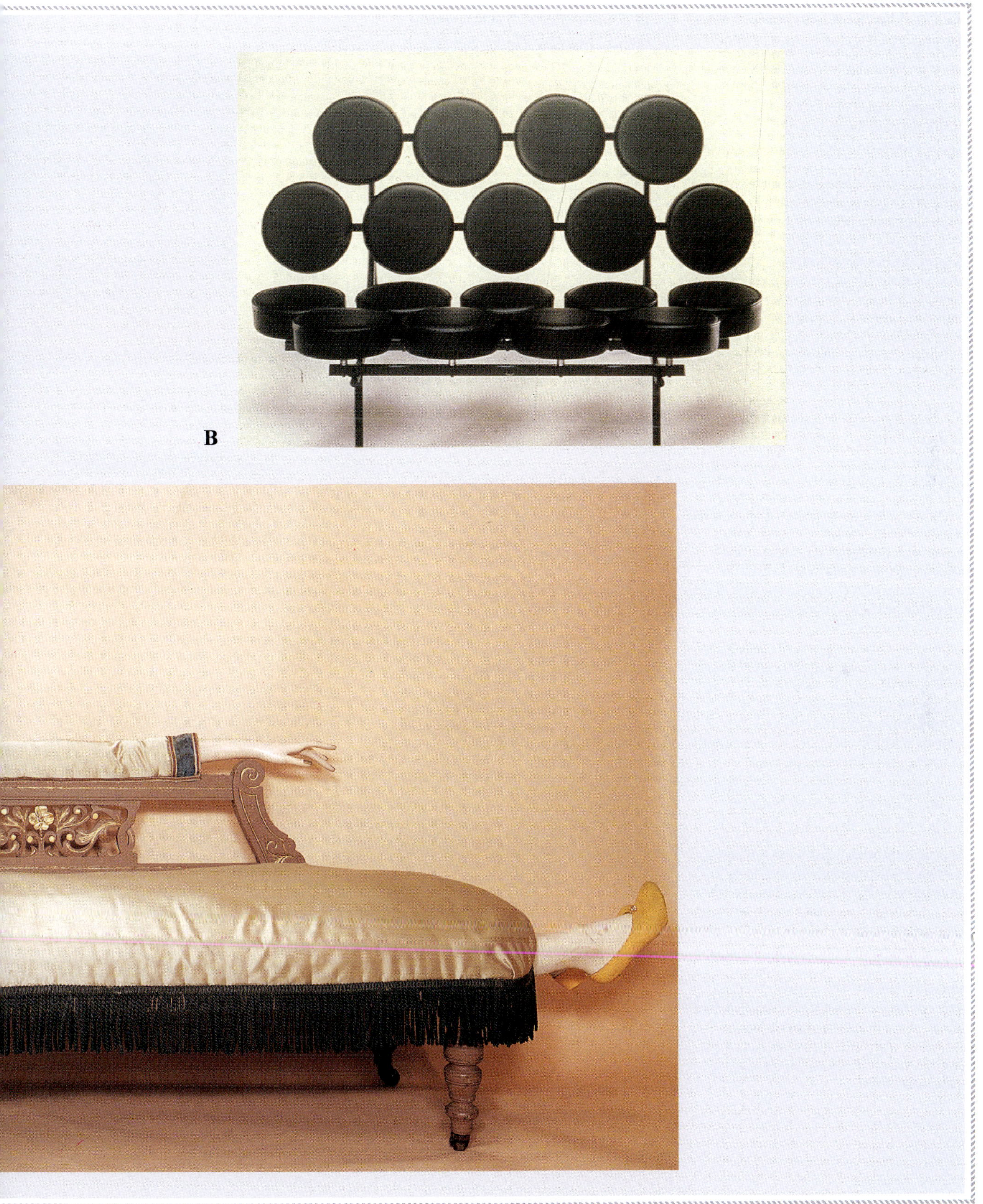

B

A . An American Leather Chaise Longue by Charles Eames, *c*1968

One of the most elegant of modern designs, this sofa is very much in the Bauhaus idiom. It was designed by Charles Eames (1907–78), perhaps the most important 20th-century American designer. This model was especially made *c*1968 for the director Billy Wilder, so he could take short rests during filming. It is typical of the best contemporary furniture, ideally adaptable to any room or environment. In the years after World War II, American designers made great advances in the use of manmade materials and mechanized furniture-making techniques. Through people such as Eames and furniture manufacturers like Herman Miller and Knoll, the philosophy of the Bauhaus became fully realized for the first time.

B . 'Boxing Gloves', a Pair of Italian Leather-Upholstered Chaises Longues by De Sede, late 1970s

The artistic eccentricity of late-1970s furniture is exemplified by this pair of chaises longues. On the borderline between sculpture and furniture, the structures were made by De Sede to form the focal point in any area where they were exhibited. Despite their Pop-Culture appearance, the sofas, leather-upholstered are both comfortable and, in a minimalist setting, very sophisticated. Pieces like 'Boxing Gloves' are, inevitably, of long term interest in terms of the history of furniture design and attract the attention of museums as well as collectors who are buying modern work as investment pieces.

C . An English Library Sofa by Floris van den Broecke, 1979

The sculptural quality of this sofa is clear to see when it is photographed out of doors. It was designed by Floris van den Broecke as a library sofa in 1979 and ranks among the most daring concepts of the period. Using the most up-to-date materials, van den Broecke claims to approach furniture design without any technical or commercial constraints but with a great concern for human scale. Although such a design would be ideally suited to factory production, the conservatism of buyers tends to restrict such structures to an exclusive intellectual market.

D . 'Chairpiece I', An English Plastic Sofa by Floris van den Broecke, 1970–74

'Chairpiece L' reveals modern furniture design at its most elegant. Developed from the organic, moulded shapes that became possible only in the 20th century, such designs could be cheaply mass-produced in plastic materials to provide economical and comfortable seating. Its designer, Floris van den Broecke, described one sofa he created as 'something settled, rigid, enclosed and private'. Another was designed for sleeping, eating, watching television and lovemaking.

C

D

B
A

1900-1999

A . 'Civitas', Seating System by Kurt Ziehmer, 1970s

Modular seating is the most significant 20th-century contribution to the general development of sofa design, providing the versatility that is necessary for both domestic and commercial use. This system, known as 'Civitas', was designed by Kurt Ziehmer, who specializes in seating units. Ziehmer also uses leather skilfully, avoiding the seams that often spoil the effect of the upholstery.

B . An English Seating System by Floris van den Broecke, 1988

This seating arrangement is a development of the brilliantly coloured 'Vis-à-Vis' form of seating, designed by Floris van den Broecke, who was born in Holland in 1945. He both designs and makes furniture and, with Peter Wheeler and Jane Dillon, formed the partnership 'Furniture Designers' in London in 1985. This highly adaptable form of seating is ideal for large areas, such as airport lounges or student common rooms, as it provides lively colour juxtapositions even when the room is empty of people. In use, the elements can be drawn together or widely separated without an interior becoming the visual mess that too often results when ill-assorted group seating is moved about.

C . An English Late 20th-Century Leather-Covered Chesterfield Sofa, 1980s

Leather-covered Chesterfields were considered the height of luxury in the early 1970s and have continued to be popular for use in commercial buildings and 'masculine' rooms. This 1980s model is deep-buttoned and finished with close nailing. It is fitted with two comfortable squab cushions.

D . 'Westbury', An English Sofa by Gordon Russell, 1980s

A product of the Gordon Russell Design Group, this sofa is part of a modular seating scheme. The soft supportive cushioning makes the sofa suitable for a domestic as well as a commercial environment. Known as the 'Westbury', it is also produced as a sofa-bed. Long sofas can be assembled by using additional single and corner units, arms and cushions. This type of modular seating is popular for island conversation units in large reception areas, or to form a rectangular seating area around a fire in the domestic setting.

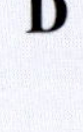

D

C

A

B

A. An English Sofa from the 'Longford' Range by Minoc Vernaschi for Gordon Russell, 1980s

Some of the better-designed modern furniture is especially made for office or hotel use, but can look good in a domestic setting as well. This sofa, from the 'Longford' range made by Gordon Russell is available with leather or fabric upholstery. The two- and three-seater versions can be used with matching armchairs to give a total look to an office. Designed by Minoc Vernaschi and using the most modern of upholstery methods, the sofa combines a high degree of comfort with crisp styling.

B. An English Sofa from the 'Segmenta' Range by Gordon Russell, 1980s

The 'Segmenta' range, designed and made by the Gordon Russell Design Group, is mainly intended for the reception areas of commercial interiors. As the emphasis is on comfortable but good, basic design shapes, sofas of this type are an attractive alternative to many of the bland structures found in High Street furniture shops. Corner sections, stools, tables, planters, concave and convex sections are all available in the range, so that a unified look can be given to a small or very large room. Office sofas are sometimes inexpensive in relation to the quality of manufacture and the design concept. It is modular sofas of this basic type that most typify the progressive mainstream style of the last quarter of the 20th century.

C. 'Eastside', An Italian Sofa by Ettore Sottsass for Memphis, 1980s

'Eastside', a beautifully structured sofa, was designed by Ettore Sottsass Jr, born in Austria in 1917 but now an Italian citizen. In this design, the headrests, which too often resemble awkwardly positioned cushions, are a pleasing feature of the composition. The statement they make is emphasized by the use of a contrasting colour. Sottsass is often considered the most outstanding Italian designer of his generation, and was a pioneer of the postwar *ricostruzione*. He is an architect, industrial designer and furniture designer, as well as an artist. For a short period in the 1970s he was involved with an avant-garde Milanese group, Studio Alchymia, designing some curious pieces for their collection. Arguably his most important work has been produced in the 1980s by the Milanese group known as 'Memphis', which Sottsass was instrumental in setting up and for which he has become the leading light.

B

C

A

1900-1999

A. 'The Fakir's Divan', An English Sofa by Danny Lane, 1980s

The fun element that often provides the focus of modern avant-garde furniture is seen in its purest form in this sofa. The traditional chair back form has been amusingly developed to form a structure entitled 'The Fakir's Divan'. Made by Danny Lane, who was born in the United States but now lives in England, it has mobile elements that can be pulled apart and reassembled to make new shapes. This ongoing involvement of the purchaser with the sofa as he or she changes its structure for different rooms or to suit a mood, opens up limitless possibilities for furniture that could be commercially mass-produced from cheaper materials.

B. An English Sofa, 1980s

The simple but classical lines of this sofa make it hard to date it to any particular period of the 20th century, but it is in fact totally modern, although constructed in the traditional manner. No foam has been used in the upholstery, and the seat has spiral springing. The cushions are feather-filled, and the sofa is covered in a Parker and Farr fabric. Such a piece is designed to suit any setting, but because of the method of its construction, it is a necessarily fairly expensive item.

C. An American 'Soft Pad' Sofa by Charles Eames, 1982

Many of the best modern designs look as good in a business environment as they do in a domestic one. This 'Soft Pad' sofa, designed before 1978 but not made until 1982, was Charles Eames's last design. It was structured to give maximum support to the shoulders and head. Eames had originally trained as an architect, but worked with Eero Saarinen on the commercial production of furniture that used modern materials such as aluminium, plastic, fibreglass and plywood. A number of his designs are beacons in the development of modern furniture and have been adapted and mass-produced.

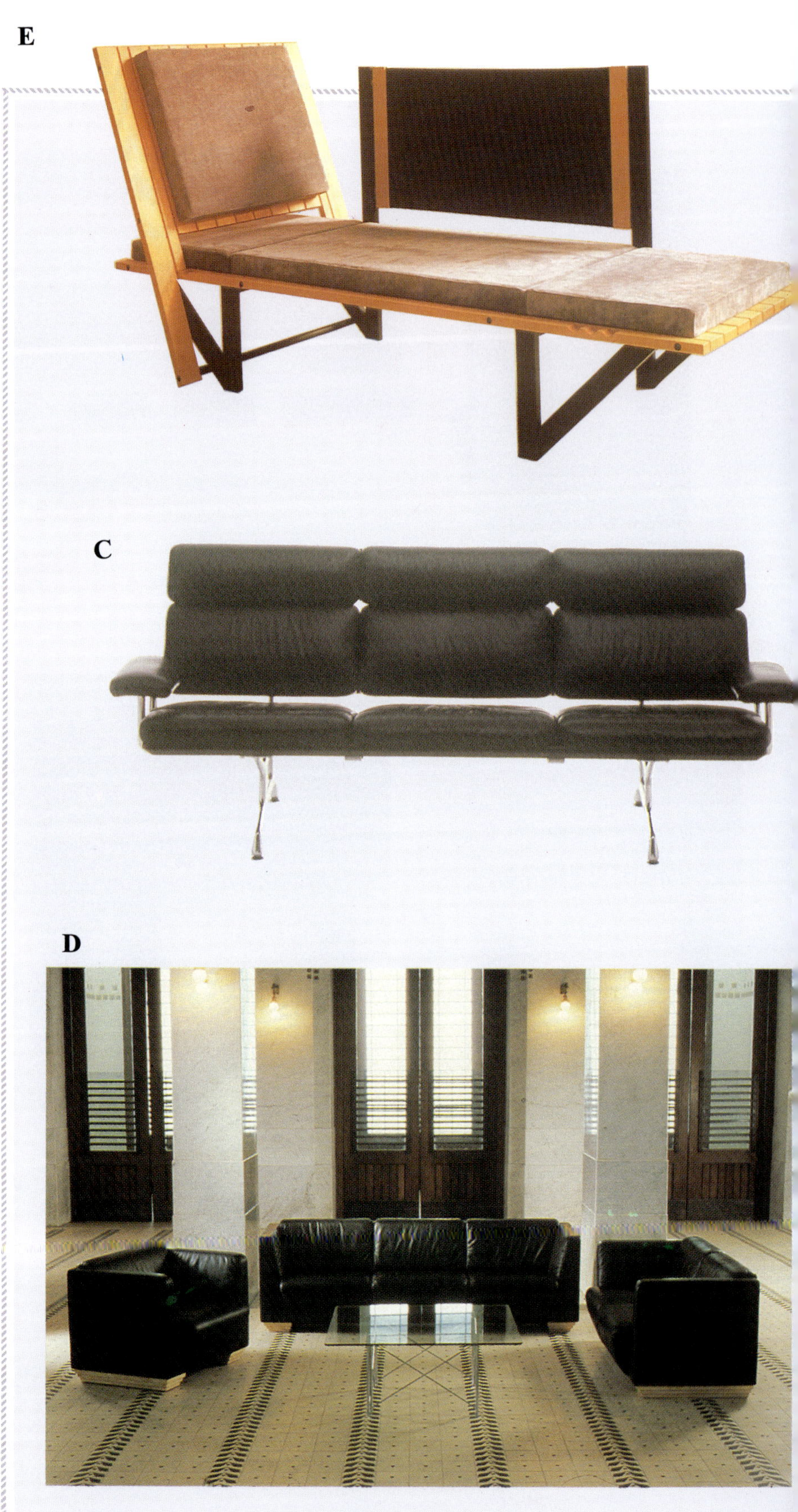

A

B

D . A Danish Leather Furniture Suite by Jørgen Kastholm, 1984

A suite of furniture that includes two- and three-seater sofas. This type of unified seating has the adaptability that is necessary both for open-plan living and for contract purchasers. It was designed in 1984 by Jørgen Kastholm (b.1931), whose work has been exhibited at the Louvre in Paris. Kastholm is a university professor and is an architect as well as a furniture designer. This suite is clearly in the northern European idiom and the clean, geometric shapes are combined with good quality basic materials. It is the type of modern furniture that looks well with works of art of any period, as well as with contrasting antique pieces. Kastholm has worked for Fritz Hansen and Ole Hagen and has had his own studio since 1964. The range of objects he has designed includes textiles, light fittings and cutlery.

E . A Chaise Longue by Eric de Graaf, 1984

During the last quarter of the 20th century, the traditional concept of special furniture for specific rooms has disappeared. This 1984 chaise longue by Eric de Graaf, for instance, would look good in a study or a drawing room. The slatted construction and the combination of natural wood with black are reminiscent of the simplicity of Japanese styles. Flat, angular cushions make the sofa comfortable and do not detract from the clean line of the construction.

1900-1999

A. 'Angaraib', An English Glass and Tree-Branch Chaise Longue by Danny Lane, 1987

An avant-garde interpretation of a primitive Sudanese rope bed, this chaise longue was designed by Danny Lane in 1987. The glass elements, locked into position by their own shape and gravity, float across two parallel branches from a storm-damaged plane tree. This mixture of technology, artistry and conservation is typical of the period, although such structures are as far removed from the lifestyle of ordinary people as the high-style Gothic Revival work of William Burges in the Victorian period. Entitled 'Angaraib', the chaise longue would provide the main focus of attention in any decorative scheme, as well as function as an art object.

B. 'Out of Babylon', An English Glass and Wood Chaise Longue by Danny Lane, 1988

Modern progressive furniture is seen at its most dramatic in this chaise longue entitled 'Out of Babylon'. Made by Danny Lane in 1988, it is a development of an all-glass 'Chaise Longhi' (*sic*) that he had previously made. This structure also incorporates wood in order to soften and humanize the piece. The original glass version had an all-glass bird beak front that has been kept but is now bolted to a winged animal form made of carved plywood and pine slats. Although it would be exciting to see such designs for sale in furniture warehouses and department stores, they have to be considered mainly exhibition pieces, whose appeal is limited to the most artistic or adventurous.

C. 'Vis-à-Vis' An English Sofa by Floris van den Broecke, 1988

This highly functional 'Vis-à-Vis' dates to 1988 and was designed by Floris van den Broecke, who is chairman of the Independent Designers Federation and visiting professor at the Royal College of Art in London. He was originally trained as a painter, and his furniture duly reveals a love of strong colour, combined with an appreciation of the basics of modern industrial design established by the Bauhaus. Van den Broecke is interested in the idea of a product-development centre, where prototypes could be nurtured. Too often, he feels, good ideas are lost because they are not immediately commercial.

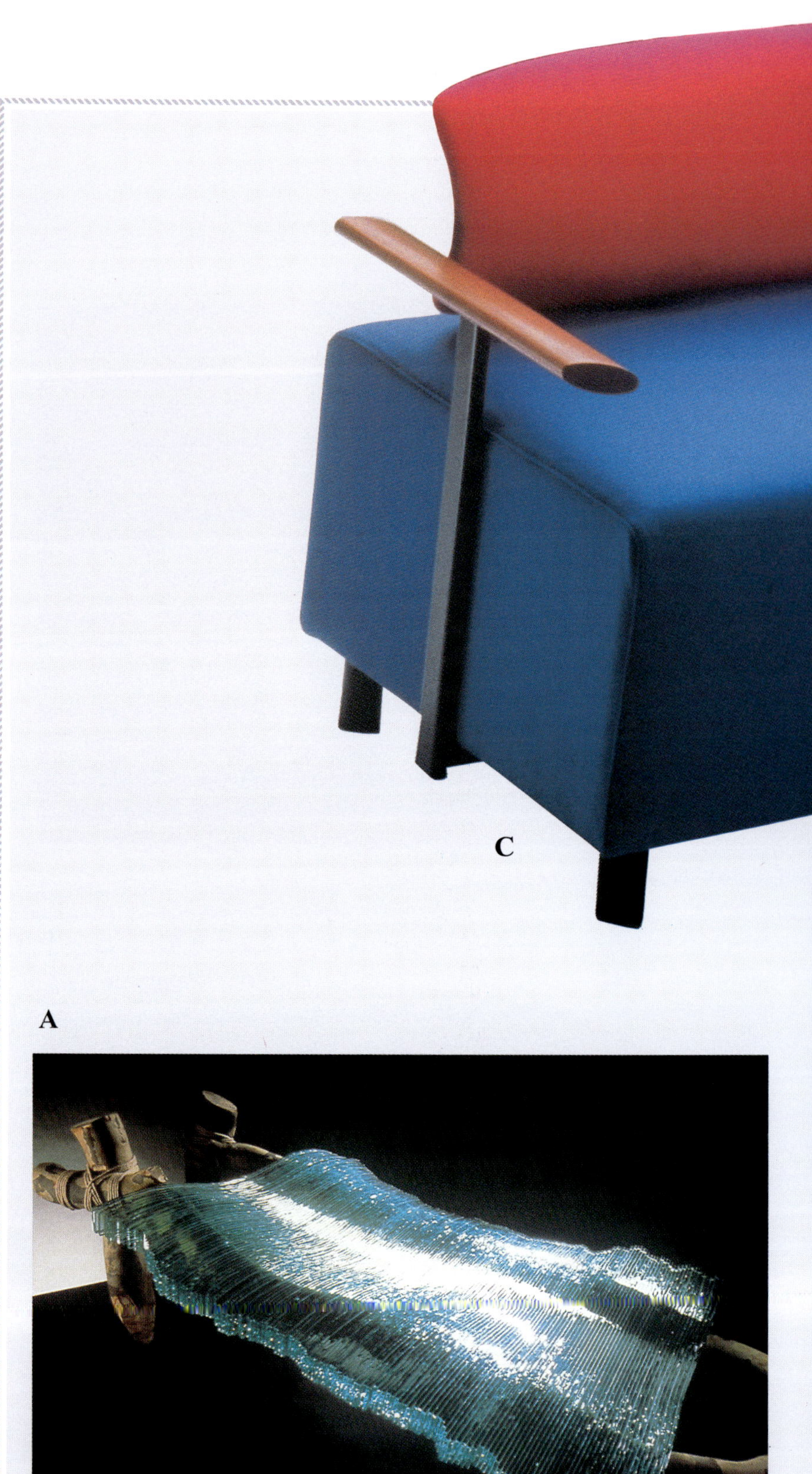

C

A

B

A . A French Revivalist Tulipwood and Ormolu Library Table, *c*1900

The French passion for revivalist 18th-century furniture reached its peak during the reign of Napoleon III, *c*1860. At first, good quality, authentic pieces were made, but after a while fidelity to the original patterns and spirit waned.

This table, produced around the turn of the century, is similar in some ways to an English centre table. It has a deep frieze, sits on a quadruped support similar to those of around 1830 and is excessively covered with Rococo ormolu decoration – too much even for a piece from the height of the Louis XV era. The overall effect is overdecorated and gauche.

B . An Edwardian Georgian Revival Mahogany Octagonal Centre Table, *c*1905

The beginning of the 20th century was ripe with new designs and designers worldwide, but the largest single area of furniture production was still revivalist. Interest in the revival of earlier styles existed widely in Europe. In France, the 19th-century concern with royal revivals of Louis XIV, XV and XVI styles continued until well into the 20th century; in Great Britain, the Edwardians turned to Georgian designs, based on the styles of Chippendale, Sheraton and Hepplewhite.

This table is a classic example of the revivalist trend and is fairly close to its true Georgian counterpart, differing in two main areas. The stretchers are more elaborate than on a typical Georgian piece, and the decoration is decidedly more excessive. The Edwardians' taste for floral inlay takes the place of the Georgians' more reserved cross-banding, and where boxwood marquetry would have been separated but perhaps in a panel on an original piece, here the boxwood marquetry is placed straight onto the mahogany base.

D

B

C . An Edwardian Oval Satinwood Painted Table, *c*1910

Although it is hard to fault this beautifully executed revival of a Georgian painted table on any one feature, a series of small clues suggest a later date. The construction of the undecorated wood frame would date it accurately, although it is impossible to see from a photograph. On a Georgian piece of this delicacy, the veneer would have been a better quailty than the wood used here – probably of a dazzling pale colour with beautiful figuring. The painted decoration in Hepplewhite style is slightly too bright and elaborate, and covers too large an area. Also, the small oval form with two tiers is an unusual Georgian combination.

All of these factors make it likely that the table dates to the late 19th or early 20th century, although copies are sometimes so good that it is impossible to be sure.

D . A French Art Nouveau 'Grotesque' Table by Emile Gallé, *c*1895

Emile Gallé (1846–1904) was a prominent founding member of the Nancy school of Art Nouveau design, based in Lorraine. Most of his output was in glass and ceramic: his cameo-glass vases with relief designs are perhaps his best-known work. Gallé produced furniture from the mid 1880s onward, inspired in part by his visit to a stockist of exotic woods. He felt that Art Nouveau motifs should be applied to conventional construction, thus believing that individuality lay in ornamentation. Hence he used blank surfaces for his subtle floral decoration.

This table is in the 'organic' style of Art Nouveau, which is highly ornamented with swirling lines and a variety of natural motifs, eg, entomological and botanical. On its upper and lower tiers, fine inlay of many different woods appears in a natural surrounding – such delicate marquetry with a lack of perspective was one of Gallé's hallmarks. The hybrid animal/insect figures on the table legs here are similar to the neo-classical sphinx, but depicted in a typical Art Nouveau manner

A . A French Art Nouveau Table by Edward Colonna, *c*1895

The work of Edward Colonna (1862–1948), one of the designers connected to the Paris atelier set up by S Bing, whose *Maison de l'Art Nouveau* gave the turn-of-the-century style its name, is representative of the Parisian school of Art Nouveau. Whereas the Nancy designers produced rather heavy work, the Parisian group (which also included Eugène Gaillard and Georges de Feure) tended to employ simpler, lighter structures, often with a minimum of decoration. The German-born Colonna was also involved with Bing's Pavillon de l'Art Nouveau at the Paris 1900 Exposition, where he jointly decorated six rooms with Georges de Feure. He also worked in Belgium and the United States.

B . A French Art Nouveau Corner Table by Georges de Feure, *c*1900

This table contains several of Art Nouveau's classic features – supports in the form of stylized flowers, an odd shape with every surface decorated and a concentration on the sinuous line. Georges de Feure (1868–1928) collaborated with Edward Colonna and Eugène Gaillard; all three were associated with S Bing. De Feure's furniture is often of gilt wood, decorated with a floral motif. He also worked as a painter, lithographer, engraver and ceramicist, taught at the Paris Ecole des Beaux-Arts, and exhibited in a variety of media at important European exhibitions.

C . A French Art Nouveau Side Table with Tea Tray by Hector Guimard, *c*1900

This walnut table has a matching tea tray with bronze handles, and is typical of the chic Parisian school of Art Nouveau, as opposed to the heavier, provincial Ecole de Nancy. It is beautifully carved with smooth, elegant lines, giving the impression of a piece of sculpture rather than furniture, and is a fine example of Hector Guimard's innovation, which often extended across different media – here, glass, bronze and wood blend together to become an integral part of the design.

Guimard (1867–1942) was the leading French architect of Art Nouveau and introduced Victor Horta, the radical Belgian architect, to Paris. Guimard's most lasting monuments are the sinuous entrances to the Paris Metro, which to most visitors symbolize exotic *fin-de-siècle* Paris.

Guimard saw architecture and furniture as a whole, and hence designed many interiors and furnishings, as well as the exteriors, of several buildings.

D . A French Art Nouveau Room Designed by Georges Hoentschel, *c*1905

This room by the Parisian architect/potter/designer, Georges Hoentschel (1855–1915), illustrates the organic quality of French Art Nouveau – the top of the table here is a conventional rectangle quartered to match veneers, but the legs have a naturalistic design: taken almost directly from nature, they are in the form of branches.

The Art Nouveau style appealed very much to the architectural discipline, and designing a whole room with sympathetic characteristics was good architectural logic. In this room, for example, it is clear that the glass-fronted cabinet matches the table and chairs. Similarly, the combination of dining table, chairs and vitrines is a traditional one, emphasizing the point that Art Nouveau decoration was generally applied to traditional forms in good-quality woods.

E . A French Writing Table and Chair by Louis Majorelle, *c*1910

Majorelle (1859-1926) was a prominent member of the Nancy school of design, a group of French architects and designers who promoted 'organic' Art Nouveau. Emile Gallé, famous for his glassware and ceramics, was active in founding the school, which is closely associated with the area around Nancy in northeastern France.

Majorelle originally trained as a painter before taking over his father's furniture business in the late 1870s. His speciality was sophisticated furniture such as that for up-market Paris restaurants like Chez Maxim, and although his early furniture was traditional, he was quick to adopt the nature-inspired forms of Art Nouveau. Much of his work is in fairly dark hardwoods, such as mahogany or walnut, with decoration on the upholstery or on the sides and drawers of tables, as here. This is relatively restrained for Majorelle, but then its date is quite late.

A

B

E

C

D

A . Scottish Furniture by Charles Rennie Mackintosh, *c*1900

Both the interior of this room and its furniture were designed by the Glaswegian architect/ designer, Charles Rennie Mackintosh (1868–1928). Among his sources were those employing strong vertical lines with horizontal grids, as well as the massive forms associated with the Scottish baronial tradition. The Japanese influence is shown through his simple, undecorated designs; he tended to ebonize his pieces, such as the table illustrated, in order to eradicate any sign of natural wood grain, and decoration was restrained, often simply cut out, as seen on the cupboards on the wall in this room.

Mackintosh's concern with minimal decoration and curve was in fact one of the main forces behind the conversion to line rather than form, an idea expanded by Josef Hoffmann and others in Vienna and Frank Lloyd Wright in the United States. Mackintosh was primarily an architect, and among his limited output of 14 buildings was the Glasgow School of Art, which shows his progression from the organic forms associated with the Art Nouveau style to the linear, geometric forms of proto-modernism (the building was completed in stages).

This ebonized table is based on medieval principles – it is extremely heavily built, plain timbered and virtually undecorated. It is arched between the legs, and is very dignified and monumental.

B . A Scottish White Painted Table by Charles Rennie Mackintosh, *c*1900

This table is quite unlike Mackintosh's atmospheric, medievalizing work. Among his 'friendlier' domestic pieces were several white chairs and tables with an enamel-like surface. This was obtained by a coach-painting technique, which was very smooth and similar to lacquer.

This example has an enamel glass inset to contrast with the large flat surface. The table legs broaden toward the floor, a form emphasizing the vertical lines and complementing the elliptical shape of the top. It structure clearly shows Mackintosh's architectural influences.

A

B

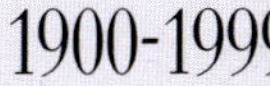

D

C

E

C, D & E. Austrian Tables by Josef Hoffmann, 1901–1910

Like Frank Lloyd Wright in America (1867–1959), the Viennese Josef Hoffmann (1870–1956) actively worked through several periods – Art Nouveau, Art Deco and the Modern movement. Hoffmann was a member of the Vienna Secession, founded in 1897, and cofounded the Wiener Werkstätte (or Vienna workshops) in 1903. Design of the turn-of-the-century period generally splits into two categories, the organic Art Nouveau school, whose motifs were based on forms such as the curves of a plant, and the geometric, linear branch, of which Hoffmann was an exponent, which concentrates on straight lines, contrasting colours and the formation of grids to define space. Hoffmann was much inspired by Scotsman Charles Rennie Mackintosh (1868–1928), who supported the Secession movement and its members.

The Wiener Werkstätte were set up to manufacture the new design styles in Vienna, and the enterprise proved enormously successful over several decades, producing mainly expensive furniture for an elite clientèle.

Around 1900, the beginnings of Hoffmann's move away from conventional curvilinear furniture were seen in the interiors of houses he designed, such as the Palais Stoclet in Brussels. This new style of furniture was also shown at the Paris exhibitions, influential platforms for innovative ideas. Table (**C**) designed in 1901, shows Hoffmann adapting traditional forms with straight lines and new materials, smooth surfaces of stained wood, and with metal details for effect and strength.

As he became better known as a designer, Hoffmann's commissions varied greatly; table (**D**) was designed for Kabarett Fledermaus, a theatre-bar in Vienna. It is strongly geometric, and uses typically smooth surfaces and restrained colour (later pieces from the 1920s and 1930s are more rounded). The model (**E**) retains the straight line, and is a classic geometric design which is still made today by the German firm, Franz Wittmann, which reproduces several other chairs and tables by Hoffmann.

1900-1999

A . The Elephant Trunk Table by Adolf Loos, c1902

This table was exhibited at the Vienna Secession in 1902; it was designed by the Austrian architect/designer, Adolf Loos (1870–1933). Also known as the Spider table, it is made of walnut with copper fittings around the lobed top and copper feet on the legs. Although not functional, the table has an intriguing design whose legs are supported on half circles appearing to combine Oriental inspiration, an interest in geometric shapes, and cabriole legs. The Vienna Secession was known for its acceptance of the new, the original and the good; this feeling for exploration and enquiry led to the Secession's, and later the Wiener Werkstätte's, leading position in the history of turn-of-the-century design.

Adolf Loos studied with Otto Wagner, an architect and *éminence grise* of the Secession, and also created designs for the influential Thonet factory, which specialized in bentwood furniture.

B . An Art Deco Partners' Desk and Chair, c1915

This functional writing desk and chair show how stylish Art Deco ideas could be incorporated into practical design. Although luxurious and high-quality work, the table's use of fruitwood veneer is not unusual, its tapering legs are not excessive and the repeated coil decoration is minimal.

It is probably the work of Paul Iribe (1883–1935), who was noted for his use of similar coils, and who was considered one of the more moderate of the avant-garde Art Deco artists. His interesting career included illustrating for design magazines; founding the magazine, *Le Témoin (The Witness)*, in 1905; designing jewellery, fabrics, interiors and advertisements; and working for Jaques Doucet in his Paris apartment on the Avenue de Bois. Having travelled to the United States in 1914 to work with the film producer-director Cecil B De Mille, he returned to France in the 1930s and was for some time associated with Coco Chanel.

C

A

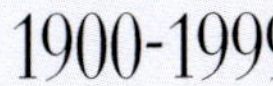

B

D

C. A Reproduction Table by Jacques-Henri Lartigue, originally designed *c*1918

This is a remake of the classic table by Lartigue (1894–1986), which was originally made of ivory and black-lacquered wood in 1918, and is now reproduced by the French designer/manufacturer Ecart.

Lartigue was known for his writing and photography as well as his furniture design, and he is associated with the Modern movement, which stressed function and utility as opposed to the sumptuous and luxurious excess of the Art Deco style. Le Corbusier's phrase, 'that houses are machines for living in', came to epitomize such ideals.

Here, Lartigue combines geometric shapes and exotic materials, which belong to the Art Deco repertoire, with the Modernist notion of structural simplicity. The bold, original, sculptural result feels quite at home in the 1980s.

D. A French Art Deco Ebony Side Table by Pierre Legrain, *c*1923

This table is undeniably from the Art Deco period, with its straight lines and smooth surfaces, and is made of an exotic wood with distinctive grain. Two influences of this era are in evidence here: the geometric shapes that were so popular give the table great elegance, and its form is directly taken from primitive art, which so fascinated French designers and artists at the start of the 20th century.

Pierre Legrain (1889–1929) was a furniture maker who pioneered this interest in the exotic – one of his most famous pieces is a low stool based on African designs and known as the *siège curule.* His designs were often made of luxurious materials, particularly lacquer, but also including mother-of-pearl and vellum. He lacked formal training as a cabinetmaker (which perhaps aided his innovative style), but found great success, working in the studio of Paul Iribe until 1914, then opening his own workshop in 1926.

A . The End Table by Gerrit Rietveld, originally designed *c*1923

Gerrit Rietveld (1888–1964) originally designed this table in 1923; this replica is made by the same cabinetmaker, G A van de Groenekan, who worked with Rietveld throughout his life on some of his most ambitious and bizarre compositions. The table was designed for the Schroeder house in Utrecht, and, like most of Rietveld's furniture, it was intended as part of an overall scheme based on basic architectural principles.

Apprenticed in the family firm, Rietveld set up his own workshop before training as an architect. Much of his early design was influenced by the principles of Dutch De Stijl (The Style) movement, which reduced objects to simple geometrical and linear elements and used the primary colours of red, blue and yellow as a contrast to the non-colours of black, white and grey. This table (and the Schroeder house generally) is a three-dimensional version of De Stijl ideas.

Rietveld's best-known work is the Red-Blue Chair, using the colours popularized by Piet Mondrian (1872–1944), who was most famous for his paintings of squares of colours. In retrospect, Rietveld could be considered the most revolutionary furniture maker of the early 20th century – he was certainly the earliest to produce radical new designs during and after the First World War.

B . The Berlin Chair by Gerrit Rietveld, *c*1923

This chair was created for the Berlin Exhibition of 1923. Like his End Table of the same date, the chair abandons all traditional preconceptions of symmetry and colour. In 1924, it was added to the Schroeder house in Utrecht, forming an unusual partnership with Rietveld's End Table.

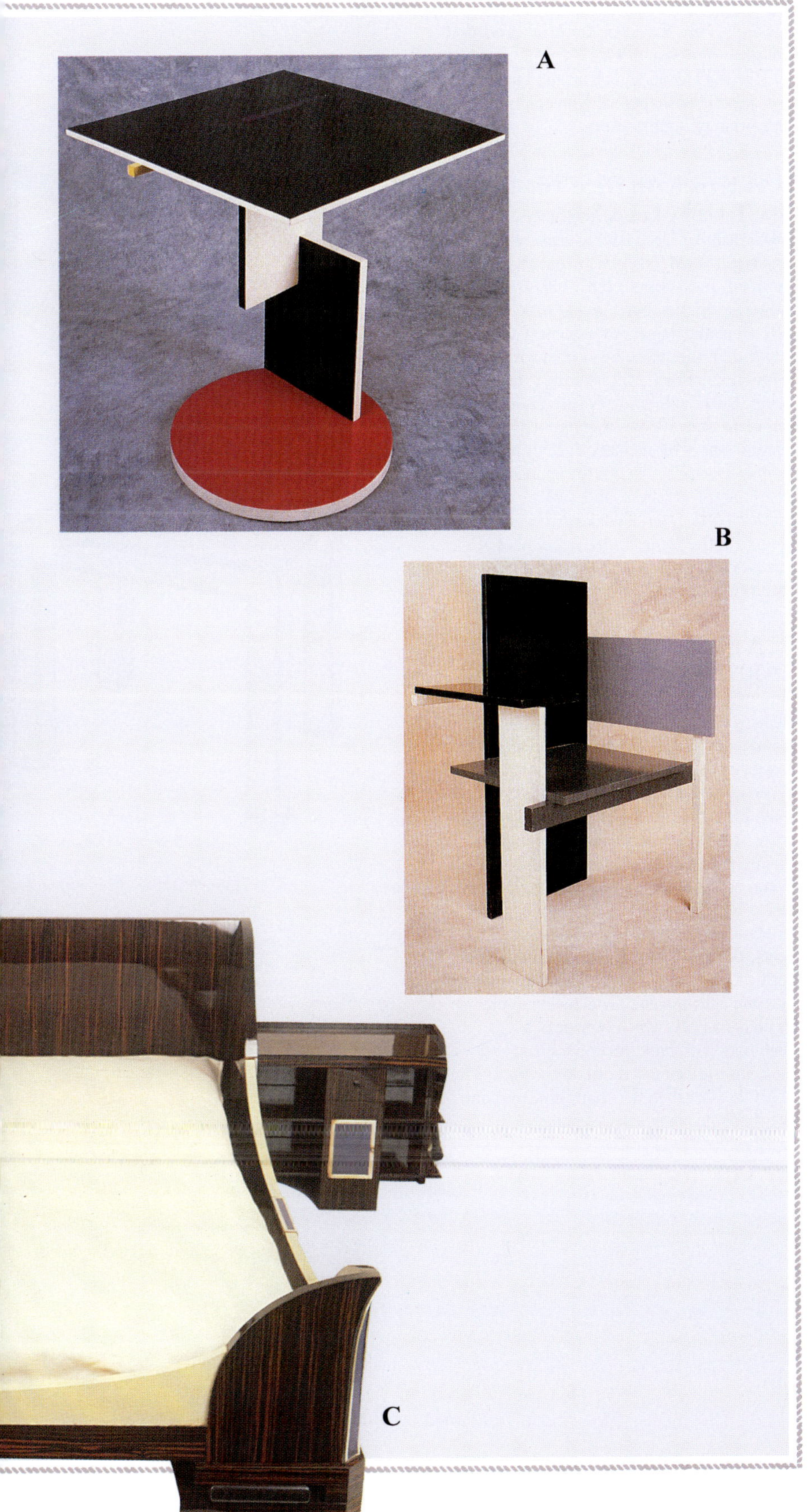

C. A French Art Deco Ebony Bed and Bedside Tables by Marcel Coard, *c*1925

The Art Deco movement reached its height during the 1920s, and was perhaps best known for its chairs, tables and interior designs. Marcel Coard (1889–1975) began designing furniture while recuperating from injuries sustained in the First World War. Afterward, he opened his own shop in Paris, first offering reproductions of period pieces, but soon creating Art Deco works for prominent clients.

Coard's most notable work was for Jacques Doucet's villa at Neuilly, outside Paris, designed by Pierre Legrain (1889–1929). Doucet, a couturier renowned for his collection of Old Master paintings 18th-century French antiques, sold this collection in 1912 and from then on concentrated on works by contemporary designers such as Coard, Paul Iribe and Eileen Gray, and painters such as Picasso, Modigliani and Henri Rousseau.

It is unusual to find a matching bed and bedside tables such as these, and especially ones so luxurious. The blue panels in the tables are lapis lazuli, surrounded by silver frames, and the wood is Macassar ebony. Elegantly simple, straight lines dominate but for the outward curve at the foot of the bed.

D. A French Art Deco Dressing Table by Emile-Jacques Ruhlmann, *c*1925

The furniture of Emile-Jacques Ruhlmann (1879-1933) is often compared to the work of the great 18th-century French cabinetmakers. Of excellent quality and made at great expense, pieces such as this table come from the peak of Ruhlmann's neo-classical phase. It is high Parisian Art Deco, with tapering legs, the use of exotic hardwoods (in this case, ebony), ivory details and panels in shagreen (sharkskin). The brass-capped *sabots* (literally, 'clogs') seen here were a particular trademark of his, echoing the mounts on 18th-century neo-classical furniture.

Ruhlmann wrote that it was 'the elite which launches fashion and determines its direction', and, not surprisingly, he was supported through much of his working life by wealthy patrons. He stated that the proportions of his furniture as a whole were far more important than their detail or ornament, but the luxury and style of his work – and especially his applied decoration – are outstanding.

A . A French Art Deco Bronze and Marble Table by Armand-Albert Rateau, *c*1925

Armand-Albert Rateau (1882–1938) was one of the most celebrated and eccentric metalworkers in Art Deco Paris; he was also a renowned interior decorator, and his extravagant designs for the apartment of the *couturière,* Jeanne Lanvin, were much admired.

His tables in particular were strikingly original. This example in bronze has a marble top in the form of a large tray, reminiscent of ancient Chinese ceremonial vessels. Its legs are the stylized forms of a bird, perhaps a peacock, and they have an archaic feel to them; indeed Rateau was directly influenced by the classical Roman furniture in metal he viewed on a visit to Herculaneum and Pompeii.

B . The Laccio Table by Marcel Breuer, *c*1925

Marcel Breuer (1902–1981) produced a design which became a near cliché of modern furniture – essentially comprising a chrome frame with leather stretched on it. The Wassily chair, also illustrated here, was made at the Bauhaus for Wassily Kandinsky's studio, and was the most celebrated example of this style; it has become a modern classic. This table originates from the same spirit.

Breuer was one of the most distinctive architects of the Modernist movement and designed extensively in Germany and the United States, where he also taught at Harvard. His interest lies in both structure and aesthetics, as can be seen from these early designs. The table is elegant and striking, with its combination of glass and chrome. These designs remain very popular, and although often associated with the 1960s, they date in fact to a time before even the motor car was popular.

C . A French Art Deco *Guéridon* by Jean Dunand, *c*1925

This table is clearly based on the traditional French two-tiered circular table form from the 18th century. Jean Dunand (1877–1942) was a radical designer from the Art Deco era, and specialized in lacquer work. The interest in lacquer in the 1920s stemmed from a search for the exotic (seen in the use of materials such as ebony and shagreen), and Dunand experimented by adding gold and silver dust, mother-of-pearl, ivory, etc, to his lacquers in the traditional Japanese style. He often worked for other designers, including Emile-Jacques Ruhlmann, on projects ranging in scale from jewellery to the interior of the Smoking Room of the *Ambassade Française,* part of the *Paris Exposition des Arts Décoratifs et Industriels Modernes* in 1925.

Dunand's tables and chairs tend to have basic geometric shapes, with an emphasis on decoration rather than form.

D . A French Art Deco Two-tier Low Table by Louis Sognot, *c*1925

This stylish Art Deco table is veneered in palissander wood, an exotic variation of rosewood. Louis Sognot (1892–1970) was known for this combination of exotic woods with a metallic frame. An influential designer in France in the 1920s, he worked with the designer, Charlotte Alix, and the Primavera atelier, before exhibiting in Paris under his own name after 1923. Other unusual commissions of his included decorating the 1st-class Doctor's cabin on the famous 1920s ocean liner, *Normandie,* and working on interiors of the liner, *Atlantique.* He also lectured at the Ecole Boulle, a school of metalwork in Paris named after the 17th-century craftsman, André-Charles Boulle.

E . A Sharkskin and Ebony Table, *c*1930

Although unsigned, this table is probably by Clément Rousseau and bears a striking resemblance to a chair made by him in 1921. Rousseau was largely responsible for the revival of the use of shagreen (sharkskin), which he tinted in a variety of colours, usually green, and combined with exotic woods. He was also patronized by Jacques Doucet, and several of his pieces can be found in Doucet's villa at Neuilly.

Made of green-tinted sharkskin and ebony, the top of this table shows the sunburst motif widely used in the Art Deco era and a favourite of Rousseau's. This is very similar to the chair of 1921, which is made of a combination of sharkskin and walnut, and also bears the sunburst motif on the back. The table is heavier than the chair, however, and probably from about a decade later.

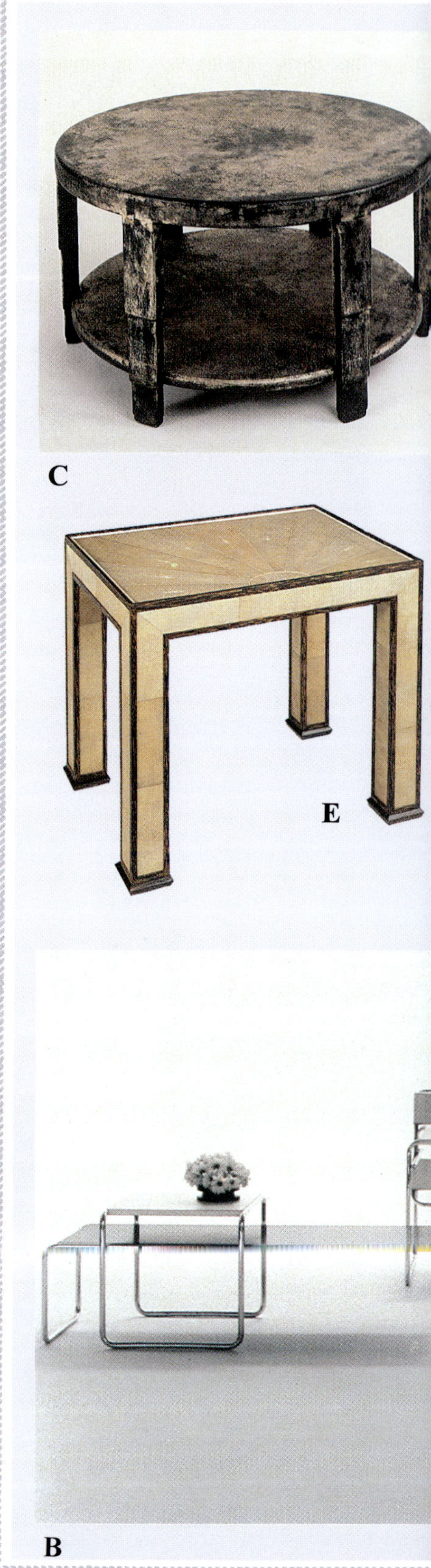

A

D

A . A Folding Writing Table by Paul Dupré-Lafon, c1930

This chic bureau was made for the family Lecroard and folds away to what must be the slimmest of desks. Supported on slender, square-sectioned shafts, a gilded leather flap folds down to form a working surface.

Little is known about Paul Dupré-Lafon (1900–1971), whose furniture in the main is unsigned. Like many Art Deco designers, he specialized in exotic materials, and his work is always of excellent quality, resulting in slim and elegant straight-edged shapes.

B . A Scandinavian Plywood Table by Alvar Aalto, c1931

The development of the simple, uncluttered wooden furniture that is today associated with Scandinavia, and especially Finland, was largely due to the work of Alvar Aalto (1898–1976). This talented and prodigious architect/designer was responsible for over 200 buildings, concerning himself with lighting, heating, acoustics and exterior surroundings as well as the basic design and construction. He saw furniture as an accessory to architecture, and believed that the human form should touch only natural materials. Wood is good acoustically as it absorbs sound, and Aalto's belief that it was pliable enough not to be cut or carved led to the development of his bent laminated plywood pieces.

One of Aalto's major projects was the Paimio Sanatorium in Finland, which he designed in the early 1930s. Much of the furniture for the hospital came from experimental design work he carried out with his wife, Aino Marsio, including this table and laminated bentwood chairs sometimes covered with a birch veneer.

C . An Oak Pineapple Coffee Table by Jean-Michel Frank, c1932

Jean-Michel Frank (1895–1941) was known for working with unusual materials and techniques. He used ordinary materials such as iron, straw and oak in luxurious pieces, often treating oak with lead to accentuate its patterned grain. Frank worked extensively with Adolphe Chanaux in the late 1920s; Chanaux had earlier worked with André Groult and Emile-Jacques Ruhlmann, leading figures of the Art Deco movement.

This table shows a typical 1930s combination of simplicity, in the flat planes of the surface, and substance, in the monumental legs. The legs are very thick compared to the elegant top, and decorated with a massive overlapping scale motif. As its title suggests, the table's decoration is taken from nature, although, like much decoration of the time, it is stylized beyond recognition.

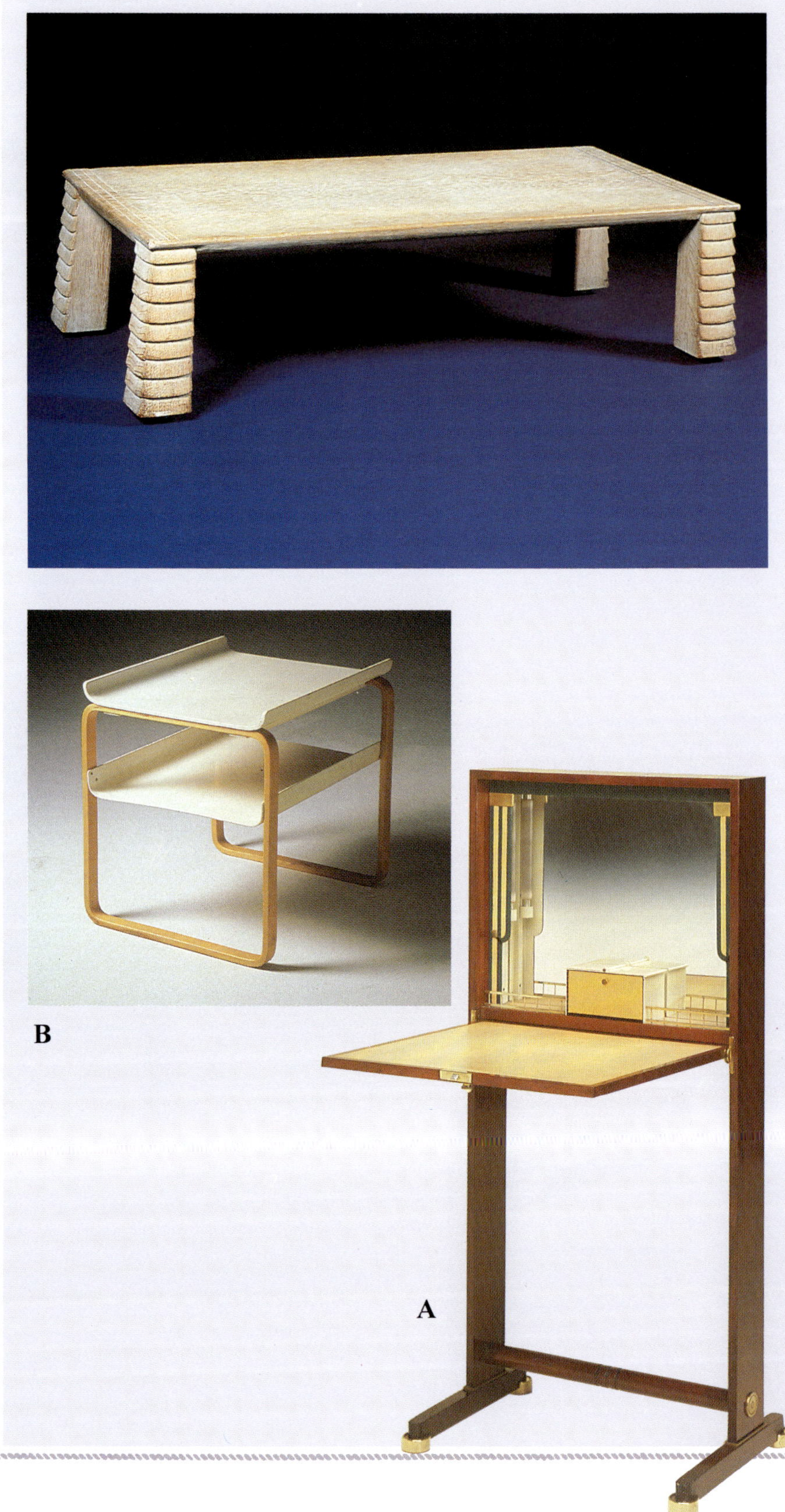

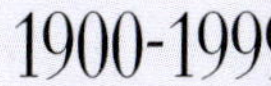

E

D

D. A French Fan Table by Pierre Chareau, *c*1933

This unusual, almost brutal, table has two fan-shaped rotating surfaces. The original design by Chareau (1883–1950) has been revived by the French furniture-making firm Ecart and is still manufactured today in Paris. Chareau was active at the 1925 Paris Exposition, and divided his time between building and furniture design: his *Maison de Verre* (House of Glass), completed in 1931, was the first to use glass tiles on the house's exterior, which later became a 1930s hallmark. Chareau's furniture was usually designed for the inside of his own commissions and was often made of highly polished woods.

Here, however, the patinated wrought iron used is simply waxed; thus it retains its industrial, utilitarian character. Although French, the table manifests a Bauhaus-like emphasis on utility.

E. A Pair of Bedside Tables by Paul Dupré-Lafon, *c*1935

These bedside tables were made for the villa, Les Myrtes, near Ste. Maxime, France. At this time, the South of France was the winter home for many of the rich and famous, including Noël Coward and Jean Cocteau, and other clients of Dupré-Lafon's included the Rothschild and Dreyfus families.

In keeping with his fascination with exotic materials, these bedside tables are covered in parchment, made out of finely stretched animal skin, and traditionally used for writing. The drawer fronts are covered in leather by the exclusive Hermès company – with which Dupré-Lafon worked repeatedly – and the tables sit on bases of black marble.

D
A

A. A French Wrought-iron Console Table by Raymond Subes, *c*1935

This breakfront table with black marble top (its centre section set slightly forward) echoes Georgian bookcases of the 18th century. The designers of the Art Deco era, especially Ruhlmann, used many neo-classical features in their designs.

Raymond Subes (1893–1970), born in Paris, studied metal engraving at the Parisian school of metalwork, the Ecole Boulle, before working with the influential architects, Borderel and Robert. In 1919 he became the director of their metal atelier, and was responsible for many influential architectural projects. He usually worked in wrought iron, but also used bronze, copper and aluminium.

Sube's work followed on from that of Emile Robert, who was responsible for the revival of metalwork as an Arts & Crafts interest in the 19th century, and the great Art Deco metalworker, Edgar Brandt (1880–1960). Brandt and Subes both worked for the top designers of the time and exhibited under their own names.

B. French *Tables Gigogne* by Frank and Chanaux, *c*1935

Gigogne is the French word for a mother of many children. These tables were originally created in oak and covered in vellum and straw marquetry. The partnership of Jean-Michel Frank (1895–1941) and Adolphe Chanaux (1887–1965) produced some original work from their design studios in Paris.

In 1927, Frank commissioned Chanaux to decorate his apartment to his own design and so began a professional association that ended only with Frank's suicide in New York, shortly after the outbreak of World War II. The two sometimes collaborated with their immediate neighbours, including Salvador Dali, Alberto and Diego Giacometti, and Pablo Picasso, and among their well-known patrons were Mr and Mrs Nelson Rockefeller, Elsa Schiaparelli and Templeton Crocker of San Francisco.

Frank/Chanaux furniture was known for its sparseness and simplicity of line and function; on visiting Frank's apartment, Jean Cocteau remarked that Frank was a nice young man, but it was a pity the burglars took everything.

C. An American Writing Table and Chair by Frank Lloyd Wright, *c*1936

This range of furniture, Cherokee Red, was made from enamelled steel and American walnut. It was designed by Frank Lloyd Wright (1867–1959), the most famous American 20th-century architect, for the Johnson Wax Building in Racine, Wisconsin. Wright's body of work covered many periods, from Victorian styles up to 20th-century post-war designs, and his furniture reflected many of these eras, in the main because they were designed for actual interiors. Wright felt that architecture and furniture were an integral whole, and he occasionally made pieces in the same shape as the buildings they were placed in. He was much influenced by Charles Rennie Mackintosh and was as equally innovative.

Wright favoured long, low shapes, as seen in his 'prairie houses' in architecture, designed to harmonize with the prairies in which they were set. The writing table featured concentrates on the horizontal; the desk and chair come from Wright's utilitarian era, and reflect his interest in unornamented design.

D. A Tea Trolley by Alvar Aalto, *c*1937

Alvar Aalto (1898–1976) was a leading architect of Modernism, a movement closely associated with the German Bauhaus. This tea trolley was exhibited at the Paris World's Fair of 1937, and is a 20th-century descendant of serving tables, sometimes mobile, which had been produced since the 17th century. The original form was the 'dumb waiter', a three-tiered table on castors which could be placed or wheeled near to the main dining table 'as soon as supper is over' so that 'our conversation was not under any restraint by servants in ye room' (Mrs Hamilton's Diary, 1874).

This trolley shows a typical freshness of design and lack of decoration; it is at once attractive and functional. Aalto founded the firm Artek in 1935, a plywood manufacturer still in operation today.

A . An Italian Card Table by Carlo Graffi, *c*1950

The influence of the Milan school, particularly its premier exponent, Carlo Mollino, is clear in Graffi's juxtaposition of materials – in this case, wood and glass – on this card table. The wood is unconventionally cut into a shape which is not inherently strong but is stressed by tensioning bars, a technique used extensively by Mollino in the 1940s and 1950s. There are also similarities to 18th-century neo-classical card tables: it is stylish, with straight legs and severe outlines, and trays for the counters slide out from each of the corners, just as candlestick holders slid out from beneath such tables in the 1700s.

Although the Milan school was responsible for countless innovative ideas, many have not endured very well. This table, with its conflicting angles and clashing horizontal and vertical lines, is energetic, but not restful.

B . Pedestal Tables by Eero Saarinen, *c*1955

Tables supported by a single pedestal reached their peak of popularity in the early 19th century; however, the weakness of design of the wooden joint generally led to stocky pedestals. Here, Saarinen uses modern materials to produce a more elegant range of chairs and tables. The Pedestal range was first produced in the early 1950s and has been manufactured ever since – one set is permanently on display in New York's Museum of Modern Art.

Finnish-born Eero Saarinen (1910–61) was the son of the famous architect, Eliel Saarinen. After studying sculpture in Paris, he graduated from the Yale School of Architecture. Despite the fact that he is basically American, his furniture shows much Scandinavian elegance and desire for simplicity. He once declared that 'the underside of typical chairs and tables makes a confusing, unrestful world. I want to clear up the slum of legs.'

C . An Italian Desk with Formica Top by Carlo Mollino, *c*1955

This pedestal desk is a curious combination of blond wood and Formica. It is typical of Mollino's post-Second World War work, when his designs were sculptural and often humorous. This table, for example, is not purely functional – the pedestal, placed on one side, could have been under the desk top, and the stretchers could have been simpler. The leg construction of this table seems to resemble a bat, or an aeroplane.

Italian design received considerable impetus after the Second World War, when so much that had been destroyed needed to be replaced economically. Designers and artists in the post-war period were keen to use new materials such as Formica, and many of Mollino's earlier designs used the cheaper plywood. His later work, such as this, echoes the stressed plywood construction of his chairs, although here he is using solid cut timber for the framework.

Mollino (1905–73) was a prominent member of the Milan school of design, which initially gained attention at the first Milan Triennale Exhibition of 1933, a fair which continues to today. His work has often been associated with Franco Albini and Guiseppe Terragni, the architects, and much of his furniture was produced by Appelli of Turin.

D . A Trapezoidal Harpies Coffee Table by Alberto Giacometti, *c*1955

This table comes from a series of bronze and glass furniture based on skeletal human and organic forms. Here, the form of a harpy – a mythical monster with a woman's head and body and limbs of a bird – is used as decoration on the twig-like legs and stretcher. The whole piece is cast in bronze.

Giacometti (1901–66) was a Swiss-born sculptor/painter/poet who trained in Italy in the 1920s; while there, he was much influenced by the Rumanian-born sculptor, Constantin Brancusi (1876-1957). In the 1930s, Giacometti produced mainly surreal work with mythological and mysterious elements, and later went on to concentrate on stick-like emaciated figures, made from a wire frame applied with plaster of Paris. His furniture is generally fairly light-hearted, and is very much prized by collectors of 20th-century work.

E . The Green Table by Allen Jones, *c*1972

This table is by the Pop Art sculptor, Allen Jones, (b.1937) and is one of a limited edition of six made of glass fibre, leather and other accessories. It is provocatively sexual, although less so than his former series, *Table Sculpture,* which featured semi-naked women wearing only gloves and boots. This has little place in the history of functional furniture, but it carries on the precedent of fantasy furniture as seen in 18th-century Rococo work, earlier Baroque pieces and the designs of the 20th-century Surrealist, Salvador Dali, who in 1936 designed a sofa after Mae West's lips. This table is a curious twist to the traditional use of human figures to support tables and other furniture, a device common in the late 17th century and early 18th century.

C
B
A

E

D

1900-1999

A. A Low Table Designed by Andrée Putman, *c*1978

This low table is clearly influenced by designers such as Jacques-Henri Lartigue, with its strong flavour of Art Deco revival – straight lines, flat surfaces and pyramidal, many-sided legs which give it a sculptural quality occupying space. The top has a low apron around it which gives the whole piece an impression of solidity. The table's feeling of monumentality is reminscent of early Art Deco designers, and the black-lacquered wood it comprises was a typical Art Deco medium.

Andrée Putman is a Parisian interior designer, many of whose furniture creations have been produced by Ecart International.

B. The Zig Zag Table by Jeremy Broun, *c*1979

Contemporary furniture production falls into three general categories – mass productions for economy; commercial designer furniture; and limited-edition designer furniture. This last provides the closest link between the maker and user, and often results in the most interesting products. This can be clearly seen in the creations of the successful craft revival begun in the 1960s.

This table is made from hyedua – an oriental hardwood – by Bath cabinetmaker and designer Jeremy Boun (b.1945). It exploits the markings of traditional manufacture, as seen by the wood joints where the top meets the legs, and is innovative in its centre joint in the table top. It is based on traditional craft design, as opposed to radical modern design; tables based on the principle of three have been made since the 16th century, but the triangular component has more usually been the tripod base rather than the top, as here.

C. The Spyder Table by Ettore Sottsass, *c*1980 and D. The Shift Table by Ettore Sottsass, *c*1980

The 1980s revival of interest in structure was an extension of ideas from Breuer and the Bauhaus of the 1920s, although most of the later pieces employ a more sophisticated combination of colour and engineering, as here, to form the central support.

Sottsass was born in 1917 in Austria, and has worked with bodies as diverse as Olivetti and the Royal College of Art, promoting the radical Memphis Collection in Milan. Describing himself as 'a metaphoric designer', he considers the object itself to be relatively unimportant; rather, he is more concerned with how it is presented. This he achieves by using bright colours and unusual shapes. His furniture is said to show a sense of irony and wit, and often refers to human or animal form – the Spyder table, for instance, is appropriately named.

The Shift Table similarly appeals for its wit; it gives the impression that it is about to collapse. Its legs are in fact pinned together, and the visible parts rest on an inner iron structure. This table is also made in marble, resembling the classical columns of antiquity.

E. The Mega Table by Enrico Baleri, 1982

The broad, flat planes of this table are without colour or ornamentation, giving it a monumental feel that seems to refer to Classical ideas. The only decorative elements, apart from the table-top texture, are the vertical lines on the legs, which are reminiscent of fluting on classical columns. This is classicism taken to an extreme, 'abstracting' some of the aspects of ancient Roman architecture.

Baleri's work was produced by Knoll International, an American firm which specializes in reproducing 20th-century classics and which also produces Ettore Sottsass's work. The interest shown here in mass and form has been central to the work of a group of 1980s designers, who also include Vico Magistretti and Giandomenico Belotti.

F. Solomon's Table by Danny Lane, *c*1988

Is this a table or a piece of sculpture? Perhaps both. Made of marble and glass, it resembles a surfboard or fish suspended by towering piles of cut glass. Glass constructions such as this have become the trademark of Danny Lane (b.1955), an Illinois native who now lives in London and ranks among the most successful of 1980s designers. Lane claims that his pieces evolve naturally out of the medium he is using.

This bold design utilizes light and colour to show the materials to good effect; very much the same principles, in fact, that designers of all periods, whether Baroque, Rococo, Regency, Federal or Bauhaus, have employed in furniture making over the centuries.

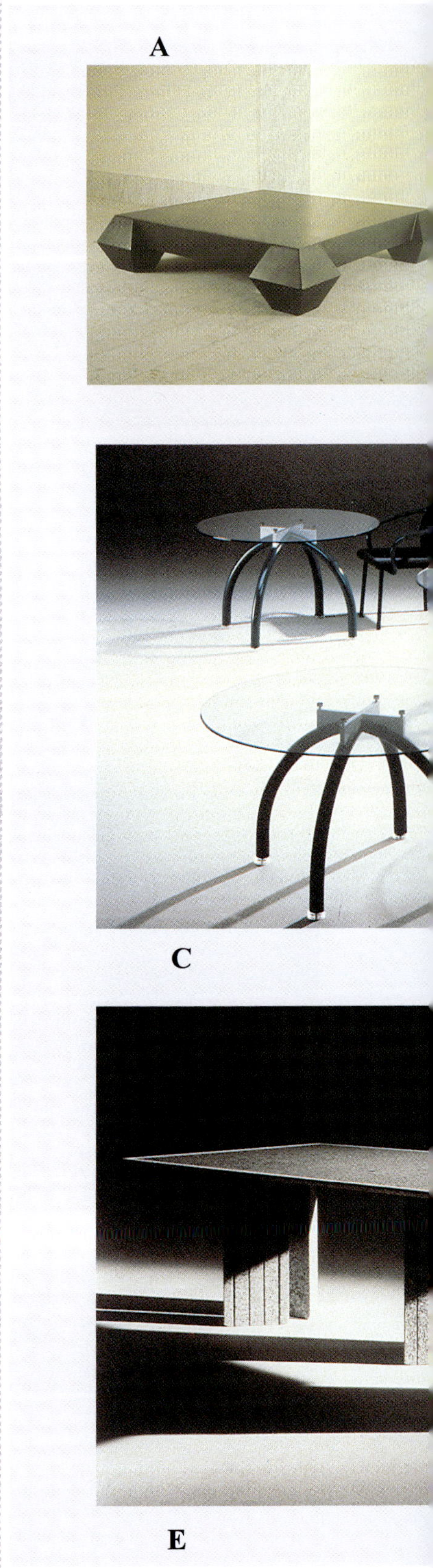
A

C

E

B

D

F

A. An American Oak Desk, *c*1900

This large piece was designed by Frank Lloyd Wright for a house at Kankakee, Illinois. Its broad overhanging top is 7ft 8in (2.34m) long, supported on two pedestals of three drawers each.

Wright is remembered as one of the most influential architects of the 20th century; he also took great care in commissioning furniture to fill the rooms of the homes he designed. Wright generally made use of massive rectangular forms, carefully balanced one against another, and was influenced, both in choice of material and simplicity of design, by the work of Arts and Crafts furniture makers.

B. An American Oak Fall-Front Writing Cabinet, *c*1902

This was designed by the architect Frank Lloyd Wright for the house he created for Francis W. Little at Peoria, Illinois. It is 5ft 9in (1.76m) high but only 1ft 9in (54cm) wide and seems to have been intended to stand on one side of a fireplace in the master bedroom, complemented by a similarly-proportioned cabinet on the other side. The mirrored door at the top opens to reveal shelves and the flap below it drops down to provide a working surface with pigeonholes behind. In the base there are five drawers. The whole is neat and sedate, designed to fit in with Wright's decorative scheme for the house.

C. A Painted Steel Office Desk, 1904

Wright again designed furniture to match the building that was to house it, and this set was designed for the administration building of the Larkin mail order company at Buffalo, New York. Wright's air-conditioned building, with its central open hall lit by skylights, was an avant garde design that was matched by equally innovative office furniture. The metal desks were built with efficiency in mind; there are banks of pigeonholes for filing along the back and an integral swivel chair without legs which can easily be pushed back and forth to make office cleaning easier. This design set a precedent for the use of metal furniture and for the creation of a single system for the entire office, which were to become standard later in the century.

B

A

C

1900-1999

A . An American Oak Fall-Front Desk with Iron Handles

2ft 6 in (81cm) wide, c1910, a typical plank-constructed product of the Stickley workshops.

Gustav Stickley was one of the most practical and successful of the American exponents of the Arts and Crafts ideal. He began his career making furniture in a variety of fashionable revivalist styles, but he took the writings of English Arts and Crafts pioneers to heart and set about putting his ideas into practice after 1898, producing simple plank-constructed pieces with tenon joints and almost no decoration. He showed a common sense that many idealists lack and was happy to use machines in his workshop where it made the work easier and the product cheaper without interfering with quality. The style soon gained the name Mission Furniture, but Stickley wrote in one of his trade catalogues 'I had no idea of attempting to create a new style, but merely tried to make furniture which would be simple, durable, comfortable, and fitted for the place it had to occupy and the work it had to do'. In many ways the American public was more ready than their European counterparts to accept a plain and simple 'non-style' which owed no debt to history and evoked the rugged life of the early settlers. Stickley's *United Craftsmen* company prospered and expanded, but it also attracted competitors and eventually went bankrupt in 1916 having opened large offices and showrooms in New York.

C

B . An American Leather-Topped Mahogany Library Table

This massively constructed piece, 4ft (1.23m) wide, was made in Gustav Stickley's workshops but is not typical of Stickley's output in that it is made of an exotic hardwood rather than an indigenous wood like oak, but it clearly shows the Stickley trademark on the inside of one of the trestle supports. It is a red transfer consisting of a joiner's compass with Stickley's signature underneath and the motto *Als Ik Kan* (As I Can), a precept taken from the 15th-century Flemish artist Jan van Eyck, in the centre.

C . An American Oak Fall-Front Desk, *c*1904

The panelled fall is inlaid with stylised motifs in pewter and various light woods and conceals an interior with a central drawer surrounded with shelves and pigeonholes. The exterior has been darkened by fuming, a favourite Stickley finish, while the interior is made of much lighter wood. This desk was designed by Harvey Ellis, who worked for Stickley for a period before his death in 1904 and introduced his characteristic inlaid ornament to the company's range. It is 2ft 6in (76cm) wide.

A . A Scottish Ebonised Oak, Mother-of-Pearl, Metal and Glass Writing Cabinet, 1904

This writing cabinet, 3ft (92cm) wide, was made for the study of the Scottish architect Charles Rennie Mackintosh to his own design. Here the desk is shown open to reveal pigeonholes and shelves over the writing surface, with an open folio stand below. The stark angular design, relieved by the sparkle of small pieces of glass and mother-of-pearl, is typical of Mackintosh's work, as is the distinctive glass and metal flower panel at the centre of the cabinet.

The desk is a copy of one originally designed for the home of Glasgow publisher Walter Blackie, Hill House, which was one of Mackintosh's most important domestic architectural commissions. His highly individual furniture forms were both influenced by and a reaction against the products of the Arts and Crafts movement and were more influential on the Continent than in Britain. In Austria designers like Hoffman and Moser showed a similarly angular response to the curves of the Art Nouveau style.

B . An English Writing Cabinet Veneered in Ebony and Holly

This beautiful piece of furniture, 4ft 5in (1.35m) high, with decorative painting and fittings and mounts of wrought iron and silver, was designed by Charles Robert Ashbee in 1902.

Ashbee was a leading figure in the British Arts and Crafts Movement in the late 19th century, and founder of the Guild and School of Handicraft at Toynbee Hall in the East End of London in 1888. Ashbee followed the basic tenets of the movement in encouraging undivided labour, with each craftsman involved in every stage of production. Like many other pioneers, however, Ashbee found it difficult to compete with commercial firms and after a move to the Cotswolds in 1902, his venture folded in 1914.

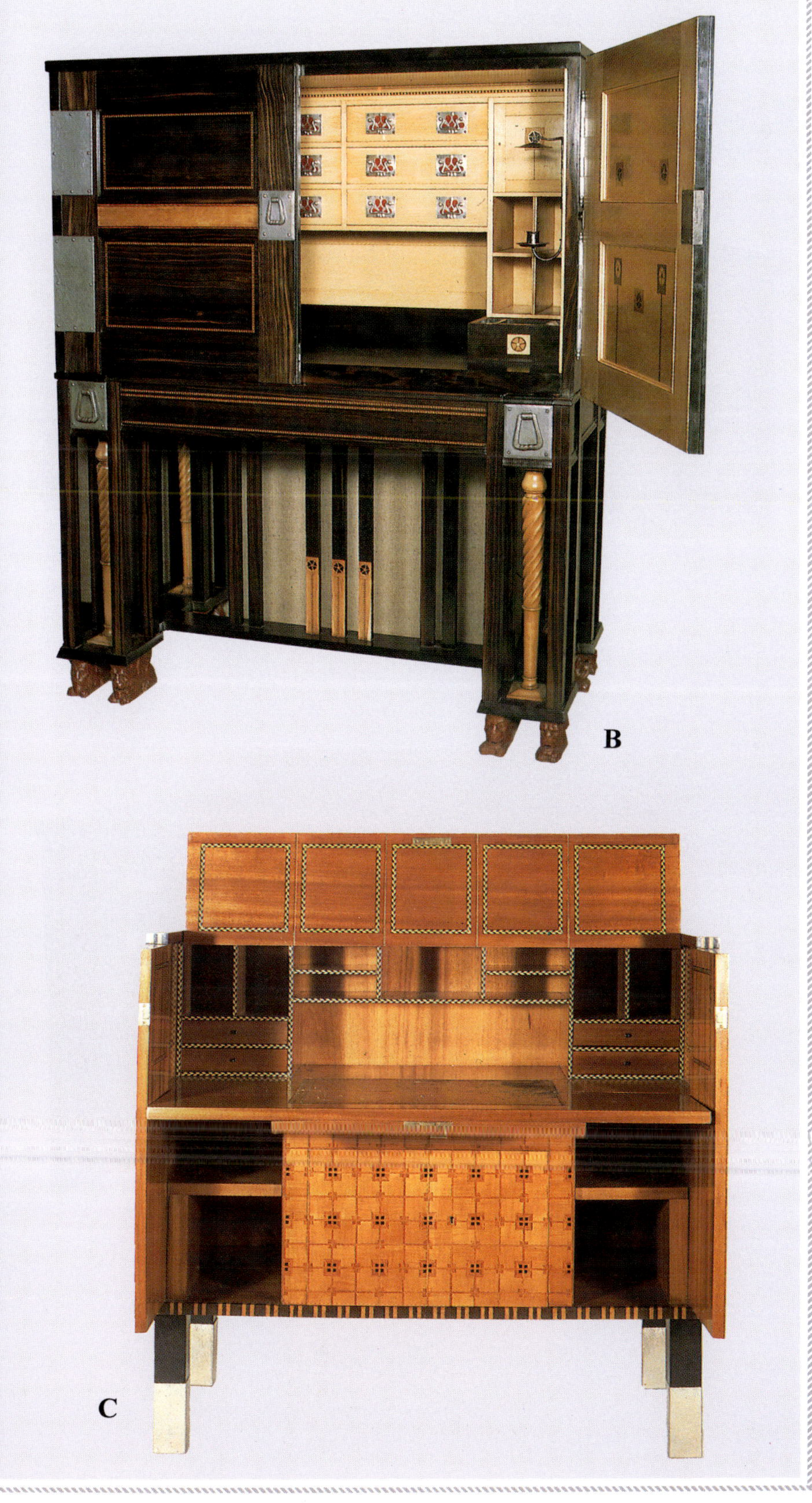

C . An Austrian Secessionist Desk, 1902

This piece, designed by the Viennese designer Koloman Moser and made of elm, ivory, mother of pearl, ebony and jacaranda, was a special commission for the Chateâu Charlottenlund near Stockholm.

It is 3ft 11in (1.20m) wide. Here it is shown open for use, and the design appears sober and symmetrical. However, when the fall-front is lifted and the two doors closed it reveals a restrained exoticism typical of the avant-garde Viennese artists of the time. The whole of the front is inlaid with a parquetry pattern of interlocking squares and the centre of the fall-front is decorated with a pair of mother-of-pearl maidens holding inlaid brass rings and flanked by stylised dolphins in ebony.

Koloman Moser was one of a group of artists (including Joseph Hoffmann, Otto Wagner, Josef Olbrich and Gustav Klimt) who broke away from the conservative Vienna Academy in 1897. The Secessionist Exhibition Gallery was opened in 1898 and in 1903 Moser and Hoffman founded the Wiener Werkstätte, a craft co-operative producing metalware, furniture and textiles. Although the Werkstätte was based on the Arts and Crafts guilds set up in Britain, the rigorous rectilinear designs of the early years were closer to the work of the Glasgow designer Charles Rennie Mackintosh than to the mainstream Arts and Crafts products or the Art Nouveau creations seen elsewhere in Europe, which relied on organic forms and sinuous curves.

D . An English Holly and Ebony Veneered Desk, 1916

The desk, which is 2ft 3in (99cm) wide, with five drawers in the front and a simple superstructure, was designed by Roger Fry at the Omega Workshops in London. It was part of a commission to furnish an entire apartment for the wife of the Belgian ambassador, Lalla Vandervelde, with the distinctive brightly painted pieces produced by Fry and the young artists who worked with him. The desk was the only marquetry piece in the commission, but it shows some of the signs of careless craftsmanship (badly fitting drawers and poor-quality marquetry) typical of the workshop, which was set up in 1913, partly as a reaction to the serious Craft Guild mentality of the post-Morris era. Fry was more concerned with spontaneity and artistic expression than with craftsmanship and technique, but he did provide many keen young artists with a means of earning a living, and by cultivating clients he managed to see the workshop through the difficult period of the First World War, finally closing it down in 1919.

1900-1999

A . A French Black Lacquer Art Deco Kneehole Desk and Chair, c1925

The desk was designed by Jean Dunand and Serge Revinski, and is 3ft 11in (1.19m) wide, with four drawers in each pedestal. The hinged central writing slope is covered with lozenges of shagreen and the top of each pedestal is hinged to give access to a compartment beneath.

Dunand was born in Switzerland and while working in Paris he learned the correct oriental technique for lacquering from the Japanese artist Sugawara. The smooth lines and surfaces of Dunand's furniture designs are among the most distinctive of the Inter-War years.

C

D

A

B

B. A French Half-Round Pedestal Desk

This unusual and attractive piece was designed as a special commission by Jacques-Emile Ruhlmann. The top is fitted with five double-hinged compartments radiating from a leather writing surface with two cut-glass inkwells. The left-hand pedestal is fitted with drawers with gilt bronze handles and the right-hand with a tambour shutter over a drawer. Both stand on gilt bronze pedestals joined by a gilt bronze stretcher. The distinctive striped veneer is macassar ebony, an exotic wood much favoured by Art Deco furniture designers for its sleek, dramatic appearance.

Ruhlmann was the leading Parisian interior decorator of the 1920s, producing very expensive but beautifully made furniture, much of which bears his mark.

C. A French Art Deco Pedestal Desk Veneered in Rosewood, by Jules Leleu, *c*1930

There are drawers in each end of the large pedestal and on one side of each of the smaller pedestals. The three-way design is unusual, but the clean straight lines, the use of rich, figured veneer in wide expanses and chromium-plated handles and bases are typical of the best quality Art Deco furniture. The whole construction measures 6ft 3¾in (1.92m) across.

D. A French Desk, *c*1928

This beautiful desk in Brazilian jacaranda, ivory and chromed steel was designed by the French architect and interior decorator Pierre Chareau. Chareau was one of the leading designers of the Art Deco movement. He produced luxurious, highly finished interiors, but also gave thought to the practical design of desks of all kinds. Here the very simple central section is flanked by a pair of swinging drawers with ivory escutcheons on one side and on the other side by a nest of four tables which expand on a central hinge to provide the writer with extra space. The tables can be separated from the desk and used on their own.

Jacaranda was a veneer popular with French cabinetmakers in the 1920s due to its rich and distinctive grain.

1900-1999

A . A British Double Architect's Desk and Matching Chair, 1935

This set of painted tubular steel and painted wood was made by by the British firm PEL (Practical Equipment Ltd). The desk has a single long frieze drawer and three smaller drawers suspended in the framework. It is attached to an adjustable drawing board, giving an overall width of 9ft (2.75m).

By the mid-1930s British firms were following the Continental lead in exploiting the strength, economy and clean modern lines of bent tubing. The principal European producer was the Vienna-based firm of Thonet. Having pioneered the mass manufacture of inexpensive bentwood furniture as early as the 1830s, they adapted naturally to the new materials, which had a similar combination of strength and flexibility.

B . An American Desk and Chair, 1936–39

This set was a standard piece designed for the administration building Wright conceived for the Johnson Wax Company at Racine, Wisconsin. The dynamic curving lines of this furniture echo the shape of the building itself. The desk consists of three round-edged worktops of polished American walnut overhanging a frame of red enamelled steel with semi-circular swing-out steel drawers. This was the basic module; Wright designed many variation for different applications throughout the building. His thoughtful creation of a modular system that was efficient and reflected the style of the building that housed what must have been the envy of many later designers. His attitude to seating was as revolutionary as his architecture – three-legged chairs encourage good posture: if you don't sit up you fall over.

A

E

C. A French Leather and Glass Desk, early 1950s

The 6ft 11in (2.10m) wide top is of boomerang form in thick red glass, supported on tubular metal legs sewn into a black leather covering, with a magazine rack on the left and two swivel drawers on the right. For an important commission this designer has used modern materials but softened the stark lines and spindly supports of typical 1950s office furniture with leather padding by Hermès.

It was designed by Jacques Adnet for the president of a French aviation company.

D. An Italian Oak Two-tier Desk of the Mid-1950s

It is stamped *Silvio Cavatorta, Roma,* but its stylish design clearly shows the influence of one of the greatest Italian designers of the period, Carlo Mollino. Supported on two K-frames, the top tier serves as a working surface over a shelf, with two angled double-drawer units below. It is 5ft 7in (1.7m) wide.

E. An Italian Office Desk of Tubular and Sheet Steel, Vinyl and Cloth

This whole concept is made up from modules of the *Spazio* system launched by Olivetti in 1961. Olivetti produced a series of standard modules that could be manufactured cheaply because they required little complicated welding or fitting, but which could be made up in a variety of combinations by the customer to fit any office or application. This is an early and stylish example of the trend towards factory-produced DIY furniture, which today is seen at its most developed in the domestic fitted kitchen.

APPENDIX

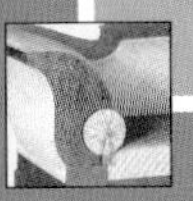

Monarchs

The names of English and French monarchs are often used to denote the period of a piece of furniture when the precise date of manufacture is not known.

In some cases a ruler is closely associated with a recognisable style; Louis XIV, for instance, saw the development of the decorative arts in France as a matter of policy and the massive formal designs of his time reflect the elaboration of life at his court. Dramatic upheavals such as the French Revolution brought about dramatic changes in style but generally changes of style were gradual and overlapped the reigns of different monarchs.

In Britain especially, the machinery of fashion tended to be more loosely linked to the sovereign and public taste was influenced by a variety of factors. This was especially true during the reign of long-lived monarchs like George III (1760-1820) and the names of the producers of cabinetmakers' pattern books, like Chippendale, Sheraton and Hepplewhite are often used quite freely to denote the style of their times. These cabinetmakers were influential not necessarily because of their designs but because they recorded contemporary styles, some of which of course may have been their own.

American furniture periods tend to be classified using a mixture of English monarchs and makers, and the dating is complicated by the fact that it took a long time for European styles to cross the Atlantic so that the American period occurs several years behind the corresponding period in Britain. For example, Queen Anne died in 1714, but the American Queen Anne style is taken to cover the period 1720-1750.

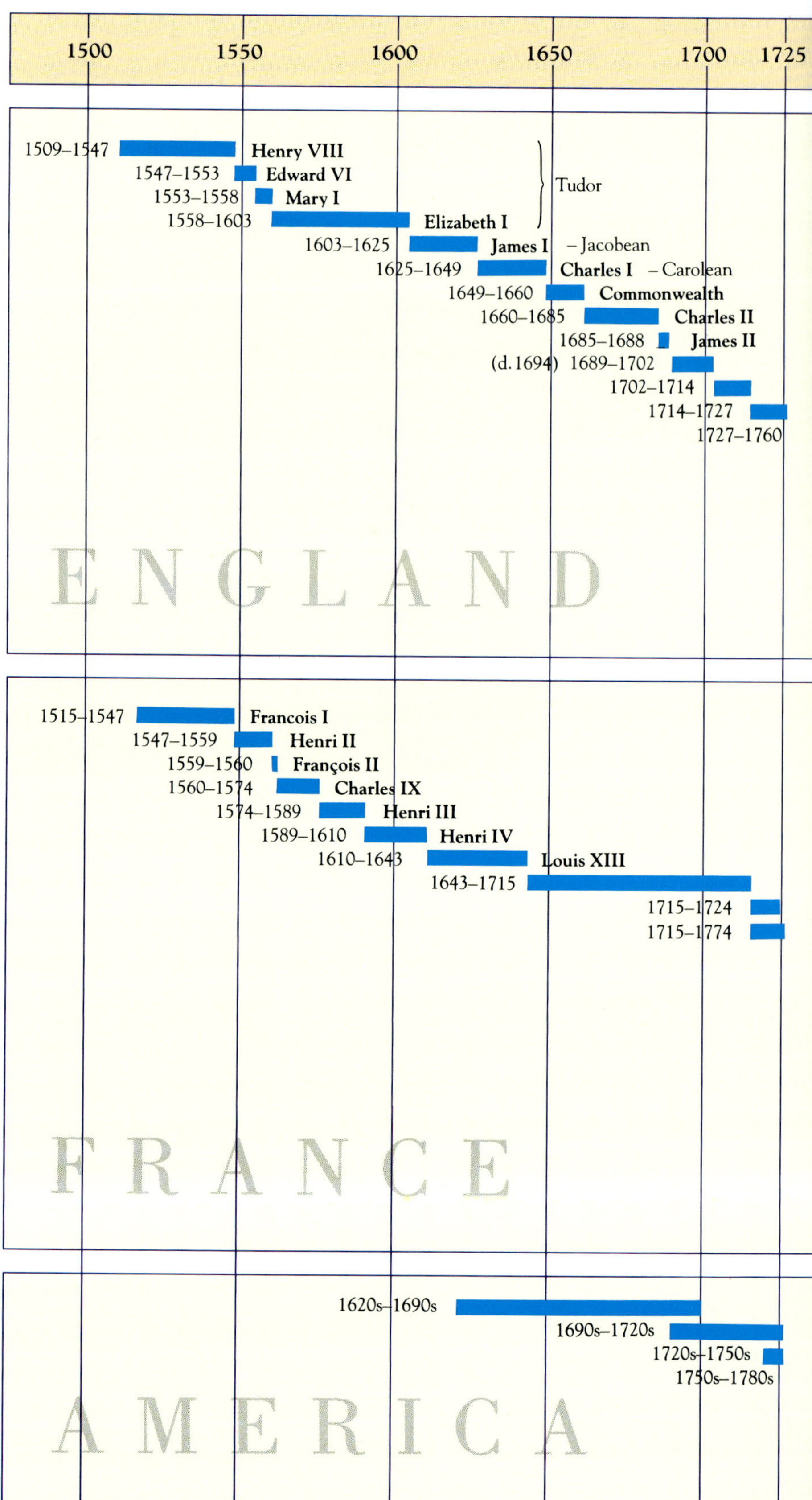

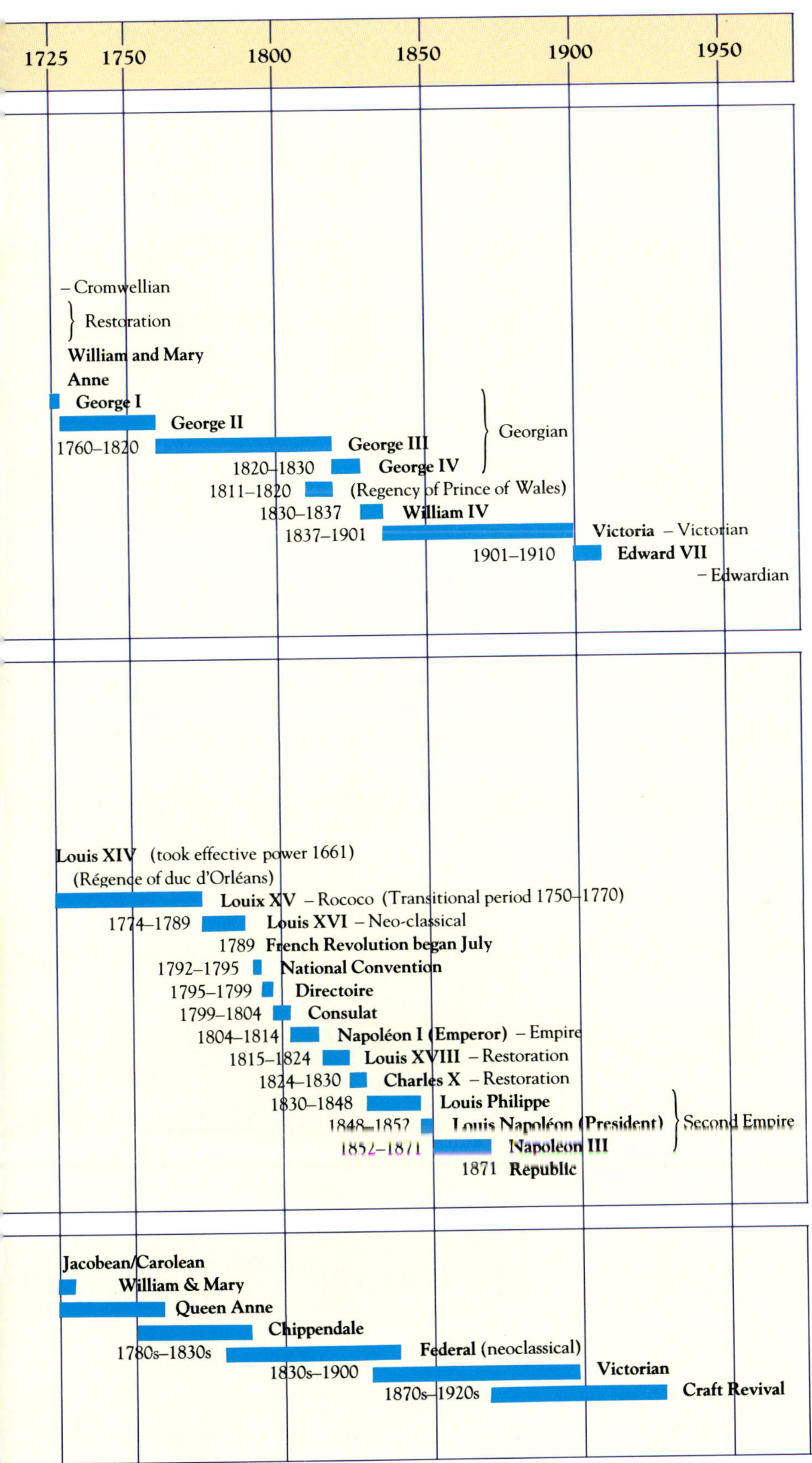

Cabinetmakers' pattern books and other influential publications

Listed here is a selection of books influential both on the furniture makers and designers of their times and on furniture historians.

Stalker and Parker, **Treatise of Japanning and Varnishing**, 1688

Thomas Chippendale, **Gentleman and Cabinet-Maker's Director**, 1754 (2nd edition 1755; 3rd edition 1762)

Ince and Mayhew, **Universal System of Household Furniture**, 1759–1762

Robert Manwaring, **Cabinet and Chair-Maker's Real Friend and Companion** 1765

Robert and James Adam, **Works in Architecture,** 1773–1778 (2nd volume 1779; 3rd volume 1822)

George Hepplewhite, **Cabinet-Maker and Upholsterer's Guide,** 1788

Thomas Shearer, Hepplewhite and others, **Cabinet-Maker's London Book of Prices,** 1788

Thomas Sheraton, **Cabinet-Maker and Upholsterer's Drawing-Book,** 1791–1794

Percier and Fontaine, **Receuil des décorations intérieurs,** 1801 (2nd edition 1812)

Thomas Sheraton, **Cabinet Dictionary,** 1803

Thomas Hope, **Household Furniture and Interior Decoration,** 1807

George Smith, **Collection of Designs for Household Furniture and Interior Decoration,** 1808

Collection of Ornamental Designs after the Antique, 1812

Cabinet Maker and Upholsterer's Guide, 1826

John C. Loudon, **Encyclopaedia of Cottage, Farm and Villa Furniture,** 1833

Augustus W.N. Pugin, **Gothic Furniture in the style of the 15th century,** 1835

The True Principle of Pointed or Christian Architecture, 1841

Bruce Talbert, **Gothic Forms Applied to Furniture,** 1867

Charles Eastlake, **Hints on Household Taste,** 1868

These drawings taken from Chippendale's *The Gentleman & Cabinetmaker's Director* are not for one-armed chairs, but are designs for suites of chairs showing how an armchair and a dining chair might look; likewise the legs are different, giving alternatives to the carver and the client.

These are very rococo chairs: all the rails are carved with rocaille, foliage, scrolls and other frippery. The cabriole legs are interesting, showing an English version with a paw foot and a dolphin as a concession to French taste.

Just as Chippendale had no hesitation bringing in elements of French designs, he combined the result with European-made 'Chinese' fabric which was very popular in the mid-18th century. The frames would almost certainly have been gilded, unlike Chinese chairs.

NINETEENTH CENTURY SWIVEL CHAIR WITH SPRING MECHANISM

FROM THE GREAT EXHIBITION AT CRYSTAL PALACE IN 1851

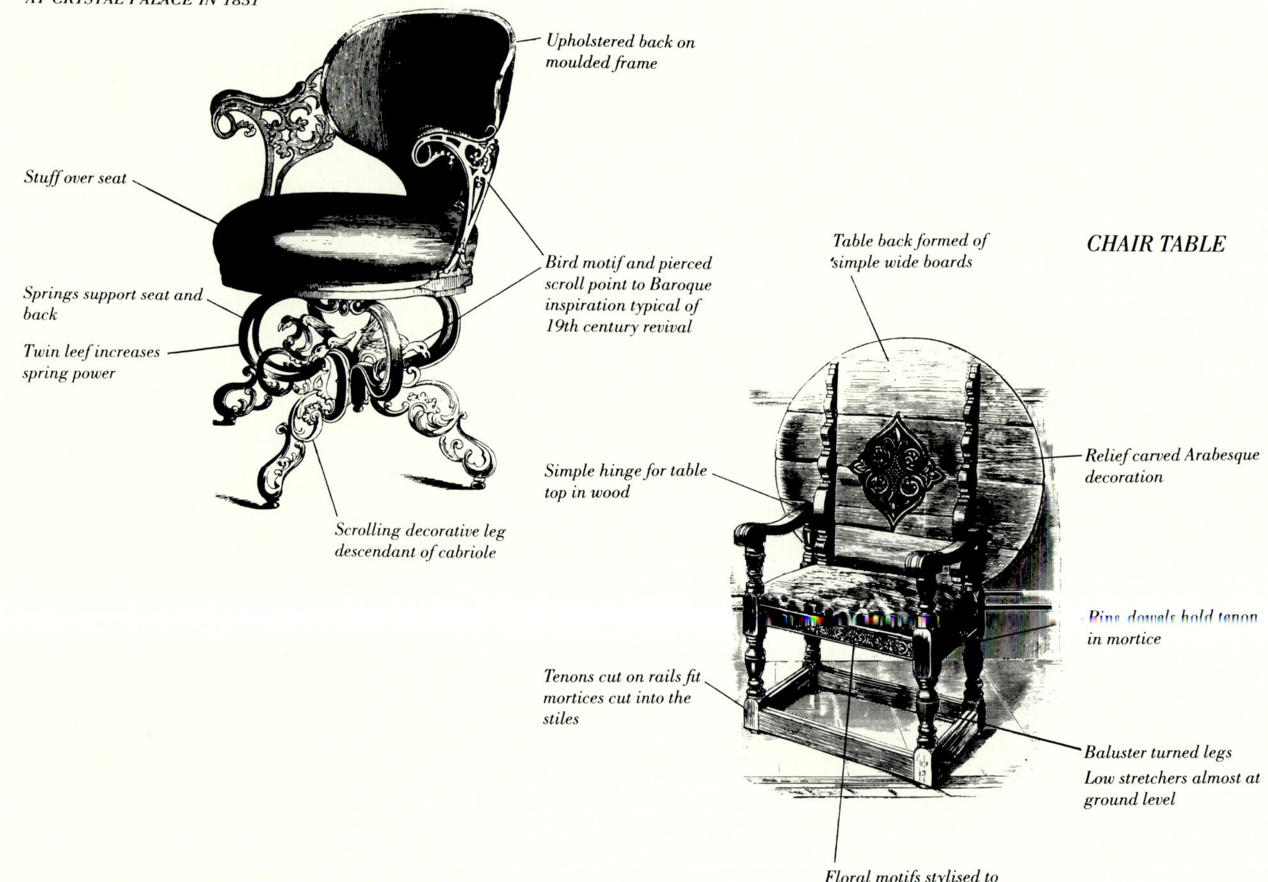

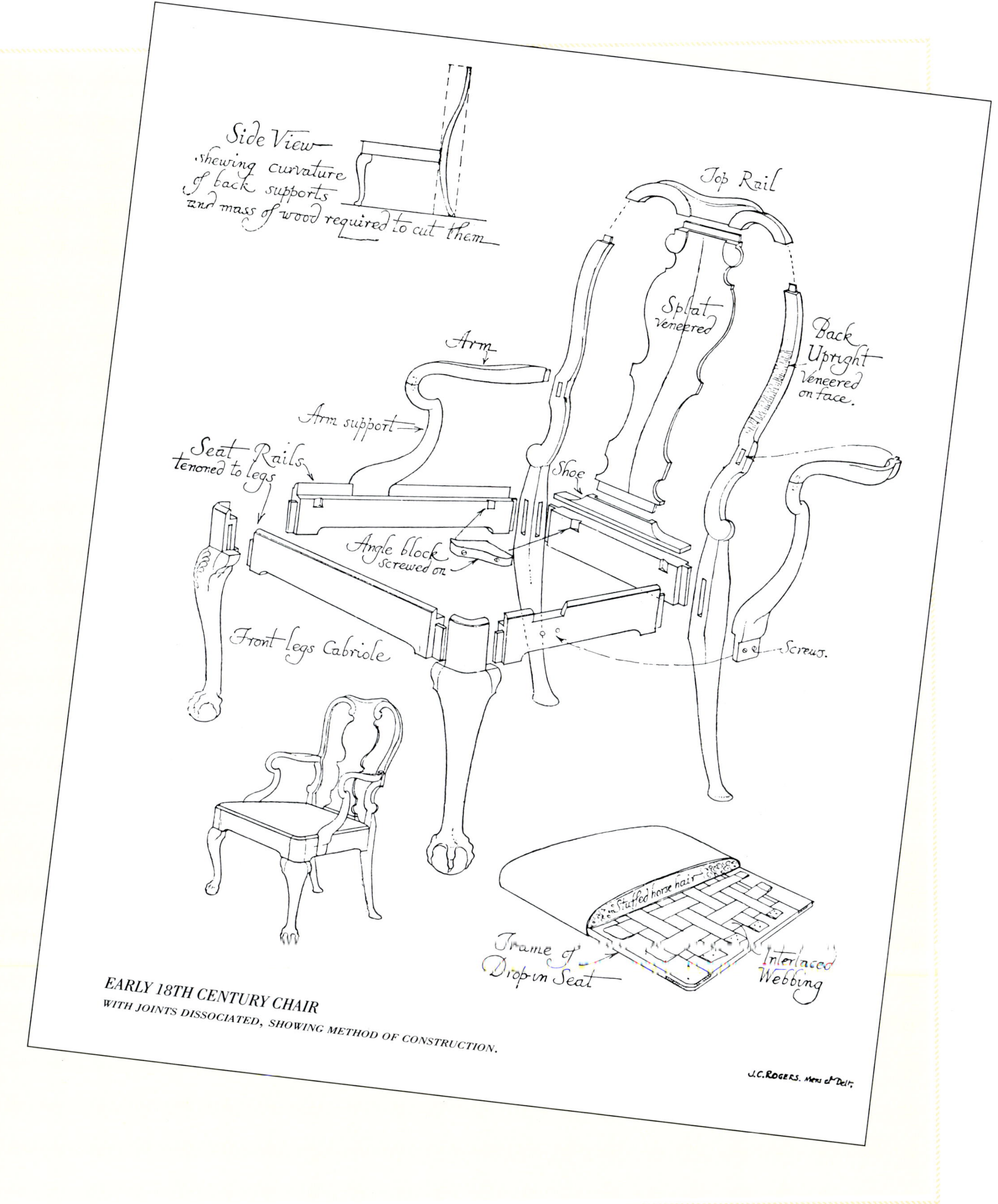

EARLY 18TH CENTURY CHAIR
WITH JOINTS DISSOCIATED, SHOWING METHOD OF CONSTRUCTION.

A DOUBLE CHAIR-BACK SOFA

EXHIBITED AT THE 1851 GREAT EXHIBITION, LONDON

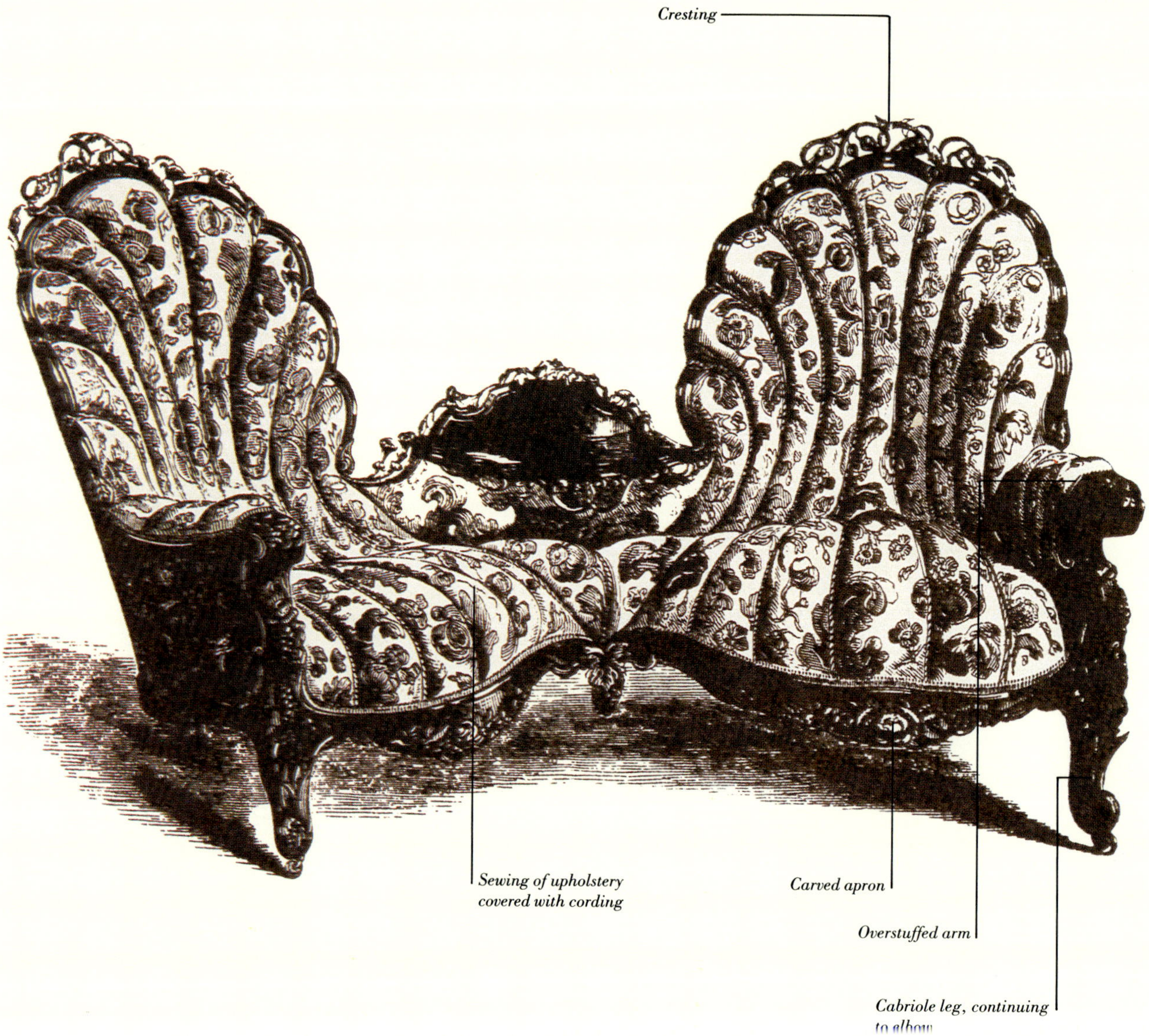

Cresting

Sewing of upholstery covered with cording

Carved apron

Overstuffed arm

Cabriole leg, continuing to elbow

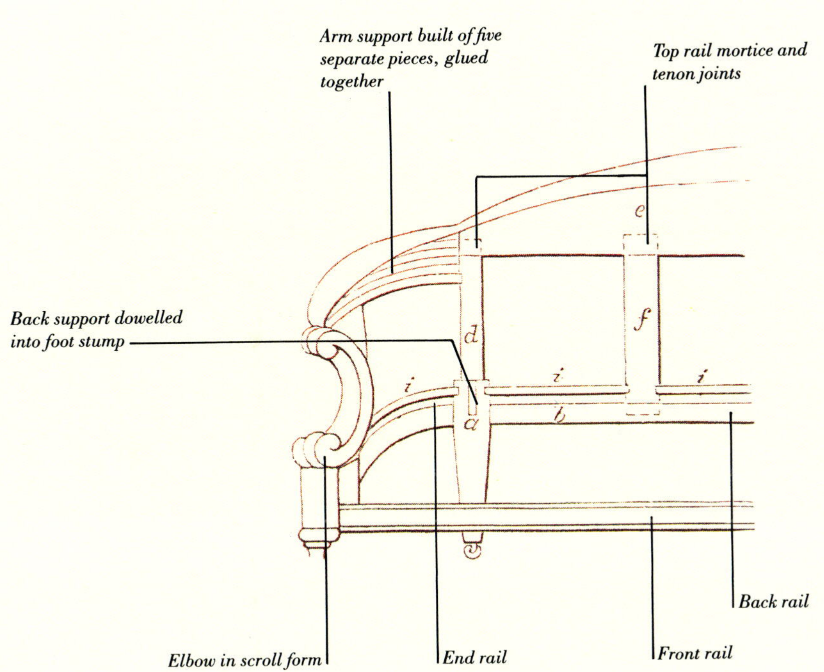

DIAGRAMS SHOWING CONSTRUCTION TECHNIQUES, FROM
THE CABINETMAKER'S ASSISTANT,
PUBLISHED IN 1853

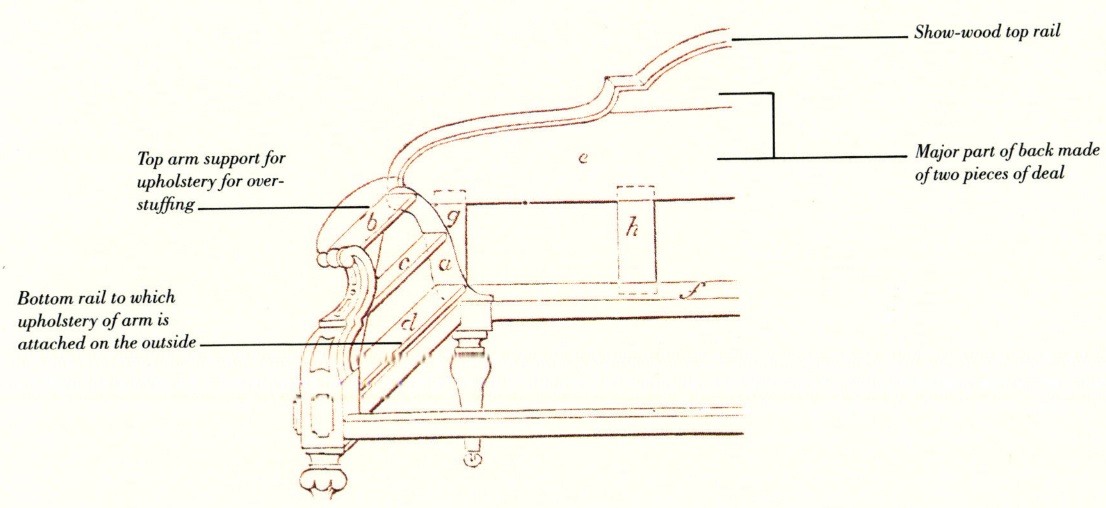

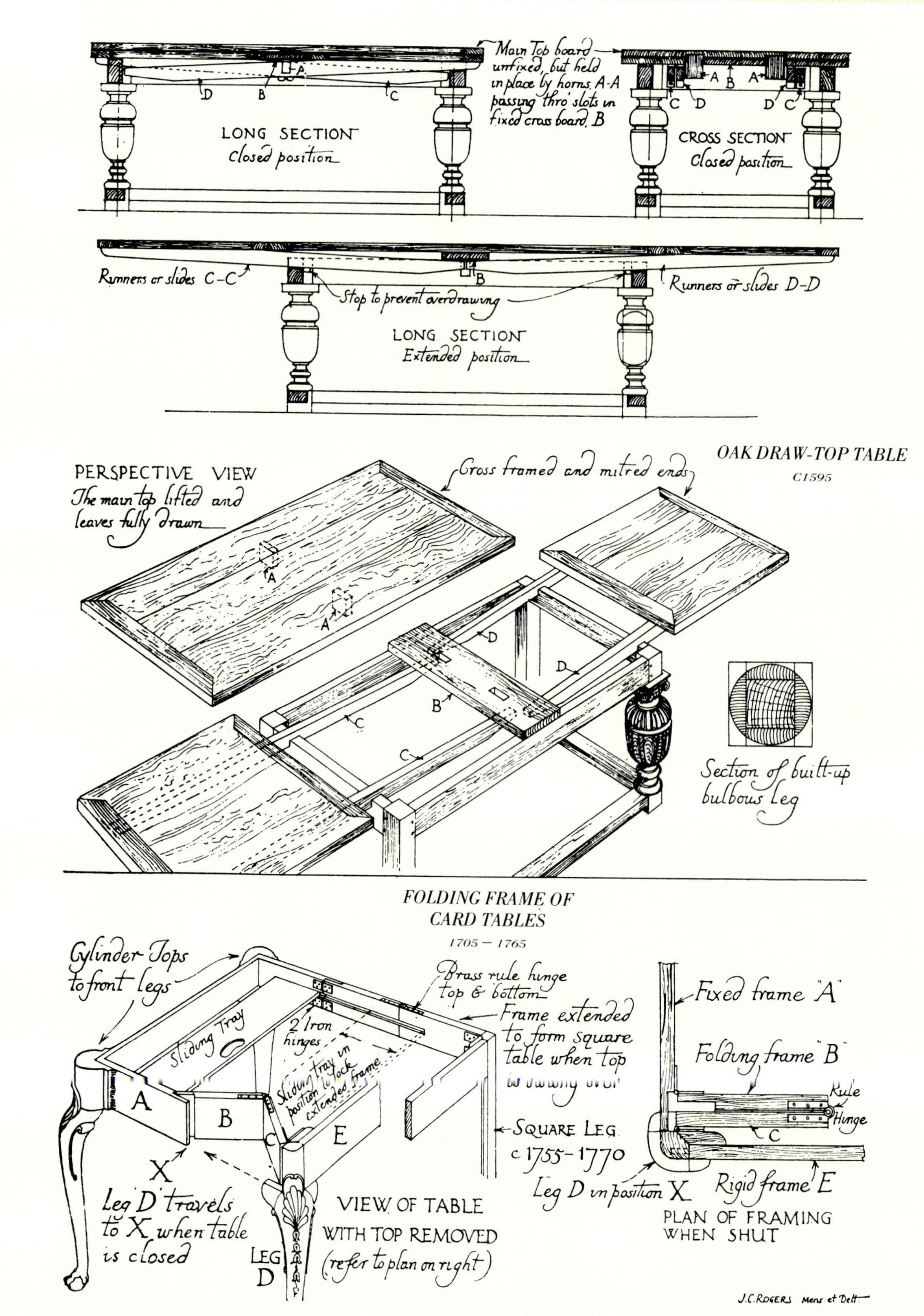

OAK DRAW-TOP TABLE
C1595

FOLDING FRAME OF CARD TABLES
1705 – 1765

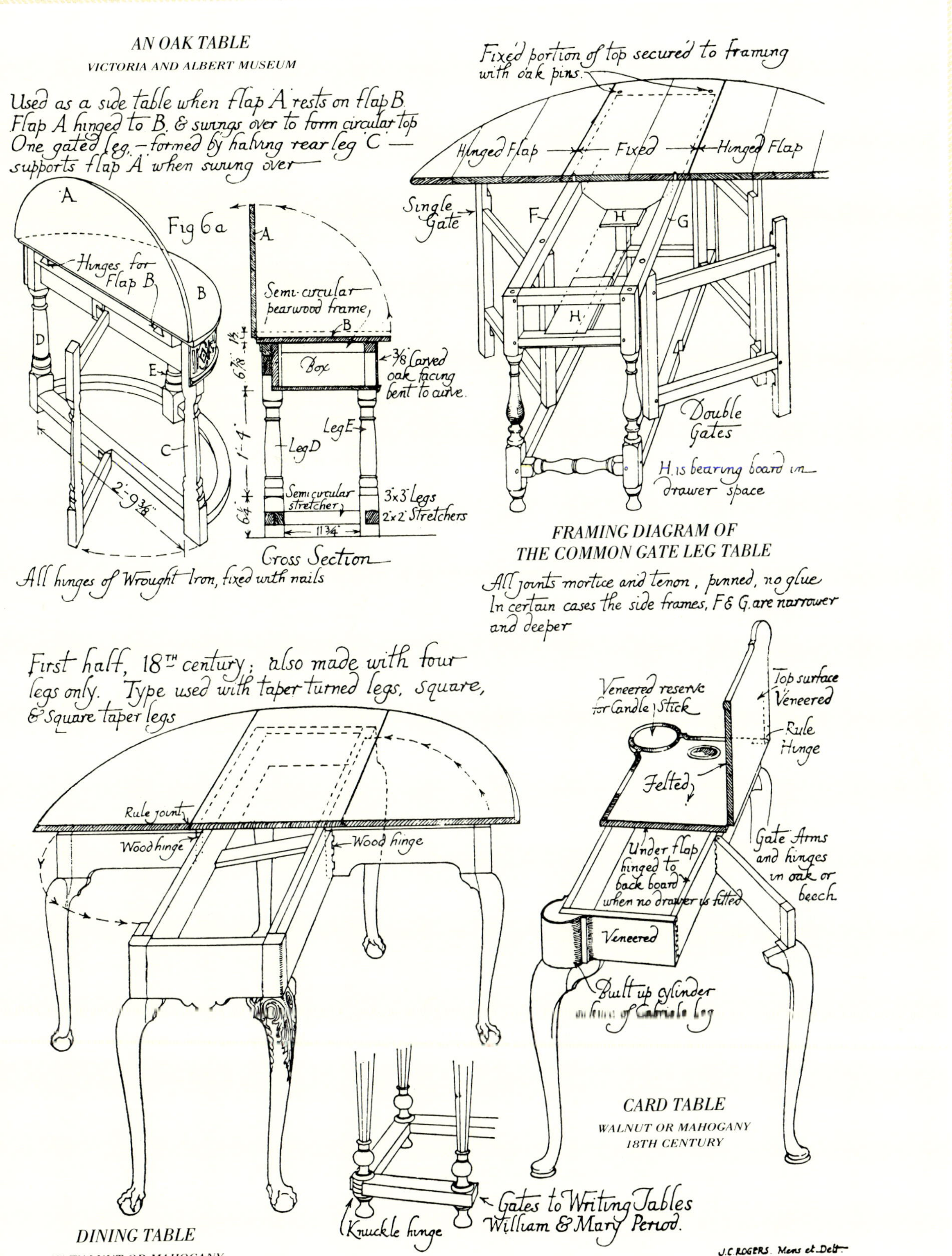
AN OAK TABLE
VICTORIA AND ALBERT MUSEUM
Used as a side table when flap A rests on flap B
Flap A hinged to B & swings over to form circular top
One gated leg, - formed by halving rear leg C -
supports flap A when swung over
Fig 6a
Hinges for Flap B
Semi-circular bearwood frame,
Box
3/8 Carved oak facing bent to curve.
Leg E
Leg D
Semi circular stretcher
3x3 Legs
2x2 Stretchers
Cross Section
All hinges of Wrought Iron, fixed with nails
Fixed portion of top secured to framing with oak pins.
Hinged Flap
Fixed
Hinged Flap
Single Gate
Double Gates
H is bearing board in drawer space
FRAMING DIAGRAM OF THE COMMON GATE LEG TABLE
All joints mortice and tenon, pinned, no glue
In certain cases the side frames, F & G are narrower and deeper
First half, 18th century; also made with four legs only. Type used with taper turned legs, square, & Square taper legs
Rule joint
Wood hinge
Wood hinge
Veneered reserve for Candle Stick
Top surface Veneered
Rule Hinge
Felted
Under flap hinged to back board when no drawer is fitted
Gate Arms and hinges in oak or beech
Veneered
Built up cylinder
CARD TABLE
WALNUT OR MAHOGANY
18TH CENTURY
Gates to Writing Tables
William & Mary Period.
Knuckle hinge
DINING TABLE
IN WALNUT OR MAHOGANY
J.C. ROGERS. Mens et Delt.

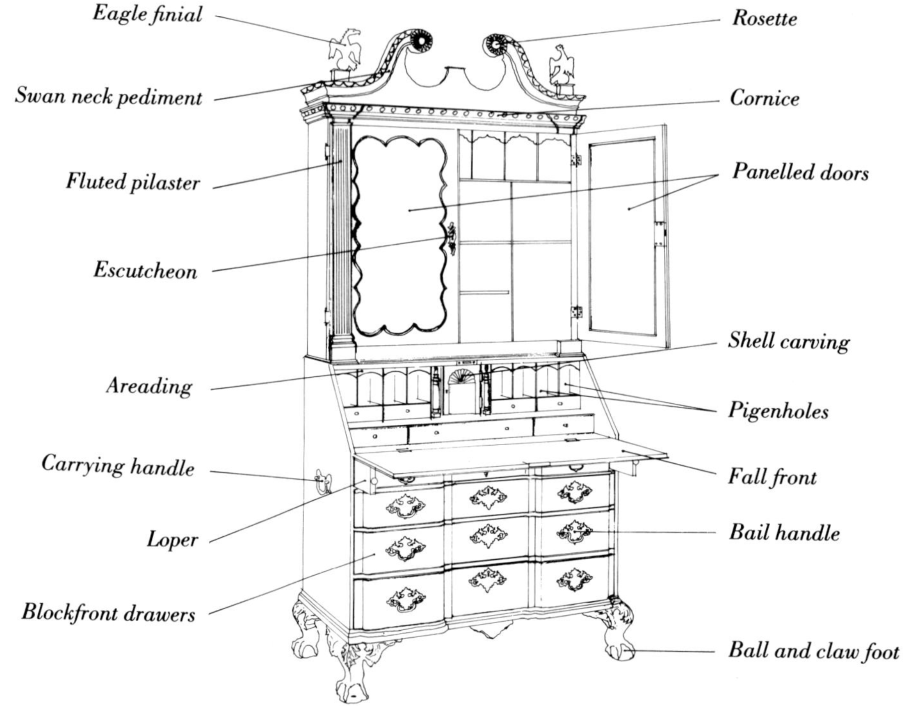

AMERICAN CHIPPENDALE DESK AND BOOKCASE, BOSTON C.1760

EARLY LOUIS XV BUREAU PLAT WITH ORMOLU MOUNTS, PARIS C.1730'S.

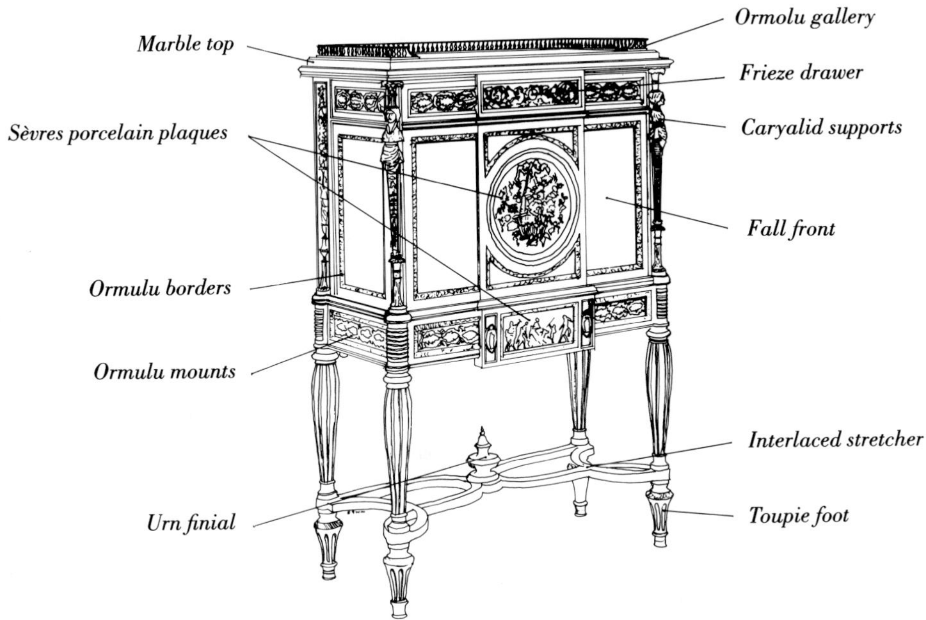

FRENCH LOUIS XVI SECRETAIRE À ABATTANT
WITH ORMOLU AND PORCELAIN MOUNTS, PARIS C.1785

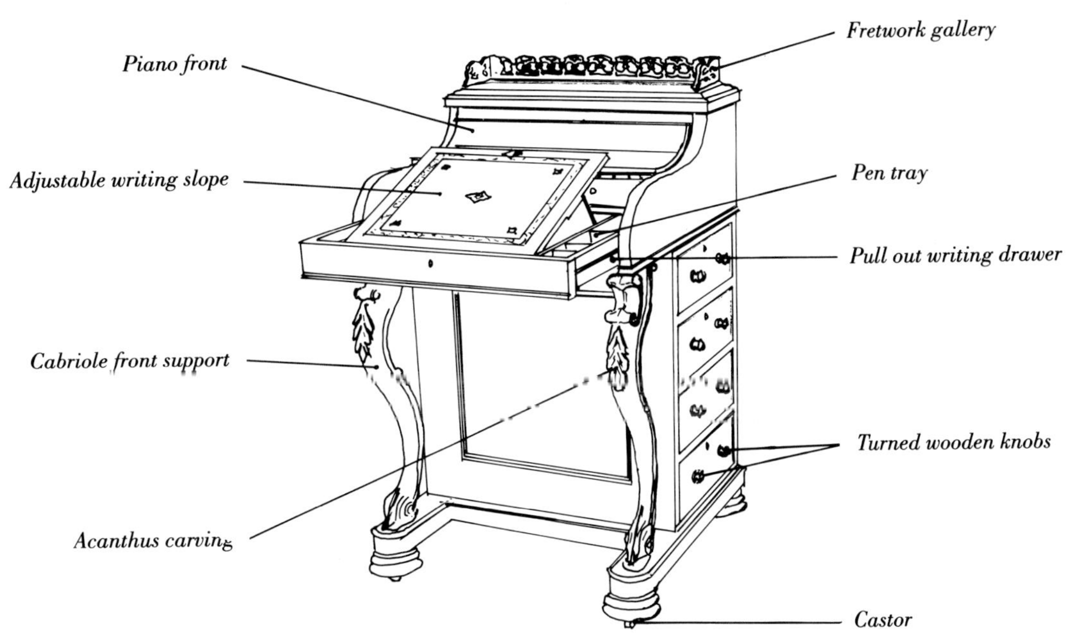

VICTORIAN WALNUT DAVENPORT,
ENGLAND C.1860

Glossary

acanthus – A classical ornamental device based on the prickly, indented leaves of the acanthus plant, used especially in the capitals of Corinthian and Composite columns.
anthemion – A classical ornament consisting of a band of alternating floral forms based on the honeysuckle flower. Also a single motif based on the honeysuckle.
apron – An ornamental projection below a rail, often shaped and carved.
arcading – A series of round-topped arches, frequently used decoratively, especially on early carved furniture.
astragal – A small half-round moulding frequently used for glazing bars.
Art Deco – Term deriving from the *Exposition des Arts Décoratifs et Industriels Modernes* held in Paris in 1925. It is generally used today to describe progressive furniture from c1910 to 1940, from luxurious and expensive Parisian pieces to Modernist examples created by industrial designers.
Art Nouveau – French term for essentially curvilinear style which was often asymmetrical and derived from organic forms, especially stems and leaves. Called *Jugendstil* in Germany and *Stile Liberty* in Italy.
Arts & Crafts Movement – Design movements of the second half of the 19th century, whose English and American exponents attempted to create beautiful, well-designed furnishings which would improve the quality of life through their daily use.
ball and claw foot – A foot in the form of a claw clutching a ball, often used in conjunction with a cabriole leg and popular in England and America in the 18th century.
baluster (banister) – A short supporting column, bulbous near the base, used in series to form a balustrade.
baluster back – A chair with a splat of baluster outline.
baluster-turned – See turned leg.
balustrade – See baluster
banding – Veneer was often used in bands to form decorative borders to the main surface. Crossbanding was cut across the grain, while feather or herringbone banding was cut with the grain at an angle so that two strips laid side by side resembled a feather.
banister – See baluster.
barleysugar-turned – See turned leg.
Baroque – A decorative style characterized by heavy and exuberant forms. Its influence varied from country to country but Baroque furniture tends to be sculptural and often architectural in form and is frequently gilded.
Bauhaus – German design school established in 1919 under the direction of Walter Gropius in Weimar. At first, artist/craftsman pieces were made, but after the move to Dessau in 1925 the main interest was in the area of good industrial design with an emphasis on functionalism.
beading – A three-dimensional decorative motif in the form of a series of round beads in a single line (see cock beading).
Biedermeier – A German term used to denote both the period 1815–1848 and the decorative style popular in Germany, Austria and Scandinavia from the 1820s to the 1840s, which was characterised by solid, unpretentious furniture in light-coloured woods. Biedermeier was a newspaper caricature symbolising the uncultured bourgoisie.
bird's-eye maple – Maple with a regular burr pattern resembling a bird's eye; very popular in the 19th century.
blind fret – A cut-work design set against a flat background.
bobbin-turned – See turned leg.
bolster – A long cushion. Can be rectangular or cylindrical, with the latter versions often used in pairs.
bombé – A[illegible]ggeratedly curved and swollen form characteristic of the rococo style.
boulle – A distinctive form of marquetry decoration making use of metal and other veneers, usually brass and tortoiseshell, to form a rich pattern. It takes its name from André-Charles Boulle, *ébéniste* to Louis XIV, who perfected but did not invent a technique known in Italy since the late 17th century.
bowfront – the front of a bureau, chest or cabinet which is formed as a single horizontal curve.
breakfast table –
breakfront –
brown furniture – A term used by the antiques trade to refer to the plain English mahogany furniture of the Georgian period.
bulb-turned – See turned leg.
bureau à cylindre **(secrétaire à cylindre)** – A French term for a roll-top desk with either a solid quarter-cylinder or a flexible tambour covering the writing surface and pigeonholes when closed.
bureau de dame – A French 19th-century term for a small writing table used by women and which would more likely have been called a *petite table à écrire* in the 18th century. The term is now used to denote all sorts of small delicate desks.
bureau en pente – See secrétaire en pente.
bureau Mazarin – A 19th-century term for the type of pedestal desk on legs joined by shaped stretchers which was popular in France at the end of the 17th century, sometime after the death in 1643 of Cardinal Mazarin who is not known to have owned a desk of this type.
bureau plat – A French term for a flat-topped writing table with drawers in the frieze and sometimes with extra slides and slopes.
burl – The American term for burr.
burr – See veneer.
butler's desk – An American term for a secretaire chest, usually with curved sides. A butler's sideboard has a secretaire drawer in the middle section.
C-scroll – A scroll in the shape of a letter C, a favourite Rococo motif.
cabochon – An oval or round boss used decoratively, usually in conjunction with other motifs.
cabriole leg – A sinuous tapering leg, curving outwards at the knee, in towards the ankle and out again at the foot.
canapé – A French sofa with arms.
canted – When legs or projected members are set at an angle to the corner of a piece they are known as canted legs or canted corners.
capital – The head of a column, usually decorated according to the different architectural orders, i.e. Doric (plain disc-like capital), Ionic (with four scroll corners), Corinthian (decorated with bands of acanthus leaves), Composite (a combination of Ionic and Corinthian).
Carlton House desk – A contemporary term for a D-shaped writing table with a bank of drawers and cupboards following the curve of the back, which was presumably named after the palace of the then Prince of Wales, later George IV.
cartonnier – A filing cabinet also known as a *serre-papiers*, introduced in France during the 18th century. Fitted with pigeonholes, the cartonnier could be an independent piece of furniture, or an accessory intended to stand on or at the end of a *bureau plat*.
cartouche – An ornamental panel, often a stylised shield, which is decorative itself but can also carry an inscription, a monogram or a crest.
caryatid – An architectural motif consisting of a column in the form of a male or female fixture which is also often found on carved furniture and as a bronze mount.
cassapanca – Italian settle with arms and back.
cassone – An Italian form of low chest, richly carved and made as a formal piece of furniture.
castors – Small swivelling wheels attached to the bottom of furniture, to make it easier to move the piece.
chair-back sofa – A sofa whose back rest gives the appearance of two to four chairs set side by side.
chaise longue – French term for a long, upholstered seat with a back rest, intended for only one person to recline on.
chamfer – A narrow flat surface formed by cutting away the apex of an angle between two surfaces, thus removing the sharp edge.
chasing – The tooling of a metal's surface. Bronze furniture mounts were chased after casting to remove blemishes and sharpen the detail before gilding.
Chesterfield – An upholstered sofa with the arms and back forming a low, unbroken line. Deeply padded and often buttoned.
chinoiserie – A Western imitation of Chinese decoration, usually more fanciful th[illegible] and frequently used to give an exotic touch to a basically European design.
chintz – Cotton or calico with a printed pattern which is sometimes glazed.
ciseleur – French for craftsman who used a variety of chisels and other tools to finish bronze mounts once they had been cast by a *fondeur* or founder. After finishing they were usually gilded by a *doreur*.
Classical – Term usually referring to the superb work of Greece and Rome, which was controlled by rules such as the Five Orders of Architecture.
classicism – Various interpretations of the Classical tradition.
cock beading – A very fine half-round moulding applied around the edges of drawer-fronts.
coffre-fort – A French term for the strong-box which was often incorporated into good quality writing desks.
confident – A sofa with attached chairs set at either end; sometimes two sofas set back to back with a chair set between at either end.
Consulate – The period of government in France between 1799 and 1804.
conversation – A sofa with seats arranged back to back or facing, so that the sitters can converse discreetly. In some Victorian pattern-books, these are described as ottomans.
cornice – An architectural term used in the description of furniture for the top moulding of bookcases and other large pieces.
cornucopia – A horn of plenty, used decoratively as a shell-like horn overflowing with fruit.
contre-partie – see boulle.
cresting – The carved ornament on the top rail of a chair-back.
cresting rail – See top rail.
cretonne – Strong, unglazed cotton with a printed pattern.
crinoline stretcher – An inward-curving stretcher designed to accommodate a full skirt.
crocket – A leaf-like projection frequently used in gothic architecture and found as a decorative device on gothic style furniture.
crossbanding – See banding.
crosspiece – A member that stretches across a piece of furniture.
cross-stretcher – A stretcher that runs across a piece of furniture.
cut-card work – A form of slightly raised decoration mainly used on silverware, consisting of thin sheets cut into patterns and soldered onto the surface.
day-bed – A sofa for one person to recline on during the day, sometimes for the formal receptions of visitors.
demilune – Half-moon shape.
desk and bookcase – The 18th century cabinetmakers' term for what would now be called a bureau-bookcase in Britain. Desk and bookcase is still used in the USA, where such pieces are also called secretaries.
dowelled – Linked with a headless pin of wood or metal.
ébéniste – A French term for a cabinetmaker, a specialist in veneered furniture, as distinct from a *menuisier* or joiner who specialised in carved pieces like chairs or beds.
écran à secretaire, écran à pupitre – A firescreen fitted with a shelf or slide at the back for writing.
écritoire – A French term for a standish, a container designed to stand on a desk and hold inkwells, sandshakers, pens, penknives, perhaps scissors or a bell to summon a servant to take the finished letter. The term is also used for a travelling writing cabinet.
escritoire – An early 18th century English term for a writing desk, now often used to refer to the large fall-front writing desk of the late 17th and early 18th century.
escutcheon – A plate surrounding and protecting a keyhole.
estampille – The stamp with the name and initials of a *maître ébéniste* which was obligatory on French furniture from about 1750 until the Revolution. The mark was struck with a cold punch rather than branded, although delicate pieces could be signed in ink. Furniture made for the crown did not have to be stamped and royal craftsmen were exempt.
fall-front – The writing flap on a secretaire which also serves to close the desk when not in use.
fauteuil – A French upholstered chair with open arms, sometimes with armrests. Term used from the late 17th century.
festoon – A neo-classical decorative motif in the form of a looped garland of flowers, fruit and foliage.
figure – The natural grain patterns of a veneer are known as figuring.
finial – An ornamental projection from the top of a piece of furniture, often a knob, ball, acorn, urn or flame.
fluting – Decorative in the form of shallow, parallel grooves, especially on columns and pilasters or on the legs of furniture.
fondeur – See *ciseleur*.
fretwork – Carved geometrical patterns, either in relief or pierced, or sawn with a fretsaw.
frieze – An architectural term for the flat surface beneath a cornice, used loosely to describe flat horizontal members in furniture.
gadroon – A form of decorative edging resembling ropetwist.
gallery – a miniature railing, often of brass, placed around the edge of a table or desk top to prevent

papers and other small objects slipping off.

gesso – A mixture of powdered chalk and size.

gilding – The application of gold to the surface of another material.

gilt – See gilding.

gimp – Simple silk or cotton braid used for concealment of joins.

Gothic – A decorative style based on the pointed arches, cluster columns, spires and other elements of late medieval architecture.

gradin – A French term for a bank of shelves or drawers, either part of a desk or free-standing; hence *bureau à gradin.*

grisaille – Monochrome decoration in tones of grey.

gros-point – French term for stitch work on canvas. The regular stitches are laid over two threads so that the effect is coarser than petit-point.

inlay – Although it is often used to mean marquetry, inlay strictly refers to decorative materials like ivory or ebony set into the surface of solid wood, unlike veneer which covers the whole surface.

japanning – The term used in America and Britain for techniques imitating Oriental lacquerwork.

joinery – Joined furniture is formed of vertical and horizontal members, united by mortice and tenon joints and supporting panels.

joint (joyned, joined) stool – A contemporary term for the mortice and tenon jointed stools of the 16th and 17th centuries, used now to refer specifically to stools with four turned legs, joined by stretchers near the feet and rails just below a rectangular seat.

lancet – An arch with a pointed top.

latticework – Pattern or structure of crossed regular lines.

lion-paw foot – Furniture foot carved in the form of a lion's paw.

lit de repos – French form of day-bed introduced in the early 17th century; intended for one person.

lowboy – A late 17th or 18th century American dressing table on legs, sometimes found combined with a slope-front desk.

love seat – A small sofa introduced in the mid-17th century. Sometimes called a 'courting chair', as two people needed to sit very closely on it.

maître – A mastercraftsman under the Paris guild system, who was entitled to own a workshop and stamp his pieces, having served an apprenticeship and paid the necessary fees. See *estampille.*

marchand-mercier – Under the Paris guild system marchands-merciers combined the roles of furniture dealers and interior decorators. They were not allowed to run their own workshops but often exerted considerable influence on fashion by acting as intermediaries between customer and craftsman.

marquetry – The use of veneers (woods of different colours, bone, ivory, mother-of-pearl, tortoiseshell, etc.) to form decorative designs like scrolls, flowers and landscapes. Abstract geometrical patterns formed in the same manner are known as parquetry.

member – Any of the structural components (rails, uprights, stretchers etc.) of a piece of joined furniture.

menuisier – See *ébéniste.*

méridienne – An 18th-century French form of day-bed, curving up at one or both ends to form scrolls.

mitred – Joint wherein the two pieces connect after they are cut at half the angle of the joint, eg, 45° for a right angle.

modular seating – Type of seating wherein complementary units, built to standard sizes, can be linked or placed against one another to form a variety of arrangements.

monopodium – Greek-derived term for a single foot, eg, as in a table which stands on a single column.

moquette – Fabric with a wool pile. Some varieties are cut in imitation of cut silk velvet.

mortice and tenon joint – The basic method of joining the framework of a piece of furniture. The tenon is a projection (usually a slim rectangle) at the end of a rail which fits exactly into the mortice, a cavity cut in the side of an upright. The tenon is normally secured by dowels.

moulding – A length of wood or other material applied to the surface of a piece of furniture. The shaped section of a moulding is usually made up from a number of curves, and there are various standard types (astragal, ogee, cavetto, ovolo) mostly of architectural origin.

mounts – Decorative motifs, usually of brass or gilt-bronze, fixed to the cabinetwork.

neo-Classicism – A decorative style based on the restrained use of Greek and Roman architectural form and ornament and characterised by a sober, rectilinear emphasis.

ormolo – Gilt bronze. A term derived from the French *or moulu* (literally ground gold).

out-scrolled – Curving outwards in a nearly horizontal plane.

outward-splayed – At a significant angle from perpendicular, the distance at the bottom between the legs being greater than that at the top.

overstuffed – Type of furniture whose stuffing and upholstery completely covers the frame.

panel – A flat surface supported by rails and stiles in joined furniture.

parcel gilt – Gilded in part only.

parquetry – See marquetry.

pediment – An architectural term used to describe an arched or triangular surmount to a bookcase or cabinet.

petit-point – French term for embroidery in small stitches on canvas, comprising at least 15 stitches to the inch.

pierced – Carved ornament is described as pierced when the decoration is cut right through the piece, as in fretwork.

pilaster – A shallow column attached to a piece of furniture.

pounce – A fine powder of pulverised sandarac, used to prevent ink spreading on unsized paper; kept in a pounce pot.

première partie – See boulle.

punchwork – Decoration achieved by the use of punches struck by a hammer.

***putto* (pl. *putti*)** – A naked infant, often winged, used as a decorative motif. Also referred to as a cherub, a cupid or an amoretto.

reeding – Decoration in the form of parallel ribbing, especially on columns and pilasters or on the legs of furniture.

Régence – Regency of the Duc d'Orléans in France (1715–24).

Rennaisance – The rebirth of ancient Roman values in the arts. Renaissance designers were inspired by the sculpture and architectural remains of the ancient world and their furniture reflects this in the profusion of carved ornament.

rocaille – Stylised and fanciful rock and shell decoration, used by extension to refer to many of the decorative forms of the Rococo.

Rococo – A decorative style which characterised by delicate curved outlines, C-scrolls, fantastic organic forms and a tendency towards asymmetry in ornamental details.

sabre leg – A furniture leg which is curved and tapered like a cavalry sabre.

salon – A French reception room.

saloon – Large, formal reception room in a stately British home.

sans traverse – A French term for a commode or desk where there are no visible divisions between drawers, and decorative motifs can continue uninterrupted.

screen writing table – see *écran à secrétaire.*

scriptor – A contemporary English term for a writing desk, now used to denote the small fall-front writing cabinets of the late 17th century.

scrutoire – A 17th century English term for a writing desk.

seat rail – The horizontal framework which supports the seat of a joined chair.

secrétaire – A French term often used for all sorts of desk, but originally denoting those where papers and documents could be kept locked behind a flap. In Britain a secretaire is a pull-out writing compartment disguised as a drawer with pigeonholes and small drawers behind a fall-front, usually part of a larger piece.

sécretaire à abattant – A French term for desk which stands against the wall like a cabinet or cupboard with a large fall-front which is vertical when closed. Also known as a *secrétaire en armoire.*

secrétaire á la bourgogne – A mechanical writing desk which resembles a *table à écrire*. When in use one half of the top rises vertically to reveal a bank of small drawers and the other hinges forward as a writing surface. Supposedly named after the Duc de Bourgogne, who was paralysed and had a mechanical desk made for him by Oeben.

secrétaire à culbute – Another form of mechanical writing table with a rising bank of drawers which swings up on a hinge along its front edge.

secrétaire en armoire – See *secrétaire à abattant.*

secrétaire en dos d'ane – A French term often used indiscriminately to refer to all sorts of slope-front desk (*secrétaires en pente*), but more correctly describing the *secrétaire à double pente* with two flaps, at which two people can write facing one another.

secrétaire en pente – A French term for a free-standing slope-front desk with a flap which serves as a lid when closed and a writing surface when open.

secretary – A Modern American term for desk and bookcase.

serpentine – In the form of an undulating curve, convex at the centre and concave on each side.

serre-papiers – see *cartonnier.*

settee – An upholstered sofa.

settle – A wooden bench-like seat with back and arms; sometimes has a box base for storage.

show-wood – Wood which is revealed on a piece of furniture; often polished.

side rail – Wooden connecting struts at the sides of chairs or sofas.

spindle – A slim, turned rod frequently used as an upright in chair backs.

splat – The central upright member of a chair back which joins the seat to the top rail.

spoon back – The back of a chair or sofa which is curved like a spoon.

squab cushion – A stuffed cushion with straight sides. Originally used in 17th-century day-beds, it is primarily connected today with modular seating, which uses rubber or foam cushions.

square-section leg – A leg which would be square if cut at right-angles, but which may also be tapering or shaped in some other way.

stile – A vertical member used in the construction of joined furniture.

strapwork – A form of decoration particularly popular in Northern Europe in the 16th and 17th centuries, resembling interlaced, pierced and scrolled bands of leather.

stretcher – A horizontal crosspiece used to join and strengthen the legs of a piece of furniture.

stringing – Thin strips of wood or metal inlay used to decorate furniture.

strung border – A border decorated with stringing.

stuff-over – A term used when the upholstery of a chair covers the framework rather than being a panel within it.

swag – A decorative motif in the form of a loop of cloth and similar to a festoon.

table à écrire – A French term denoting a writing table, generally smaller than a *bureau plat* and provided with a slope or slides and a fitted writing drawer.

table ambulante – An 18th century French term for any light, portable table, usually intended for writing.

table en chiffonière – A small 18th century French work with a high gallery around the top and several drawers in the frieze.

tambour desk – A desk where the writing compartment is hidden behind vertical slatted shutters when not in use (see also roll-top desk).

tempera – Powder colour mixed with thinned egg yolk. The paint work dries quickly and gives a tough surface.

tête-à-tête – Various constructions wherein the seats are angled towards one another. See *confident.*

thrown chair – See turned chair.

timbers – Another name for the heavy wooden framework of a piece of furniture.

top rail – The topmost horizontal member which joins the uprights of a chair back. Also known as a yoke rail or a cresting rail.

tracery – Ornamental openwork.

turned chair – A chair made up entirely of turned uprights and rails, often incorporating large numbers of decoratively turned spindles.

turned leg – A leg shaped on a lathe, usually circular in section. Turned legs are found in many traditional patterns, e.g. bobbin, bulb, barley sugar or barley twist, vase and baluster.

under-frame – The supporting structure of a piece of furniture, including legs, stretchers and any other braces.

uprights – The vertical parts of a chair back, formed as continuations of the rear legs.

vase-turned – See turned leg.

veneer – A very thin sheet, usually of wool, applied to the surface of a piece of furniture. Veneers cut from knotty areas of the tree are particularly decorative and known as burrs, hence burr walnut.

vernis martin – A generic term for all varnish and lacquer (japanning) used in France in imitation of oriental lacquer, but specifically referring to the four Martin brothers, who were granted a monopoly on imitation relief lacquer in 1730.

vitruvian scroll – A classically-derived ornamental device in the form of a series of scrolls resembling waves.

x-frame – An arrangement of diagonal stretchers joining the front and back legs of a piece of furniture and crossing to form an X.

yoke rail – See top rail.

Index